Incomes and the Welfare State

Incomes and the Welfare State

Essays on Britain and Europe

A. B. ATKINSON
Nuffield College, Oxford

Published by the Press Syndicate of the University of Cambridge
The Pitt Building, Trumpington Street, Cambridge CB2 1RP
40 West 20th Street, New York, NY 10011-4211, USA
10 Stamford Road, Oakleigh, Melbourne 3166, Australia

© Cambridge University Press 1995

First published 1995

Printed in Great Britain at the University Press, Cambridge

A catalogue record for this book is available from the British Library

Library of Congress cataloguing in publication data
Atkinson, A. B. (Anthony Barnes)
Incomes and the Welfare State: essays on Britain and Europe / A. B. Atkinson.
p. cm.
Includes bibliographical references (p.).
ISBN 0 521 46250 9
1. Income distribution–Great Britain. 2. Poverty–Great Britain. 3. Public welfare–Great Britain. 4. Social security–Great Britain. 5. Income distribution–Europe. 6. Poverty–Europe. 7. Public welfare–Europe. 8. Social security–Europe. I. Title.
HC260.I5A868 1996
339.2′2′0941 – dc20 95-3398 CIP

ISBN 0 521 46250 9

VN

Contents

III Targeting and the future of social security policy

Figures

Tables

Preface

The essays in this volume were written over the period 1989 to 1994 as part of the Welfare State Programme at STICERD, London School of Economics. It is a pleasure to begin by thanking Michio Morishima, founder Chairman of STICERD, who encouraged me to draw up a research programme on this subject, Suntory Limited and its then Chairman and President, K. Saji, for supporting the first four years of the Programme, and the ESRC which provided financing from 1988 to January 1993 under its Welfare Research Programme (Grant X206 32 2001). Secondly, I have a great debt to those who made up the Welfare State Programme, including Julian Le Grand, John Hills and Howard Glennerster, who jointly acted as directors, and Jane Dickson, the Programme Secretary. The essays in this book owe a great deal to members of the Programme, particularly Holly Sutherland, now Director of the Microsimulation Unit at Cambridge. In addition, chapter 2 builds on a joint project carried out with Lee Rainwater and Tim Smeeding as part of the Luxembourg Income Study, and chapters 9 and 10 draw on joint research with John Micklewright of Queen Mary Westfield, London, and the European University Institute, Florence. At the same time, I should emphasise that no one apart from me is responsible for the views expressed.

A number of the chapters make use of material from the Family Expenditure Survey made available by the Central Statistical Office (CSO) through the ESRC Data Archive by permission of the Controller of HM Stationery Office. Neither the CSO nor the ESRC Data Archive bears any responsibility for the analysis or interpretation of the data reported here.

I am grateful to the following for permission to reprint previously published material (the place of the original publication is indicated in brackets):

Chapter 1 © the British Academy (*Proceedings of the British Academy*, vol. 82, 1992 *Lectures and Memoirs*, 317–51),

Chapter 4 The World Bank (*World Bank Economic Review*, vol. 5: 3–21),
Chapter 5 Macmillan Press Ltd and St Martin's Press (A. B. Atkinson and M. Rein, editors, *Age, Work and Social Security*, 1992, chapter 6),
Chapter 7 Longman Group UK (T. and D. Wilson, editors, *The State and Social Welfare*, 1991, chapter 7: 121–42),
Chapter 8 Nomos Verlag (W. Schmähl, editor, *The Future of Basic and Supplementary Pensions in the European Community*, 1991: 117–34),
Chapter 9 Ethics (*Ethics*, vol. 100: 569–85),
Chapter 10 The MIT Press (P. Dasgupta, D. Gale, O. Hart and E. Maskin, editors, *Economic Analysis of Markets and Games*),
Chapter 11 The Geneva Association (*Geneva Papers on Risk and Insurance Theory*, vol. 16: 113–31),
Chapter 13 Macmillan Press Ltd, St Martin's Press and the International Economic Association (D. Bös, editor, *Economics in a Changing World*, vol. 3: 121–39),
Chapter 14 The Institute for Fiscal Studies (*Fiscal Studies*, vol. 13: 41–53),
Chapter 16 The Age Concern Institute of Gerontology (*State Pensions for Today and Tomorrow*, David Hobman Annual Lecture, 1994).

It should be noted that the papers do not appear in exactly the same form as originally published; they have been edited to form a coherent whole.

Introduction

The Welfare State has in recent years been rediscovered by economists. When I first began work on the economics of social security in the 1960s, the subject scarcely appeared in the economics literature. The study of poverty was regarded as a matter for social administration, social policy or other disciplines. Even with the War on Poverty and the negative income tax experiments in the United States, the subject still tended to remain outside the mainstream of economics.

The situation has altered dramatically. The economics of the Welfare State is now centre stage, entering debates about the macro-economy and about the wealth of nations. Reform of the Welfare State is seen as one of the key policy issues of the 1990s. In OECD countries there have been calls for cuts in social security spending in order to solve the fiscal problems of national governments. In the European Union, social protection is being reviewed with regard to its impact on international competitiveness. In the world at large, the World Bank is calling for rethinking of the role of pensions under the title of 'Averting the Old Age Crisis' (World Bank, 1994).

The present collection of essays may be seen as contributing to an active policy debate on the future of the Welfare State, with particular reference to social security. There are, however, two important differences from much of the recent economic writing. First, I believe that the role of the Welfare State can only be assessed in relation to the objectives which it is intended to accomplish. Too often when reading critiques one gets the impression that social security performs no useful function. Yet the programmes were introduced to meet certain goals, and one has to ask how far these goals could be achieved if the programme were cut or eliminated. Moreover, there is a tendency for the function of social security to be equated with the relief of poverty, whereas this is only one of several objectives of programmes such as retirement pensions, child benefit or unemployment insurance. The Welfare State is designed to provide a sense of security to all, not just to focus on those below the poverty line.

The second important difference from much of the recent writing is that I do not start from the position that the Welfare State must necessarily have a negative impact on the working of the economy. If one reads what economists write about social security, one learns that unemployment insurance has caused a rise in the 'natural' rate of unemployment, that payment of disability benefits has caused people to leave the labour force early, and that pay-as-you-go state pensions have lowered the rate of capital accumulation. This focus on the disincentive effects in turn has led to calls to scale back spending. However, as is increasingly being recognised in economic theory, we are not starting from a first-best position, from which any government intervention must cause a distortion. In a world of uncertainty and imperfect information, income transfers can have a positive influence. Income maintenance not only alleviates poverty, but also provides a sense of security, thus contributing to efficiency objectives. People are more willing to take risks, to retrain or change jobs, in a society where there is adequate social protection. Historically, social insurance grew up alongside the modern employment relationship, providing a guarantee against catastrophic loss of income through unemployment, sickness or accident. This was a positive inducement for workers to enter the formal market economy, just as retirement pensions may form part of an active labour market policy. There are positive, as well as negative, effects on economic efficiency and growth.

The existence of positive functions for the Welfare State does not mean that it is not in need of reform. Indeed, I have been proposing reforms of social security in the United Kingdom for more than a quarter of a century. The persistence of poverty even at times of relatively full employment was evidence of shortcomings in the post-war Welfare State and of the need for change to meet changing social and economic circumstances. Challenges have come from demographic developments, from new patterns of family formation and dissolution, from the increased participation of women in the labour force, and from the new economic climate. The essays in part III deal with various aspects of reforming social security. They treat, among other issues, the fashionable solution of increased targeting and the European dimensions of social security; and they introduce new ideas for reform in Britain, such as a Participation Income and the Minimum Pension Guarantee, both designed to move in the opposite direction from the current policy of reliance on means-tested benefits.

Such proposals for reform are based on analysis of the existing Welfare State in part II. This analysis does not consider all aspects of spending, concentrating on social security transfers and within this field giving particular attention to retirement pensions and unemployment benefits. The essays stress the need to look at the fine structure of transfer programmes. I do not believe that the Welfare State can simply be analysed as an aggregate. Different programmes have different objectives and different effects. The term 'Welfare State' is indeed understood in different ways in different countries.

The essays in this book are largely concerned with the impact of the Welfare State on the incomes and living standards of individuals and their families. Two ways of reducing the proportion of GNP spent on social security may have quite different implications at the individual level. The wider availability of evidence from sample surveys has allowed these effects to be analysed, and the results are used in a number of chapters. This perspective also means that the role of the Welfare State has to be seen in the wider context of the distribution of resources. Since 1979 we have witnessed a rise in income inequality in the United Kingdom, the United States and certain other countries – although not in all European countries. Part I of this book describes the background of income inequality and poverty, against which the calls for a reduction in the Welfare State have to be assessed.

The essays do not form a continuous narrative. At the same time, they are linked closely together by the themes outlined above. In what follows, I provide a brief introduction to each of the three parts – the distributional background (part I), analysis of the current Welfare State (part II) and future policy (part III). It also has to be borne in mind that the chapters were written at different dates between 1989 and 1994, and that the factual information has not been updated.

I Income inequality and poverty in Britain and Europe

The subject of the first part of the book is the distribution of income and poverty in the United Kingdom and in Europe. It is concerned with the problems – conceptual and empirical – of measuring the extent of inequality, and with inquiry into what lies behind the observations.

Chapter 1 is entitled 'What is happening to the distribution of income in the UK?'. It was widely believed for a long time in the post-war period that income differences were gradually declining in advanced economies. In terms of the popular Kuznets curve, we were in the second phase of the $\cap$-shaped relation between inequality and national income. Chapter 1 shows that in the UK this ceased to be the case towards the end of the 1970s. Measured income inequality increased substantially during the 1980s.

Decomposition of the observed changes in income inequality in the UK suggests that several factors were in operation. Between the mid 1970s and the mid 1980s there was a discrete reduction in the proportion of families with income from work, resulting from unemployment, disability and sickness, from earlier retirement, and from non-participation in the labour force. This was combined with rising dispersion in the distribution of earnings, which continued steadily over the 1980s. After the mid 1980s, there was also a significant decline in the relative incomes of those not in work, associated with the fall in state benefit levels relative to average earnings. Those dependent on state benefits began to fall behind.

Some of these factors leading to increased inequality may be expected to apply to all advanced countries, such as the widening gap between low-paid and high-paid workers. Other factors, such as the policy towards benefit levels, are likely to differ from country to country. It is therefore interesting to ask how far the experience of the UK is the same as that in other European countries. **Chapter 2** examines the evidence about income inequality in 15 European countries (and the United States, as a point of reference), drawing on evidence from the Luxembourg Income Study and national sources, and written jointly with Lee Rainwater and Tim Smeeding. The first purpose is to establish what is known about the relative *levels* of inequality in the different countries. Such an exercise faces a number of problems, and the first section warns readers that they are about to enter a statistical minefield. In contrast to some earlier international comparisons, a clear pattern emerges, with distinctly lower income inequality in Scandinavia and Northern Europe, and a higher level in Southern Europe and Ireland, which are closer to the United States in this regard. The Gini coefficient, for instance, ranges from around 20 per cent in Scandinavia to 30 per cent or more in Italy, Switzerland and Ireland.

The rise in inequality in the UK – some 8 percentage points in a decade – is large in relation to these international differences. Moreover, it stands out in comparison with the trends in other countries. While there are a number of countries in which inequality appears to have increased during the 1980s, after a period of falling inequality, the changes are typically smaller in size. In some countries there is no marked trend, and in others the downward trend continued.

As the general level of incomes has risen, those at the bottom have tended to fall behind. This has led to concern about poverty in the European Union, measured concretely by the European Commission in terms of a poverty line set at half of each member country's average income. **Chapter 3** describes the progress which has been made in improving knowledge about low incomes in the European Union and the problems in making substantive progress in reducing poverty. The chapter was written in 1989. Since then the situation has improved in terms of knowledge, particularly on account of the work at Erasmus University, led by Aldi Hagenaars, whose early death in 1993 was such a great loss. The substantial situation in terms of the extent of poverty has not, however, shown a great improvement. According to the most recent estimates of the European Commission, in 1988 16 per cent of the population of the twelve member states were living below the poverty standard (European Commission, 1993a, p. 100).

The measurement of poverty raises many conceptual problems. Even an apparently clearcut standard like 50 per cent of average income is susceptible of different interpretations. These aspects are examined both in chapter 3 and in **Chapter 4**, which is concerned with the approaches adopted in the measurement of poverty in a range of OECD countries. The measurement of poverty is not purely a technical matter, and the choice of definition depends on social judgements. An obvious example is the selection of equivalence scale used to compare the needs of different sizes of households. This affects not only the magnitude but also the composition of the low-income population. Poverty among children may appear to be a priority with one scale, but the elderly to have higher priority with another. The role of these and other differences is illustrated in chapter 4 by case studies of France, West Germany and the UK.

In order to understand more fully the causes of poverty and of rising income inequality, we need to look behind the overall distribution. **Chapter 5** takes one particular group in the UK – the early retired. In examining distributional issues, it is often convenient to consider sub-groups defined by their employment status, or other characteristics, and I have referred to the decline in the relative income of those not in work. However, within these sub-groups there may be very sizeable inequality. In the case of the elderly we have seen increasing polarisation, or what Titmuss (1955) called 'two nations in old age'. In chapter 5, Holly Sutherland and I ask whether the same is true of the early retired, a question prompted by the sharp rise in the proportion of men aged 55–64 who are economically inactive. While any classification is to some extent arbitrary, we find that there are three identifiable groups within the early retired: those retiring with a substantial portion of their income from occupational pensions, those deriving their income largely from health-related benefits, and those dependent on Income Support. A corollary is that there is one group (occupational pensioners) where there is some relation between retirement income and past earnings, and two groups whose living standard is largely influenced by flat-rate benefit levels.

The discussion of social security in chapter 5, and earlier in chapter 1, may be seen as a bridge to the review of the existing Welfare State in part II.

II Analysis of the Welfare State

The essays in this part of the volume seek to provide an economic and institutional analysis. Both elements seem important. One can only examine the economic impact of transfer programmes within a fully specified economic model. Such models provide a framework for thought and point to relationships which may not otherwise be apparent. It is not, for instance, widely known that it is theoretically possible that a cut in unemployment insurance benefits may *reduce* total employment (chapter 10), or that a switch from state to private pensions may *reduce* the rate of capital formation (chapter 6). At the same time, social security programmes do not arise in a vacuum. We need to look at their historical origins, examining how methods of dealing with poverty in pre-industrial societies broke down with the advent of the modern employment relationship (chapter 11). We have to consider the political economy of benefit determination (chapters 7 and 9). My aim in these essays is to illustrate these points with regard to certain features of the social security system.

Much of the recent economic evaluation of the Welfare State has reached negative conclusions, arguing that it needs to be reconsidered and – in some views – dismantled. **Chapter 6** examines the indictment of the Welfare State and the specific charge that it is a barrier to economic growth. The purpose is not to reach a definite conclusion, but to clarify the precise nature of the case made by the opponents of the Welfare State. Such a clarification seems necessary since the argument is often not made transparent. Concentrating on the long-run potential growth rate, rather than on the failure of the economy to reach its potential, I consider the impact of transfers as illuminated by the recent studies of economic growth, with especial reference to retirement pensions and the financing of education. In part the analysis makes use of standard growth theory, showing how the substitution of a private for state pension may affect the rate of savings. In part it is necessary to extend the model, for instance by introducing an explicit investment function and examining the operation of the capital market. In such a richer model, the switch from state to private pensions may negatively affect the rate of capital formation, reversing the conclusion which is conventionally drawn.

Recent critiques of the Welfare State do indeed provide a good illustration of the role of rhetoric in public debate. The ambiguities in such discourse are the subject of **Chapter 7**, which traces the evolution of thinking about a national minimum in Britain and its relation to the determination of benefit levels. This is of particular interest in view of the distributional significance of benefit levels identified in chapters 1 and 5. How is the level of benefit determined? Is it the government's view of the desirable national minimum? Or is it a compromise between this objective and the desire to control public spending? Beveridge gave the impression that these two could be reconciled, but the position remains ambiguous. If, as in the United States, the UK government were to adopt an official poverty line, then this would make apparent the gap between promise and performance.

The impact of the Welfare State depends a great deal on its institutional fine structure. **Chapter 8** is the first of four dealing with retirement pensions (chapters 8 and 11) and unemployment benefits (chapters 9, 10 and 11). The chapter provides a thumbnail sketch of the evolution of state pensions in Britain, and is particularly concerned to set them in a European context. By international standards, the rate of replacement offered by the state pensions system, flat-rate plus the state earnings-related pension, is not generous, and it will become even less so if the present policy is continued of allowing benefit levels to fall relative to average earnings. Nor does Income Support guarantee an adequate safety net. For these reasons, consideration needs to be given to reform – see chapters 14–16.

Income maintenance for the unemployed in the UK has been put severely to the test since the late 1970s. As is shown in **Chapter 9**, the reaction of the government to mass unemployment has been to make unemployment benefits less extensive and less generous. Why has this been so? I examine some of the answers which may be given to this question, drawing on the theory of public choice. The account in chapter 9 gives prominence to the interests and concerns of voters but recognises that these may be influenced by the ideological views of politicians and by the goals of civil servants. The relative contribution of these different explanations is relevant to those, such as myself, making the case for reform. Are they arguing against the expressed wishes of the democratic majority? Is it possible that people vote for a harsh political platform but would prefer not to be offered this choice?

The need to investigate the fine structure of the benefit system is exemplified by the frequent references in the economics literature to unemployment benefit as 'the wage when not working'. As is shown in **Chapter 10**, the institutional features of unemployment insurance are essential to understanding its economic impact. Contrary to what is typically assumed in economic models of the labour market, receipt of unemployment insurance depends on the past employment record: people may be ineligible where they have been dismissed for industrial misconduct, and benefit may be terminated where an unemployed person refuses a job offer or fails to search for new employment. This casts serious doubt on the standard job search model, since the unemployed cannot with impunity reject job offers which fall short of their reservation wage. It casts doubt on the efficiency wage model where workers dismissed for 'shirking' are assumed to receive benefit. In chapter 10, I describe a model which takes account of these institutional features and which demonstrates that unemployment insurance can play a rather different role from that usually assumed. The model is one of a 'dual' labour market, with a primary sector (typified by large-scale industrial enterprises), in which employers pay an efficiency wage premium but job separations occur continually, and a less-favoured secondary sector. Unemployment insurance is *complementary* to employment in the primary sector of the economy. Seen in this way, cutbacks in unemployment insurance, as with the 1994 Jobseeker's Allowance, makes primary-sector employment less attractive, encouraging a shift from 'good jobs' to 'bad jobs'.

The relation between social insurance and the labour market is the subject of **Chapter 11**. Continuing the theme of chapter 10, I argue that the development of social insurance is best understood in terms not of failure of the insurance market but of the operation of the labour market. State retirement pensions and unemployment insurance arose with a particular form of labour market, and their role may be expected to evolve as that labour market situation changes. Put another way, the risks against which social insurance provides protection are themselves social constructions. In order to understand the role of state benefits, and of parallel private provision, which exists for pensions but not typically for unemployment, a richer model of the labour market is necessary, and a sketch of such a model is given in chapter 11. The model goes beyond the dual labour market structure of chapter 10, allowing for both permanent and contract workers in the primary sector. Incorporation of such features of the labour market is necessary to understand the past formation of social insurance and to assess the implications of proposals for reform.

III Targeting and the future of social policy

In the lexicon of the debate about reform of the Welfare State, two of the most popular concepts are those of 'targeting' and 'social safety net'. The essays in part III may be seen as an attempt to sharpen the way in which these terms are used.

Targeting is an attractive idea. Many people have seen it as the solution to achieving greater effectiveness while reducing total spending, replacing expensive 'universal' programmes with cheaper 'targeted' benefits. **Chapter 12** seeks first to set out the theoretical argument implicit in many of the calls for greater targeting, and to show how the assessment of relative efficiency depends on the formulation of social objectives. Here it is necessary to remember, as noted at the outset, that the alleviation of poverty is only *one* of the objectives of the Welfare State. Even if, as in chapter 12, attention is focused on the poverty objective, the attractiveness of targeting depends on how precisely it is formulated – we have the same problems as with the measurement of poverty discussed in chapters 3 and 4. The second main point of chapter 12 is that the choice of benefits is considerably richer than is suggested by a simple opposition of uniform and income-tested transfers, a point which is illustrated specifically by reference to family benefits. In principle family benefits can be differentiated in many ways, which may be combined with income relation; income testing itself may take different forms. A review of European countries, Australia and Canada indicates that a wide variety of types of family benefit have been implemented in practice.

Thirdly, the design of effective targeting faces the problems of imperfect information and of work incentives. These arise with both income testing and categorical conditions, but there are some reasons to suppose that they are more serious in the former case. Translating a scheme into practice in the face of imperfect information on the part of both administrators and potential recipients is particularly demanding for transfers that require evidence of current income. Experience indicates that there is a major problem of securing adequate take-up of income-tested benefits. Concerns about work incentives, whether based on empirical findings or notions of desert, may limit the acceptable degree of income targeting.

The role of the social safety net has come to the fore in a number of contexts. **Chapter 13** was given in 1992 as a lecture in Moscow (in the same hall where Yuri Gagarin held a press conference on returning from his first flight in space). Much had been written, and continues to be written, about the need for a social safety net to protect the poorest against the costs of economic transition. Much less is written about the *form* of such a safety net, and about whether it is indeed practicable. The aim of this chapter is to see what can be learnt from the experience of Europe and the United States. What is the meaning of safety net? How successful have Western nets proved to be in practice? It is argued that a safety net is not easy to design and typically has only limited effectiveness. The choice of policy at the macro-level should not place too much weight on the safety net.

Issues of the design of the safety net at a European level are the subject of **Chapter 14**. This is essential if we are to take seriously the social dimension of the European Union. At what level of government such a safety net is to be provided depends on the interpretation of 'subsidiarity', and this is the first topic addressed. It is argued that, whatever machinery is used to achieve social protection, the *objectives* of the proposed action are to be determined at a European level. There is moreover the question as to how far individual national governments are able to provide effective social protection in the face of pressure from fiscal competition. It is suggested that potentially the most worrying of such arguments are those arising from political pressure – a political economy, rather than a migratory, constraint on national policy.

A social safety net at the level of the European Union raises many questions, particularly about its form and scope. The problems with means testing would apply to a pan-European scheme, and the UK experience is in this respect instructive. It is therefore highly regrettable that the British government is not currently taking part in the formation of the social dimension of Europe post-1992. I refer in chapter 14 to 'exit' and 'voice' as possible reactions. The British government has chosen the former, but I believe that it would be much more valuable at this stage to be exercising voice.

The final two chapters consider the future of social security in the UK, seen within a European context. **Chapter 15** was given as a lecture on the fiftieth anniversary of the publication of the Beveridge Report. It asks how we should seek to provide a national minimum – and, more broadly, a European minimum – in the years to come. It argues that Beveridge was right to reject means testing, and that the objections are strengthened when we take account of the new circumstances. The means test only make sense when applied to the family or household as the unit, but this runs counter to the major change in social attitudes towards independence, as evidenced by the separate taxation of husbands and wives. Turning to the European context, and looking ahead to the ways in which European policy may be aligned, I believe that the complexity of means-tested benefits makes them unsuitable for this purpose.

The proposals examined in chapter 15 are to replace the present emphasis on means testing with a modernised social insurance scheme and a new version of a basic income. While basic income is usually seen as an *alternative* to social insurance, in my view it is more productive to see them as complementary, with the function of basic income being to reduce dependence on means-tested social assistance. Moreover, it is proposed that the basic income should be subject to a condition of *participation*, not limited to paid work but with a wider definition of social contribution.

Chapter 15 is primarily concerned with those of working age; **Chapter 16** examines state retirement pensions. It argues that the present pension provisions in Britain cannot guarantee an adequate minimum standard of income in old age, and that, unless there is a change in policy, particularly with regard to state pensions, then the problem of poverty in old age is likely to remain with us. What then can be done? The simple answer is an increased basic National Insurance pension linked to net average earnings. Two objections are typically made. First, there is the cost; secondly, the second tier of pensions has evolved, and what people are seeking is different, including an understandable desire for greater individual choice. I do not myself find these objections overwhelming, but I sense that I am in a minority. It may therefore be helpful to identify an intermediate route, and this is described in the form of a *Minimum Pension Guarantee*. In its most straightforward form, the guarantee would make sure that everyone retired with at least a specified minimum pension from state, occupational and personal pension sources, and that this was indexed with average earnings after retirement. It should be stressed that this would not involve a means test. There would be no assessment of assets; nor would savings income be taken into account. If introduced, it would do a great deal to reduce the dependence of pensioners on means testing, and help the very poorest pensioners who do not claim Income Support.

The essays in this part make no pretence of providing a fully worked out plan for the reform of social security. They have the more modest intention of suggesting some new ways of thinking about the design of such reform and of canvassing some ideas – such as the Participation Income and the Minimum Pension Guarantee – which seem worthy of further attention.

Part I

Income inequality and poverty in Britain and Europe

1 What is happening to the distribution of income in the UK?

The question examined in this chapter has been out of fashion in recent years. In this respect, there is a marked contrast with the situation 20 years ago. At that time, there was considerable discussion about the distribution of income and about the distributional consequences of government policy. In the 1960s, there had been the rediscovery of poverty in Britain and the launching of the War on Poverty in the United States. New measures for income maintenance were being planned and issues of fairness were much debated with regard to incomes policies.

Along with public interest came scientific research. In the United States, the War on Poverty was accompanied by large-scale research projects, including the negative income tax experiments, and by the founding of the Wisconsin Poverty Research Institute. In Britain, there was a considerable improvement in the availability of official statistics, including the fuller exploitation of existing household surveys such as the Family Expenditure Survey and administrative sources such as the estate duty returns. In the second half of the 1970s, the Royal Commission on the Distribution of Income and Wealth was established.

The position today is different. For the last 10 years there has been little public concern in Britain about the distribution of income, and it does not appear to be high on the political agenda. Yet this is a period which one suspects has seen major changes in the distribution of income. The evidence, as we shall see, is limited in its coverage and in the degree to which it provides an up-to-date picture. But it seems clear that income inequality increased over the 1980s. To see the significance of this development, it is important to place it in historical perspective, and it is with this perspective that I begin.

Before reviewing the evidence about income inequality, I should however make clear that I am *not* considering in this chapter the reasons why there should be – or why there should not be – concern about inequality, or why income, rather than some other variable, should be the focus of our concern. The mere existence of income differences does not necessarily imply economic injustice, and what one means by injustice depends on underlying moral judgements. These are important matters, but they are not my subject here. In what follows, I am simply assuming that the distribution of income, measured in a conventional manner, is one of the elements which enters social judgements about the state of contemporary Britain.

A second important disclaimer is that I do not discuss in any systematic way the conceptual problems that arise in measuring income inequality. There are major issues concerning the way in which the data are collected and analysed: the definition of the income unit, the treatment of different-sized units, the period over which income is measured, and the definition of income (see Atkinson, 1983, chapter 3, and Atkinson and Micklewright, 1992, section 3.4). In what follows, the evidence in general relates to the distribution of annual after-tax income among family units, with adjustment for family size, weighted according to the number of individuals. Departures from this 'Base Definition' are noted where applicable.

1.1 The post-war decades

In the post-war years, there was a widespread feeling that the distribution of income in Britain was moving in the direction of equality. In 1962, Titmuss summarised prevailing opinion as follows:

> Much has been written in recent years about the strongly egalitarian effects of the social and economic policies pursued by British Governments since the end of the Second World War. ... Full employment ... was leading to a steady reduction in wage and salary differentials. ... the wealthy were a disappearing class in Britain. (1962, p. 15)

Kuznets argued in his Presidential Address to the American Economic Association in 1955 that, on the basis of evidence for pre-tax incomes in the United Kingdom (UK), the United States (US) and Germany:

> the relative distribution of income ... has been moving towards equality, with these trends particularly noticeable since the 1920s but beginning perhaps in the period before the first world war. (1955, p. 4)

It was in this Address that Kuznets put forward the hypothesis that income inequality tended to increase in the early stages of economic growth but that in mature economies inequality tended to fall as per-capita income increased. This hypothesis of an inverted U-relation between inequality and income came subsequently to be known as the 'Kuznets curve'.

Table 1.1. *Blue Book estimates of the distribution of personal after tax income in the UK 1949–84/5*

	Share of		Gini coefficient
	Top 10%	Bottom 50%	
1949	27.1	26.5	35.5
1954	25.3	26.3	35.8
1959	25.2	25.0	36.0
1962	25.6	25.8	35.6
1963	25.4	25.8	35.6
1964	25.9	25.2	36.6
1965	25.4	25.8	35.4
1966	24.5	26.8	33.7
1967	24.3	26.8	33.5
1968/9	23.6	26.6	33.2
1969/70	23.6	26.4	33.5
1970/1	23.9	26.1	33.9
1971/2	24.1	25.9	34.2
1972/3	23.6	26.8	33.1
1973/4	23.6	27.0	32.8
1974/5	23.2	27.0	32.4
1975/6	22.3	27.4	31.5
1975/6	23.1	26.7	32.6
1976/7	23.2	26.9	32.6
1977/8	23.3	26.5	33.0
1978/9	23.4	26.2	33.5
1981/2	25.6	25.2	36.0
1984/5	26.5	24.9	36.0

Notes: (a) The data are based on the Survey of Personal Incomes (SPI); only those years are included for which a survey was carried out (from 1949 the survey was quinquennial, with estimates for intervening years being made by extrapolation, the survey becoming annual in 1962).

(b) There is a break in continuity in the series in 1975/6; the earlier figures deduct mortgage interest and other tax-deductible items.

(c) The figures relate to the distribution of tax units; no adjustment is made for differences in unit size.

(d) The figures show the distribution of annual income, net of income tax paid; no adjustment is made for part-year units.

(e) The Gini coefficient is equal to half the expected absolute difference in incomes, relative to the mean, between any two tax units drawn at random from the population: for example, a value of 36 per cent means that, on average, the absolute difference between the incomes of any two tax units is equal to 72 per cent of the mean.

Sources: 1949 to 1976/7 from Royal Commission on the Distribution of Income and Wealth (1979), table A.3, p. 167; 1977/8 from National Income and Expenditure, 1980, p. 113; 1978/9 to 1984/5 from *Economic Trends*, 1987, table A (Gini coefficient for 1978/9 from National Income and Expenditure, 1982, p. 110).

According to Kuznets' observations, the US and the UK were comfortably on the second part of the ∩ shape.

These conclusions about falling inequality were not accepted by all. The purpose of Titmuss' (1962) essay *Income Distribution and Social Change* was to provide a critique of the evidence on which popular impressions were based. He rightly drew attention to the limitations of the official statistics. To take just one example, the definition of income fell considerably short of a comprehensive measure of command over resources. Awareness of the weaknesses of existing statistical information was one of the reasons that led to the setting up in 1974 of the Royal Commission on the Distribution of Income and Wealth, chaired by Lord Diamond. An important function of the Commission was to improve the available statistics. The distribution of annual after-tax income among tax units shown in table 1.1 is based largely on its reports. This is the main official series on the distribution of income, widely known as the 'Blue Book series'.

Before looking at what it shows, I should emphasise that the Blue Book series is still far from perfect. It is still the case, for example, that measured income excludes the imputed rent on owner-occupied houses and major items of fringe benefits. National Insurance contributions are not deducted in arriving at 'after-tax' income. Nor, to take another example, do the estimates make any correction for people who only appear in the statistics for part of the year.[1] For these, and other, reasons, table 1.1 can give only a partial picture of the distribution of economic well-being.

Moreover, the Blue Book series departs in certain respects from the Base Definition described above. Table 1.1 takes no account of family size, so that an income of £10,000 is regarded the same whether it has to support one person or a family of four, and each tax unit is counted once whatever its size. While we would not necessarily want to divide the income by four, yielding per-capita income, we may want to make an adjustment for family size by means of an 'equivalence scale' which varies with family size and composition. Having calculated 'equivalent income' by dividing by this scale, we may then want to count as many incomes as there are people in the tax unit.

Bearing these qualifications in mind, we can see that the Blue Book series in table 1.1 shows that in 1949 the top 10 per cent and the bottom 50 per cent of tax units both received about 27 per cent of total after tax income. The fact that the shares were virtually the same means that the top 10 per cent were on average about 5 times better off than the bottom half of the population: in fact 5.1 times. There was however a gradual downward trend until the mid 1970s in the share of the top 10 per cent, there being a total fall of 4.8 percentage points (from 27.1 per cent to 22.3 per cent). At the same time, the share of the bottom 50 per cent rose slightly from 26.5 per cent to

27.4 per cent. This led to a decline in the ratio of their average incomes from 5.1 to 4.1. A different indicator of inequality, the Gini coefficient favoured in official statistics, fell over the quarter century by 4 percentage points.[2]

The fall in income differences between 1949 and 1976 was a noticeable one.[3] At the same time, as we have just seen, the share of the bottom 50 per cent did not itself rise very much. Most of the redistribution was from the top 10 per cent to the next 40 per cent, or the upper middle-income group. It was those already in the upper middle of the income range who gained, not those at the bottom. This may give some indication why a period of recorded income equalisation still gave rise to concern about the persistence of relative poverty.

1.2 What do we know from official statistics about the recent period?

So far I have discussed the situation up to the mid 1970s. What has happened since then? The first point to be made in answering this question is that our knowledge in this area remains distinctly limited; indeed the situation with regard to statistics on the overall distribution of income has in certain respects worsened since the 1970s.

A comparison with the situation in Eastern Europe is striking in this respect. In work with Micklewright (Atkinson and Micklewright, 1992), I have been looking at what was known about the distribution of income in Eastern Europe prior to 1990. At the outset, our expectations regarding data availability were not high, influenced by the case of the Soviet Union, of which Bergson has written: 'Concerning income inequality in the USSR, the Soviet government apparently prefers to withhold rather than to release information' (1984, p. 1091). The situation in Eastern Europe was however quite different. The Central Statistical Offices of a number of Eastern European countries have an impressive record of publications. Evidence about the distribution of *earnings* in Poland has been collected and published since 1955 (Vielrose, 1978, p. 229), whereas in Britain the regular collection of statistics on the earnings distribution (the *New Earnings Survey*) began only in 1970, or 15 years after Poland. In the case of *incomes* in Poland, information was (in Autumn 1991) available on the household distribution for a range of years up to 1989; data were available for Czechoslovakia on the household distribution of income covering the period 1958–88; and those for Hungary covered the years 1962–87.

In contrast, in Britain in Autumn 1991, the Blue Book income distribution series covered only the period up to 1984/5. The Blue Book series has indeed had a rather chequered history, a history which illustrates how political factors play a role in the availability of statistics in market as well as in Communist countries. After being produced for many years, the series was dropped by the government in 1970. It was reinstated some five years later by the Royal Commission. When the Commission was abolished by the newly elected Thatcher government in 1979, this improvement was commended and reference made to the work being continued by official statisticians.[4] However, within two years, the Review of the Government Statistical Services (Privy Council, 1981, p. 4) reduced the frequency of production of estimates of the distribution of personal income from every year to every three years. We have therefore only figures for 1978/9, 1981/2 and 1984/5, as shown in the lower part of table 1.1. The last of these was published in November 1987, so the figures for 1987/8 are overdue. On telephoning the Central Statistical Office in July 1991, we were however told that there were no definite plans to publish the next set of results.

The official income distribution data in Britain are therefore considerably less up to date than those of Eastern Europe. Now you may say that there is a difference in the quality of the data. The Eastern European statistics have been criticised for not including, for political reasons, the 'nomenklatura', or the party elite, who derived benefits ranging from the ability to buy in foreign currency shops to privileged housing or medical care. This is true, but it has to be remembered that the UK figures too leave out much of the benefits in kind paid to top earners. So-called fringe benefits are far from minor in importance and include some of the same items, such as privileged medical care.[5]

The lack of recent Blue Book income distribution data is frustrating, since what the figures up to 1984/5 show is very interesting. As may be seen from table 1.1, the share of the top 10 per cent in after-tax income has begun to rise, after falling for several decades. Between 1975/6 and 1978/9 the increase in inequality was slight, but between 1978/9 and 1984/5, a period of six years, the share rose by 3.1 percentage points – wiping out two-thirds of the fall between 1949 and the mid 1970s. But it was not a simple reversal of the previous trend: the upper middle-income group did not absorb all of the fall, and the share of the bottom 50 per cent fell – see table 1.1 – to the lowest level recorded in the post-war period. This intensified the widening in the distribution and the top 10 per cent were back to having more than 5 times the average of the bottom half.

1.3 Evidence from the Family Expenditure Survey

The Blue Book series on which I have drawn so far 'seeks to combine the best features of the available sources' (*Economic Trends*, November 1987, p. 100). To this end, the Central Statistical Office (CSO) takes the Inland Revenue Survey of Personal Incomes, based on income tax returns, as its starting point but supplements this with information from the Family

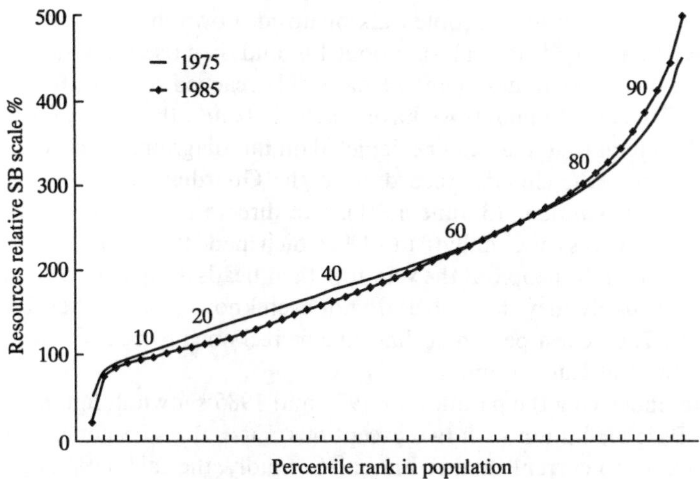

Figure 1.1 Income parade 1975 and 1985
Note: The values for 1985 have been adjusted proportionately to give the same mean as for 1975 (222 per cent of the SB scale). The mean for 1985 was 211 per cent of the SB scale in that year. The percentile points are plotted from 2 per cent to 96 per cent.
Source: FES Base Tapes.

Expenditure Survey (FES), particularly on those with low incomes.[6] The way in which it is done means however that one cannot have access to micro-data on individual families. In order to explore more fully what lies behind the changes, we have to rely solely on the FES, which has been used extensively in distributional analysis: see for example Jenkins (1991) and Townsend (1991). The FES is an excellent survey, but differential non-response and underreporting of income mean that it provides less satisfactory coverage of the top incomes than does information based on the tax records.[7] It should also be stressed that, being based on a *household* survey, the FES data do not cover those people who sleep on the streets of London or those living in institutions.[8]

Results from our own analysis of the FES – work done jointly with Holly Sutherland and Karen Gardiner – are shown in figure 1.1, comparing the years 1975 and 1985.[9] The representation is a little different. In statistical terms, figure 1.1 shows the percentiles of the distribution. These are the numbers 10, 20, etc. marked on the graph, with '10' indicating the person 10 per cent from the start of the distribution.

In more popular terms, figure 1.1 is like the parade of incomes described by Pen (1971). He imagined a parade in which everyone marches past in an hour, with their height corresponding to their income. The height of the marchers begins – after some people walking upside down (businessmen or investors who have made losses) – at about 1′6″ and then rises very slowly, so that even by the 30 minute point we have only reached some 4′. By the beginning of the last 3 minutes we have reached 10′ and then it begins to shoot up. Much more so than can be depicted on this diagram, which stops $2\frac{1}{2}$ minutes before the climax. According to the Guardian Index of Top Executive Pay (*Guardian*, 13 June 1991), five directors received annual remuneration in excess of £1 million in 1990, which made them over 500 feet tall. As Pen said of the people at the very top 'their heads disappear into the clouds and probably they themselves do not even know how tall they are' (1971, p. 53). The richest person at that time he reckoned to be J. P. Getty with a height of at least 10 miles.

The data underlying the parades for 1975 and 1985 shown in figure 1.1 follow the Base Definition with two exceptions. First, the FES concept of income is closer to current than to annual. Secondly, the calculations are based not on income but on 'net resources', which is income net of income tax, National Insurance contributions and outgoings on housing. The deduction of housing costs means that we are considering resources disposable after this relatively fixed item of expenditure has been deducted.[10] This measure of living standards has been applied for many years in the official study of 'Low Income Families' (Department of Health and Social Security, 1988a), but is clearly open to debate – see, for example, Johnson and Webb (1990). It does however avoid some of the problems which arise in securing comparable estimates for 1975 and 1985.[11]

Earlier, I noted that the Blue Book series made no allowance for differences in family size. Here net resources are divided by the relevant long-term Supplementary Benefit (SB) scale, SB being at that time the minimum income guarantee programme (now called Income Support). This scale is used primarily to allow for differences in family composition (an equivalence scale), but it also expresses an official view of the movement over time in the minimum safety net standard. The parade shows for 1975 people's position in relation to the official safety net level, this being measured on the left-hand axis. It may be seen that a significant minority of the population are below this level, with, for example, the person 10 per cent from the start of the 1975 parade having net resources around 100 per cent of the SB scale. This reflects the fact that a proportion of those entitled to SB do not in fact claim and that those in work are not covered by the safety net.

The main focus of figure 1.1 is on the comparison of the two years, for which purpose the figures have been normalised to have the same mean. The two parades do not of course contain the same people: they are representative of the population at two different dates. Between 1975 and 1985 some people have died and others have been born. Of those present on both occasions, most will be in a different place in the two parades. We cannot follow the individual life histories, to see who has moved up and who has moved down (although this will become possible with the panel study being carried out at the University of Essex). What figure 1.1 indicates is the income of the 'corresponding person' who has the same position in the parade. It shows that in the first part of the 1985 parade the corresponding person has a lower income than in 1975 (the 1985 line marked with diamonds lies below), and this continues until we are about two-thirds of the way through the parade. Then we see the 1985 people appearing over the top. At high incomes, such as the ninetieth percentile, they are distinctly taller. Incomes in 1985 were such that those in the lower two-thirds of the distribution had a lower relative income than their counterparts in 1975, whereas those in the top third had a higher relative income. In this sense, the tall have got taller and the short have got shorter.

If, instead of the parade, we were to draw the Lorenz curves, taking the shares in total income of the bottom 5 per cent, 10 per cent, 15 per cent, up to the bottom 95 per cent, then the Lorenz curve for 1985 lies at all those points below that for 1975. The share of the bottom 25 per cent, for example, was 11.3 per cent in 1975 but 10.4 per cent in 1985, and the share of the bottom 50 per cent was 30.3 per cent in 1975 but 27.9 per cent in 1985. The share of the top 10 per cent was 22.6 per cent in 1975 and had risen to 24.4 per cent by 1985.

The increase in income inequality from 1975 to 1985 is also demonstrated by summary measures of inequality, a selection of which are shown in table 1.2. The Gini coefficient, already used, shows an increase from 28.9 per cent to 32.1 per cent. The other measures of inequality in table 1.2 all belong to the 'generalized entropy class' (Cowell and Kuga, 1977, and Shorrocks, 1980). The different values of the parameter c appearing in the index I_c attach differing weights to different aspects of inequality. The value of the index when $c=2$ is equal to half the squared coefficient of variation, and this increased by 3 percentage points from a value of 20.9 per cent in 1975 to 23.9 per cent in 1985. The value $c=0$ corresponds to a logarithmic welfare function (Atkinson, 1970), and this increased from 16.4 per cent to 19.0 per cent.

What has happened since the mid 1980s? Table 1.2 also shows estimates for 1988, indicating that there was a further – indeed sharper – rise in inequality between 1985 and 1988. The Gini coefficient increased from 32.1 per cent to 37.5 per cent in 1988. Judged by past changes, this is a large increase. The share of the top 10 per cent increased from 24.4 per cent to 29.2 per cent, a rise of nearly 5 percentage points. The value of the generalised entropy index corresponding to a logarithmic welfare function increased from 19.0 per cent in 1985 to 28.0 per cent in 1988.

These findings are confirmed by official studies using the FES data. The CSO study of the effect of taxes and benefits on household incomes, referred to as the 'CSO series', compares the distribution of equivalent disposable income in 1977 with that in 1988. These figures differ from those quoted so far, and from the Base Definition, in that the unit of analysis is the household rather than the family unit and that each household counts for 1, regardless of its size. The definition is closer to the Base Definition in that the CSO makes an estimate of annual as opposed to current income.[12] As is stressed by the authors, the CSO series is not fully consistent over time, but the broad trend is clear. According to the official summary:

> the distribution of household income has become more unequal. The bottom quintile group's share of disposable income fell [between 1977 and 1988] from 9.7 per cent to 7.6 per cent whilst the share of the top fifth of households went up from 36 per cent to 42 per cent. (*Economic Trends*, March 1991, p. 107)

The CSO results for the period 1977 to 1988 are shown in figure 1.2 in terms of the Gini coefficient (left-hand axis) and the ratio of the share of the top 20 per cent to that of the bottom 20 per cent (right-hand axis). It may be noted that the rise in the share of the top 20 per cent, and the fall in the share of the bottom groups, was particularly marked after 1985. The Gini coefficient increased by 6 percentage points between 1985, when it was 29 per cent, and 1988, when it was 35 per cent. This change is in line with that recorded in table 1.2 and bears out the finding that there was a more rapid movement towards inequality in the period 1985 to 1988.

Further confirmation of a sharp rise from 1985 to 1988 is provided by a recent addition to the range of official statistics: the series on 'Households Below Average Income', referred to as 'HBAI'. This again relates to households, rather than families, and is based on current income, but otherwise corresponds to the Base Definition. The series shows the share of the bottom 20 per cent in net income before housing costs falling from 9.8 per cent in 1985 to 8.9 per cent in 1987, and that of the top 20 per cent rising from 36.2 per cent to 39.1 per cent (*Social Trends*, 1991, table 5.16). The figures for net income *after* housing costs, more comparable to those in table 1.2, show the share of the bottom 20 per cent falling from 8.6 per cent in 1985 to 7.6 per cent in 1987, and that of the top 20 per cent rising from 37.6 per cent to 41.0 per cent. Expressed as a ratio, the share of the top 20 per cent relative to that of the bottom 20 per cent rose from 3.7 in 1979 to 4.4 in 1985 and then by considerably more to 5.4 in 1987.

Conclusions: *income inequality in the UK in the 1980s*

To sum up, the traditional – and most extensive – Blue Book set of official estimates of income inequality, those in table 1.1, show inequality in the

Table 1.2. *Summary measures of income inequality in the UK 1975–88*

	1975	1985	1988
Gini coefficient (%)	28.9	32.1	37.5
Generalized entropy index (%)			
$c=2$ ($\frac{1}{2}$ squared coefficient of variation)	20.9	23.9	47.3
$c=0.5$	15.1	17.8	27.2
$c=0$ (logarithmic welfare function)	16.4	19.0	28.0
$c=-0.5$	20.3	22.8	34.3

Notes: (a) The generalised entropy index is defined for $c \neq 0$ or 1 as

$$I_c \equiv 1/[c(c-1)]\ 1/n\ \Sigma\{(Y_i/y)^c - 1\}$$

where Y_i denotes the income of person i, y denotes mean income, and n is the number of people. The case where $c=0$ is given by

$$I_0 \equiv -1/n\Sigma \mathrm{Ln}(Y_i/y)$$

where Ln denotes the natural logarithm.

(b) The distribution refers to net resources, defined as income net of income tax, National Insurance contributions and housing costs. It is expressed as a percentage of the relevant long-term Supplementary Benefit scale.

(c) Earnings are 'normal' earnings and include certain payments in kind. Self-employed income is adjusted by an index to bring it to the mid point of the relevant year, and is increased by 19.5 per cent to make an approximate allowance for underreporting. Social security benefits are those in current receipt. Where individual net income is negative, it is set to zero.

(d) The distribution is calculated for family units, with each unit receiving a weight equal to the number of individuals in the unit.

Source: FES Base Tapes, summary indices calculated using the INEQ programme written by F. A. Cowell from data grouped into 23 ranges.

UK as increasing between the mid 1970s and the mid 1980s, a reversal of the previous downward trend. Evidence from the Family Expenditure Survey shows that there can be little doubt that inequality was higher in 1985 than in 1975. The increase in measured inequality is large by historical standards, and there are grounds to believe that the rise between 1985 and later years in the 1980s was even more marked (see chapter 2 for more recent estimates).

1.4 Understanding the changes: the balance of conflicting forces

I have described the breakdown of the Kuznets hypothesis, at least as far as Britain is concerned, but I suspect that Kuznets himself would scarcely have been taken aback by the finding that the inverse-U shape no longer

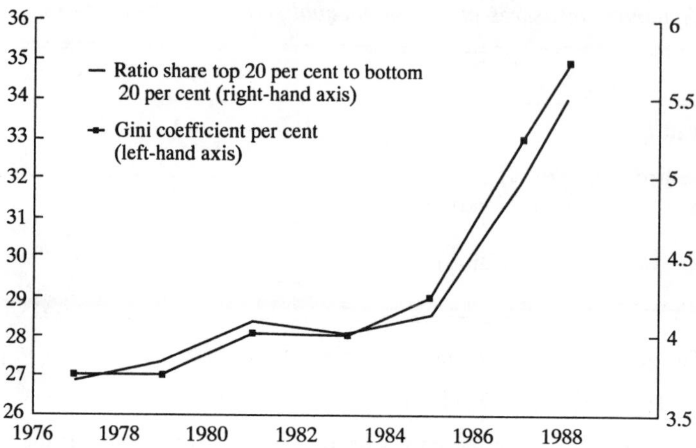

Figure 1.2 *Economic Trends* estimates 1977–88
Source: *Economic Trends*, March 1991, table N and O, p. 118.

applies, since he referred frequently to the balancing of conflicting effects. Changes in the distribution of income are the outcome of several forces operating in different directions. As the balance of these forces varies, we may expect the resulting trend in inequality to change direction. In the same way, alternative explanations will have differing importance at different dates.

The balancing of conflicting forces is evident from what is perhaps the most important legacy of Kuznets' approach: the analytical framework for examining the contribution to overall inequality of different sectors of the economy. Suppose that the population can be divided into two groups, A and B, and that θ denotes the proportion in sector A. Overall inequality depends on θ, on the degree of inequality within each sector, and on the difference between the mean incomes in the two sectors. This is illustrated in part A of table 1.3 for the case where the degree of income inequality is measured by the square of the coefficient of variation, V^2, this being the member of the generalised entropy family that allows a familiar variance decomposition –see equation (1) in table 1.3. Overall inequality is the sum of three terms, involving the inequality within sectors (the first two terms) and the inequality between sectors (terms in square brackets).

It is this kind of decomposition that underlay Kuznets' original discussion of the impact of the shift from the agricultural to the non-agricultural sector associated with economic development. Using a numerical example, he examined the implications for overall inequality of a decline in the proportion engaged in agriculture. As the proportion in the

Table 1.3. *Decomposition of inequality measures*

(A) Squared coefficient of variation

$$V^2 = \theta\,(y_A/y)^2\,V_A{}^2 + (1-\theta)\,(y_B/y)^2\,V_B{}^2 + [\theta(y_A/y-1)^2 + (1-\theta)\,(y_B/y-1)^2] \quad (1)$$

or

$$1 + V^2 = [\theta\lambda^2(1+V_A{}^2) + (1-\theta)(1+V_B{}^2)]/[\theta\lambda + 1 - \theta]^2 \quad (1')$$

(B) Generalized entropy ($c \neq 0$ or 1)

$$1/c(c-1) + I_c = \{\theta\lambda^c[1/c(c-1) + I_c{}^A] + (1-\theta)[1/c(c-1) + I_c{}^B]\}/[\theta\lambda + 1 - \theta]^c \quad (2')$$

(C) Generalised entropy ($c = 0$)

$$I_0 = \theta\,\{I_0{}^A - \text{Ln}[\lambda/(\theta\lambda + 1 - \theta)]\} + (1-\theta)\{I_0{}^B - \text{Ln}[1/(\theta\lambda + 1 - \theta)]\} \quad (3')$$

Notes: (a) $\frac{1}{2}V^2 = I_2$

(b) $y_A/y = \lambda/[1-\theta+\theta\lambda]$; $y_B/y = 1/[1-\theta+\theta\lambda]$.

The following definitions apply:

θ proportion of the population in sector A

y overall mean income

y_i mean income in sector i (i=A,B)

V_i^2 squared coefficient of variation in sector i

λ relative mean incomes, y_A/y_B

I_c generalised entropy measures with parameter c

I_c^i generalised entropy measure with parameter c in sector i

two sectors, here represented by θ, varied, he held constant the relative inequality within the sectors (here V_i^2) and the relative mean incomes in the two sectors. This means that the overall mean income, y, must change with θ. For this reason, it is better to replace the terms in y_A/y by ones involving θ and the relative mean incomes in the two sectors, denoted here by λ – see the alternative version of equation (1) in table 1.3, denoted by (1′). Parts B and C of table 1.3 show the corresponding expressions for the generalised entropy measures. As is clear from these expressions, and as Kuznets emphasised, the effect of a switch in the importance of the two sectors is not clear cut. Not only does it depend on the degree of inequality within the sectors and on the relative mean incomes, but also it is non-monotonic in θ. For example, with the same level of inequality in both sectors, overall inequality measured by the squared coefficient of variation rises with θ until the latter reaches a value of $1/(1+\lambda)$, and then falls.

This sectoral framework was applied by Kuznets to help understand the effects of industrialisation. It may appear attractive to apply the analysis in reverse to the de-industrialisation of the British economy. However, it is not clear to me that the explanation of the distribution of personal incomes in Britain today should begin with the generation of factor incomes. There are a number of stages between the determination of factor incomes and the final distribution of income among families. The factor distribution is important for the personal distribution, but there are several intervening mechanisms. Since the days when classical economists could identify payments to factors with payments to individuals, there has been a growth in the role of intermediaries, not least in the role of the state, and its function of taxation and payment of transfer incomes. I am therefore going to reverse the traditional approach, not working from factor incomes to personal incomes, but back from the elements which directly affect the personal distribution.[13]

1.5 The shift from work

Of the elements which affect personal incomes, one of the most important is whether or not the family is supported by a person in work, which determines whether or not the family has access to the single largest component of factor income – that from wages or self-employment.[14] In this respect there has been a major shift since the 1970s, as is brought out by figure 1.3, which shows the composition of household gross income in the Family Expenditure Survey (there is a break in the series in 1983 as a result of changes in housing benefit). In the mid 1970s, income from work (earnings plus self-employment income) accounted for more than 80 per cent of the total; by 1982 it had fallen to 73 per cent. There appears to have been a discrete shift between the mid 1970s and the mid 1980s, with the proportion remaining more or less steady since then.

The implications of this shift in the importance of work income depend on how it has been shared. At one extreme, all earned incomes may have been scaled down (or other incomes scaled up) proportionately; at the other extreme, a fraction of the population may have seen their earned incomes reduced to zero. Evidence that the fall in income from work has not been spread proportionately across the population is provided by figure 1.4, which shows the percentage of households where the head was in work (employed or self-employed). This fell by 6.3 percentage points between 1975 and 1981 (when there was a break in the series), and by 3.5 percentage points between 1982 and 1985. Since then it has levelled out. It did not return to its previous level with the decline in recorded unemployment in the latter part of the 1980s.

It may be thought that this shift in income from work between the mid 1970s and the mid 1980s is simply associated with the ageing of the

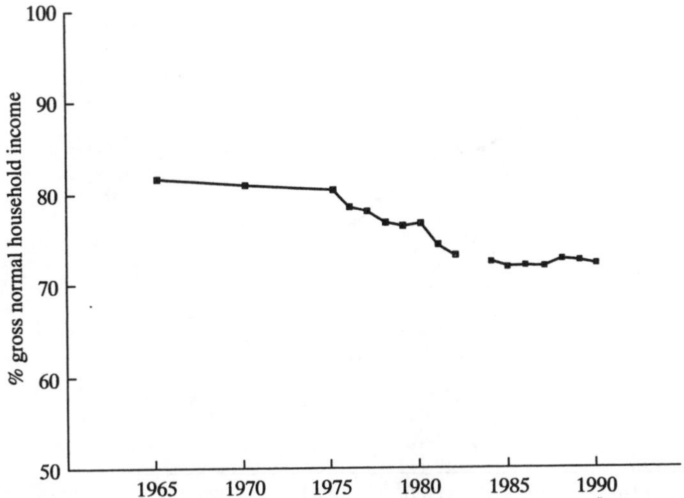

Figure 1.3 Per cent of income from work
Sources: 1965–78: Family Expenditure Survey (FES), 1978, table 40. 1979: FES, 1979, table 46. 1980–2: FES, 1983, table 22. 1984–6: FES, 1986, table 22. 1987–8: FES, 1988, table 22. 1989: FES, 1989, table 22, corrected using FES 1990, table A. 1990: FES, 1990, table 22. There is a break in the series in 1983 and the figure for that year is not shown.

population. However, Britain is ageing less markedly than other countries. Between 1975 and 1985 the proportion of people living in families headed by a person aged over 65 rose by little more than 1 percentage point.[15] And while it is true that early retirement has expanded in Britain over this period, those aged 55 plus only account for about a third of the increase in the size of the group without a person in work.[16] If we look at the ages at which the size of the not in work group has increased, then we find increases at all ages: the age group 35–54 contribute less proportionately but broadly the same number absolutely as those aged 65 plus. It is therefore a more general phenomenon than retirement.

This decline in the importance of work cannot but have affected the distribution of income, and I now use the data from the Family Expenditure Survey to explore how far this accounts for the observed increase in inequality between 1975 and 1985.[17] For this purpose, let us consider two groups of the population: those families where either the husband or wife is in work, denoted by the A, 'Active', sector and those where neither is in work, denoted by B.[18] It may be noted that in treating husbands and wives symmetrically the breakdown differs from that in figure 1.4, which refers to the 'household head'.

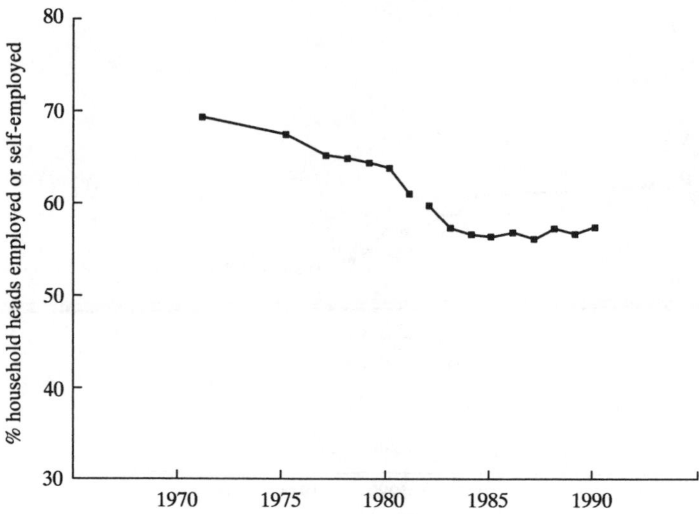

Figure 1.4 Per cent of household heads at work
Sources: Family Expenditure Survey, table 1 for all years except 1975 (table 40) and 1977 (table 39). There is a break in the series between 1981 and 1982, when there was a change in the definition of people 'at work' – see FES 1982, annex A.

To see how such a decomposition may help us learn about the trends, an example may be helpful. In a study of the early retired in the years 1975 and 1985, we found (chapter 5 below) that there had been a significant change over this period in the distribution of income for the cohort of men aged 55–64. However, if one considers the two sub-groups of those who had retired and those in the labour force, then *within* these groups there had been little change in the distribution. The overall shift reflected the trend to lower rates of labour force participation. For example, the incidence of low incomes could be almost totally accounted for by the change in the relative size of the group in the labour force.

In the case of the whole population, there has been a similar reduction in the proportion 'in work'. In 1975, 80.6 per cent of families contained an adult in work; by 1985 this had fallen to 69.1 per cent – see table 1.4. There was a downward shift of 11.5 percentage points. The effect of this shift depends on the income differential between the two sectors, and we may note that those in work had on average net resources just short of twice that of families without a person in work. This ratio was higher in 1985 than in 1975, but the difference for the two years is not very large.

The effect of the shift from sector A to sector B depends also on the distribution *within* the two sectors. It is commonly believed that income

Table 1.4. *Decomposition of individual distribution of family net resources in the UK 1975, 1985 and 1988*

	1975	1985	1988
θ share of sector A (those in work)	80.6	69.1	70.3
λ relative income in A and B	1.87	1.91	2.20
Inequality among those in work (A) percentage points			
Gini	25.7	27.8	32.8
I_2	17.8	19.0	40.5
$I_{0.5}$	12.2	13.7	22.0
I_0	13.1	14.4	21.4
$I_{-0.5}$	16.1	17.0	25.0
Inequality among those not in work (B) percentage points			
Gini	27.0	28.0	34.0
I_2	23.3	21.8	37.8
$I_{0.5}$	15.1	15.3	21.7
I_0	16.1	16.2	23.1
$I_{-0.5}$	19.9	19.3	27.6

Source: FES Base Tapes, summary indices calculated using the INEQ programme written by F. A. Cowell from data grouped into 23 ranges.

inequality is greater among the working population than among those not in work, particularly in Britain with its largely flat-rate benefit structure. In fact, this is not true. Typically, for those not in work there is more inequality at the top and the bottom of the income scale. The Lorenz curves for the two groups cross, with that for sector B lying *outside* at the top and the bottom. As the results for 1975 and 1985 in table 1.4 show, all five summary inequality measures used here record higher inequality among those not in work. This difference in sectoral inequality has to be taken into account in assessing the impact of the shift between 1975 and 1985: it is in the direction of the more unequal sector.

To quantify the effect of the shift from work, suppose that we take the generalised entropy measure, I_0, with $c=0$, which corresponds to a logarithmic welfare function. The overall rise in inequality from 1975 to 1985 was from 16.4 per cent to 19.0 per cent, a rise of 2.6 percentage points. If in the formula for I_0 (in table 1.3, part C) we take the values for 1975 but replace the proportion in the A sector by that for 1985, then the calculated change is a rise of 1.5 percentage points, or more than half the observed change.

In contrast, the effect of the change in relative sectoral incomes is small. If we replace the 1975 value for λ by that for 1985, the difference is 0.2

percentage points; similarly, replacing inequality in the B sector by its 1985 value, the change would be less than 0.1 percentage point. The other main element is the rise in inequality *among those in work*. If we replace the 1975 value for inequality in the A sector by its 1985 value, then the calculated increase is 1.0 percentage point. Together, the shift in the size of the working population and the rise in inequality among those in work 'account' in an arithmetic sense for almost all of the difference in inequality between 1975 and 1985.

The quantification of the different effects may depend on the choice of inequality measure. Taking the generalised entropy measure with $c=0.5$, we may calculate that the shift between sectors accounts for a rise in inequality of 1.3 percentage points, and the rise in inequality in A for 1.2 percentage points, compared to a total increase of 2.7 percentage points. With a value of $c=-0.5$, the figures are 1.8 percentage points and 0.6 percentage points, compared with a total increase of 2.5 percentage points. To give a quite different measure, we may note that in 1975 the proportion of the population living in families with incomes below the SB scale was 9.5 per cent; by 1985 this had risen to 15.1 per cent. While the proportion below this level has risen in both sectors, the shift in weight of the two sectors alone could account for a rise of 3.3 percentage points, or 60 per cent of the change.

On this basis, it appears that the shift from work accounts for around half of the observed rise in inequality. At the same time, it appears from figures 1.3 and 1.4 to have been a structural shift rather than a secular trend. We would not therefore expect the same explanation to apply to the changes post-1985. From table 1.4 it may be seen that the size of the A sector did not fall further from 1985 to 1988, in fact it increased slightly. The inequality within the A sector, on the other hand, continued to increase, and this accounted for some 60 per cent of the observed increase in inequality from 1985 to 1988. Inequality also increased between 1985 and 1988 in the B sector, and there was a sizeable rise in the relative income of the A sector, which in three years rose from 1.9 to 2.2 times that in B. These two elements, which played little or no role in the difference between 1975 and 1985, accounted almost equally for the remainder of the change between 1985 and 1988.

In what follows I examine in greater depth the determinants of the incomes in the two sectors identified here, considering both their relative level (λ) and their distribution within the sector.

1.6 Those not in work and transfer income

In considering sources of income, one tends to think of the complement of income from work as being income from capital: rent, dividends and

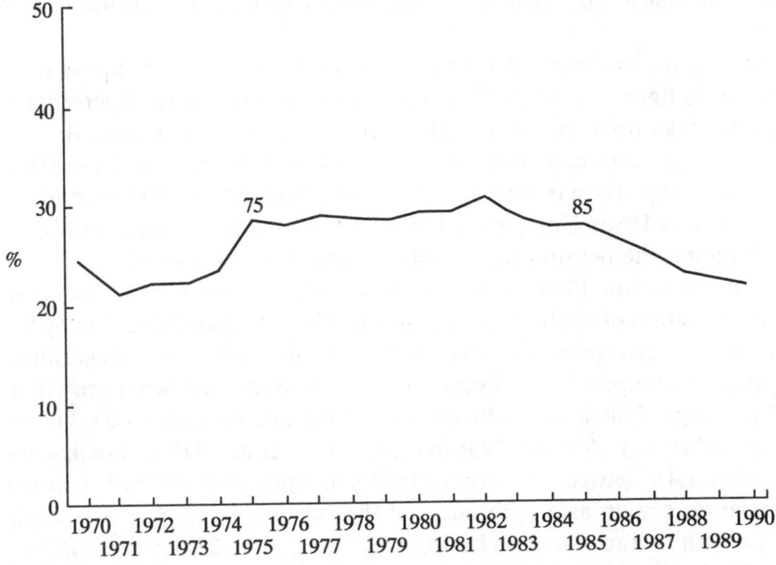

Figure 1.5 Pension as per cent of net earnings
Sources: Department of Social Security, *Social Security Statistics*, 1991, tables H3.06 and H3.10. Earnings are the average of those of all adult full-time workers (male and female) whose earnings are unaffected by absence, after deduction of the income tax and National Insurance (not contracted out) contributions paid by a single person. The earnings series is adjusted for the change in definition in 1983 using overlapping figures for that year.

interest. This is the classic division by factor shares. However, as far as the household sector is concerned, the second most important source, after income from work, is that of social security benefits. Social security is an example of an intermediate distributional mechanism, as of course are private transfers such as those from occupational pension funds. The social security schemes and the pension funds are institutions that stand between the factor and personal distributions of income.

It is on state transfers that I wish to concentrate here, since through the level of benefits the government has a direct impact on the distribution of income. The weekly net take-home pay of a single person with average earnings rose from £40.70 in April 1975 to £137.90 in November 1985, or an increase of 238.8 per cent (*Social Security Statistics*, 1989, table 46.13, with adjustment for break in series in 1983). Over the same period, the rate of unemployment benefit rose from £9.80 to £30.45 a week, or an increase of 210.7 per cent. These figures may sound very similar, but they mean that the ratio of income in work to income out of work rose from 4.15 in 1974 to 4.53 in 1985.

Pensioners have been treated more generously than the unemployed, as is shown by figure 1.5, where the single pension is expressed as a percentage of the net take-home pay of a single person with average earnings. In 1974 the Labour government made a distinct improvement in the position of the flat-rate state pension relative to the net earnings, and this was maintained until the early 1980s. Comparing 1975 and 1985, the two years identified on the diagram, the pension was a similar percentage in both years.

From the middle 1980s, however, there has been a marked decline in the relative position of the basic state pension. This reflects the decision by the Conservative government to change the basis for up-rating from earnings to prices, a change which is important in view of the significant growth in real earnings. This is undoubtedly one of the factors responsible for the sharp fall between 1985 and 1988 in the relative income of those not in work (see table 1.4). Between November 1985 and April 1988 the basic pension for a single person as a percentage of the net take-home pay of a single person with average earnings fell from 28.5 per cent to 23.5 per cent (*Social Security Statistics*, 1989, table 46.15).

The level of social security benefits has an important influence on the relative incomes in the two sectors. If, in 1985, all social security benefits (not including rent or poll tax rebates) had been reduced by 20 per cent, then the relative income of those in work would have risen to 2.22 times that of those not in work, which is almost exactly the increase observed between 1985 and 1988 (see table 1.4). (Since this is only an illustrative calculation, no attempt has been made to allow for the income tax payable on benefits or the reduction in housing rebates.) Overall inequality in 1985, measured in terms of half the squared coefficient of variation, would have been increased by some 3 percentage points. This is large by historical standards (although less than the very large increase recorded from 1985 to 1988 in table 1.4).

The impact of social security benefits on the overall distribution comes about not just on account of the change in the relative average incomes but also because of the effect on the *distribution* among those not in work. In figure 1.6 are plotted the frequency distributions for the two sectors, the horizontal scale being percentages of the Supplementary Benefit (SB) scale, and the frequencies being expressed as percentages. The frequency distribution for those in work (solid) has the expected hump shape, but that for those not in work is more complex. There is a heavy concentration around the SB level, but there are more at the very bottom and a long upper tail. It is this combination that generates a distribution where there is less relative inequality in the middle, but more at the bottom and at the top.

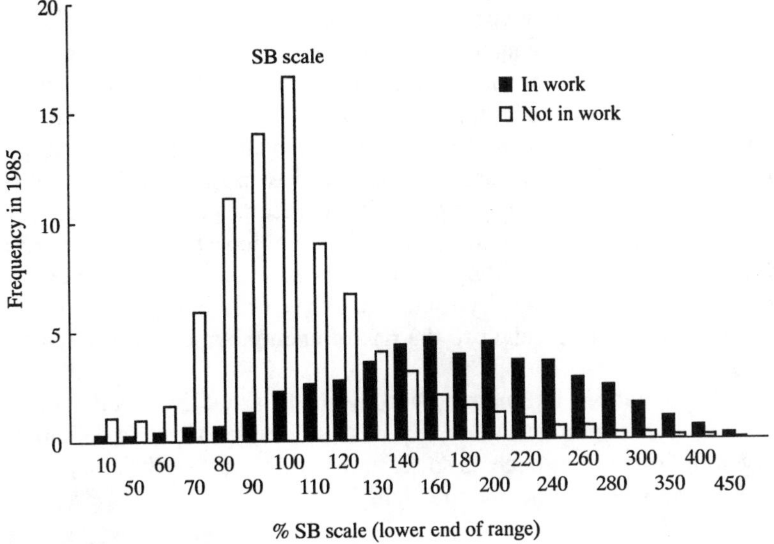

Figure 1.6 Distribution in relation to SB level
Source: FES Base Tape for 1985. Frequencies shown in percentage points per 10 per cent intervals of the SB ratio up to 500.

A cut in benefits, while holding the SB scale constant, has the effect of shifting the central mass downwards, away from those with other sources of income, such as occupational pensions, and towards those who are ineligible for or do not claim state transfers. In the case of the retired, it would widen the gap between what Titmuss (1955) described as 'two nations in old age': one group relatively fortunate, benefiting from occupational pensions and private savings, the other group receiving only the basic state pension, which left them dependent on means-tested assistance. What is striking is that the position does not seem to have altered greatly since Titmuss wrote. The aim of the state earnings-related pension scheme introduced in 1975 was to provide adequate pensions for those not covered by occupational schemes, but its build up has been slow and it has been seriously scaled down by the 1986 Social Security Act.

This analysis highlights the importance of social security benefits. This in turn brings us to the question as to what determines benefit levels. As public choice economists have emphasised, the government's actions cannot be treated as purely exogenous. Explaining the distribution of income requires an explanation of government behaviour. Does the change in direction of policy reflect a change in social judgements? Have our concepts of equity changed, becoming less relative and more absolute, so that purely inflation proofing of benefits is now regarded as an acceptable target? Why has the response in the 1980s to higher unemployment been to make the benefit system less generous to the unemployed? One answer is that there has been a change in the model of unemployment on which the government bases its decisions, with it now apparently believing in the largely voluntary nature of unemployment. But has there also been a decline in altruism? Has *ex ante* electoral support for the policy of providing an income guarantee given way to *ex post* self-interest? One can see how this might have happened if people had voted for the welfare state for motives of insurance, but once the recession arrived, the majority found that they were not at risk, and so ceased to give as much weight to the risk of unemployment (see chapter 9 below).

This is speculation. The main point to be made is that the explanation of trends in the income distribution requires an analysis of public decisions. Intervening institutions such as social security are part of the story as to what has happened to income inequality.

1.7 Those in work and earnings inequality

Families with a person in work have on average enjoyed a marked rise in prosperity over the 1980s, but amongst them was a distinct rise in inequality. In part this rise is due to the behaviour of transfer payments, such as child benefit, received by those in work; in part it reflects the changes made to the structure of income taxation and National Insurance contributions. According to the estimates of Johnson and Webb (1993), the application of the 1979 tax and benefit system to the 1988 distribution of household incomes would have reduced the Gini coefficient by about 3 percentage points.[19] And the reductions in top income tax rates may have led at the upper levels to a larger proportion of remuneration appearing in the statistics.

The rise in inequality among those in work also reflects the increased dispersion of pre-tax earnings, which brings us closer to the factor distribution of income. Moving from the level of the family or household to that of the individual, we can find evidence in the *New Earnings Survey* of widening inequality in individual gross earnings. Figure 1.7 shows the changes between 1975 and 1990 in the distribution in Great Britain for all full-time workers. The degree of inequality is measured by the ratio of the top decile (earnings of the person 10 per cent from the top) to the bottom decile (earnings of the person 10 per cent from the bottom), referred to as the 'decile ratio'. In 1975, the person at the top decile earned about 3 times the person at the bottom decile; from 1980 the ratio increased, reaching 3.2 in 1985 and 3.36 in 1988. Put another way, the earnings at the top decile

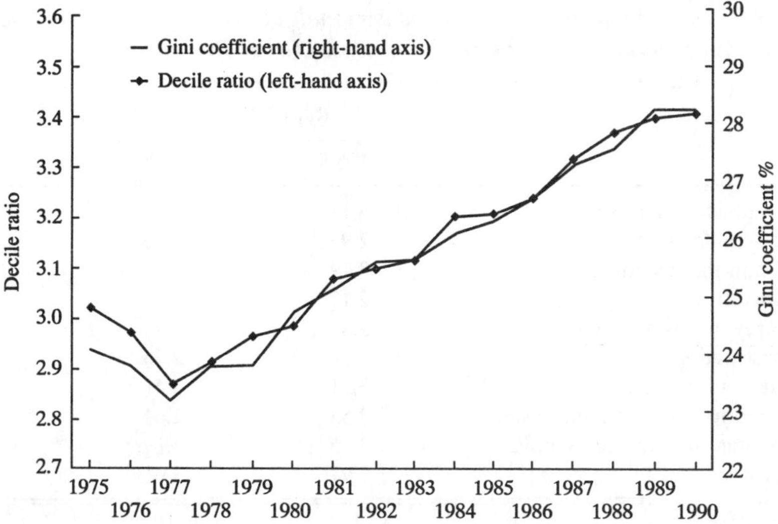

Figure 1.7 Earnings distribution 1975–90
Source: Atkinson and Micklewright, 1992, table BE1.

rose from 167.5 per cent of the median in 1975 to 186.5 per cent in 1990. The higher earners did particularly well.

To what is this increase in earnings dispersion due? There are a large number of potential explanations which may be derived from the literature on the determination of pay differentials (see Phelps Brown, 1977, for a wide-ranging review). In the Preface to his *Theory of Wages* in 1932, Hicks referred to:

> The historical fact which dominates the wage-history of the present century . . . is the growth of Trade Union power and the development of State Regulation of Wages. (Hicks, 1932, p. x)

One possible explanation is that there has been a reversal of these historical facts. It certainly seems possible that pressures for equalisation have been reduced by the abandonment of incomes policies (see Adams, 1988), and the dismantling of much of the Wages Council provisions to protect low-paid workers. A role may also have been played by the changes in social security provisions which have had the effect of making people accept jobs paying less than in their previous employment. How far union bargaining power has been reduced at shop floor levels is more open to question, as is the impact of reduced union power on earnings dispersion.

Alternatively, is increased dispersion attributable to Kuznets-like inter-

Table 1.5. *Earnings inequality by industry: all full-time employees paid on adult rates (earnings not affected by absence) Great Britain*

	Ratio of top to bottom decile	
	1986	1990
All industries and services	3.11	3.30
All manufacturing	2.93	3.10
All non-manufacturing	3.19	n/a
Agriculture, forestry and fishing	2.17	2.50
Energy and water supply	2.49	2.83
Construction	2.57	2.96
Distribution, hotels and catering	3.11	3.41
Transport and communication	2.53	2.64
Banking and financial services	3.75	4.19
Other services	2.97	3.01

Note: The lower part of the table shows the results for all single digit SIC codes outside manufacturing.
Source: 1986: *New Earnings Survey* (NES), 1986, part B, table X2. 1990: *NES* 1990, part A, table X2.

sectoral shifts – the de-industrialisation hypothesis? Employment has moved away from manufacturing towards services, but are services characterised by greater inequality? In table 1.5 are shown the changes in earnings dispersion by industry between 1986 and 1990, measured by the decile ratio. The figures relate to workers paid on adult rates (and hence are different from those in figure 1.7, which cover all workers). It appears that the service industries are not unambiguously characterised by greater earnings dispersion. If we take the distributive trades, hotels and catering, then the ratio in 1986 was exactly equal to that for the work force as a whole, bearing out the truth of Napoleon's statement that we are a nation of shopkeepers! For banking and financial services the decile ratio is greater (a ratio of 3.75), but for construction, transport and communication, and 'other services' it is less. Moreover, within each of the industrial groups, the decile ratio increased between 1986 and 1990. For example, the decile ratio increased from 3.11 to 3.41 in distribution; in banking it went from 3.75 to 4.19. All the industrial groups examined, including manufacturing, show a significant rise in inequality, apart from 'other services'. It appears that we have to explain what has happened within industrial sectors as well as between these sectors.[20]

Moreover, the explanation cannot be peculiar to the policies of the British government, since the trend is found in other countries. Green,

Coder and Ryscavage (1992) made use of data on five OECD countries (Australia, Canada, Sweden, US and West Germany) from the Luxembourg Income Study, covering two dates: broadly the beginning of the 1980s and the mid 1980s. The data, which cover the wages and salary income received by male heads of households aged 25 to 54 years working full time and year round, suggest that the 'earnings of the highest paid men in each of the countries examined were becoming more concentrated in the 1980s' (Green *et al.*, 1992, p. 11). In all five countries, the share of the top 20 per cent in total earnings increased. Outside North America, there was little change at the bottom, and it was Canada and the US that showed the largest overall increase in dispersion, the Gini coefficient rising by 3 and 4 percentage points, respectively. Gottschalk and Joyce (1991), adding France, Netherlands and the UK to the sample, show that, despite the large differences in the movements in average real wages in the eight countries, in all cases the upper percentiles performed better. The decile ratio widened by amounts varying from 1 per cent per year (Australia and Netherlands) to 4 per cent per year or more in North America.

Conclusions

There are many aspects of the distribution of income which I have not discussed in this chapter. I have said nothing about the distribution of capital. What about the attempts by Mrs Thatcher to create a property-owning democracy through privatisation?[21] I have not discussed the gender distribution of income and such difficult, and important, issues as the distribution of income within the household. I have not discussed income mobility – either within a lifetime or across generations.

Much therefore remains undiscussed. At the same time, I have tried to do two things. The first is to document the changes which are taking place. Whether or not income inequality is increasing is a contentious subject, and statistical evidence can be abused and misused. As I have stressed, the resources devoted to this area have diminished; we have no body comparable to the Royal Commission. In the first part of the chapter, I have looked at the evidence from different directions, setting it in historical context. It is clear to me that the 1980s have seen a departure from the historical trend, with a definite rise in inequality. There are grounds for believing that the rise between 1985 and later years in the 1980s was even more marked.

The second aim has been to identify some of the elements which should enter an explanation of the trend to increased inequality. I have highlighted two aspects – the shift from work and the rise in earnings inequality – which in my judgement need to receive particular attention when considering the rise in inequality between the mid 1970s and the mid 1980s. The subsequent rise after 1985 can again be attributed to increased earnings dispersion, but the period also saw a widening income difference between those in work and those not in work, and a rise in inequality within the latter group. In seeking to explain these different parts of the story, economic factors undoubtedly play an important role. The observation that the earnings dispersion has increased in a range of countries suggests that there may be common economic determinants. But these are less relevant to the substantial proportion of the population (now three in ten families) without income from work. We need also to give weight to considerations which do not typically appear in the textbook account of the distribution of income. I have stressed the role of intervening institutions, such as the social security system and the political process that determines transfer payments. Differences in national policies are one reason why there may be less similarity of experience across countries when it comes to the distribution of *income*.

I have not provided an answer to the question posed in the title to this chapter, but I would like to leave you with one concluding reflection. It has been suggested to me in the past that the distribution of income did not change much and that it was therefore either unimportant or uninteresting. Changes in the distribution were of second-order importance. Now, such stability may have resulted from a general tendency to immobility or it may have reflected the fact that, at certain periods, there was a broad balance between a variety of forces operating in different directions. It is my impression from the evidence of the 1980s that the latter is the case. There are certainly a variety of mechanisms at work and there is no reason to expect that they will always balance each other, nor that the same explanations will apply at all dates. The future is likely to be, in this respect, an interesting one.

2 Income distribution in European countries

(WITH LEE RAINWATER AND TIM SMEEDING)

The aim of this chapter is to assemble empirical evidence about the personal distribution of income, and the trends in income inequality over time, in the countries of Europe in the 1980s. It encompasses 15 European countries: the Nordic countries, Switzerland, and all 12 members of the European community apart from Greece. The United States is included as a point of reference.

Empirical facts are treacherous objects. The subject of income distribution is littered with 'facts' that have ceased to hold or which proved on closer examination to be mere statistical artefacts rather than genuine economic regularities (remember Keynes' constancy of the share of labour?). The value of empirical generalisations has more often been found in the theoretical process used to explain them than in the empirical observation itself. It can be argued that the – very substantial – contribution of Kuznets' Presidential Address (1955) lay in his analytical framework rather than in the celebrated Kuznets curve indicating that inequality first rises and then falls as a country develops. This chapter starts therefore from a position of modesty as to what can be achieved by a summary of the empirical evidence. Not the least of the reasons for this are the difficulties in making such comparisons, and it is with their limitations that the chapter begins in section 2.1.

The second difficulty in writing a chapter on empirical facts is that these have many dimensions. Here we have chosen to concentrate on the comparison of income inequality across countries, and across time. Sections 2.2 and 2.3 summarise evidence for 14 of the European countries about the extent of income inequality in the 1980s, drawing largely on data from the Luxembourg Income Study (LIS). (The country not covered in these sections is Denmark.) Do all distributions have broadly the same shape? Can one identify distinct groupings of countries with different degrees of inequality?

Sections 2.4 and 2.5 are concerned with the changes over recent years. Is there a worldwide trend towards greater inequality? In addressing this question, use is made not only of the LIS data but also of the findings of individual national studies in different European countries (now including Denmark). These studies, carried out by government statisticians or academic researchers, are not typically designed to be comparable with those in other countries, but are an important complement to the LIS data, providing a point of comparison and typically allowing a longer time series to be examined.

Even within the field delimited above, any compilation of empirical facts is bound to be selective, and there is a high probability that the tables and graphs in this chapter fail to answer the particular questions in the reader's mind. It is in fact our belief that this method of dissemination should be supplemented by one which takes advantage of modern micro-technology. We should move to a situation where subsets of variables from full micro-datasets are made available in a form where the reader can choose, within limits, the method of presentation. This however requires a change in the rules of official statistical agencies, and for the present we can only apologise for the straitjacket imposed on the micro-data.

Finally, it should be noted that the title refers to income inequality in *European countries*, not to income inequality *in Europe*. It would be a valuable, but challenging, project to produce income distribution estimates for Europe as a whole.

2.1 On entering the minefield

The comparison of income distributions across countries, or across time, raises many problems. (For discussion of the problems of comparability across countries, see, among others, Lydall (1979), van Ginneken and Park (1984) and Atkinson and Micklewright (1992).) We need to decide what we want to measure and how far we can measure it on a comparable basis.

Inequality of what among whom?

In the empirical results, attention is concentrated on the distribution of *disposable money income*, that is income after direct taxes and including transfer payments. Several points should be noted:

(a) income rather than consumption is taken as the indicator of resources;
(b) the definition of income falls considerably short of a Haig–Simons comprehensive definition, typically excluding much of capital gains, imputed rents, home production, and income in kind;
(c) no account is taken of indirect taxes nor of the benefits from public spending (other than cash transfers) such as health care or education or subsidies;

(d) the period of assessment is in general annual (although the UK evidence relates to weekly or monthly income).

These points mean that the variable measured may depart from that regarded as ideal. They also mean that the results may not be comparable across countries: for example, one country may help low-income families through housing benefits (included in cash income), whereas another provides subsidised housing (not taken into account).

To the question 'among whom', the standard answer here is the simplest: the distribution is that among *individuals*. The standard unit of assessment is however taken as the household, in that the incomes of all household members are aggregated and then divided by an equivalence scale to arrive at individual *equivalent income*. The equivalent scale is taken, for simplicity, to be the square root of the household size, so that the income of a household of four persons is divided by 2.0. The choice of the household, rather than a narrower unit such as the spending unit or the family, is open to debate. It assumes a degree of income sharing within the household which may not take place. Moreover, the choice of unit may affect comparisons across countries on account of differing household structures and/or differences in the form in which data are collected. The same applies to the choice of equivalence scale, and the alternative of taking per-capita incomes is considered in section 2.2.[1]

Problems in ensuring comparability

The problems in ensuring a reasonable degree of comparability may be illustrated by reference to one of the most widely cited international comparisons – that carried out by Sawyer (1976) for the OECD. Table 2.1 summarises his main findings for the size distribution of post-tax income for 12 OECD countries around 1970. The countries are ranked in order of the Gini coefficient (highest at the top). The countries fall into three main groups (the breaks correspond to differences in the Gini coefficient of more than 2.5 percentage points):

France, Italy, Germany[2] and the United States,
Spain, Canada and Netherlands,
United Kingdom, Japan, Australia, Norway and Sweden.

This grouping is rather surprising: it does not correspond to what might be expected in view of the known features of these societies. For this, and other, reasons, the Sawyer study met with lively reactions, notable from the French government, which published a reply (Bégué, 1976). There are

Table 2.1. *International comparison by Sawyer 1976*

Country	Year	Gini %	Comments
France	1970	41.4	*
			Based on tax records
Italy	1969	39.8	
Germany	1973	38.3	Synthesis of different sources
United States	1972	38.1	*
Spain	1973–4	35.5	
Canada	1969	35.4	
Netherlands	1967	35.4	Based on tax records Relates to tax unit rather than household
UK	1973	31.8	*
Japan	1969	31.6	*
			Excludes agricultural, forestry workers and fishermen
Australia	1966–7	31.2	Only households in urban areas
Norway	1970	30.7	Based on tax records
Sweden	1972	30.2	

Note: * Estimated by applying average tax rates to pre-tax data.
Source: Sawyer (1976), tables 4 and 6.

indeed a number of serious problems, some of which are indicated in the 'Comments' column of table 2.1:

(a) The data are derived from different types of source. In the majority of cases, the source is a household survey, such as the US Current Population Survey, but in other cases the data are based on tax records (France, Netherlands and Norway) or a synthesis of different sources (Germany). Some indication of the consequences is provided by Sawyer's additional memorandum items for Germany (which replaces the synthetic estimate by one from a household income and expenditure survey) and the UK (which replaces the expenditure survey figure by a synthetic estimate[3]): the Gini coefficients are

	Synthetic estimate	Survey estimate
Germany	*38.3*	31.2
United Kingdom	33.5	*31.8*

(Sawyer (1976), table 6.)

Table 2.2. *Sources of data used*

Country (abbreviation)	Years	Source
Belgium (BE)	1985, 1988	Household panel study
Finland (FI)	1987, 1990	Household income survey
France (FR)	1979, 1984	Income tax records
Germany (GE)	1984	Socio-economic panel survey
Ireland (IR)	1987	Household income survey
Italy (IT)	1986	Household income survey
Luxembourg (LU)	1985	Household panel study
Netherlands (NL)	1983, 1987	Household survey of the use of public services
Norway (NO)	1979, 1986	Household income and wealth survey
Portugal (PO)	1980/1, 1989/90	Household income and expenditure survey
Spain (SP)	1980/1	Household income and expenditure survey
Sweden (SW)	1981, 1987	Household income survey
Switzerland (CH)	1982	Household income and wealth survey
UK	1979, 1986	Household income and expenditure survey
US	1979, 1986	Household income survey

To use the italicised figures, as in table 2.1, provides a rather misleading picture of the relative income inequality in the two countries.

(b) In two cases the data do not cover the whole population (Japan and Australia). The exclusion of part of the population may be expected in both cases to reduce the recorded degree of inequality.

(c) Sawyer did not have access to the original micro-data, and had in some cases to make aggregative adjustments, particularly in going from pre-tax income to post-tax income (the countries marked by a * in the Comments column). As described by Sawyer

> one of these distributions had to be estimated from the other by utilising data on the average amount of tax paid by each income class ... inequality tends to be under-estimated since households have not been ranked by the derived income concept. (1976, p. 12)

(d) The distributions relate to household income, but in the main figures no adjustment is made for differences in household size.

Approach adopted here

The approach adopted here does not overcome all of the problems of making comparisons across countries and across time, but reduces them significantly. Although the data are still drawn from different types of source (table 2.2 lists the countries covered and the origin of the data used in sections 2.2–2.4), the great majority are now drawn from household income surveys, or their equivalent, and no use is made of synthetic data. (Synthetic data may well give a more accurate picture of the distribution; they are not however typically available as micro-data.) The main qualification concerns the French data, which come from tax records.

The major advantage compared to the situation in 1976 when Sawyer made his study is the availability of micro-data. The aim of the Luxembourg Income Study has been to assemble in one place a database containing survey data from many countries and to place them as far as possible on a consistent basis.[4] Access to the micro-data means that it is possible to produce results on the same basis starting from individual household records.[5] It is therefore possible to make any desired adjustment for household size (eliminating problem (d) above). Aggregate adjustments, such as that from pre-tax to post-tax income (problem (c)), are not necessary, although in some cases imputations are necessary at the household level. The data all cover, at least in principle, the whole population (avoiding problem (b)).

The aim of the LIS project is to increase the degree of cross-national comparability, but it is important to emphasise that *complete* cross-national comparability is not attainable. Comparability is a matter of degree, and all that one can hope for is to reach an acceptably high level. Moreover, comparability does not imply accuracy. A critic may say that it reduces all data sets to the lowest common denominator. There may remain serious shortcomings in the extent to which we can measure economic advantage and disadvantage. These qualifications must be borne in mind when reading this chapter. We have some idea as to where the mines are located, but we have to tread very carefully.

2.2 Incomes in European countries in the 1980s: the shape of the distribution

This section looks at the shape of the distribution of disposable income in 14 European countries and the United States. In the majority of cases, the results refer to the period 1984–7, but some relate to the start of the 1980s (Portugal, Spain and Switzerland). Comparisons across countries may be sensitive not just to the data comparability but also to the form of presentation. We begin by considering disposable income per equivalent adult, using an 'intermediate' equivalence scale of household size to the power of a half, and by looking at percentiles of the median.

Table 2.3. *Income distribution in 1980s: percentiles of median and decile ratio*

	P_{10}	P_{25}	P_{75}	P_{90}	P_{95}	P_{90}/P_{10}
Belgium 1988	58.5	74.5	128.8	163.2	190.8	2.79
Finland 1987	58.9	76.5	125.5	152.7	173.6	2.59
France 1984	55.4	72.1	139.7	192.8	233.5	3.48
Germany 1984	56.9	75.0	132.7	170.8	201.7	3.00
Ireland 1987	49.5	66.7	150.9	209.2	252.2	4.23
Italy 1986	48.9	68.8	145.0	197.9	233.8	4.05
Luxembourg 1985	58.5	75.1	132.7	184.0	228.1	3.15
Netherlands 1987	61.5	75.7	135.0	175.0	206.4	2.85
Norway 1986	55.3	76.0	128.7	162.2	187.3	2.93
Portugal 1980/1	47.4	69.2	143.5	203.2	252.7	4.29
Spain 1980/1	46.3	68.1	143.4	203.0	248.1	4.38
Sweden 1987	55.6	75.6	125.1	151.5	170.4	2.72
Switzerland 1982	53.9	73.6	134.3	185.1	244.6	3.43
UK 1986	51.1	67.6	144.6	194.1	232.1	3.79
Memorandum item:						
US 1986	34.7	61.7	149.6	206.1	247.3	5.94

Sources: Portugal: see Rodrigues, 1993.
Spain: see Mercader, 1993.
All other from Atkinson, Rainwater and Smeeding (1994), table 4.1.
Notes: *a* The results are for the distribution among persons of household disposable income adjusted by an equivalence scale equal to (household size)$^{0.5}$.
b The results for Portugal and Spain are not produced from the LIS dataset and are less comparable with those for other countries.

Percentiles of the distribution

The first method of presentation (table 2.3) expresses the percentiles of the distribution as percentages of the median, denoted by P_i. For example, the tenth percentile (bottom decile), P_{10}, in the UK is around a half (51.1 per cent) of the median, and the ninetieth percentile (top decile), P_{90}, is nearly double (194.1 per cent) the median. The ratio of the top to bottom decile, referred to as the *decile ratio*, is shown in the final column; and in the case of the UK is approaching 4.

The overall picture in the 14 European countries are shown in the left-hand column of table 2.4, where the countries are ranked according to the value of the decile ratio. From this we can see that there is a group of countries with higher ratios, in excess of 4, including Italy, Portugal, Spain and Ireland. Switzerland and France are quite close to the UK, but there

Table 2.4. *Decile ratios for European countries on two different bases*

Decile ratio	Equivalised	Per capita
5.0		
4.9		
4.8		Ireland
4.7		
4.6		
4.5		
4.4		UK
4.3	Spain	France Italy
4.2	Portugal Ireland	Switzerland
4.1		
4.0	Italy	
3.9		
3.8		
3.7	UK	
3.6		
3.5		Germany
3.4	Switzerland France	Netherlands
3.3		Luxembourg
3.2		
3.1	Luxembourg	
3.0	Germany	Belgium
2.9	Norway	Sweden Norway
2.8	Netherlands	
2.7	Sweden Belgium	Finland
2.6		
2.5	Finland	

Note: 3.0 denotes that the decile ratio lies between 3.00 and 3.09.
Sources: Table 2.3 and Atkinson, Rainwater and Smeeding (1994), table 4.9.

are distinctly lower ratios in Benelux, Germany and the Nordic countries. The decile ratios appear to be inversely related to latitude, if Ireland is included with Southern Europe. It is interesting to note that the decile ratio in the United States, included in table 2.3 as a memorandum item, is close to 6, and this is the largest value recorded here. It is in fact off the scale in table 2.4.

Before looking at what lies behind these decile ratios, we should consider their sensitivity to the methods of calculation. This issue is examined in Atkinson, Rainwater and Smeeding (1994) and here reference is only made to the results shown in the right-hand part of table 2.4, which are intended to test the sensitivity to the method used to calculate equivalent income. It shows the ranking according to the decile ratio of per-capita income (Portugal and Spain excluded). Although standard practice in Eastern Europe (see Atkinson and Micklewright, 1992), per-capita distributions are rarely presented in OECD countries.[6] For all countries, except Norway, the decile ratio is increased, but the difference varies quite a lot across countries. The decile ratio in Sweden increases from 2.72 to 2.95, whereas that in the Netherlands increases from 2.85 to 3.46, taking it out of the 'less unequal' group. France, Switzerland and the UK are now more in line with Italy. While the broad picture is not greatly changed by the use of different equivalence scales, both the level of measured inequality and the position of individual countries *can* be materially affected.

Shape of the distribution

The high value of the decile ratio in the US is due in large part to the low value of the bottom decile relative to the median. This is brought out in figure 2.1a, which shows the countries ranked according to the bottom decile. (We have reverted to the square root equivalent scale.) In the US, the bottom decile is only slightly over a third of the median, compared with values of around 46–9 per cent in the next group of countries. The bottom decile is in excess of 55 per cent in Belgium, Finland, France, Luxembourg, Norway, Sweden and Germany. In the estimates for the Netherlands, the bottom decile is over 60 per cent of the median.

At the upper end of the distribution, the United States is less obviously different. Figure 2.1b shows the top decile relative to the median. The US cannot be distinguished from Southern Europe and Ireland. Comparing the two parts of figure 2.1, we can see that higher inequality in one country at one point in the distribution does not necessarily imply higher inequality elsewhere, as it would for example in the case of the two-parameter log normal distribution. The relative positions of Ireland and the US are one instance. Sweden performs less well with respect to the bottom decile than Netherlands and Luxembourg, but better at the top.

The shape of the distribution is shown more generally in figure 2.2 for France, Sweden and the US. This shows the logarithm of the income level corresponding to different percentiles. The diagram is like Pen's parade of incomes (see chapter 1), except that the heights have been adjusted so that the median person in each country passes through at eye level (0 on the scale) and that the differences are shown in relative rather than absolute terms.

The parade starts with the bottom decile. As we know, incomes at this point are a lot lower in the US. The height rises more steeply to reach the median, but beyond that point increases at almost the same rate. France

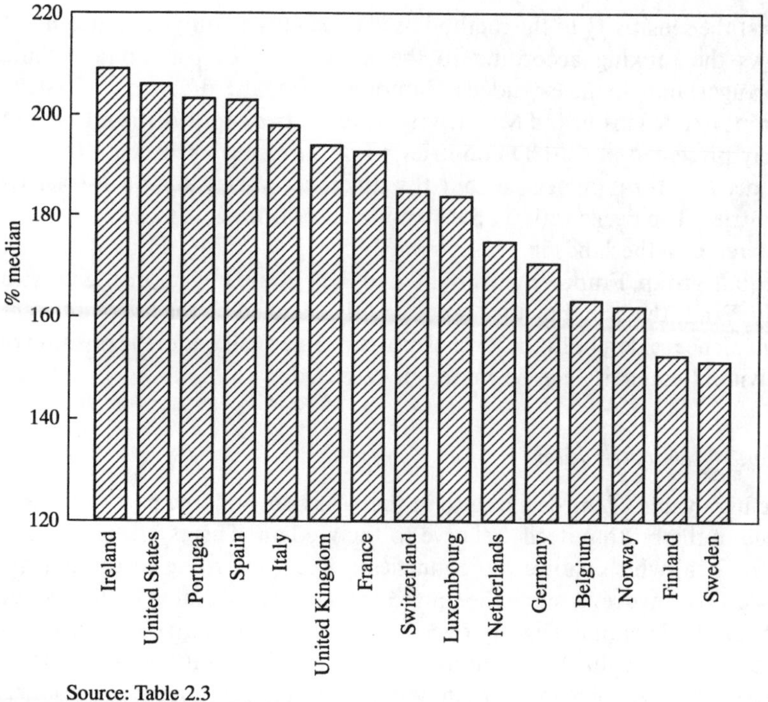

Figure 2.1a Top decile as per cent of median
Source: Table 2.3.

and Sweden start at the same level as each other, but the heights rise more quickly towards the median in Sweden. After the median, they rise more slowly in Sweden, and France is closer to the US. It may be seen that incomes in Sweden are more centred on the median than in the other two countries. If we take a band from 80 per cent of the median to 125 per cent, as indicated in figure 2.2, then only around a quarter (27.8 per cent) of the US population are found in this central range. In France, the proportion is around a third (35.9 per cent), whereas in Sweden it is approaching one half (46.4 per cent). This is an interesting difference between the income distributions in the different countries. From the results of Atkinson, Rainwater and Smeeding (1994), it may be seen that the middle-income class is also large in Belgium, Germany, Luxembourg and Norway. The middle-income class is small in Ireland, Italy and the UK, in addition to the US.

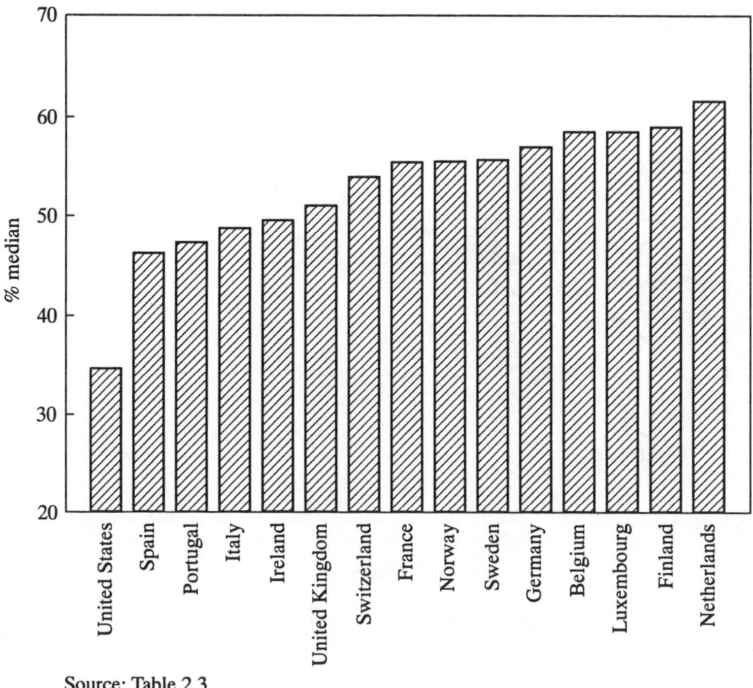

Figure 2.1b Bottom decile as per cent of median
Source: Table 2.3.

2.3 Income inequality in European countries in the 1980s

A more common form of presentation of income distribution statistics is in terms of shares of total income, which are the ingredients for the conventional Lorenz curve. Table 2.5 shows the cumulative shares by decile groups, where S_{10} denotes the share of the bottom 10 per cent, S_{20} denotes the share of the bottom 20 per cent, etc. The countries are listed in order of the share of the bottom decile group, S_{10}, which ranges from some 2.5 per cent in Ireland to 4.5 per cent in Finland. The ranking is not identical to that according to the bottom decile, P_{10}, since the share depends on the shape of the distribution in the bottom decile group, as well as on the mean, rather than the median. In considering the results of table 2.4, it should be borne in mind that those for Portugal and Spain were produced independently, and may be less fully comparable. They are therefore shown in brackets.

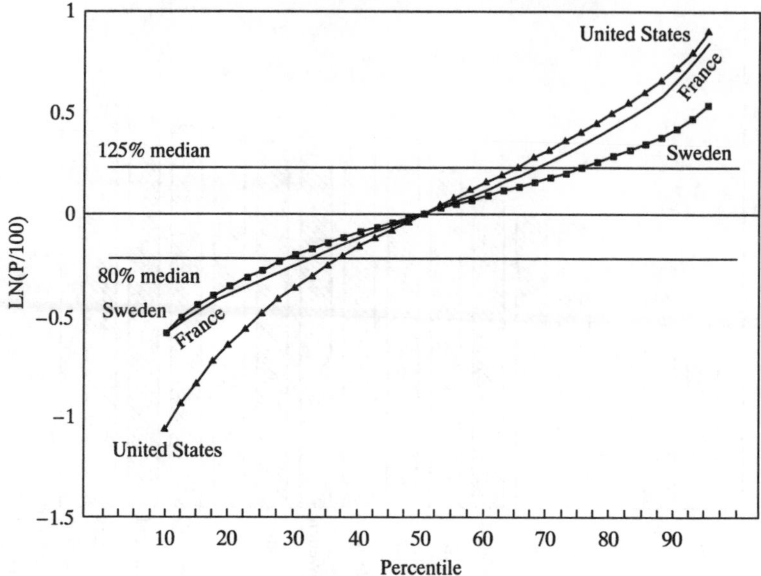

Figure 2.2 Relative incomes at different percentiles
Source: LIS data set.

The share of the bottom decile group gives the initial ranking of the Lorenz curves, but the Lorenz curves may subsequently cross. The decile shares are used in table 2.6 to test whether or not the Lorenz curves cross. A + or (+) in the table indicates that the Lorenz curve for the country shown in the left-hand column remains everywhere above that for the country shown on the horizontal axis; and a ? indicates that the Lorenz curves cross. Treating any difference as significant, there are in fact a high proportion of situations where a Lorenz comparison can be made. Of the 91 possible pair-wise comparisons of the 14 European countries, there are 70 cases where one Lorenz curve dominates the other. If, to make approximate allowance for the errors surrounding the estimates, cases are excluded where the differences for all decile shares are less than 1 percentage point (those cases marked (+) in table 2.6),[7] then there are 67 cases of Lorenz dominance. In over 70 per cent of cases we have an unambiguous ranking.

The partial ordering resulting from the Lorenz comparisons (taking only those cases where the difference is 1 percentage point or larger) are summarised in figure 2.3 in terms of a *Hasse diagram*. The countries towards the top of the diagram have the lower levels of inequality, and where a line can be traced downwards from country A to country B this implies that the Lorenz curve for country A is superior to that for country B.

Table 2.5. *Income distribution in European countries 1980s: cumulative decile shares of total income (per cent)*

	S10	S20	S30	S40	S50	S60	S70	S80	S90
Finland	4.5	10.8	18.1	26.4	35.6	45.6	56.6	68.6	82.2
Luxembourg	4.3	10.2	17.1	24.8	33.5	43.1	53.9	66.0	80.4
Belgium	4.2	10.2	17.1	25.0	33.8	43.5	54.3	66.4	80.3
Netherlands	4.2	10.2	17.1	25.0	33.8	43.5	54.3	66.4	80.3
Germany	4.0	9.8	16.6	24.2	32.9	42.5	53.2	65.3	79.4
Norway	3.9	9.8	16.9	24.9	33.9	43.7	54.6	66.7	80.6
Sweden	3.3	9.5	16.9	25.3	34.6	44.8	55.9	68.2	81.9
Italy	3.1	8.0	13.9	20.7	28.7	38.0	48.7	61.2	76.2
(Portugal)	3.1	7.8	13.8	20.1	28.7	37.9	48.3	60.6	75.8
France	3.0	8.3	14.6	21.8	29.9	39.1	49.5	61.6	76.3
Switzerland	2.8	8.0	14.1	21.0	29.0	37.8	47.7	58.9	72.5
(Spain)	2.8	7.4	13.2	20.1	28.2	37.5	47.9	60.2	75.5
UK	2.5	7.5	13.5	20.5	28.7	38.2	49.1	61.8	77.1
Ireland	2.5	7.1	12.6	19.3	27.1	36.3	47.0	59.6	75.1
US	1.9	5.7	11.2	18.0	26.2	35.7	46.9	60.2	76.3

Note: The results are for the distribution among persons of household disposable income adjusted by an equivalence scale equal to (household size)$^{0.5}$.

Sources: Portugal and Spain: see table 2.3. All other from Atkinson, Rainwater and Smeeding (1994), table 4.3.

Finland dominates all countries, followed by Benelux and Norway and Sweden. There appears to be a clear grouping of mainland Northern Europe at the top. At the bottom, neither Ireland nor Switzerland dominate any other country. In the middle are France, Italy, the UK and Portugal, which cannot be ranked one against the other. The Lorenz curves for Italy and Portugal are close; those for France, and even more the UK, start off lower and end up higher.

Summary measures of inequality

Where the Lorenz curves cross, the use of a summary measure of inequality yields a complete ranking, although different measures may generate different such rankings. In table 2.7 are shown the Gini coefficient and equally distributed equivalent (Atkinson) measures with inequality aversion parameters 0.5 and 1.0. (Portugal and Spain are not included.)

Table 2.6. *Lorenz comparisons (based on decile points)*

	LU	BE	NL	GE	NO	SW	IT	PO	FR	CH	SP	UK	IR	US
FI	+	+	+	+	+	+	+	+	+	+	+	+	+	+
LU		?	+	+	?	?	+	+	+	+	+	+	+	+
BE			+	+	?	?	+	+	+	+	+	+	+	+
NL				(+)	?	?	+	+	+	+	+	+	+	+
GE					?	?	+	+	+	+	+	+	+	+
NO						?	+	+	+	+	+	+	+	+
SW							+	+	+	+	+	+	+	+
IT								(+)	?	?	+	?	+	?
PO									?	?	(+)	?	+	?
FR										+	+	?	+	+
CH											?	?	?	?
SP												?	+	?
UK													+	+
IR														+

Source: Calculated from table 2.5.

The results for the Gini coefficients suggest the following broad groupings:

Scandinavia (Finland, Sweden, Norway), Belgium and Luxembourg: 20–4 per cent
Germany and Netherlands: 25–7 per cent
France, UK, Italy and Ireland: 30–2 per cent

This ranking of countries is rather different from that of Sawyer (1976), who found a higher value for the Gini coefficient in West Germany than in the US. The results with the Atkinson indices are broadly similar. Cases where European countries move up the ranking compared with the Gini coefficient are shown in italics in table 2.7. With an inequality aversion parameter of 1.0, Luxembourg moves up to second place and Sweden drops to fifth, below Germany; Italy moves ahead of France and the UK.

2.4 Recent trends in income distribution: evidence from the LIS dataset

There is considerable interest in how the distribution of income has been changing over time, particularly over the 1980s.[8] For eight of the 14 European countries discussed in the previous section we have comparable

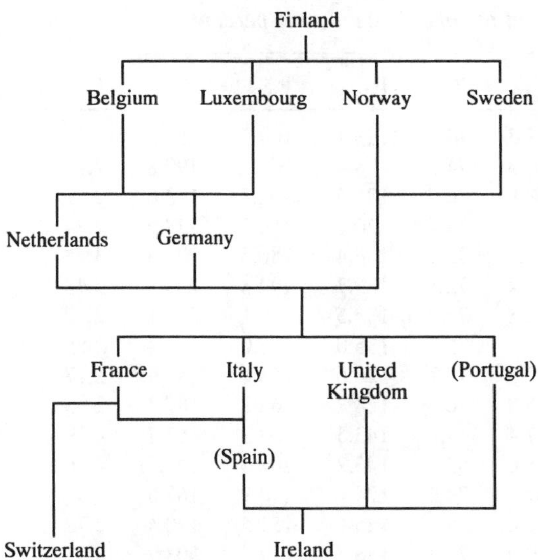

Figure 2.3 Ranking of countries (Hasse diagram)
Source: Table 2.5.

Table 2.7. *Summary measures of inequality*

Country	Year	Gini	Atkinson Measure parameter	
			0.5	1.0
Finland	1987	20.7	3.6	7.5
Sweden	1987	22.0	4.6	10.3
Norway	1986	23.4	4.6	*9.5*
Belgium	1988	23.5	4.9	10.3
Luxembourg	1985	23.8	*4.6*	*9.2*
Germany	1984	25.0	5.2	10.1
Netherlands	1987	26.8	n/a	n/a
France	1984	29.6	7.7	16.0
UK	1986	30.4	8.2	18.1
Italy	1986	31.0	*8.0*	*15.3*
Switzerland	1982	32.3	9.9	18.4
Ireland	1987	33.0	*9.3*	18.8
United States	1986	34.1	9.9	21.2

Note: In these calculations the data have been bottom-coded with the lowest value set at 1 per cent of mean disposable income.
Source: See table 2.5.

Table 2.8. *Trend over time in income distribution: percentiles of median*

		P_{10}	P_{25}	P_{75}	P_{90}	P_{95}	P_{90}/P_{10}
Belgium	1985	59.3	74.7	128.7	162.5	187.2	2.74
	1988	58.5	74.5	128.8	163.2	190.8	2.79
Finland	1987	58.9	76.5	125.5	152.7	173.6	2.59
	1990	57.0	76.4	126.2	156.2	178.5	2.74
France	1979	53.6	72.5	138.4	186.5	232.3	3.48
	1984	55.4	72.1	139.7	192.8	233.5	3.48
Netherlands	1983	64.8	77.2	135.5	176.1	208.1	2.72
	1987	61.5	75.7	135.0	175.0	206.4	2.85
Norway	1979	57.0	76.7	126.6	158.1	181.9	2.77
	1986	55.3	76.0	128.7	162.2	187.3	2.93
Portugal	1980	47.4	69.2	143.5	203.2	252.7	4.29
	1990	48.6	69.0	143.2	202.4	248.5	4.16
Sweden	1981	61.5	79.2	124.4	150.9	167.0	2.45
	1987	55.6	75.6	125.1	151.5	170.4	2.72
United Kingdom	1979	50.9	70.4	138.5	179.7	208.9	3.53
	1986	51.1	67.6	144.6	194.1	232.1	3.79
United States	1979	38.1	64.5	141.8	187.6	221.9	4.93
	1986	34.7	61.7	149.6	206.1	247.3	5.94

Note: The results are for the distribution among persons of household disposable income adjusted by an equivalence scale equal to (household size)$^{0.5}$.
Sources: Portugal: see table 2.3. All other from Atkinson, Rainwater and Smeeding (1994), table 4.5.

information for two dates: Belgium, Finland, France, Netherlands, Norway, Portugal, Sweden and the United Kingdom. These cover a range of countries, both with regard to their intrinsic features and with regard to what we have seen about the degree of income inequality. However, the two data points are not the same in each country, and the results need to be interpreted with care in view of the differing macro-economic climate at different dates and in different countries.

Percentiles of the distribution

The changes in the percentiles are shown in table 2.8. In considering the changes over time, little significance can be attached to small changes, such as the fall in the bottom decile in Belgium from 59.3 per cent of the median to 58.5 per cent. On the other hand, more significance can be attached to the

Table 2.9. *Trend over time in income distribution: cumulative decile shares of total income (per cent)*

		S10	S20	S30	S40	S50	S60	S70	S80	S90
Finland	1987	4.5	10.8	18.1	26.4	35.6	45.6	56.6	68.6	82.2
	1990	4.3	10.5	17.7	26.0	35.1	45.1	56.0	68.1	81.8
Belgium	1985	4.2	10.3	17.3	25.1	34.0	43.9	54.8	66.9	80.9
	1988	4.2	10.2	17.1	25.0	33.8	43.5	54.3	66.4	80.3
Netherlands	1983	4.4	10.6	17.4	25.0	33.4	42.8	53.3	65.3	79.4
	1987	4.1	10.1	16.9	24.5	33.0	42.5	53.2	65.3	79.4
Norway	1979	4.1	10.2	17.4	25.6	34.6	44.4	55.2	67.2	80.9
	1986	3.9	9.8	16.9	24.9	33.9	43.7	54.6	66.7	80.6
Sweden	1981	4.0	10.6	18.3	26.7	36.0	46.1	57.2	69.2	82.9
	1987	3.3	9.5	16.9	25.3	34.6	44.8	55.9	68.2	81.9
Portugal	1980/81	3.1	7.8	13.8	20.1	28.7	37.9	48.3	60.6	75.8
	1990/1	3.4	8.0	13.9	20.9	28.9	38.1	48.5	60.8	75.8
France	1979	3.1	8.4	14.6	21.9	30.0	39.2	49.7	61.6	76.0
	1984	3.0	8.3	14.6	21.8	29.9	39.1	49.5	61.6	76.3
UK	1979	3.5	8.7	15.1	22.6	31.1	40.8	51.8	64.4	79.2
	1986	2.5	7.5	13.5	20.5	28.7	38.2	49.1	61.8	77.1
US	1979	2.1	6.4	12.4	19.7	28.4	38.3	49.6	62.7	78.3
	1986	1.9	5.7	11.2	18.0	26.2	35.7	46.9	60.2	76.3

Note: The results are for the distribution among persons of household disposable income adjusted by an equivalence scale equal to (household size)$^{0.5}$.
Sources: Portugal: see table 2.3. All other from Atkinson, Rainwater and Smeeding (1994), table 4.7.

rise in the top decile in the UK from 179.7 per cent to 194.1 per cent.

The decile ratio increased in Finland, Netherlands, Norway, Sweden, the UK and (slightly) in Belgium. It remained unchanged in France and fell modestly in Portugal. In broad terms, this summarises the picture that emerges throughout this section. The majority of countries covered here show a rise in inequality, but this is not universal and the extent of the increase differs. There is diversity of experience across countries.

Moreover, the pattern of change has distinctive features. Even among those countries where inequality increased, we find differences. If, for instance, we look at the top decile relative to the median, then we find little change in the Netherlands and Sweden, where it is the decline in the relative position of the bottom groups that is responsible for the rise in the decile ratio. In contrast, the rise in the decile ratio in the UK over this period is the product of the rise in the relative position of the top decile. In the US, both the top decile rose and the bottom decile fell.

In the US, the changes between 1979 and 1986 were associated with a contraction of the central-income group: the proportion between 80 per cent and 125 per cent of the median fell from 31.1 per cent to 27.8 per cent. There were increases in the size of both the lower- and the upper-income groups. Over a similar period (1981–7) the percentage in the central group fell also in Sweden, from 49.3 per cent to 46.4 per cent, but the increase was almost entirely in the lower group. In contrast, in France the proportion in the central group did not change between 1979 and 1984.

Lorenz curves

The changes in the Lorenz curves are shown in table 2.9 for the eight European countries and the US. In France, the Lorenz curves cross, but they are virtually identical for the two years, the maximum difference in the cumulative decile shares being 0.3 percentage points. In Portugal the Lorenz curve moves upwards, the maximum difference over ten years being 0.8 percentage points. For the remaining six European countries, and the US, the Lorenz curve moves downwards, to varying degrees.

In both Netherlands and Norway the share of the bottom 50 per cent fell on average by 0.1 percentage point per year (in Belgium the fall was smaller), whereas the average rate of fall was larger in Finland, and was 0.2 percentage points or higher in Sweden, the UK and the US. As far as changes over time are concerned, the US does not appear to be an outlier. In the US, the total difference over the seven-year period in the cumulative decile shares is at least 1 percentage point from the third decile upwards, whereas in Sweden (over a six-year period) this is true from the second decile and in the UK for all decile shares. The maximum difference in the Lorenz curve in the US is 2.7 percentage points, which is the same as in the UK.

A similar picture is shown by the summary measures of inequality. The rise in the Gini coefficient is 3.2 percentage points in the US and 3.4 percentage points in the UK (Atkinson, Rainwater and Smeeding, 1994, table 4.8). By historical standards this is a noteworthy increase. The rise in Sweden is 2.1 percentage points, and that in Norway around half this amount. In France the Gini coefficient remained virtually unchanged between 1979 and 1984; in Portugal there was a modest decline over the 1980s. Again there is diversity of experience: the upward trend in income inequality is exhibited to differing degrees in different countries, and is not to be found in some countries.

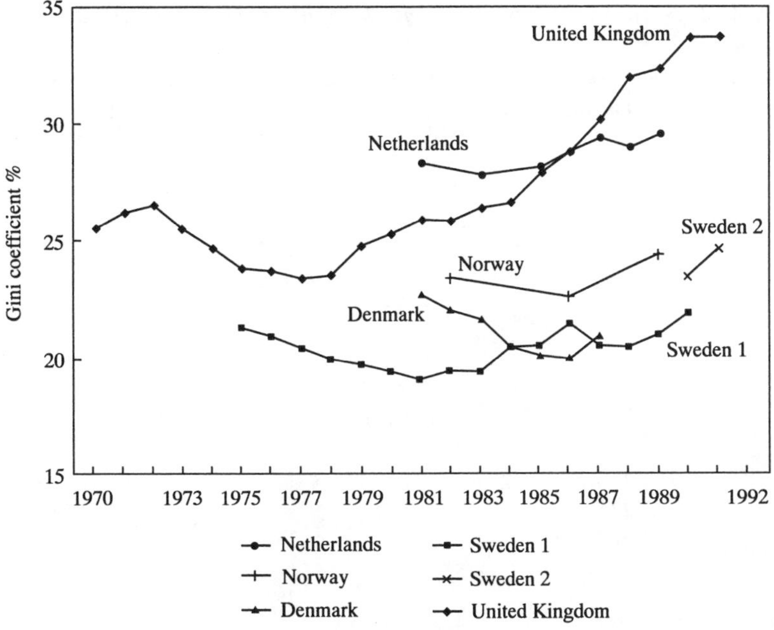

Figure 2.4 Trends in inequality I
Source: Table 2.9.

2.5 Recent trends in income distribution: evidence from national studies

In this section, we set the earlier results in the context of national studies of income inequality and extend the coverage to include Denmark. In reviewing the evidence available from other studies, we do not attempt a comprehensive survey of all published material. Rather, our purpose is to build a bridge between the LIS dataset, with its emphasis on raising the degree of comparability of the data employed, and the much more disparate national studies, which for understandable reasons have employed a wide variety of sources and definitions. Since we are concerned to compare the LIS dataset with other approaches, we do not refer to other studies which are based on the LIS dataset, such as Smeeding, O'Higgins and Rainwater (1990).

The Gini coefficients in table 2.10 are drawn from national studies of income inequality which are not designed for purposes of international comparison, and they are not necessarily based on the same types of sources, the same concepts of income or the same methods of calculation. For example, the US series, unlike those for other countries shown, relates

Table 2.10. *National studies of income distribution: Gini coefficients from 1970*

Year	Belgium	Denmark	Finland	France	Germany	Ireland	Italy
1970				39.8			
1971			27.0				
1972							
1973					25.4	36.7	
1974							
1975				38.4			
1976			21.6				
1977							34.9
1978					25.4		33.4
1979				36.4			33.8
1980						36.0	31.2
1981		22.7	20.6				30.6
1982		22.0					28.7
1983		21.6			25.5 / 25.0		29.2
1984		20.5		37.2			30.1
1985	22.5	20.1	20.0		26.0		
1986		20.0	20.5				30.2
1987		20.9	19.9		25.2	35.2	31.9
1988	23.4		20.4				
1989			20.5				29.7
1990			20.4		26.0		
1991			20.2				29.2
1992	23.7		19.9				

Notes and Sources:
Belgium: Cantillon *et al.* (1994), table 30; equivalent (scale 0.7 for the second adult and 0.5 per child) disposable income with person weights.
Denmark: Hansen (1993), table 3.4; equivalent disposable income with family weights.
Finland: Uusitalo (1989), table 5.4 and Uusitalo (1994); equivalent (scale 0.7 to the second adult and 0.5 per child) disposable income with person weights.
France: Canceill and Villeneuve (1990), p. 71; household income with no adjustment for household size, and with household weights.
West Germany: Hauser and Becker (1993), table 7; equivalent (social assistance scale) disposable income with person weights; excludes households with non-German head.
Ireland: Callan and Nolan (1993), table 4; household disposable income with no adjustment for household size, and with household weights.
Italy: Brandolini and Sestito (1994), table 2a; equivalent disposable income with household weights.

Table 2.10 (cont.)

Year	Netherlands	Norway	Sweden	UK	US
1970				25.5	39.4
1971				26.2	39.6
1972				26.5	40.1
1973				25.5	39.7
1974				24.7	39.5
1975			21.3	23.8	39.7
1976			20.9	23.7	39.8
1977			20.4	23.4	40.2
1978			20.0	23.5	40.2
1979			19.7	24.8	40.4
1980			19.4	25.3	40.3
1981	28.3		19.1	25.9	40.6
1982		23.4	19.4	25.8	41.2
1983	27.8		19.4	26.4	41.4
1984			20.4	26.6	41.5
1985	28.1		20.5	27.9	41.9
1986		22.6	21.4	28.8	42.5
1987	29.4		20.5	30.2	42.6
1988	29.0		20.4	32.0	42.7
1989	29.6	24.4	21.0	32.4	43.1
1990			21.9/23.5	33.7	42.8
1991			24.7	33.7	42.8
1992					43.3

Netherlands: Data supplied by Central Bureau of Statistics, see Atkinson, Rainwater and Smeeding (1994), chapter 4; household disposable income (deducting from net income interest paid, health care and life assurance premia, wealth tax payments, and alimony paid) with no adjustment for household size, and with household weights.
Norway: Epland (1992), table 4; equivalent (scale of 0.7 for second household member and 0.5 for subsequent members) disposable income with person weights.
Sweden: Gustafsson and Palmer (1993), annex; equivalent (social assistance scale) disposable income (including an allowance for imputed rent on owner-occupied homes) with person weights.
UK: Goodman and Webb (1994), p. A2 (BHC); equivalent (HBAI scale) disposable household income with person weights.
US: US Department of Commerce (1993), table B-3, p. B-6; household gross income (not including food stamps) unadjusted for household size, and with household weights.

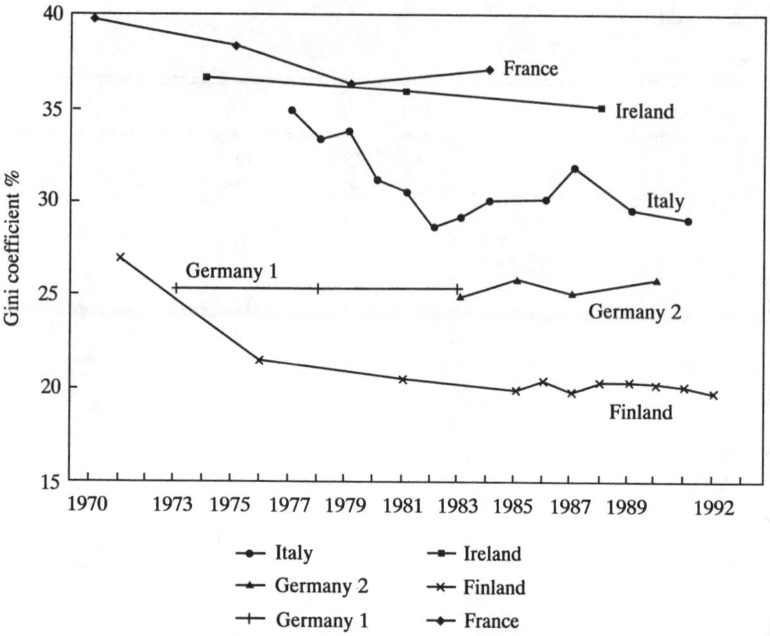

Figure 2.5 Trends in inequality II
Source: Table 2.9.

to the distribution of gross income (before taxes) and is not adjusted for household size. We have chosen series which give a reasonable span of years and which are themselves intended to be consistent over time. They therefore may serve to give an indication of the relative *trends* in different countries, but it should be stressed that one can draw no conclusions from these figures about the *relative* degree of inequality in different countries. (The main respects in which the series differ from those in earlier sections of the chapter are identified in the notes to table 2.10.) In view of the differences in definitions, sources and timing, we would not necessarily expect the results from the national studies to show the same level of inequality as we found in earlier sections. Nor need the trends be the same, in that the differences may have a different impact at different dates. The trends in the national studies are however of particular interest in view of the fact that the estimates typically cover a longer time period and include more observations.

We saw in section 2.4 that in the first half of the 1980s there was a marked rise in income inequality in Sweden and the UK. This rise is the more striking in that it came after a period in which inequality fell: there was a reversal of the previous trend. The U-shaped pattern – the inverse of that predicted by the Kuznets hypothesis – is illustrated in figure 2.4. As may be seen, the pattern in the Netherlands, Norway and Denmark has some similarity, although in Denmark it is only the last year (1987) in which there is any indication of an upturn in inequality. But in other countries, such as those shown in figure 2.5, the pattern is less clearly U-shaped. In Finland and France, it appears to be a case of the trend towards reduced inequality having come to a stop; in Germany there is no marked trend; in Ireland and Italy the downward trend continued, in the latter case with a cyclical component.

The pattern across countries does not therefore appear to be a uniform one. While it is possible that the countries in figure 2.5 are lagging behind the UK and Sweden, and that the 1990s will see a rise in income inequality more generally, this has yet to be demonstrated. Moreover, among the countries where inequality is rising, the rate of increase differs, with the UK standing out for the sharpness of the rise in recorded income inequality in the second half of the 1980s.

It may be noted that there is no apparent relation between the trend over the 1980s and the overall level of inequality. Inequality has increased both in the United States, with a high level even before the increase, and in Sweden, where inequality has historically been relatively low. Inequality has fallen in Italy, but risen in the UK, both occupying intermediate positions in the mid 1980s.

A brief conclusion

This review of evidence for different European countries is only partial, but it suggests two broad conclusions. First, certain groupings may be made. The Scandinavian countries, Benelux and West Germany have apparently distinctly less inequality in disposable equivalent income; Southern Europe and Ireland have distinctly higher inequality, with France and, to some degree, the UK and Italy, occupying an intermediate position. The ranking of countries is rather different from that of the earlier study by Sawyer and more suggestive of explanatory hypotheses – such as the differing form and extent of social protection, and the role of redistributive income taxation. Secondly, we can no longer assume that all European countries are comfortably on the downward part of the Kuznets curve, with inequality falling over time. Continuing progression towards *reduced* inequality was in the 1980s the exception rather than the rule. In a number, but not all, of the countries studied, inequality increased.

3 Poverty, statistics and progress in Europe

The first section (3.1) in this chapter will consider the important changes in poverty measurement in Europe. This is the first interpretation of the word 'progress' in the title 3.1. There have been significant developments, and our knowledge is substantially better than it was a few years ago. Calculations of the number with incomes below 50 per cent of the national average, taken as a low-income cut-off by the European Community, can now be much more firmly based. At the same time, there are ways in which the methods used in the measurement of poverty need to be advanced, or the emphasis shifted, and the role of future research receives particular attention.

The second interpretation of the word 'progress' concerns progress towards the development of the European Community. Here I have in mind not just rates of growth of GNP, but also progress of a more qualitative kind towards greater European unity, including the assessment of poverty on a Community-wide basis rather than relative to national incomes per head. In section 3.2, I consider the impact of economic growth on poverty in the Community under different assumptions about its assessment.

This brings us to policy, and in the concluding section I am concerned with the relation between poverty statistics and policy. What is the role of statistics such as that of 44 million people in the European Community living at below 50 per cent of national average income? Who should provide such statistics? Who are the intended audience?

3.1 Progress in the measurement of poverty and areas for future research

There have been major advances in our knowledge about poverty in Europe.[1] To begin with, the sheer volume of information is now much greater. A country with which I am not very familiar – Greece – provides a striking example of the improvement in availability of evidence about poverty. When the issue of poverty in Greece was discussed in 1984 the commentator said that 'studies on poverty are almost non-existent' (Hadjipanayotou, in Spahn, 1985, p. 77). When I enquired into the position in the Summer of 1989, I found that – in addition to the work of the Consultants to the European Poverty Programme – there have been studies by Kanellopoulos (1986), by Loizides and Giachalis (1989) and by Tsakloglou (1988 and 1990). There is a much richer availability of evidence at the national level.

At the same time, there are important ways in which the available information about poverty in Europe needs to be developed. In the rest of this section, I discuss some of the methodological issues, but I begin with a more general aspect – the integration of statistical information with that of a qualitative kind. It is evident from the *Exchange* bulletin that the Community Action Programme of the Second Poverty Programme provides a source of evidence quite different from, and complementary to, that based on statistical sources. In Atkinson (1989), I stressed that the secondary analysis of sample surveys needed to be complemented by studies in greater depth of localities and communities. We need to know how many of those in poverty are to be found in the inner urban areas which have been the focus of action projects like the Porte Verte projects in Brussels. How many are to be found in isolated rural communities such as the mountains of Greece?

There are several reasons why it is essential to link more closely the statistical and the qualitative research on poverty. First, sample surveys typically exclude either by design or through non-response many of those on the margins of society. The people settling down to spend the night in cardboard boxes on the streets of London are not included in the Family Expenditure Survey on which the poverty statistics are based, because they are not part of the household population. Similarly, one suspects that surveys in other countries do not cover adequately those marginal to society, such as the groups to whom projects like the Compagnons d'Emmaus in Paris and the Simon Community in Dublin are addressed. Is it not possible to build some kind of link with information about the homeless and other marginal groups?

A second important consideration is that most national sample surveys do not allow analysis on any larger unit than the household. They do not allow people to be seen in the context of the community in which they live, or allow us to investigate the influence this has on people's risk of poverty. In technical terms, is there spatial auto-correlation? There are of course surveys which examine this geographical dimension, including Townsend's *Poverty in the United Kingdom* (1979), which had special concentrated sub-samples covering Belfast, Glasgow, Neath and Salford. But it seems to me that there is a strong case for a greater degree of clustering in sample design in order to allow the local nature of poverty to be more fully explored. The macro-economic analysis may have overemphasised the regional dimension, not showing sufficient awareness of poverty in rich regions, but the micro-analysis of poverty has gone too far in the opposite direction and should pay more attention to geography.

A third example of the potential role of qualitative evidence concerns the definition of the poverty line. The adoption of a standard like the European Community 50 per cent of average income has the great merit of transparency. It is easily explained. At the same time, the implications of adopting such a standard would have more meaning if it could be linked to actual circumstances. In terms of standards of living, what is a family at 50 per cent of the average actually able to consume in each of the Community's countries? Asking this question is to reverse the usual process. Rather than working from living standards to a poverty line, we would be working from a poverty line to the implied levels of living. Here qualitative information on how families actually live would be most valuable. A video of families living at 50 per cent and 200 per cent of the average in each of the Community countries – if it could be made in such a way that it did not intrude unacceptably on their privacy – would be a valuable complement to the statistical evidence. As Abel-Smith has argued, one of the important functions of poverty studies is to 'educate public opinion on the causes, extent and effects of poverty so as to change the attitudes of the more affluent' (1984, p. 73). To help achieve this, we need closer links between the statistical work on poverty measurement and the action projects of the European Poverty Programme.

International comparability

In recent years, there has been distinct progress in the degree of international comparability of data on poverty and in the awareness of the associated conceptual problems. This is illustrated by the work of O'Higgins and Jenkins (1989), which is the basis for the 44 million figure cited earlier. Even if this estimate does not stand the test of time, the framework set out by these authors will make a lasting contribution, highlighting as it does a number of important definitional issues which may lead to quite different findings. The same applies to the interesting work being undertaken by Deleeck and colleagues (e.g. Deleeck and van den Bosch, 1989) evaluating four different types of poverty line in seven European countries, building on the research of van Praag, Hagenaars and others (e.g., Hagenaars and de Vos, 1988). The Luxembourg Income Study, by assembling micro-data sets for different countries (see chapter 2), has raised international comparisons of this kind to a new level (e.g., Buhmann *et al.*, 1988). While the resulting estimates are not going to be fully comparable, and indeed this may be an unattainable goal given the differences between societies, the placing of the data sets on the same basis is in itself a very valuable discipline and it allows sensitivity analysis to be carried out to assess the implications of differences in methods.

At the same time, there is considerable need for further research on international poverty comparisons, as becomes evident when one examines the estimates for individual countries in detail. Suppose for example that we compare the official United Kingdom government figures for low incomes in 1979 with the figures for that country used in two of the international comparisons cited in the previous paragraph.[2]

The official figure, published in Households Below Average Income (HBAI) shows 7.1 per cent of the Great Britain population as living in 1979 in households with disposable income below 50 per cent of the average.[3] The O'Higgins and Jenkins (O'HJ) figure, based on the same statistical source, for 1980 is 9.2 per cent; the Luxembourg Income Study (LIS) figure, also based on the same source, is 8.1 per cent for 1979 (Buhmann *et al.*, 1988, table 10, taking the STAT equivalence scale). Can we conclude from these figures that the incidence of low incomes, defined in this way, in Britain is around 7–9 per cent?

At face value, the degree of agreement is reassuring. Closer examination reveals, however, the following differences in method:

(i) The LIS takes the average as the *median* rather than the *mean* used in HBAI and O'HJ. Since we may expect the mean to be several percentage points higher than the median, the comparable figure may therefore be rather higher than found in the other two studies.[4]

(ii) The official HBAI figures relate to *Great Britain* (GB), whereas O'HJ and LIS both refer to the *United Kingdom* (UK), thus also including Northern Ireland, where the incidence of low incomes is significantly higher. We would expect UK figures on this account to be higher.[5]

(iii) The *equivalence scales* used to adjust for differences in household size are different: the quoted O'HJ and LIS figures are based on a scale that treats a couple with two children as equivalent to 2.7 single adults, the official HBAI figures treats them as equivalent to 1.93–2.82 depending on age. Buhmann *et al.* show the sensitivity of the findings to the choice of equivalence scale. Adopting a scale similar to that embodied in the social assistance scheme (and closer to the lower end of the HBAI range), the proportion with less than 50 per cent of the average rises from 8.1 per cent to 11.4 per cent (Buhmann *et al.*, 1988, table 10). On this account, we would expect the official HBAI study to give a higher estimate.

(iv) The official and O'HJ estimates are based on the *household unit*, consisting of people, related or not, who live at the same address and share common housekeeping. The LIS figures refer to a *family unit* which considers only people in a household who are related by blood, marriage or adoption. (Other people in the household form a separate unit(s).)[6]

The differences described above work in different directions and may cancel each other out. For example, the LIS figure would increase if the mean were used rather than the median but would be reduced if the household rather than the family unit were chosen. Nevertheless, it should be clear that the choices made can affect the outcome. In making an international comparison, it may matter appreciably *which* national estimate is selected. Matters which are often relegated to footnotes – or not even mentioned – may significantly affect the poverty estimates.

Poverty and the unit of analysis

The choice between such different definitions should not be based solely on the securing of international comparability; the choice should reflect the underlying social objectives. A good example is provided by the selection of the unit of analysis – the household, the family, the inner family or the individual.

The answer depends in part on whether one sees poverty as concerned with

standards of living

or concerned with the

right to a minimum level of resources

On a standard of living approach, the choice of unit becomes essentially an empirical question. Does the 21 year old living at home share the same consumption as his or her parents? Although evidence is limited, such income sharing is believed to be widespread and this was one of the arguments advanced in the UK for adopting the household unit: 'there are many instances of [people] with low incomes living in relatively well-off households and in practice being substantially supported by them' (Department of Health and Social Security, 1988, p. 23). On the other hand, the minimum rights approach directs our attention to the individual and the nature of his or her relations to the other household members. One can see in this case that our concern may be with the independence of the individual. Certainly it is an often expressed goal of social policy that old people should be financially independent, even if they live with their children. As it was put by Goodin, 'depending on their families for assistance subjects beneficiaries to the "arbitrary will of another"' (1988, p. 351).

What about the treatment of married couples? On a standard of living basis, to take the couple as a unit is to assume that inter-spousal obligations of support exist and are fulfilled, so that the couple enjoy a comparable standard of life. Whether this is so is an empirical question. However, on a minimum-rights basis, we may question whether the dependency of one partner, typically the woman, on the other is acceptable. Even where resources are equally shared, this may not be on equal terms. This idea has been developed by Millar and Jenkins (1989), who relate the issue to Sen's concept of personal capabilities and positive freedom, and make suggestions as to how it may be made concrete.

One approach to learning more about the distribution within the family is to consider the allocation of income according to its actual recipient. As an illustration, Sutherland (1990) has taken the Family Expenditure Survey data for couples in the UK and apportioned the income between couples according to its receipt, so that wives are assumed to have a right to their earnings, their investment income and transfers to which they are entitled in their own right. Child benefit for example is paid to the mother. The individuals are classified according to their income relative to the Income Support level (IS), this being a legislative standard. The figures are projections of the situation in April 1990, using the LSE tax benefit model TAXMOD (see Atkinson and Sutherland, 1988). Taking couples as a unit, one finds that 9 per cent had incomes below the IS level. If we look at the position of men and women separately, taking a standard of half this amount, then we find about 5 per cent of husbands and about 50 per cent of wives are below. The existence of a difference is not unexpected but the magnitude is striking. This provides some measure of the potential significance of this issue, an issue which can only be resolved by reference to basic social objectives.

Panel studies

The last area of progress on which I want to comment is the mounting of panel studies, which allow study of the experience of low-income families over time. There is a great deal that can be learned from this type of data that cannot be obtained from one-off cross-section surveys.

It is clear from the more qualitative studies of low-income families that fluctuations are the norm rather than the exception. To quote from a recent report on 40 extended interviews with families in Britain eligible for income-tested family credit:

> the whole tenor of their lives appeared to be in a state of flux, with little indication of anything other than brief periods of stability. Partners went into and out of work; children shuttled between their natural father and mother or even lived for periods with grandparents and other relatives; council accommodation changed with their circumstances such as following the break-up of a marriage. (MIL Research, 1988, p. 10)

The extent of changes in family composition should be stressed, since it seems to be a general phenomenon. To take just one example, the Berlin Panel study shows that 30 per cent of single parents interviewed in 1984 had ceased to be living as single parents by 1985 (Witte in Krupp and Schupp, 1988, p. 28).

The evidence already available suggests substantial turnover in the low-income population. In the UK, Hancock (1985), using panel data from the Family Finances and Family Resources Surveys, found that 32 per cent of families with low resources (net income less housing costs) in 1978 did not have low resources when re-interviewed in 1979. Deleeck and van den Bosch (1989, table 11) report that some 40 per cent of those found to be poor in Belgium in 1985 were not found to be poor in 1988. The Michigan Panel Study finds that the proportion classified as poor in adjacent years is between 54 per cent and 65 per cent over the period 1969 to 1978 (Duncan, 1984, p. 40).

How should one react to these figures? Is this degree of mobility large or small? According to Rainwater, in his Introduction to Duncan (1984), there is 'an astonishing amount of turnover' (p. 3). The article in the Institute of Social Research Newsletter which described the Duncan study carried the headline: 'Poverty Turnover High'. But what does 'high' mean? After all, we would expect there to be some mobility. There is an important life-cycle element to the incidence of poverty. As Rowntree pointed out at the beginning of this century: 'the life of the labourer is marked by five alternating periods of want and comparative plenty' (1922, pp. 169–70). The periods of want were childhood, when he himself had children, and old age; and the picture today is not too different in this respect. We may well expect some of the couples with children interviewed in Belgium in 1985 to be without them in 1988 as the children have grown up and left home. Hancock in her study of families with children found that 6 per cent acquired more children within the year, and 11 per cent had fewer children when interviewed a year later.

What we need therefore is a benchmark against which to interpret the degree of mobility, a benchmark which takes account of the changes in poverty status which would be expected as part of the life cycle. Some part of the observed exits from poverty may be due to the life cycle of family needs and we may regard these differently from a situation where there has been an improvement in, say, the earning power of the family head.

The second point to be made about the use of panel data to investigate the dynamics of poverty is that we would like ideally to separate 'genuine' changes in poverty status from those that are temporary or the result of imperfections of measurement. The position of the unemployed worker recruited to a permanent position with job security and good prospects is quite different from that of one who finds precarious work as Father Christmas in a department store, even if in the short-run the effect on family incomes may appear to be the same. This of course raises the question of the time period over which income is measured, and whether indicators can be devised which distinguish between temporary and permanent fluctuations. This may involve taking income averaged over a longer period or bringing in other dimensions such as assets or stocks of consumer durables. In these respects, the Enquête Multidimensionelle carried out by INSEE in France (Villeneuve, 1989) appears to be of considerable interest.

3.2 Economic progress and the European Community

According to the European Commission,

> the prospect of the single internal market will generate a higher rate of economic growth but unless the Community takes appropriate action and mobilizes its resources more effectively, poverty will continue to exist. (European Commission, 1989, p. 7)

My purpose here is to explore some simple arithmetic as to the possible effects of economic growth. But the first consideration concerns the nature of the objective. If the Community continues to assess poverty purely in national terms, taking 50 per cent of national average income, then the impact of growth on poverty in the Community will depend solely on what happens *within* each country. However, a central question concerns the possibility of moving to a Community-wide poverty line, with the same standard applied in all countries. In that case, the effect of growth on the extent of low income is affected by the relative growth rates of different member countries.

A Community-wide poverty line would mean that low income is assessed in terms of 50 per cent of the Community average income, denoted by Y_{EC}. It would mean that the same cut-off was being applied in terms of purchasing power on both sides of the Channel, just as at present the same

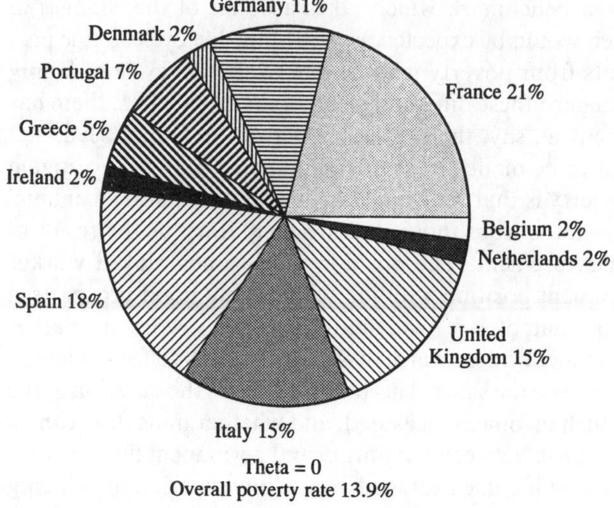

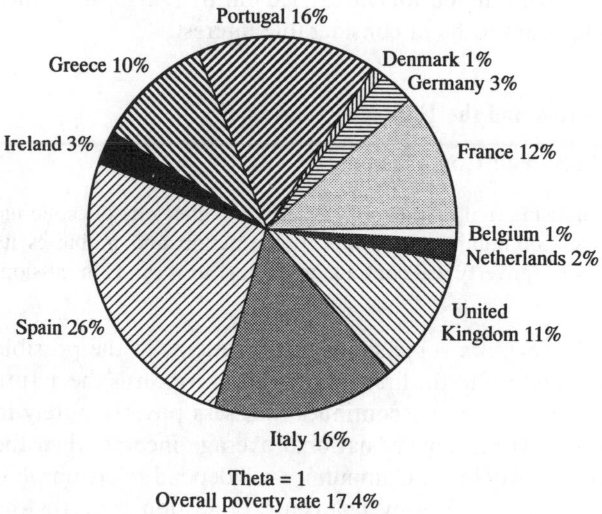

Figure 3.1 Poverty in Europe: comparison of results with national and Community-wide poverty lines
Note: Luxembourg is not shown separately.

standard is applied to the Isle of Wight as to Hampshire. It would mean for example that in Spain the poverty line would become some two-thirds of its national average rather than a half.[7] As such the extent, and particularly the composition, of the low-income population would be changed.

The effect of adopting a Community-wide poverty line is illustrated in figure 3.1, which is based on the 1985 information collected for the O'Higgins and Jenkins (1989) estimates and some approximate interpolation (for this reason the figure should only be regarded as illustrative). The upper part of the diagram corresponds to the use of national poverty lines, as in the O'Higgins and Jenkins study. The overall poverty rate is 13.9 per cent. The countries with significantly below Community average incomes (Spain, Ireland, Greece and Portugal) account for 32 per cent of those in poverty. The lower part of the diagram shows the position with a Community-wide line. The overall poverty rate is 17.4 per cent, and Spain, Ireland, Greece and Portugal account for 55 per cent of those in poverty.

We can image intermediate situations, where the poverty line in country i is based on both its average income, Y_i, and the Community-wide average. Suppose for example that the poverty line is set at

$$\text{50 per cent of } Y_{EC}{}^{\theta}\ Y_i{}^{(1-\theta)} \tag{3.1}$$

so that values of θ between 0 and 1 give intermediate poverty lines. For example, θ equal to a half corresponds to a line which is 50 per cent of a geometric average of the national and Community averages. The poverty line in Spain would be 57.7 per cent rather than 50 per cent of average income, and in the case of Germany the line would be reduced to 45.3 per cent of the national average. With this value of θ, the four lower-income countries account for 43 per cent of those in poverty.

Effect of growth

Turning now to the effects of economic progress, one's first reaction is that the first crucial aspect is the extent to which growth is uniform across the Member Countries and, if there are differential rates, whether they are divergent or convergent.

The Padoa-Schioppa Report referred to the 3.5 per cent per annum growth which was the basis for the Community's 'co-operative growth strategy' and the possibility that the internal market programme might raise this for a period of years by up to a further 0.5 per cent per annum. The authors saw the achievement of growth as crucial in integrating the new Member States, and argued that 'the countries of the periphery of the Community should be able to look ahead to a period of rapid growth, as they raise productivity levels closer towards average European standards'

Table 3.1. *Poverty in the European Commuunity under different assumptions about objectives and growth*

Percentage below the poverty line			
	Purely national poverty line (θ=0)	'Geometric average' poverty line (θ=0.5)	Community-wide poverty line (θ=1)
In 1985	13.9	15.2	17.4
With convergent growth	unchanged	14.8	16.3
With divergent growth	unchanged	15.4	17.8

Notes: The poverty line is 50 per cent of national average income adjusted by $(Y_{EC}/Y_i)^{\theta}$, where Y_i is national income and Y_{EC} is the Community average.

Convergent growth involves the poorest country (Portugal) growing by 53 per cent while the richest (Luxembourg) grows by 27 per cent, with the other growth rates being interpolated linearly on the basis of 1985 average per-capita GDP at purchasing power parity.

Divergent growth involves the poorest country growing by 32 per cent, while the richest grows by 42 per cent, the other growth rates being interpolated.

(Padoa-Schioppa *et al*., 1987, p. 110). Particularly if coupled with more effective redistribution within the Community, as proposed in the Padoa-Schioppa report, the co-operative growth strategy could lead to a convergence of incomes per head. For example, an overall increase of 37 per cent in income per head (which could be the result of 4 per cent growth for eight years, or 2.5 per cent for 13 years) could be associated with a 53 per cent growth for the lowest-income country (if it grew at 5.5 per cent per annum for eight years or 3.5 per cent for 13 years) and a growth of half that amount for the richest country (if it grew at 3 per cent for eight years or rather under 2 per cent for 13 years). This would raise Portugal for example from 46 per cent to 52 per cent of the Community average per-capita GDP at purchasing power parities. This is referred to below as a convergent strategy. On the other hand, growth may be divergent, in that the countries with higher incomes may reap more of the benefits and enjoy faster rates of growth. For example if the 0.5 gain from the internal market accrues to the richer countries, and there are no offsetting Community measures, then the gain for the richest country would be 42 per cent and that for the lowest-income country 32 per cent, compared with an overall increase of 37 per cent. This is referred to below as the divergent case.

The calculations in table 3.1 show the consequences of different assumptions about the growth of national incomes for the incidence of poverty. In these calculations, it has been assumed that the national distribution of income remains unchanged in relative terms. The second and third lines compare the impact of convergent and divergent growth. Convergent growth leads to some reduction in the overall poverty rate, and to some reduction in the share of the bottom four countries in the total poverty population. But perhaps the most striking feature is the small size of these effects. With $\theta = 0.5$, the poverty rate only falls from 15.2 per cent to 14.8 per cent. The share of the bottom four countries in the total poverty population only declines from 43 per cent to 41 per cent. Despite the fact that the average income in Portugal would rise relative to that of Germany by some 20 per cent, there would be only a limited effect. Conversely, divergent growth, according to which Portugal would fall behind Germany, would only raise the overall poverty rate to 15.4 per cent.

The moral seems to be that the crucial effects of growth are likely to be the impact on the distribution *within* countries. This obviously depends crucially on policy decisions, at national and Community level. It depends on the form that economic growth takes, including the regional pattern, and on the extent of harmonisation in areas such as minimum-income provisions. Here I will simply make the point that one cannot rely on growth itself being equalising in its impact. The UK government for example has made much of the performance of the British economy in the past decade, a matter about which I would be more guarded than they are, but there can be little doubt that the benefits have been unequally shared (see chapter 1). This indicates that consideration of poverty should be more closely linked to the discussion of economic policy, both Community-wide and nationally. Much of the debate, particularly in the UK, has treated the economic and the social dimensions as quite separate, whereas Tawney recognised as long ago as 1913 that

> the problem of poverty ... is primarily an industrial one. It is to be studied first at its sources [by which he meant in the mill, in the mine or at the docks], and only secondly in its manifestations ... in casual wards or on the Embankment. (1913, p. 12)

Concluding comments: poverty statistics and policy

Finally, I would like to comment on the relation between poverty statistics and policy.

What is the function of poverty statistics? One role is that of a call to action, a part of the political rhetoric of setting national targets. Historically, this has been most important, as is well illustrated by the American War on Poverty. This made extensive use of the poverty analysis carried out first by the Council of Economic Advisers and then by Orshansky (1965) at the Social Security Administration, of whose work Haveman has written:

> the 1965 study was a milestone in the field of poverty analysis, and adoption of 'the Orshansky line' as the official measure of poverty represents an important example of the effect of research, combined with a certain amount of political compromise, on policy-making. Its adoption is in fact viewed by many as one of the more lasting and significant achievements of the War on Poverty. (1987, p. 55)[8]

A second important function of poverty statistics is in the design of policy at both national and Community level. Room (1989) has referred to the allocation of Community funds, and the use of poverty indicators in identifying regions which merit particular assistance. At a national level, one important question that should be asked of any proposed government spending – or other intervention – is what does it do for the poor? There is a need for statistical information about poverty which can be accessed readily in policy debate. To answer this kind of question what is needed is to combine the micro-data on income poverty with the models of the tax and benefit system that allow one to predict, at least in an approximate fashion, the consequences of changes in policy. That is one has to make calculations of the impact for individual families, to see whether the new policies take people above or push them below the poverty line. This is one of the roles of tax benefit models of the type that have been developed for quite a number of European Community countries, including France, Ireland, Italy, the United Kingdom and West Germany.

Who should produce poverty statistics? What is the role of each member of the triangle formed by the Community, the governments of Member countries, and independent researchers within those countries? It may be useful here to distinguish between the production of statistics and the legitimisation of statistics. To put myself for a moment in the shoes of EUROSTAT, I can see that it has the task first of obtaining national estimates of the extent of poverty and then of being confident that it can use these in the public debate without their being disowned –either by national governments or by independent researchers.

In considering the role of EUROSTAT, it seems to me that there is a strong case for it taking an even more active role than to date, and in particular that EUROSTAT should seek to collect the raw micro-data from national governments, so that it has its own independent access to the data, and so that the estimates of poverty can be produced centrally. A major reason for saying this is that the problem of measuring poverty is a complex one and the simple transmission of a number or set of numbers, as requested for example by O'Higgins and Jenkins (1989), is going to raise as many questions as it answers. Anyone who has had experience of working with sample surveys is aware of the large number of detailed points which have to be resolved (as we have seen in section 3.1) and that the cumulative effect of the decisions taken may make an appreciable difference to the resulting estimate. It may seem trivial to worry about such questions as – how does one treat couples where one partner is absent, or how does one treat the self-employed who have made losses – but it is among those with low incomes that one finds a disproportionate number of such cases. Any estimate of poverty conveyed by the national statistical office, or rapporteur, involves a decision about such detailed matters, as will become clear as soon as one seeks to reproduce the figures from the raw data. For example, we have tried to reproduce the definition of 'children' used by other researchers and it proves remarkably difficult, even if you know the cut-off age used. What do you do about those over the cut-off age who are at school? Or those below the cut-off age who are living on their own? Can people be both children and parents?

The question of access brings me finally to the question – for whom are poverty statistics provided? Much of the discussion has been in terms of policy makers, but I would like to end by entering a plea for a wider view of the potential audience. Concern about poverty is not limited to governments and civil servants. It is an issue which is of concern to individuals and groups, such as churches, welfare organisations, claimants' unions, etc. But there is a great risk that discussion of Community policy and its social dimension will be confined to experts.

This is not to suggest that the debate should descend to the level of anecdote or tabloid journalism. In the Athenian democracy the herald may have issued a general invitation – who wishes to speak? – but the assembly was intolerant of those who did not know what they were talking about. According to Plato, 'In technical matters anyone who was not considered an expert, even if he was "quite a gentleman, wealthy and well-born", was ... jeered and booed until he gave up or was removed from the speaker's platform' (Sinclair, 1988, p. 34). Today, just as then, in technical matters access to information is crucial, and what I am arguing is that the tools developed to analyse poverty in the Community should be ones which can be made accessible outside government. Statistics Canada now markets its Social Policy Simulation Database and Model covering 100,000 individuals and which runs on a personal computer. I would like to see a poverty analysis model for Europe available along the same lines. In this way, the debate can be widened to include more of the many people who are concerned about poverty in the Community.

4 Comparing poverty rates internationally: recent studies in OECD countries

The *World Development Report 1990* (World Bank, 1990) estimates that a third of the population of the developing world had incomes below US$370 a head in 1985, but that the proportion varied from about half in Sub-Saharan Africa and South Asia to a fifth in East Asia and Latin America. Investigating the reasons for such differences is an obvious first resort in evaluating the success of different policies in reducing poverty, and in identifying priorities. To take a second example, estimates produced for the European Commission show the proportions in different member countries with incomes below 50 per cent of the national average (O'Higgins and Jenkins, 1989; see chapter 3): such figures may be used to draw conclusions about the relative effectiveness of, for instance, the minimum wage policy in France as against the extensive social assistance network of the United Kingdom. Equally important, poverty statistics for different countries may be the basis for allocating investment and readjustment funds by supranational bodies such as the European Community.

If international comparisons of poverty are to be used in this way, it is vital to identify and examine the concepts on which they are based; the objective of this chapter is to provide a selective review of the principal issues involved, complementing that provided in chapter 3. The illustrations are from countries that belong to the Organisation for Economic Cooperation and Development (OECD).

4.1 Conceptual issues in the measurement of poverty

The issues that arise in comparing poverty rates across countries are similar to those that arise at a national level, but the explicitly comparative approach gives a different perspective. Methods of measurement differ considerably, and any international comparison has to recognise this diversity of approach. The choices made affect findings on the composition as well as on the size of the poor population: whether, for instance, there appear to be more elderly poor in the United Kingdom than in the United States may depend on how the poverty standard is defined, and the policy response will differ accordingly.

The four central conceptual issues considered in the chapter are the choice of poverty indicator, the determination of the poverty line, the unit of analysis, and the choice of equivalence scale. The studies of poverty or low incomes in OECD countries selected to illustrate these issues are listed in table 4.1. The selection is intended to be illustrative, not exhaustive: many OECD countries for which data exist are not shown; and for some of the countries that are shown, only one of several available studies has been selected. The countries nevertheless cover a range of income levels and types of social welfare system. Some of the studies are made by official bodies, others by independant research bodies or academics. Because the primary purpose is to bring out the extent of similarities and of differences, and their implications for international comparisons, I concentrate not on the findings (which are not shown in the table) but on the methods.

The choices of indicator, poverty line, unit of analysis and equivalence scale are frequently discussed in the literature, but even when these have been determined significant differences remain between the ways in which poverty is measured in different countries. The need to resolve these in an international comparison is demonstrated in the more detailed case study of France, Germany and Great Britain which closes the article.[1] Even if statisticians are provided with an apparently tightly defined brief – to measure income poverty, taking a standard of 50 per cent of the national average, using the household as the unit of analysis – serious questions, of policy as much as of techniques, still remain to be answered.

Note too that the measurement of poverty cannot be seen in isolation from the design of anti-poverty policy measures. In several countries, particularly those in which a social assistance scheme exists that aims to provide a guaranteed minimum income, the poverty standard has been closely linked to social security programmes. Not only does this mean that national poverty measures reflect the nature and form of policy concerns, but also the operation of the programmes may affect the conclusions drawn when other standards are applied in an international comparison (based, for example, on a standard of 50 per cent of average incomes).

Choice of poverty indicator

For the purposes of this chapter, poverty is assumed to be defined in terms of a single broad indicator of economic resources. This assumption in itself

Table 4.1. *Poverty and low-income studies in selected OECD countries*

	Studies considered in case study				
Item	Great Britain[a] (low-income families)	Great Britain[a] (households below average income)	France	Germany	Ireland
Period covered	1972–7 1979 1981 1983 1985	1979 1981 1983 1985 1987	1984–5	1963 1969 1973 1978 1983	1980 and 1987
Poverty indicator	Disposable income net of housing costs (≡resources), 'normal'	Disposable income, current *or* disposable income net of housing costs, current[b]	Disposable income, annual	Disposable income, annual	Disposable income, current[b]
Poverty line	Supplementary Benefit scale (+ 10 per cent, 20 per cent and 40 per cent), adjusted over time as benefit increased	50 per cent of mean income (also 60, 70, 80, 90 and 100 per cent)	50 and 60 per cent of median income	40 per cent and 50 per cent of mean income (also social assistance level)	40, 50 and 60 per cent of mean income
Unit of analysis	Inner family (≡benefit unit)	Household	Household	Household	Household
Equivalence scale (single person = 1) for couple and for child (aged 15 or under)	Couple = 1.62 Child = 0.34–0.62[d]	Couple = 1.64 Child = 0.15–0.44[d]	Couple = 1.70 Child = 0.50	Couple = 1.8 Child = 0.45–0.75[d]	Couple = 1.6–1.7 Child = 0.3–0.5
Reference	Department of Health and Social Security (1988a)	Department of Social Security (1990)	Assémat and Glaude (1989)	Hauser and Semrau (1988)	Nolan and Callan (1989)

Notes: [a] Excludes Northern Ireland.
[b] Self-employment and investment income averaged over a longer period.
[c] Disposable income is the most relevant variable, but in Canada and the United States pretax income has been used because of data limitations.

Finland	Sweden	United States	Canada	Australia	Greece
1966 1971 1976 1981 1985	1967 1975 1978 1980–5	1959–present	1961–present	1966, 1972–3, 1978–9, 1981–2, 1985–6,	1974 and 1982
Disposable income, annual	Disposable income, annual	Gross income, annual[c]	Gross income, annual[c]	Disposable income, annual (also disposable income net of housing costs)	Consumption expenditure, weekly
National pension level, adjusted over time as benefit increased *or* 50 per cent of median income	Social assistance level in 1985 (allowing for housing costs), adjusted by price index	Official poverty line, adjusted over time by consumer price index (also 125 per cent of this line)	Statistics Canada low-income cutoff, adjusted by consumer price index, and revised in 1969, 1973, 1978 and 1986	Henderson poverty line, adjusted initially by average earnings, since 1981 by household disposable income per capita	2/3 median consumption expenditure per equivalent adult
Family	Family	Family	Family	Inner family	Household
Couple = 1.7 Child = 0.5	Couple = 1.59 Child = 0.44[d]	Couple = 1.25 Child = 0.21–0.46[e]	Couple = 1.36 Child = 0.18–0.37[e]	Couple = 1.41 Child = 0.34 (simplified scale)	Couple = 2.0 Child = 0.25–0.40[d]
Gustafsson and Uusitalo (1990)	Gustafsson and Uusitalo (1990)	US Bureau of the Census (1981)	Wolfson and Evans (1989)	Saunders and Whiteford (1989); Bradbury and Saunders (1990)	Tsakloglou (1990)

[d] Depending on age.
[e] Depending on position in family.

is restrictive. If the concern about poverty takes the form of concern about basic needs, such as food, housing and clothing, the focus should be on individual items of consumption, and poverty would need to be measured in a multi-dimensional way, rather than in terms of a single indicator. The same consideration may apply if we are concerned about time as an input and about 'time poverty' as well as deprivation of commodities. Or concern about poverty may relate to social or demographic indicators, such as life expectancy or literacy. These multi-dimensional aspects of poverty are not considered here, even though they may influence comparisons across countries. Countries may differ in the extent of their social provision, and this may affect the interpretation to be placed on a specified level of economic resources. In determining the appropriate relative poverty lines in, say, France and Sweden, account has to be taken of differences in the public provision of medical care, education, and so on. Do parents have to buy school books for their children? For this reason, a method that encompasses a number of indicators – see, for instance, table 2.1 of World Bank (1990) – has a lot to recommend it.

If the measure of disadvantage is limited to a single index of economic resources, then a natural choice may appear to be total consumption, or expenditure plus home-produced goods and services. A household is then said to be poor if its total consumption is below a specified amount. But most studies of poverty in advanced countries record poverty on the basis of total income rather than consumption – income is in fact the basis for all the studies listed in table 4.1 apart from those in Greece.

Why is income used? The first answer is that it is taken as a proxy for living standards, because these are hard to quantify. As such, assessments of poverty based on income have to be qualified: income may understate or overstate the level of living. If a family can dissave or borrow, its current level of living is not constrained by current income. Temporary variations in income may be smoothed out (though such borrowing may be expensive, with serious consequences for the future). A family that can share in the consumption of others may have higher living standards than its income would permit. An elderly person living with his or her children may benefit from their expenditure. Such considerations would lead one to expect the estimates of poverty to be lower, other things equal, in Greece than in the other countries shown in table 4.1.

Conversely, income may overstate the level of living when money alone is not sufficient to buy the necessary goods, for instance, if there is rationing or if goods are not available. An obvious implication is that one would have to be careful in making comparisons across countries with different market structures, particularly with regard to housing. It would certainly be unwise to compare the studies in table 4.1 with those for Eastern European countries, without taking this consideration into account (see Atkinson and Micklewright, 1992).

The second reason for using income rather than consumption is that it may be seen as intrinsically preferable as an indicator of resources in the measurement of poverty. One argument is that people may choose a low level of consumption, whereas income is closer to a measure of the opportunities open to a family and not influenced by the consumption decisions made: the concern then is with the budget constraint, not with consumption choices. Alternatively, we may move away from the conception of poverty as concerned with standards of living to poverty as concerned with minimum rights to resources (chapter 3, and Atkinson, 1989, chapter 1). In this view, people are seen as entitled, as citizens, to a minimum income, the disposal of which is a matter for them. This right to a minimum income may be regarded as a prerequisite for participation in a particular society, as a guarantee of 'positive freedom'.

The conception of poverty adopted will in turn affect more detailed choices about how best to measure it. If income is being used as a proxy for consumption, permanent income may be a closer match than current income, so that in practical terms annual income may be a better indicator than income in a week or month. The choice of time period for income depends in this case on matters of fact. How important are seasonal fluctuations? How far can people in reality borrow to tide their families over bad times? Adoption of the minimum rights standpoint, conversely, involves judgements about interpretation. On the interpretation that the right is to a guaranteed minimum below which no one should fall, even temporarily, current weekly income may be the better indicator.

The definition of poverty chosen will also affect the way income is defined. A standard of living definition will include an estimate of income in kind. (Home production of food is an example, as is the receipt of transfers in kind such as food stamps.) But a minimum rights interpretation might not count income in kind, because it may be cash income that is necessary for people to participate in society. More generally, different items of income may make greater or lesser contributions to the objective in question. The receipt of income may be subject to conditions that reduce its effective value. On a minimum rights interpretation, for example, we may want to apply a discount to income received subject to a means test that is regarded as a social stigma.

The choice of indicator has to be addressed in the design of social security programmes that aim to ensure some minimum standard. Such programmes have for evident reasons not taken expenditure as an indicator and typically involve an income test. This test is, however, often accompanied by an assets condition. Those eligible are people with incomes below a qualifying level whose net worth does not exceed a specified level, which conditions may be seen as taking account of the person's capacity to finance consumption by dissaving. Such an approach takes us back to a multi-dimensional measure of poverty.

The institutional arrangements for Income Support in OECD countries also identify the special role of housing expenditure. In Great Britain, for example, Income Support takes the form of a cash amount intended to cover needs other than those of shelter, the latter being met (approximately) in full by housing assistance. Accordingly, the benefit-based poverty standard in Great Britain has been measured on the basis of 'net resources', or income after deduction of housing costs (see the first column in table 4.1); the same has been done in Australia. As a result, the poverty cutoff in terms of total income for a particular family depends on its own housing costs. Such an approach may be seen as treating housing expenditure as an unavoidable outlay, or as adjusting for variation across people in the prices faced for housing (for example, where there are rent controls). It may be justified on the grounds that the measure of income does not capture the full benefit to owner-occupiers from the services of the house they own: if the imputed rent of owner-occupiers is not included in income, then the subtraction of the rent actually paid by tenants would put the two tenure groups on the same footing. The institutional features of the housing market in individual countries need to be taken into account.

Determination of the poverty level

If standard of living is the concern, then the most straightforward way to determine the poverty line is to specify a basket of goods, denoted by the vector x^*, purchasable at prices p, and to set the poverty standard as a subsistence standard

$$(1+h)p \cdot x^* \tag{4.1}$$

where h is a provision for inefficient expenditure or waste, or a provision for items not included in the list x^*. This was in effect the method followed in the United States in the derivation of the official poverty line, where x^* represented food requirements and h made allowance for spending on other goods. The list x^* was based on the US Department of Agriculture's 'economy food plan' for households of different composition, and the multiplier to allow for other goods was 3. This method differs from, but has some relation to, the definition of the poverty line as the income at which households spend a specified proportion on necessities. The Canadian low-income cutoff was based originally on the income level at which more than 70 per cent was spent on food, clothing and shelter (Poduluk, 1967).

As was recognised when the US official poverty line was introduced, there is room for considerable disagreement about the subsistence standard. Political judgement played a considerable role in determining the '$3,000 for a family of four' that featured prominently in the speeches launching the War on Poverty, as did the use by the European Commission of a benchmark of 50 per cent of average national income in measuring poverty in Europe. (As may be seen from table 4.1, the same benchmark approach, with differing percentages, has been used in several European studies.)

These two examples serve also to illustrate the difference between a poverty line such as that depicted in equation (4.1) adjusted for changes in prices, and often referred to as an 'absolute' poverty standard, and a 'relative' line related to contemporary levels of living. The latter may follow naturally from the minimum rights approach, where poverty is seen in terms of people being excluded from the 'living conditions and amenities which are customary, or at least widely encouraged or approved, in the societies to which they belong' (Townsend, 1979, p. 31), or what is often referred to as a participation standard. In adopting its definition, the European Community stated: 'The poor shall be taken as to mean persons, families and groups of persons whose resources (material, cultural and social) are so limited as to exclude them from the minimum acceptable way of life in the Member State in which they live' (Council Decision, 19 December 1984).

The choice between an absolute and a relative standard takes on particular importance in international comparisons. *World Development Report 1990* (World Bank, 1990) used a common dollar figure, adjusted by purchasing power parities, across countries, to reach its US$370 poverty standard; such a method evidently leads to quite different conclusions from those reached applying a specified percentage of national average income. This applies even when countries at relatively similar stages of economic development are compared, as shown for European Community countries in figure 3.1, chapter 3.

The adjustment of the poverty line may take an intermediate form; for example, in some countries the line has been adjusted regularly for price increases, with additional real increases from time to time as a result of a special decision. In Canada, the Special Senate Committee on Poverty argued in 1971 that there should be a real increase 'to take account of changing socioeconomic conditions over the last decade' (quoted by Wolfson and Evans, 1989, p. 12). The ensuing policy changes led to the real value of the poverty line following a step pattern over time. Alternatively, the line may rise steadily in real terms, but less than the increase in other incomes. Subjective definitions of poverty, based on survey responses to questions about the minimum necessary income, have produced such an outcome. In the United States, the Gallup Poll has regularly asked the question: 'What is the smallest amount of money a family of four needs each week to get along in this community?' An analysis of the responses over the period 1957–71 by Kilpatrick (1973) showed that they tended to rise about 0.6 per cent for each 1 per cent rise in per-capita income. He notes that on this basis the poverty line would have increased in real terms by some 25 per cent between 1959 and 1971, and that the poverty rate would have fallen, not from 22 per cent to 12 per cent (as with the poverty line kept constant in real terms), but only from 22 per cent to 18 per cent. In Australia, where the Morgan Gallup poll collects similar data, the average reported minimum amount doubled in real terms between the 1950s and the 1970s (Saunders and Bradbury, 1989).

The relation of the poverty line to the objectives of economic and social policy is also important. The US official poverty line was designed quite independently of benefit programmes. The Council of Economic Advisers stressed that 'no measure of poverty as simple as the one used here would be suitable for determining eligibility for particular benefits' (US Council of Economic Advisers, 1964, p. 58).

In contrast, post-war studies of poverty in the United Kingdom, following Abel-Smith and Townsend (1965), have in several instances taken the scale of entitlement to social assistance (called National Assistance from 1948 to 1966, then Supplementary Benefits until 1988) as the basis for defining low incomes. In Finland, Germany and Sweden, studies have also used benefit scales. One immediate implication is that adjustments of the scale over time have been in line with benefits rather than prices or average incomes. In the case of Finland, the scale appears to have risen about 0.7 per cent for each 1 per cent real increase in the median income (on the basis of the estimates of Gustafsson and Uusitalo, 1990), and in Germany the rise appears to have been around 0.9 per cent for each 1 per cent real increase in the average net wage (on the basis of the estimates made by Hauser and Semrau, 1989).

The measurement of poverty may also be affected by income maintenance policy if the latter leads to a concentration of people at a particular income level. Taking an international yardstick, such as 50 per cent of average income, may lead to misleading conclusions about the proportion in poverty if country A has a social minimum of 47.5 per cent of the average and country B has a social minimum of 52.5 per cent.[2]

Unit of analysis: residence, spending and relationships

The unit of analysis refers to the group of persons for whom resources are assumed to be combined when poverty status is being assessed. A range of

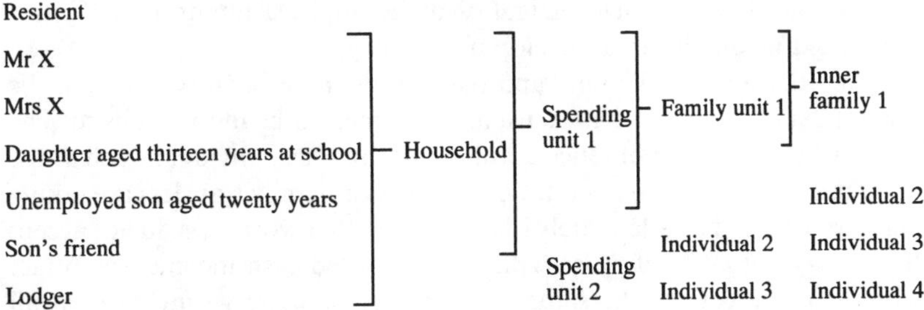

Figure 4.1 Illustration of different units of analysis

different definitions of the unit of analysis is in use – see table 4.1. The definitions are based on a number of different elements:

Common residence, with a household comprising those resident in a dwelling and sharing some degree of common housekeeping; this typically constitutes the most extensive unit of analysis

Common spending, where the spending unit is defined as those taking spending decisions to a considerable degree in common, where this may cover people who have no family relationship

Blood or marital relationship, where members of the family unit are related by marriage or cohabitation or by blood relations

Dependence, as where the unit is defined to include a single person or couple plus any dependent children; this constitutes the inner family.

The different possibilities are illustrated in figure 4.1. As set out there, the criteria are typically applied cumulatively, so that the family unit refers to those members of the family resident in the same household.

In considering the choice between different units, it is helpful to consider first the standard of living approach. Some items of consumption, such as food, are essentially individualistic, whereas others, such as housing, have some of the attributes of public goods as far as individuals in the household are concerned. For the latter, the spillover may be such that all members of the household enjoy broadly equal levels of living, but for the former there may be considerable inequality within the household or according to gender. The distribution of benefits within the unit is extremely difficult to observe. It is not therefore surprising that in practice many studies have based their analysis on the spending unit, assuming that all within the unit share the same standard of living, or on the household – allowing for the difficulties in treating housing outlays (see table 4.1). But in ignoring the potential for intra-household inequality, these assumptions about resource sharing may misrepresent the extent and nature of poverty (see Haddad and Kanbur, 1990, for an investigation of the empirical importance of intra-household inequality in a developing country).

When the minimum rights approach to defining poverty is taken, the theoretical concept of rights is usually assumed to be individualistic. The case for considering in practice a wider unit than the individual, such as the inner family, rests on an assumption that within-family transfers are taking place that cannot be adequately observed. In other words, we do not accept that a large number of those with zero recorded cash income are in fact without resources. At the same time, it may be quite wrong to treat all married couples as having equal rights to the joint income. Even if within-family transfers are such that total family income is equally divided, one cannot treat all sources of income as equivalent: $100 earned by the wife may be valued more highly than $100 given by her husband to pay for the housekeeping. Within the household, transfers from children to elderly parents may be conditional (for example, on the old person going to live with the children) and may induce dependence. From the minimum rights standpoint, there is a strong case for attempting to measure poverty on an individual basis, using, for example, information on the original source of income (this being easier to observe than the distribution of consumption). It is only in this way that issues such as the feminisation of poverty can be adequately discussed.

The significance of the choice of unit of analysis may be demonstrated by a single example. Until 1985, the official statistics for Great Britain were based on the inner family unit (table 4.1). The new Households Below Average Income series is based on the more extensive unit of people 'living at the same address having meals prepared together and with common housekeeping'. Among the arguments for this change were that most people in such units are closely related, so that the household is close to the family unit as defined above, and that the living standards of its members are more likely to be related to the total income than to their individual income. (In terms of figure 4.1, the son is likely to be better off than would be indicated by his unemployment benefit.) The effects of the change in definition on the results for 1983 have been investigated by Johnson and Webb (1989), who show that the proportion of the population with income below 50 per cent of the average is 11.1 per cent on an inner family basis and 8.1 per cent on a household basis. In other words, the changed unit of analysis reduces the number of people with low incomes by 25 per cent. And the change to a household basis also affects the composition of the low-income population: the proportion of single non-pensioners below half the national average becomes 8 per cent, as against more than 20 per cent on an inner family basis (Johnson and Webb, 1989, p. 75).

Equivalence scales

If a unit of analysis other than the individual is used, the equivalence scales to be applied to different-sized units need to be considered. An equivalence scale gives the relation between the poverty line for, say, a couple and that for a single person. Equivalence scales may be relevant even on an individual basis, if we wish to make allowance for differing needs according to age, degree of handicap and so on. The different methods used to arrive at such scales can produce very different results. Table 4.1 illustrates the variation in the scales applied in the different studies. The scale for a couple, relative to a single person, varies between 1.25 and 2.0. Although there is some clustering in the range 1.6 to 1.7, more than half lie outside. The scale for a child varies between 0.15 and 0.75.

More generally, the differences between equivalence scales have been conveniently summarised by Buhmann *et al.* (1988) in terms of the following formula

$$\text{equivalent income} = \text{total income} \ / \ N^s$$

where N denotes the number of members of the unit and s is the elasticity of family 'need' with respect to family size. A value of $s = 0$ corresponds to making no adjustment for family size, and $s = 1$ corresponds to taking per-capita income. Equivalence scales based on subjective evaluation (of what is needed 'to get along') tend to produce relatively low values for the elasticity; Buhmann *et al.* take a value of 0.25 as representative. Estimates based on observed consumption patterns, and identifying assumptions, tend to be higher; Buhmann *et al.* take a representative elasticity of 0.36. Estimates used in policy making – those embodied in benefit scales or the official US poverty line – are quite substantially higher: around 0.55. And those used in statistical studies by the OECD and other bodies are represented by an elasticity of 0.72.

Buhmann *et al.* use these representative elasticity values to explore the consequences of using different equivalence scales; a selection of their findings is shown in table 4.2 for the OECD countries included at that time in the Luxembourg Income Study data set (see Smeeding, O'Higgins and Rainwater, 1990). The choice of scale can significantly affect conclusions as to the extent and composition of the low-income population. Although the proportion below 50 per cent of the median changes little for the Netherlands and the United States, that in Norway and the United Kingdom is approximately halved on moving from the subjective to statistical scales. The United Kingdom ranks third on the former basis and sixth (out of nine) on the latter. In Norway, older people account for 55 per cent of the poor when the subjective scale is employed, but 23 per cent with

Table 4.2. *Proportion of population with income below 50 per cent of the median*: *results for different equivalence scales* (*Luxembourg Income Study*)

Country	Type of scale			
	Subjective	Observed consumption	Policymaking	Statistical
United States	17.9	17.8	17.2	17.2
	(30.5)	(28.3)	(24.3)	(20.7)
Australia	16.0	14.8	12.3	11.7
	(37.1)	(32.7)	(18.7)	(8.9)
United Kingdom	15.2	14.0	11.4	8.1
	(66.2)	(64.9)	(55.4)	(34.9)
Canada	15.0	14.4	13.2	12.3
	(32.3)	(29.9)	(22.7)	(15.1)
Switzerland	10.5	9.8	8.5	8.3
	(45.4)	(39.9)	(30.1)	(19.0)
Norway	10.3	8.9	5.1	5.2
	(54.6)	(49.3)	(22.5)	(18.4)
Sweden	7.9	6.5	5.4	5.3
	(34.8)	(25.3)	(11.6)	(5.1)
Germany	7.6	6.6	5.2	5.4
	(64.3)	(60.2)	(50.4)	(34.3)
Netherlands	7.3	7.2	8.0	8.8
	(15.7)	(12.8)	(10.8)	(9.4)

Note: Numbers in parentheses are the percentage of those poor households in which the household head is aged 60 years or more. The data used here are not necessarily the same as those referred to in table 4.1.
Source: Buhmann *et al.* (1988, tables 10 and 13).

the policy-making scale, and 18 per cent with the statistical scale. Using the subjective scale, the older group constitutes the majority of the poor in Germany, Norway and the United Kingdom, but with the statistical scale the highest proportion is a third (in the United Kingdom and Germany).

4.2 A case study of an international comparison: France, Great Britain and Germany

The discussion so far has illustrated the strong influence the differing methods used in the studies may have on the conclusions drawn. To illustrate the corresponding difficulties that beset comparison of such findings, we now describe the results of an attempt to compare poverty in three of these countries – France, Great Britain and Germany – using the studies indicated in table 4.1.

The starting point for the investigation is the European Community calculation; the poverty standard is therefore taken as 50 per cent of the national average income. Of the two studies for the United Kingdom, the Households Below Average Income study is thus the more apt to the purpose. According to this study (UK Department of Social Security, 1990, p. 21), in 1985, 9.2 per cent of the population of Great Britain lived in households with an income below 50 per cent of the mean. In France (Assémat and Glaude, 1989, p. 5), in 1984–5, 10.9 per cent of households had income below 50 per cent of the median. In Germany (Hauser and Semrau, 1989), in 1983, 7.0 per cent of the population lived in households with incomes below 50 per cent of the mean.

Can we conclude from these figures that in the mid 1980s low incomes were less prevalent in Germany and (somewhat) more prevalent in France than in Great Britain? No, for – despite their apparent comparability – the differences in the methods by which the estimates are made are still significant.

The poverty indicator is taken to be net of tax income for the studies in all three countries (the figure for Great Britain being that for income rather than income minus housing costs). But the British figure is for current (weekly or monthly) income, whereas the data for the other two countries are for annual income.[3] Thus difference is likely to affect the measured extent of poverty (making the figure for Great Britain higher) and the composition of the poverty population (if pensioners, for example, are less subject to income fluctuations).

The three studies are comparable in using a household unit of analysis, although the precise definition may vary from country to country. But the equivalence scales employed are noticeably different. For a couple with two children, the scale (single person = 1) is: France, 2.7, corresponding to an elasticity of 0.72; Germany, 2.7–3.3 (depending on age of children), corresponding to an elasticity of between 0.72 and 0.86; and Great Britain, 1.79–2.15 (depending on age of children, these being less than 15 years), corresponding to an elasticity of between 0.41 and 0.55.

Such differences are not as large as those between the subjective and statistical scales discussed earlier, but they are nonetheless sizeable. Without access to the micro-data in each country, it is not possible to evaluate the quantitative impact on the measured extent of low incomes, but the differences in equivalence scales could change the ranking of the three countries.

Nor is this the end of the problems. Examination of the calculation of the poverty line reveals further divergences. To begin with, in France the median rather than the mean is employed. For the French data cited earlier, the mean is 13 per cent higher than the median, so that this difference in definition causes the poverty rate to be understated, relative to that in the other two countries, by about one-third (Atkinson and Cazes, 1990). Second, the mean (or median) is calculated in different ways (see O'Higgins and Jenkins, 1989), as follows:

(Household $h = 1, \ldots, H$ has total income y_h, contains n_h persons, and e_h equivalent adults. The equivalent income for the household is y_h/e_h.)

Method Alpha: $\frac{1}{H}\Sigma_h\left(\frac{y_h}{e_h}\right)$

Method Beta: $\frac{\Sigma_h\left\{\left(\frac{y_h}{e_h}\right)\cdot e_h\right\}}{\Sigma_h e_h} = \frac{\Sigma_h y_h}{\Sigma_h e_h}$

Method Gamma: $\frac{\Sigma_h\left\{\left(\frac{y_h}{e_h}\right)\cdot n_h\right\}}{\Sigma_h n_h}$

In France (Method Alpha), the average is obtained by taking the equivalent income for each household and treating each household as one unit irrespective of the number of people. In Germany (Method Beta), the average is obtained by weighting each household by the number of equivalent adults, which is the same as dividing total income by the total number of equivalent people. In Great Britain (Method Gamma), the weights are the number of persons. The method can again make a noticeable difference: applying Method Beta to French data for 1979 reduces the mean, relative to that obtained by Method Alpha, by 12.5 per cent (O'Higgins and Jenkins, 1989, background information). Third, the related question arises of the weighting adopted in the poverty count. In Great Britain and Germany, the figures count the total number of people; in France, the figures show the total proportion of households. This is important to the extent that the poverty rate differs by size of family.

The significance to be attached to the observed differences in poverty rates depends also on the reliability of the data sources. The studies are all based on household budget studies, but two of them compare the results from different data sources. Assémat and Glaude (1989) have access to a matched sample of households who appear in both the budget survey (Enquête Budgets) and the tax records (Enquête Fiscale), and show that the estimated poverty rate is about 20 per cent lower in the latter case. Two of the reasons that they identify for the divergence are illustrative of the kinds of problem that arise. First, the fiscal data attribute to all eligible elderly the minimum guaranteed income to which they are entitled. In view of the evidence that a non-negligible proportion of the elderly do not in fact claim, the number with low incomes will be understated. However, the budget survey is based on reported receipt of transfers, and there is evidence of underreporting, so that the number of elderly with low incomes is overstated. Second, the budget survey shows a larger proportion of farmers and self-employed below the low-income cutoff, and it may be that there is a tendency for this sector to understate income.

The underreporting of income is similarly given as one reason for the divergence in Germany between the results just quoted, which are based on budget survey data, and those derived from the Socio-Economic Panel, although in this case the budget survey is considered to be more complete. The proportion found to be below 50 per cent of the mean is about twice as high in the Panel Study. Hauser and Semrau (1990, p. 34) argue that the more extensive procedure of the budget survey allows cross-checking and more comprehensive recording than the single interview of the Panel. There is, however, a second possible explanation which they advance. For both surveys participation is voluntary, but whereas the Panel is a random sample, the budget survey is based on a call for volunteers. In both cases a reweighting procedure is applied, but it is believed that low-income households remain underrepresented in the budget survey (Kitterer, 1986).

The case study just described should serve as a warning of the difficulties involved in making detailed inter-country comparisons. Even if statisticians are provided with an apparently tightly defined brief – to measure poverty in terms of income, taking a standard of 50 per cent of the national average, using the household as the unit of analysis – there may still be serious divergences in the methods and findings. The case study made use of existing results, and some of the differences could be eliminated by returning to the raw micro-data. The equivalence scales could be harmonised; the methods of calculating the poverty line could be brought into line; the sensitivity of the results to different adjustments for underreported income could be assessed. But some differences would remain that could not be resolved without changes in the raw statistics collected. The time period of income is an example, as is the differing design of the samples. A full-scale comparative exercise is therefore likely to entail a substantial statistical effort which, to be effective, would require the participation of people familiar with the situation in the countries studied – in relation both to the statistical data and the institutional context.

4.3 Concluding comments

The aim of this chapter has been to emphasise the need for clarity about the concepts employed in studying poverty. The 'mischievous ambiguity of the word poor', to use the phrase of the British Poor Law Report of 1834 (quoted by Himmelfarb, 1984, p. 523), may be inescapable in political rhetoric, but behind the rhetoric there must be explicit analysis as to what one means by poverty. Clear understanding of the terms of reference becomes even more important when poverty is compared across countries, where terms carry differing significance and where their implications are affected by differing social institutions.

The definition of the poverty indicator, of the poverty level, and of the unit of analysis is not a purely technical matter. It involves judgements about the objectives of policy. Any cross-country comparison of poverty has therefore to consider the purposes of the analysis and the relation between its objectives and those pursued within the countries studied. If the purpose is to measure the relative extent of need in different countries, then external criteria may be appropriate. A supra-national body may, for example, decide to measure poverty on an individual basis because it is particularly concerned with gender inequality, even though national governments do not attach the same priority. If, however, the purpose is to assess the comparative effectiveness of anti-poverty policy, then national objectives become relevant. A country that gives high priority to the needs of children, and provides generous family support, may score well if the equivalence scale treats children as close to adults, but much less well on another scale.

The inter-relation between policy and measurement means that it is important to relate the observed statistics to the underlying economic and social institutions. This applies even to countries as close geographically and economically as those of Western Europe. Woolf (1986) has drawn attention to the differences among Protestant countries such as Denmark, England and the Netherlands, where outdoor relief was established early as an obligatory parish function, and the Catholic countries, where it remained a matter of charity. The Beveridge tradition of flat-rate social security benefits is different from the earnings-related benefits found in other countries influenced by Bismarck. Such historical differences leave their traces today in the differing forms of Income Support, and these in turn influence the observed distribution of income.

5 Two nations in early retirement? The case of Britain

(WITH HOLLY SUTHERLAND)

In 1955, Richard Titmuss described Britain as having 'two nations in old age': one group relatively fortunate, benefiting from an occupational pension and being able to draw on savings privileged under the income tax, the other group receiving only the basic state pension, which left them dependent on means-tested assistance (the successor of the Poor Law). There were:

> greater inequalities in living standards after work than in work; two contrasting social services for distinct groups based on different principles, and operating in isolation of each other as separate, autonomous, social instruments of change. (1955, p. 166)

At that time, the position of the early retired was relatively little discussed, for the simple reason that those ceasing work before the minimum retirement age constituted only a small proportion of the age group. Of men aged 55–64, who are the focus of this chapter, in 1961 the proportion in England and Wales who were employed or self-employed was 89 per cent, and only 5.6 per cent described themselves as 'inactive' (Trinder, 1989, table 2.1). The labour force participation rate decreased slightly up to 1975 – see figure 5.1 – but then began to fall sharply, first for the 60–4 age group, and then after 1981 for those aged 55–9. By 1987 the proportion of the whole age group 55–64 classified as 'economically inactive' had reached 32.3 per cent (Trinder, 1989, table 2.1).

This major shift in the employment status of men aged 55–64 raises the question as to whether there are also 'two nations in early retirement'. This could arise in at least two different ways. First, among those in this age group who have retired, there could be the tendency to polarisation described by Titmuss for those above the pension age. Is there one group relatively fortunate, in receipt of an occupational pension, for whom retirement was a welcome choice, and another group largely dependent on means-tested assistance, or other state benefits, for whom early retirement

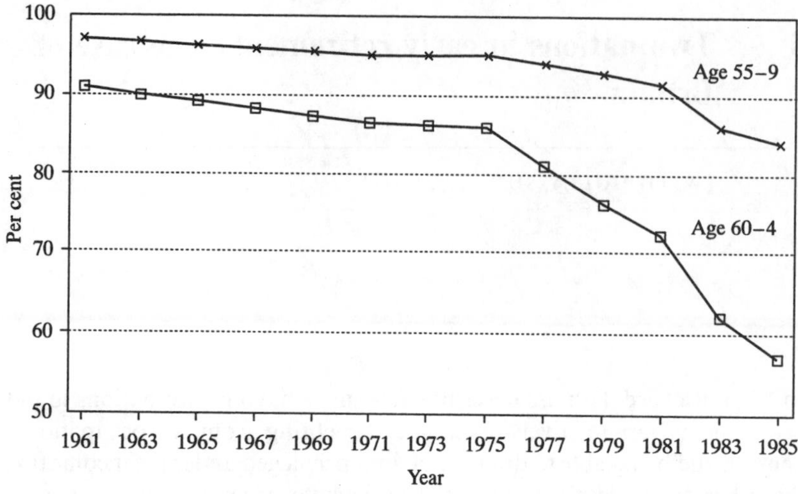

Figure 5.1 Male labour force participation rate in Great Britain 1961–85
Source: Casey and Laczko, 1989, table 1, series interpolated at 1971.

is a euphemism for terminal unemployment? In the US, Gordon has suggested that early male retirees could:

> be classified into two quite different groups: a majority consisting of low-income men who suffer from reduced earning capacity, and a minority with more positive attitudes toward retirement and a superior retirement income prospect resulting from entitlement to an employer pension on top of social security benefits. (1988, p. 90)

Or, in a different sense, there could be two nations in that the early retired as a whole are a disadvantaged group relative to those who continue in work. How does the position of the early retired compare with that of those aged 55–64 in employment or self-employment? Is the development of early retirement one of the ways in which polarisation has become manifest in the economy as a whole?

Such a characterisation in terms of 'two nations' may be seen as a recognition of the segmented nature of economic and social life. The polarisation represents a continuation out of the labour force of the divisions found in employment. In terms of the dual labour market theory (see, for instance, Doeringer and Piore, 1971), the primary sector, with its stable employment and well-developed internal career structure, is likely to be associated with generous occupational pension provisions (the economic rationale of such provisions has been discussed by Lazear, 1979). In contrast, the secondary sector, where employment tends to be of short duration, with a loose attachment between employers and workers, occupational pensions are less widespread, and low wages are likely to have restricted the capacity for private saving. In the case of the second interpretation of the two nations hypothesis, employers from both sectors of the economy may find the redundancy of older workers the least costly method of adjusting to economic recession. The less advantageous treatment of the early retired relative to those who continue in work may reflect the economic logic of a market economy.

On the other hand, the two nations hypothesis may be seen as imposing too tight a straitjacket, presupposing a degree of uniformity within the two classes which does not in reality exist. The circumstances of the early retired are characterised by great heterogeneity, and the hypothesis may be seen as oversimplifying a situation where there is a diversity of experience and motives. Within the early retired there may, for example, be great differences between those who would refuse a job if offered and those who have become discouraged from seeking work but would be glad to accept a job offer. Moreover, the circumstances of any one person may be difficult to classify in any definite way. The concept of labour force participation is one of considerable ambiguity, and neither administrative category nor self-definition may prove a reliable guide. This may in turn cast doubt on the wisdom of seeking to distinguish a group of 'early retired'.

In order to assess the merits of these views, it is necessary to examine in detail the circumstances of individual people. For this purpose, access to *micro-data* is important. Whereas a lot can be learned from aggregate statistics, or from the variation across geographical units such as counties (as in Piachaud, 1986), the degree of individual heterogeneity is essential to the story. The use of such micro-data was, of course, one of the characteristics of early social research in Britain, such as that of Rowntree (1901), who went out and collected his own material. Today, it is more likely to take the form of secondary use of survey data carried out by another body (typically a government department) or collected for another purpose.

There have been a number of interesting studies of the economic position of the early retired using national micro-data for the United Kingdom. The sources of evidence include the special survey carried out in 1977 by the OPCS (Parker, 1980), the annual Family Expenditure Survey, used for 1970–7 by Altmann (1982), and the annual General Household Survey, used for 1980–2 by Laczko, Dale, Arber and Gilbert (1988). The present chapter is primarily based on the Family Expenditure Survey, but differs from the studies just cited in that it focuses on a *comparison* of two age cohorts: the position in 1975 of those aged 55–64 and the position in 1985 of those of that age.

The choice of 1975 and 1985 is intended to span the period when the labour force participation rates changed significantly for the group we are considering and when there were major changes in policy with regard to early retirement. It may be compared with 1971 and 1981, used by Piachaud (1986), where the decline for the younger part of the age group (55–9) was barely evident by the latter year – see figure 5.1. It may be compared with 1979 and 1986 used by Casey and Laczko (1989), where a number of the policy changes had already been made before 1979 (for example, the Job Release Scheme was introduced in 1977), and the participation rate for those aged 60–4 fell nearly 10 percentage points between 1975 and 1979 (figure 5.1).

The two cohorts on which we concentrate are described in the next section (section 5.1). We draw attention to the differences in the labour market conditions at the two dates, and the immediately preceding years (when early retirement is likely to have taken place). This change in the labour market led in turn to differences in UK policy with regard to early retirement, which are described briefly. The observed fall in participation may also result from a longer-term trend towards increased leisure, and in this respect we need to consider the experience of the two cohorts over a longer time perspective.

The characteristics of the men in our two cohorts are the subject of section 5.2, where we consider the extent to which there are discrete differences in labour market status, sources of income and health. The first of these involves examination of the different ways in which early retirement may be defined and of the ambiguity of individual circumstances. Sources of income may provide an alternative indicator of labour market status, as well as being of interest in their own right. Particular attention is paid to occupational pensions and to state transfers, including those linked to ill-health or disability, this being one of the few indicators of health status contained in our main data set.

The idea of a relatively 'fortunate' group is assessed in this chapter in terms of economic status measured in relation to the assistance (Supplementary Benefit) scale. This is the subject of section 5.3. In the first part of the section we consider the evidence concerning polarisation within the early retired population, and its relation to the discrete characteristics identified in the preceding section. In the second part of the section, we compare the position of the early retired, defined in different ways, with that of the cohort as a whole, and consider how far changes in labour market participation have led to changes in the overall distribution of economic status. In this way, we seek to relate the findings for one particular cohort to the wider debate about polarisation and increased income inequality.

In the final, concluding, section, we bring together the main findings and

Table 5.1. *Numbers in different age groups*

	1975	1985
Age 55–6	196	200
Age 57–8	175	166
Age 59–60	197	202
Age 61–2	213	177
Age 63–4	192	206

summarise the implications for policy, as they affect the early retired specifically and social policy more generally.

5.1 Two cohorts of men aged 55–64 and their context

The basic source of empirical information on which we draw in this chapter is the United Kingdom Family Expenditure Survey (FES), which is a continuous nationwide survey designed to collect expenditure information for updating the weights in the Retail Prices Index. It covers approximately 11,000 households per year, with a response rate of about 70 per cent, and it gives detailed information on expenditure, income and personal characteristics (for further information, see Kemsley *et al.*, 1980).

The surveys used here are those for 1975 and 1985. In each case, we take as the sample to be studied all family units headed by a man aged between 55 and 64 at the survey date. The family unit includes his wife and any dependent children (defined to be aged under 16 or under 19 and in full-time education). The sample number are 973 in 1975 and 951 in 1985.[1] In the latter year the sample constituted 15 per cent of all adult males in the FES. At various points we consider individual two-year age groups, containing the numbers shown in table 5.1.

The first of the two years studied (1975) pre-dates the massive rise in unemployment which occurred in the late 1970s and early 1980s. In 1975 the average level of unemployment was below 1 million (4.1 per cent); in 1985 it averaged $3\frac{1}{4}$ million (11.8 per cent).[2] In other words, in the latter of the two years we study, unemployment is some three times larger than in the former.

Given that decisions to retire may have been made several years earlier, it should be noted that the average unemployment rate over the period 1971–5 was around 3 per cent, compared with 10 per cent or more over 1981–5. The two cohorts therefore faced very different labour market conditions. Comparison of the experience of the early retired is of interest on these grounds alone.

The different labour market conditions led in turn to different government attitudes towards early retirement. In the post-war Welfare State, income support for the early retired had been implicit rather than explicit and the stated government aim was to encourage people to remain in the labour force. In proposing a minimum retirement age of 65, with a retirement condition for the receipt of the pension, coupled with an incentive to postpone retirement beyond that age, Beveridge saw it as important that:[3]

> The conditions governing pension should be such as to encourage every person who can go on working after reaching pensionable age, to go on working and to postpone retirement and the claiming of pension. (1942, p. 96)

And he suggested that:

> The natural presumption from the increasing length of total life is that the length of years during which working capacity lasts will also rise, as health improves [and as] the physique and the courage of the citizens are maintained. A people ageing in years need not be old in spirit. (1942, p. 99)

This prediction has proved in recent years to be wide of the mark in two important respects: high levels of unemployment in the late 1970s and 1980s led governments to see early retirement as a part of labour market policy, and, over a longer timescale, rising living standards have led to a preference for increased leisure and early retirement by choice.

The change in government policy towards early retirement came more naturally to the Labour Party. From the 1930s there had been trade union pressure for early retirement, both to help reduce unemployment among younger workers and to provide a longer period of leisure in later life. After the Second World War, 'the Party experienced considerable problems in adjusting its policy to one of delaying retirement' (Harper and Thane, 1989, p. 48). In the late 1970s, the Labour government responded to the changed conditions by, for example, introducing in 1977 the Job Release Scheme for older workers, allowing them to retire with a special allowance providing that the employer undertook to recruit as soon as possible a registered unemployed worker, although not necessarily for the same job. The conditions of eligibility varied over time: for example, in 1985 it applied to disabled men aged 60–3 (who received a taxable allowance of £58.35 a week) and all men aged 64 (who received a tax-free allowance of £49.95). (These amounts are for a single person and may be compared with the single pension at that time of £35.80 a week.) The take-up of the Job Release Scheme appears to have been modest: in 1978/9 it is estimated that about

7 per cent of the eligible 64-year-old men had taken retirement (Bosanquet, 1987, p. 23). (In the reversal of policy which post-dates the period considered in this chapter, the scheme was ended in January 1988.)

Probably more important are the measures taken to extend entitlement to social security benefits. In November 1981, the long-term rate of Supplementary Benefit (means-tested assistance) was extended to unemployed men aged 60 and over, so that if unemployed for more than one year, and no longer registered as unemployed, they received the higher rate of benefit. From May 1983, *all* unemployed men aged 60 and over were no longer required to be available for employment and became eligible for the higher benefit. A role has also been played by the development of Invalidity Benefit and other provisions for the long-term sick and disabled. As has been noted in other countries (for example, Wolfe *et al.*, 1984), disability transfers may act as a surrogate early retirement programme. The introduction in 1971 of Invalidity Benefit, replacing Sickness Benefit for those off work for 28 weeks or more, acquired particular significance as the rates of benefit began to diverge (in 1985 Invalidity Benefit was some 25 per cent higher than unemployment benefit).

The second reason why retirement ages have fallen rather than risen is of a longer-term nature, reflecting rising living standards, with early retirement 'attributable principally to the decision by an increasingly affluent nation to consume part of its growing wealth as leisure' (Aaron, 1980, p. 62). In this respect, we should consider the experience of the two cohorts over a longer time perspective. The cohort aged 55–64 in 1975 were born in the decade 1911–20 (see figure 5.2). They reached the age of 15 between 1926 and 1935, so that they entered the labour market at a relatively unfavourable time. Being aged between 19 and 28 in 1939 they are likely to have served in the Second World War. If they retired early in the 1970s they are unlikely to have had more than some 25 years of uninterrupted employment. They have a lower probability of being covered by an occupational pension scheme: coverage in 1956 (around the mid point of their career) was only 35 per cent (Bosanquet, Laing and Propper, 1990, table 4.1).

In contrast, the cohort aged 55–64 in 1985 were born in the decade 1921–30, and this ten years' difference may have been highly significant. The older members of the cohort will have served in the War, being aged 18 in 1939, but the youngest members will have entered the labour market after the War. If they retired early in the 1980s they are likely to have had some 30–5 years of uninterrupted employment. In 1967, around the mid point of their careers, the coverage of occupational pensions was over half of the labour force (and since 1978 the state earnings-related pension was in operation for those not so covered). The labour market conditions in which

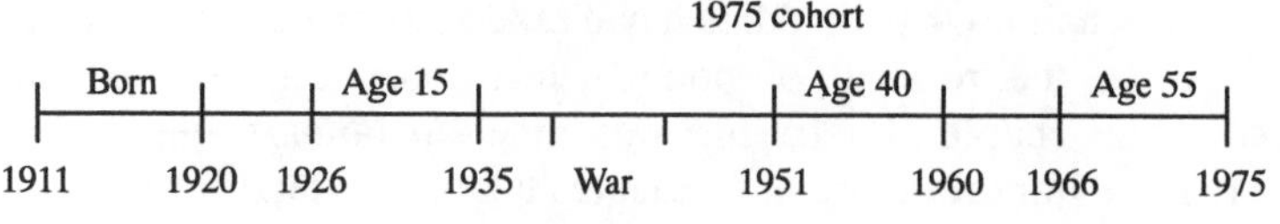

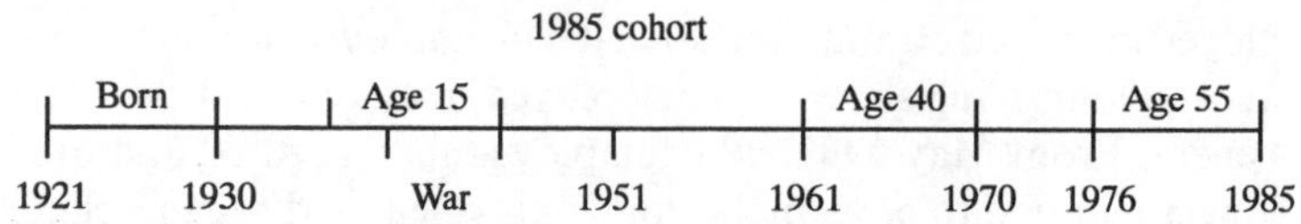

Figure 5.2 The life experience of the two cohorts

they retired were certainly less favourable; and this may to some extent have offset their earlier advantage. However, the transition has certainly been eased by earlier retirement options within occupational pension schemes or special provisions (such as those covering university teachers) or by redundancy payments. Firms appear to have made extensive use of early retirement options to bring about reductions in manpower (see Laczko *et al.*, 1988, p. 321).

There are therefore likely to be significant differences between the lifetime experiences of the two cohorts studied here. These may provide insight into the consequences of different labour market conditions and policy reactions. They may also give rise to issues of generational justice (Thomson, 1989).

5.2 Discrete characteristics: labour market status, sources of income and health

Labour market status

The difficulty in defining 'retirement' has been well recognised. As has been described by Fields and Mitchell, in some cases it is straightforward:

> Suppose that at age 65 you leave your lifelong job, accept an employer-provided pension, begin to collect social security benefits, leave the labour force, and depart for a life of sunshine and tranquillity on a Caribbean island. (1984, p. 3)

(In this case, of course, you will not be covered in our FES sample.) But other cases are less easily determined:

> Suppose you leave your life-long employer at age 61 with a year's terminal sabbatical. Starting at age 62, you become eligible for a private pension from your employer's fund, which you accept. At age 65 you file for social security. You

Table 5.2. *Labour market status of two FES cohorts*

	1975 cohort		1985 cohort	
Status (variable A201)	Number	%	Number	%
At present working as employee (1)	736	75.6	477	50.2
Self-employed or employer (2)	79	8.1	92	9.7
Out of employment but seeking work (3)	30	3.1	74	7.8
Sick/intending to seek work (4)	10	1.0	13	1.4
Sick/not intending to seek work (5)	74	7.6	117	12.3
Retired (6)	38	3.9	140	14.7
Unoccupied (7)	6	0.6	38	4.0
Total	973	100.0	951	100.0

continue to earn a few thousand dollars a year as a part-time consultant.... Have you retired? If so, at what age? (1984, p. 3)

In the present case, we are utilising secondary data, so that we can only use the information contained in the FES, limiting our capacity to draw fine distinctions. The most relevant variable is that based on a question: 'Are you doing any kind of paid work at present?' If the answer is 'no', the interviewer is instructed to 'probe the situation'. On this basis, respondents are classified as shown in table 5.2. The variation of the main categories by two-year age groups is shown in figure 5.3.

The proportion in work, employed or self-employed, fell from 83.8 per cent in 1975 to 59.8 per cent in 1985. The rise in unemployment, while noticeable, did little to offset this, and we have seen that the government took measures to reduce the numbers in this age group registered as unemployed. From figure 5.3, it may be seen that the rise in unemployment was most marked below the age of 61. The proportion classified as retired or unoccupied[4] rose from 4.5 per cent to 18.7 per cent. From figure 5.3, there is a marked age gradient, but the increase for this category between 1975 and 1985 appears to have affected all age groups. Overall, the picture is not dissimilar to that found in the aggregate statistics and in other studies.[5]

The most obvious definition of 'early retirement' would include those people who classify themselves as retired, unoccupied or not seeking work (categories 5, 6 and 7). This gives a total of 118 in 1975 (or 12.1 per cent) and

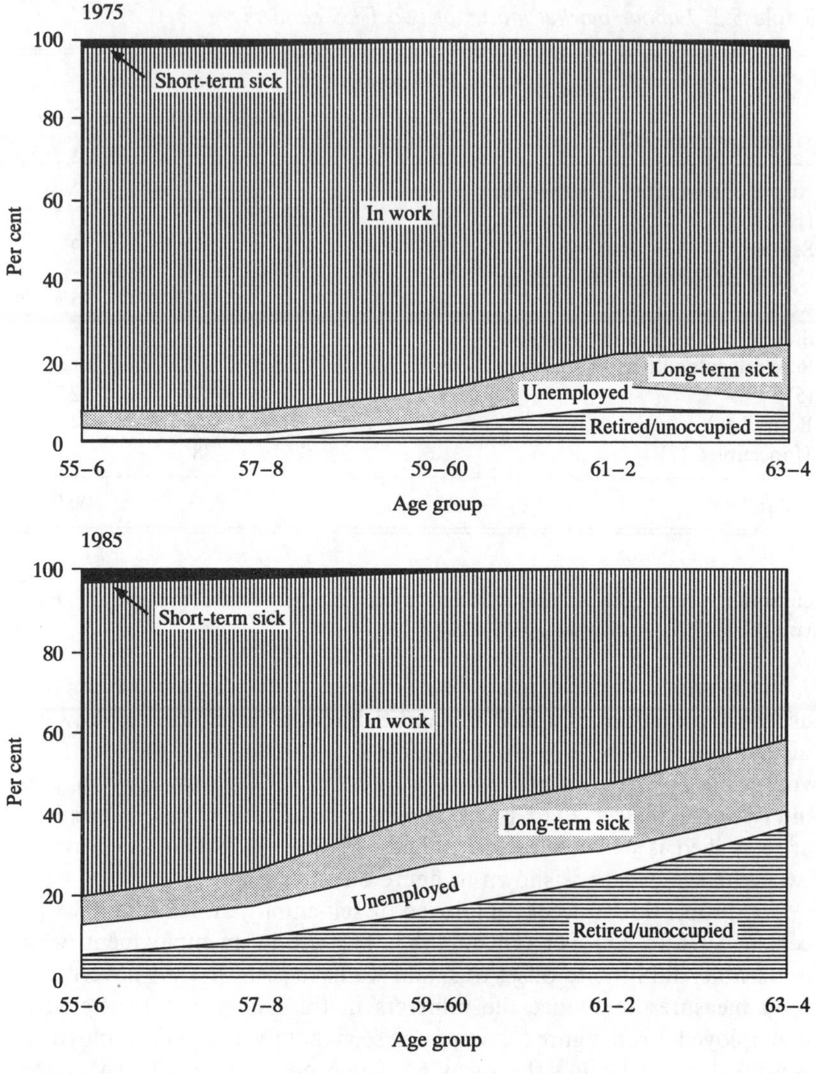

Figure 5.3 Labour market status by two-year age groups

of 295 in 1985 (or 31.0 per cent). At the same time, we would expect to find differences within this group – this indeed being one of the main subjects of our investigation. Laczko *et al.* (1988, p. 314) have emphasised, for instance, the need to distinguish those who are long-term sick, and we consider separately the position of the latter group (category 5), this providing one index of the degree of heterogeneity. From figure 5.3, it may be noted that there is a less pronounced age gradient for the long-term sick than for those classified as retired/unoccupied.

More generally, the classification has been criticised by Casey and Laczko on the grounds that the term 'early retired' 'is an unhelpful, indeed deceptive one, and that its use deflects concern away from the labour market problems experienced by many older workers' (1989, p. 509). Using data from the Labour Force Survey, they distinguish a category of 'discouraged' workers, who are not seeking work because they believe no jobs to be available. The information available to us in the FES does not allow such a group to be identified. Casey and Laczko also feel that the category of 'unemployed' is ambiguous, drawing attention to the difference between the labour market classification and the receipt of benefit – a point to which we will return.

The definition of 'early retirement' may also be augmented by other information in the FES, notably that about hours of work or receipt of occupational pension. The part-time consultant instanced by Fields and Mitchell would have been classified as employed according to our definition, but we might want to exclude people who reported working less than 35 hours a week, of whom there were 21 in 1985. More importantly, a sizeable fraction of those classified as in employment were in receipt of occupational pensions. Of the 815 in work in 1975, 60 were receiving occupational pensions, and they were virtually half of those with such pensions (121 in all). For 1985, the number with occupational pensions was much higher – 271 in all – of which 77 were in work. In view of this, we also define a category of 'semi-retired' consisting of those with an occupational pension or working less than 35 hours a week (not including teachers). This gives the breakdown shown in table 5.3.

Income and its sources

The FES provides information about the total income of families and about its composition.[6] For the cohort as a whole, and for the different sub-groups distinguished above, we have the figures for total family income[7] shown in table 5.4.

The levels of income in 1985 follow a not unexpected pattern, with those in the labour force having a total income about two-thirds higher than that of those classified as early retired (with the semi-retired being particularly well favoured). Within the early retired, there is a sizeable difference in average income, with those classified as retired having about 25 per cent more than the long-term sick. This difference was even more marked in 1975.

In considering the 1985 figure relative to that in 1975, shown in the last column of table 5.4, it must be remembered that there have been important

Table 5.3. *Early retired and semi-retired in two cohorts*

	1975		1985	
	Number	%	Number	%
Early retired	118	12.1	295	31.0
Semi-retired	85	8.7	123	12.9
Remainder in labour force	770	79.1	533	56.0

Table 5.4. *Total income (£ per week) of different groups*

	£ per week		ratio
	1975	1985	1985/75
Total cohort	52.45	148.02	2.82
Early retired (5–7)	34.31	102.11	2.98
Long-term sick (5)	29.55	94.24	3.19
Retired (6)	45.77	117.13	2.56
In labour force (1–4)	54.95	168.54	3.07
Semi-retired	60.05	181.82	3.03
Remainder	54.39	165.63	3.05

changes in the magnitude and composition of these groups. The smaller increase in the overall average (by a factor of 2.82) than for the early retired sub-group (by a factor of 2.98) and for those in the labour force (by a factor of 3.07) reflects the changing weight attached to these sub-groups. Moreover, within the groups there have been compositional changes.

To put these figures in perspective, we may note that the Retail Prices Index increased by a factor of 2.78 between 1975 and 1985, and that between April 1975 and April 1985 average earnings for adult males increased by a factor of 3.22.[8] It is also interesting to make a comparison with the position of those over the minimum retirement age (65 for men), as shown in an official study (Dawson and Evans, 1987). They show the average net income of pensioner households as increasing by a factor of 3.39 between 1975 and 1985, so that the younger age groups did less well. Although the figures are not strictly comparable, they also suggest that the average income for the early retired was about a quarter higher than the average for those over the minimum pension age. On this basis, the early retired had an advantage, but one which narrowed over the period.

The sources of income of the different groups may be classified as follows:

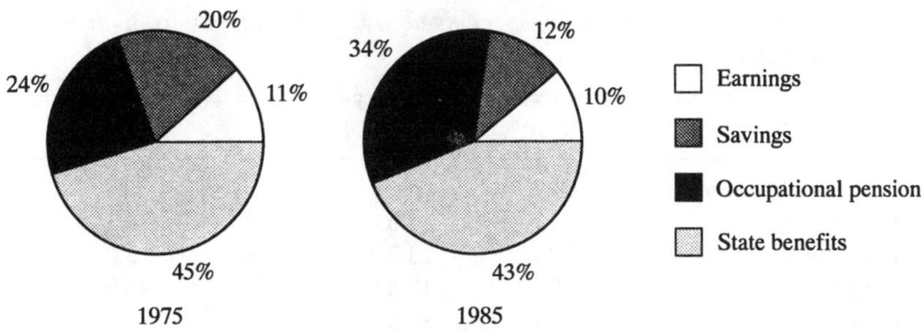

Figure 5.4 Sources of income of the early retired

earnings and self-employment income
social security benefits
occupational pensions
investment income.

(There is a fifth residual category.) The relative importance of these types of income in 1975 and 1985 is shown in figure 5.4 for the early retired. The proportionate contribution of state benefits, the single most important source of income, changed little over the period, as did the (much smaller) share of earnings. The major change was the growth in the contribution from occupational pensions, with a fall in the role of private savings. Each of the categories is considered in more detail below.

Earnings

For the group in the labour force, earnings from employment and self-employment constituted the major part of the net income: 90.2 per cent in 1975 and 81.8 per cent in 1985, with most of the fall due to the increase in 'semi-retirement' and the associated receipt of occupational pensions. For the early retired group, the earnings of their wives provided on average about 10 per cent of total income – see figure 5.4. However, this was limited to a small minority: about one in five had wives with earned income (20.3 per cent in 1975 and 16.6 per cent in 1985).

Savings

In 1975 income from savings (bank accounts, savings banks, stocks and shares, etc.) constituted 20 per cent of total income of the early retired and averaged £6.87 a week. To have kept up with inflation, this average would have had to increase to over £19, but the 1985 figure was £12.40 a week. Average income from this source was therefore smaller in

Table 5.5. *Proportion of income received by early retired from different sources in 1985*

	<10%	10–30%	30–50%	≥50%
Occupational pensions				
All early retired	47.5	15.6	12.9	24.1
Long-term sick	70.1	13.7	10.3	6.0
Retired	19.3	18.6	17.1	45.0
Unoccupied	81.6	10.5	5.3	2.6
State benefits				
All early retired	27.1	7.8	10.8	54.2
Long-term sick	4.3	4.3	10.3	81.2
Retired	49.3	10.7	12.1	27.9
Unoccupied	15.8	7.9	7.9	68.4

real terms for the 1985 cohort; and, as may be seen from figure 5.4, it contributed a much smaller share. In contrast, the income from savings of those continuing in work increased significantly in real terms.

Occupational pensions

These have constituted a rising share in the incomes of the early retired – up from a quarter of total income to a third (see figure 5.4). The average amount per recipient was virtually constant in real terms, so that the rising share reflects the extension of coverage: in 1975, of the early retired, 42.4 per cent were in receipt, but by 1985 this had risen to 58.0 per cent. There are however important differences within the early retired group. In 1985, 81.4 per cent of the retired group (6) had an occupational pension (80.0 per cent in their own right). For the long-term sick (5), the proportion was 41.0 per cent.

A much smaller fraction of the long-term sick were in receipt of an occupational pension, and the proportion falls to a third if we consider only those cases where the man was receiving the pension in his own right. It is interesting to note that the proportion of cases where the wife of an early retired man received an occupational pension increased from virtually zero in 1975 to one in eight in 1985. The differing significance of income from occupational pensions is illustrated by table 5.5, which shows the proportion of total income received from such pensions in 1985. (The picture for 1975 is similar.) Unlike investment income, which reaches 50 per cent in only 6 per cent of cases, occupational pensions account for at least half of total income for nearly a quarter of the early retired. These people

Table 5.6. *Families with more than 50 per cent of income from one source*

Status (variable A201)	Wages/self-employment	Occupational pension	SB	Health benefits
Employee of self-employed (A201 = 1, 2)	533 (94)	11	2	4
Out of employment but seeking work	10 (14)	18 (24)	25 (34)	0
Sick/injured (A201 = 4, 5)	10	9	7	**93 (72)**
Retired	7	**63 (45)**	**18 (13)**	5
Unoccupied	3	1	**22 (58)**	4
Total	564	102	74	107

Note: The figures in brackets show the percentage of that group, rounded to the nearest 1 per cent, where the percentage exceeds 10 per cent.

are heavily concentrated amongst those classified as retired. The distribution for the 'unoccupied' is much more similar to that for the long-term sick than for the retired. In the case of both the long-term sick and the unemployed, a large proportion receive more than half their income in the form of state benefits.

State benefits

State benefits are relatively unimportant for those continuing in work, but for the early retired they represent about 45 per cent of total income, a proportion which has changed little between 1975 and 1985. In terms of coverage, there has been a modest decline (from 82.2 per cent to 76.6 per cent) but this still means that the proportion of the age group as a whole financed (at least in part) by state benefits has risen from 26 per cent to 48 per cent. The average benefit per recipient has risen by about 7 per cent in real terms. Table 5.5 shows that for 54 per cent of the early retired state benefits provide over half of the total income. This is much less likely to be the case for the group classified as retired (around a quarter), whereas four out of five of the long-term sick depended on the state for more than half their total income.

The reliance of different groups on different sources of income is shown in more detail for 1985 in table 5.6. This gives the number who receive more than half of their total income from a single source: categories which are non-exhaustive but which are exclusive.[9] For those in work we would expect wages or self-employment income to account for at least half of total income in the great majority of cases, and it does for 94 per cent. The table also brings out again the importance of occupational pensions for those classified as retired. Of particular interest for the other groups is the disaggregation of state benefits into Supplementary Benefit (SB) and health benefits. We find that means-tested Supplementary Benefit was much more important for the unoccupied group: 63 per cent were in receipt and for nearly all of these it accounted for more than half of total income. There was also a group of similarly dependent recipients among those classified as retired – see table 5.6. In contrast, the percentage of the sick and injured receiving SB was 15 per cent and very few received more than half of their income from this source. Not surprisingly, 68 per cent of them received Invalidity Benefit, and 88 per cent received a benefit related to sickness or disability, with 72 per cent receiving more than half their income from this source. In these figures, we have combined all of the sick and injured, whether or not they intend to seek work (the group intending to seek work contains only 13 people in 1985), and this applies below when we refer to the total of all 'sick and retired' (A201 = 4–7), so that the total number is 128 in 1975 and 308 in 1985.

The position in terms of sources of income suggests that certain distinct groups can be identified amongst the sick and retired:

those classified as retired who received more than half of their income from occupational pensions, referred to as 'occupational pensioners'. This group was small in 1975 (only 17 people) but has increased to 63 people in 1985;

the 'health benefit beneficiaries', or those sick and injured who receive more than half of their income from state benefits linked to their medical condition. This group constituted over a third in 1975 (52 people), but has grown proportionately less (in 1985 it was 93 people, or about 30 per cent);[10]

those classified as retired or unoccupied who receive more than half of their total income from Supplementary Benefit (SB), referred to as 'SB dependants'. Only five people were in this position in 1975, but the number had increased to 40 in 1985.

These groups, identified in bold figures in table 5.6, account for 64 per cent of the total in 1985 and 58 per cent in 1975. They receive particular attention in the next section.

5.3 Economic status and the two nations hypothesis

In this section, we consider the economic status of different groups in our two cohorts. The 'two nations' hypothesis is essentially concerned with differences in standards of living, and as such may turn critically on how this is defined. One particular problem is that of comparing the economic status of those not in work with those in work. To begin with, we leave this on one side by considering only those who are 'sick or retired' (A201 = 4–7).

In assessing economic status, we make two adjustments to net income, both in line with the practice of calculating entitlement to Supplementary Benefit (in 1985 or 1975). The first is to deduct actual housing costs, so as to measure 'net resources' available after payment of rent or other housing costs, with the objective of adjusting for the different housing costs and circumstances.[11] The second is to express net resources relative to the long-term Supplementary Benefit (SB) scale, which between 1 January and 27 November 1985 was £35.70 a week for a single householder and £57.10 for a married person (in other words a couple are treated as equivalent to 1.6 single persons). The post-27 November 1985 rates were £37.50 and £60.00. The corresponding scale in 1975 was:

1 January–6 April	£10.40 single/£16.35 couple
7 April–16 November	£12.00 single/£18.85 couple
17 November–31 December	£13.70 single/£21.55 couple

There was a different scale for non-householders and also allowances for children. In studies of low-income families, particular attention has been focused – following the lead of Abel-Smith and Townsend (1965) – on those with net resources less than 140 per cent of the SB scale. (For discussion of the Supplementry Benefit scale and its use for this purpose, including the official 'Low Income Families' statistics, see, for example, Atkinson, 1983, chapter 10.)

The net resources of the person and his family (wife and any dependent children) are expressed as a proportion of the SB scale, to give the *relative net resources ratio* (RNR). The distribution of this ratio for all sick/retired in 1985 is shown in figure 5.5 (b). The modal range is from 100 to 120 per cent of the SB scale. Half (156 out of 308) are below 140 per cent of the SB scale, with a broadly declining frequency in the higher ranges. We would expect the group dependent on SB to be concentrated at the bottom: 40 have an RNR below 140 per cent of the scale.[12] What figure 5.5 (b) brings out is that there is also a concentration of health benefit beneficiaries at the bottom, a pattern which is not found for the group with more than half its income from occupational pensions: 55 out of 93 of the health benefit group

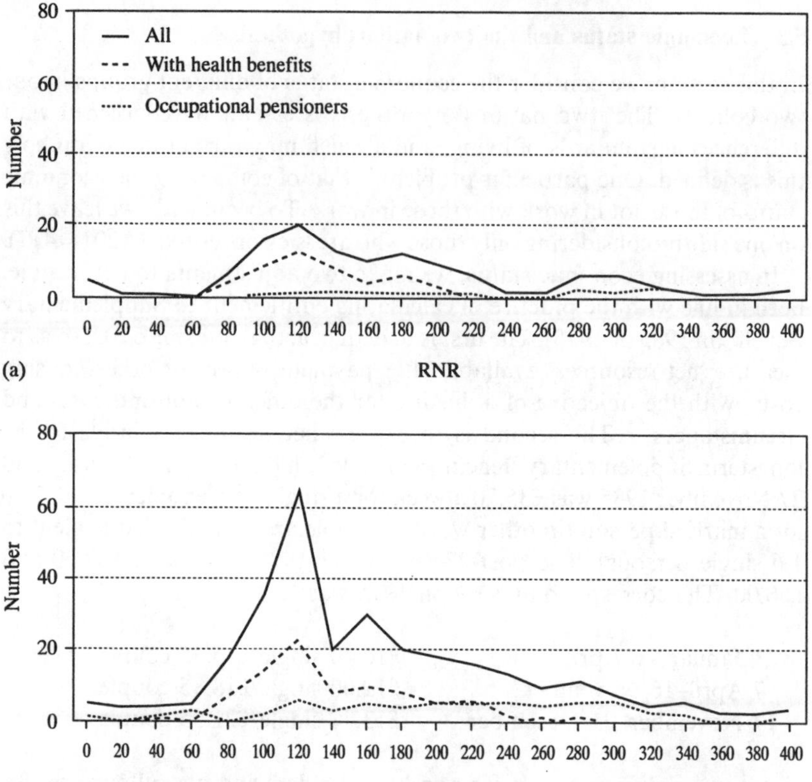

Figure 5.5 (a) Distribution of relative net resources 1975 (b) Distribution of relative net resources 1985

are below 140 per cent of the SB scale compared with 16 out of 63 of the occupational pension group.

Turning to the distribution in 1975,[13] we see from figure 5.5 (a) that the mode is again at 120 per cent of the SB scale, although less pronounced. Again about half (63 out of 128) are below 140 per cent of the SB scale, and more than half of these (35 people) are health benefit beneficiaries (there are only four occupational pensioners).

Comparing the two figures for 1975 and 1985, it appears that – apart from the more pronounced mode in the latter year – the growth in numbers has left the overall shape of the distribution little changed. Figure 5.6 shows the *relative* distributions for 1975 and 1985. The emergence of a group of people dependent on SB has enlarged the peak of the distribution around the SB level; the growth in occupational pensioners has increased the

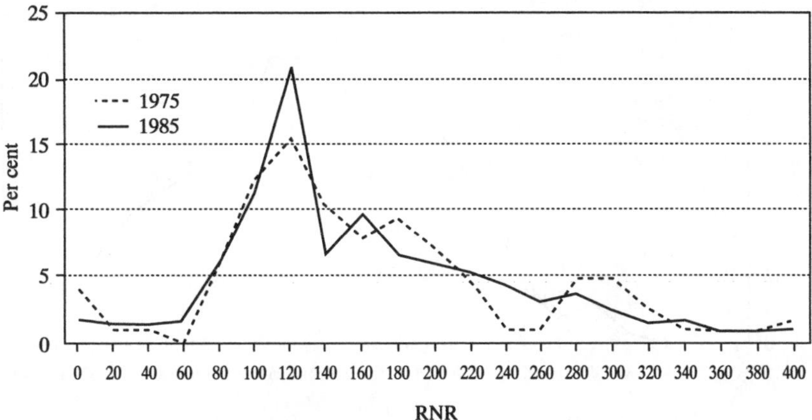

Figure 5.6 Comparison of the sick/retired for 1975 and 1985

numbers from 140 per cent upwards. Taken together, the two influences have not greatly changed the overall shape of the distribution.

Relation with those in work

The change in the overall distribution of living standards amongst the age cohort depends on both shifts within groups and between groups. We have seen that the distribution within the 'sick/retired' group has not changed greatly; from figure 5.7 we can see that the same is also true of those in work (employed or self-employed). Given that there has been a large reduction in the size of this group (from 815 in 1975 to 569 in 1985), we might have expected the shape to have changed: for example, if the early retired came from the middle and upper-middle ranges, or if those forced to leave work on account of ill-health were drawn from the low paid. We also know that the aggregate distribution of earnings has shifted towards greater inequality: the lowest decile for adult men was 67.4 per cent of the median in 1975 and 61.5 per cent in 1985 (adjusting for the break in continuity in 1983).[14] The stability shown in figure 5.7 is therefore striking.

Since there has been relatively little change in the distribution within the two groups, the change in the overall distribution must reflect the shifting balance of the two groups. In figure 5.8 we show the distributions for the entire age cohort for both years.[15] There is a clear leftward shift. The proportion with RNR below 140 per cent rises from 17 per cent to 27 per cent.

The effect of the shifting balance may be seen if we consider the two groups of those at work (A201 = 1 or 2) and those not at work (A201 = 3–7).

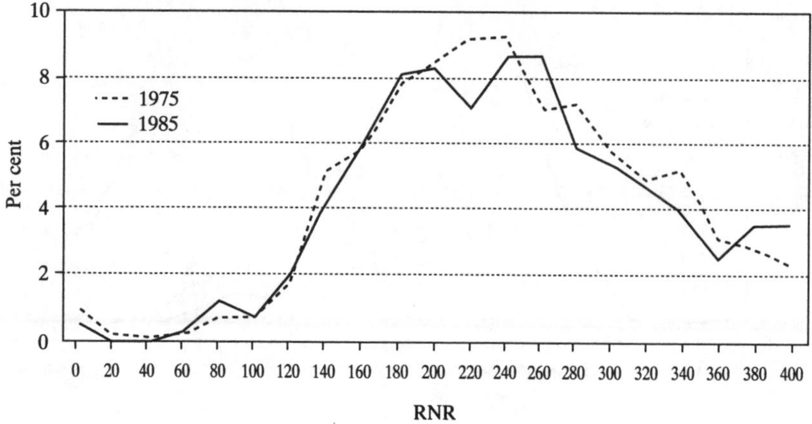

Figure 5.7 Distribution among those in work 1975 and 1985

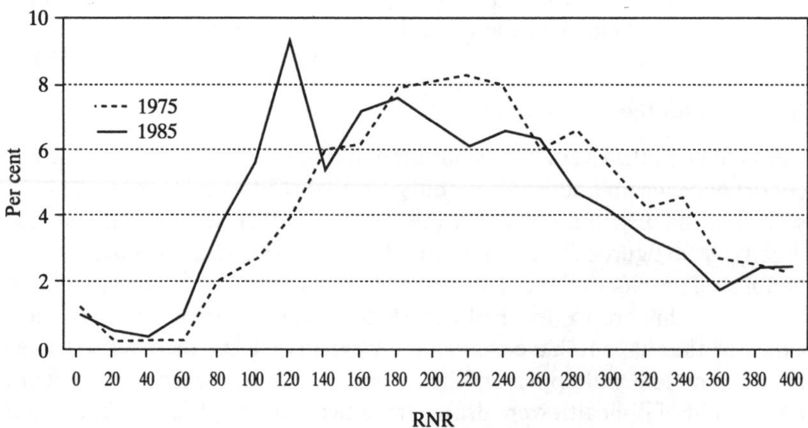

Figure 5.8 Comparison of whole cohort 1975 and 1985

The proportions with RNR below 140 per cent in 1975 were 10 per cent and 53 per cent, respectively, and these hardly changed in 1985. But the proportions in the two groups changed from 84 : 16 in 1975 (rounding to the nearest 1 per cent) to 60 : 40. This structural change may be seen as 'accounting for' the ten percentage point increase in the overall proportion with RNR below 140 per cent ($0.24 \times 0.43 = 0.10$).

The conclusions which can be drawn from this accounting exercise are limited by the fact that we have not made any adjustment for the costs of work and foregone leisure. These are reflected in the fact that the target

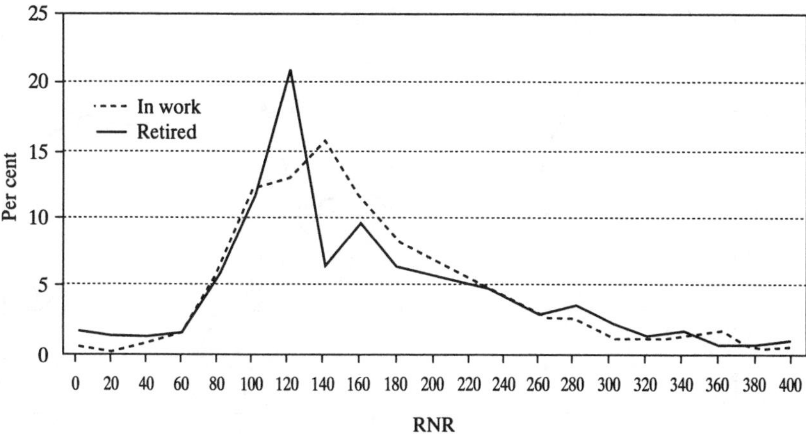

Figure 5.9 Comparison of distributions of sick/retired and those in work scaled down by replacement rate of 0.57 for 1985

replacement rate in pension schemes is typically less than 100 per cent. Seen in these terms, the average replacement rate in our sample of sick and early retired in 1985 is 57 per cent: for the sick and retired (A201 = 4–7) the mean RNR is 163 per cent of the SB scale, for those in work (A201 = 1, 2) it is 285 per cent.

One simple calculation is then to compare the *relative* distributions, dividing in each case by the mean (figure 5.9). This is equivalent to comparing the distribution of income among those not in work with that obtained with a replacement rate of 57 per cent. It may be seen from figure 5.9 that we cannot obtain one distribution from the other by such a simple transformation. The upper tail is reasonably represented, but there is a deficiency in the ranges from 120 to 220 per cent of the SB scale, and an excess in the range around the SB scale.

The argument of Titmuss regarding two nations was not based on statistical evidence, but on a consideration of the underlying transfer mechanisms. The constant replacement rate calculation of figure 5.9 corresponds to a 'continental' model of proportional income replacement.[16] The UK social security system, on the other hand, gives more weight to the flat-rate element. The combination of a flat-rate state scheme and an earnings-related occupational (or SERPS) element could in theory be redistributive, reducing the relative income differences in retirement. However, Titmuss emphasised the differential coverage of the two types of provision. In extreme form, we have a fraction of the population receiving an earnings-related pension and the remainder dependent on the flat-rate benefit. These fractions probably vary with the level of income. In the

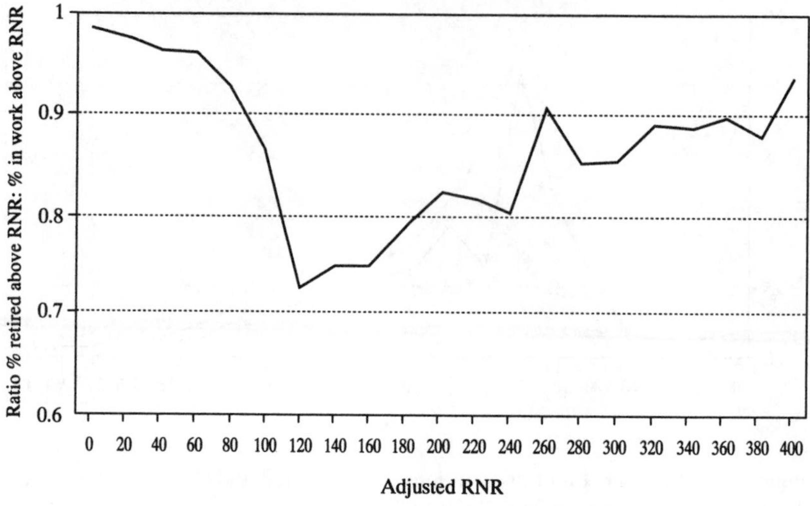

Figure 5.10 Cumulative proportions above specified levels: comparison of sick/retired and those in work scaled down by replacement rate of 2/3

present case, we have the further consideration that the incidence of early retirement varies with the level of income. On the one hand, the better-off are more likely to be able to choose to retire early; on the other hand, the low paid may be more exposed to redundancy and sickness.

Some insight into the combined impact of these two mechanisms is provided by figure 5.10. In constructing this figure, we have taken a replacement rate of 2/3, which is closer to that which may be expected under an occupational scheme, and plotted the cumulative distribution of the income of the sick/retired *relative* to that of those in work (reduced by the replacement rate). We know that not everyone could have such a replacement rate, since the average for those sick/retired is only 57 per cent. The diagram shows the cumulative percentage above specified income levels and that, taking for example 300 per cent of the SB scale, we find that 9.1 per cent of the sick/retired have an income above this amount, compared with 10.7 per cent of those in work (even adjusted by the 2/3 factor), giving the *relativity* shown in figure 5.10 of 0.85. This falls as one moves to the left in the diagram, indicating that the coverage/incidence of early retirement falls, being offset by the large excess in the range from 80 to 120 per cent (where there are 32.5 per cent of the sick/retired, compared with 18.3 per cent of those in work).

This calculation involves an 'as if' experiment but is certainly consistent with the story described in the previous paragraph, with the distribution of income among the sick/retired being generated by the 'mixture' of a distribution generated by incomes in work (adjusted by a replacement rate), selected with a probability that increases with earnings, and of a largely flat-rate distribution.[17]

Concluding comments

In this chapter we have presented the results of an exploration of the incomes of men in the UK aged 55–64 in 1985, compared with the position of the same cohort in 1975. Between the two years there had been a substantial rise in the extent of early retirement, associated in part with worsening labour market conditions and in part with a longer-run trend.

In the absence of longitudinal data covering the changing experience of individuals, we have attempted to draw inferences from the changing distribution over time. The overall distribution has shifted between 1975 and 1985, but there is relatively little change *within* the groups of those in work and those who are sick/retired. This directs attention to the impact of the substantially increased numbers in the latter category. Within this group there is considerable heterogeneity, but there are several sub-groups which appear to be fairly clearly identifiable:

those retiring early with a substantial proportion of their income from occupational pension;
those who derive a substantial proportion of their income from health-related benefits;
those largely dependent on Supplementary Benefit (now Income Support).

While the idea of 'two nations' is no doubt an oversimplification, we feel that there are indeed discrete differences between different sets of circumstances. The overall distribution may be seen as a 'mixture' of the distribution of incomes in work, scaled down appropriately, and of a distribution concentrated around the Supplementary Benefit level. The probability of 'escaping' this latter level of income depends on the level of income in work and is much higher among those in receipt of occupational pensions than among those with health-related benefits.

In this sense, the main thrust of Titmuss' argument has validity today – applied to the early retired – and it raises several issues of policy importance. Here we identify just three of these issues. The first is the role of health-related benefits and the extent to which they are appropriate to provide income support for the early retired. The second is the level of flat-rate benefits and Supplementary Benefit (now Income Support). The redistributive potential of the UK social security system depends on the level of benefits relative not just to prices, which have been the focus of recent policy, but also to earnings. If benefits continue to fall in relation to earnings levels, the polarisation identified in this chapter will be intensified. This leads to the third question, which is the extent to which occupational and other sources can be relied upon to provide adequate support for the early retired on a universal basis. The 'two nations' story reflects the uneven coverage of occupational provision. With the introduction of personal pensions in 1986, allowing people to contract out of both occupational and state earnings-related schemes, there is risk that the inequality amongst the retired will increase.[18]

Part II

Analysis of the Welfare State

6 Is the Welfare State necessarily a barrier to economic growth?

There has recently been a groundswell of opinion among economists that the scale of the Welfare State is one of the elements responsible for slower economic growth and that a retrenchment in state spending on social security is necessary if growth is to be revived in Europe. The Welfare State is indicted with the charge of being a barrier to economic growth.

Two widely discussed documents are illustrative of this view. The Swedish Economics Commission, chaired by Assar Lindbeck and including distinguished economists from other Nordic countries, has referred to 'the crisis of the Swedish model', arguing that it has

> resulted in institutions and structures that today constitute an obstacle to economic efficiency and economic growth because of their lack of flexibility and their one-sided concerns for income safety and distribution, with limited concern for economic incentives. (Lindbeck *et al.*, 1994, p. 17)

The social security system is one area which they seek to reform. In order that 'the social-security (or social insurance) system should not overburden the economy through distorted incentives or large deficits' (Lindbeck *et al.*, 1993, p. 238), they say that 'cuts in benefit levels constitute an important step in this direction' (Lindbeck *et al.*, 1993, p. 238) leading to a 'mandatory benefit level, which is low enough for large groups to find it attractive to acquire additional insurance by themselves' (Lindbeck *et al.*, 1994, p. 106). On an international level, the World Bank has similarly been arguing for a reduced weight of the state in the provision of welfare benefits, with, for instance, a larger role for private pensions.

The second document is the paper on 'Growth and employment: the scope for a European initiative', prepared by Jacques Drèze and Edmond Malinvaud, on the basis of discussions with a group of Belgian and French economists. This report provides a clear endorsement of the basic justification for the Welfare State, but goes on to list three major criticisms:

(i) measures of income protection or social insurance introduce undesired rigidities in the functioning of labour markets;
(ii) welfare programmes increase the size of government at a risk of inefficiency; their funding enhances the amount of revenue to be raised, and so the magnitude of tax distortions;
(iii) ... welfare programmes may lead to cumulative deficits and mounting public debts. (Drèze and Malinvaud, 1994, p. 95)

They stress that there is no case for dismantling the Welfare State, but conclude that 'the agenda should be to make the Welfare State leaner and more efficient' (Drèze and Malinvaud, 1994, p. 82). While recognising the diversity of national circumstances within Europe, and that in some countries spending may be too low, their overall recommendation is to 'reduce expenditure in some countries, perhaps by 2% of GDP or so' (Drèze and Malinvaud, 1994, p. 98).

The present chapter does not attempt to determine whether or not the charge against the Welfare State is proven. In my view, this would be premature. The aim is rather to clarify the nature of the indictment and the lines along which a defence might be mounted. What exactly is being alleged by the prosecution? Are there arguments on the other side?

In considering these questions, I limit the treatment in three important respects. First, I do not consider the positive benefits provided by the Welfare State in terms of providing security, alleviating poverty, or redistributing income (these are discussed in other chapters). This side of the balance sheet clearly needs to be part of any final decision as to whether to reduce spending. Secondly, I concentrate on income transfers and do not discuss Welfare State spending on health care or education. In view of the direct role that the latter may play in human capital formation, I am tackling the areas where the indictment seems most likely to apply. Thirdly, in examining the economic impact of the Welfare State, I focus on the long-run determination of potential output, rather than on the failure of the economy to achieve its potential.

6.1 Circumstantial evidence and the empirics of growth

I consider first the empirical evidence, which appears to underlie much of the case for the prosecution. In particular, one piece of evidence advanced in the indictment of the Welfare State is the relatively poor economic performance of countries with large welfare spending. Sweden is a widely cited example, where the Lindbeck Commission argue that productivity growth (GDP per person employed) has been significantly slower than the OECD average. It is not my intention here to enter into discussion of the Swedish case, which is clearly controversial (see, for example, Klevmarken,

1994). It does however illustrate one of the points which I wish to make, which is the need to distinguish between two different charges which may be levelled:

(a) arguments based on disincentives embedded in the structure of the Welfare State, and
(b) arguments against the Welfare State based on cost of financing, via taxation or debt.

Both of these appear to concern the Lindbeck Commission, who refer to the macro-economics of public finance and to the detailed structure of social security benefits. Similarly, the argument (i) of Drèze and Malinvaud corresponds to (a), and their arguments (ii) and (iii) correspond to (b).

This distinction is important. It affects the kind of defence which is mounted. If the indictment is (b), then the defence can point to other forms of government spending as equally culpable. The Welfare State is no more than a co-defendant with other elements of the state budget. Macro-economic considerations, say, determine the overall total of spending, and we have a question of the relative desirability of different types of government spending. The question is one of *differential expenditure* analysis, to use Musgrave's terminology (Musgrave, 1959). And if the issue is tax *rates*, rather than total taxation, then tax expenditures can also be brought into the dock. Why not, the defence may ask, reduce income tax allowances for children rather than child benefit? The case on which I concentrate is (a): that the Welfare State has a specific disincentive impact on growth.

Implicit in the critique of Swedish performance is a cross-country comparison, and this could be elaborated to a full international cross-section study. Following the recent literature on growth empirics (Barro, 1991 and Mankiw *et al.*, 1992), one could introduce Welfare State spending as an explanatory variable in international cross-section regressions with the rate of growth as the dependent variable. There are noticeable differences between OECD countries in the level and timepath of welfare spending. Figure 6.1 shows social security transfers as a percentage of GDP in four OECD countries. Whereas one tends to associate large Welfare States with Scandinavia, in the 1960s it was in fact West Germany which had the higher spending. In the early 1970s Sweden and West Germany were at a similar level; the difference was that spending remained broadly constant in Germany but increased substantially in Sweden.

The relation between post-war growth (1960–85) and the level of state transfers, relative to GDP, in 13 OECD countries has been examined by Persson and Tabellini (1994). They conclude that 'the data do not seem to be at odds' with the proposition that greater transfers in proportion to

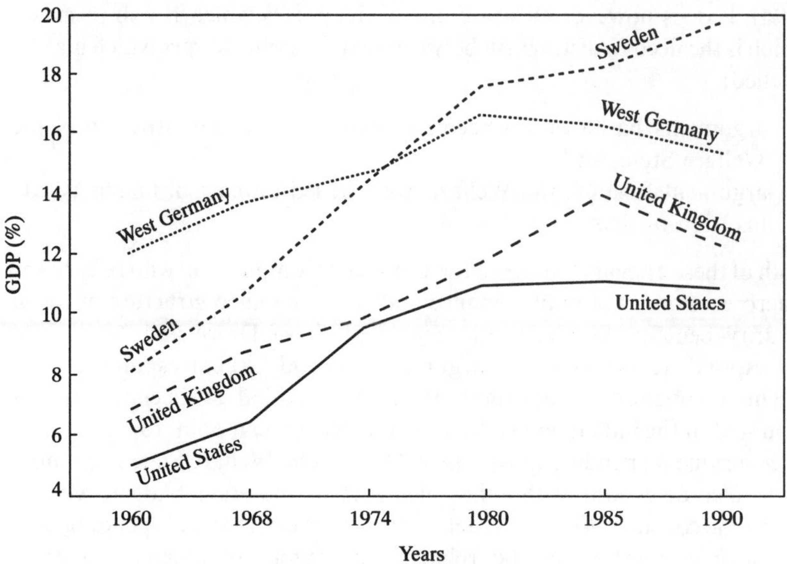

Figure 6.1 Social security transfers as a percentage of GDP
Source: OECD, 1992, tables 6.2 and 6.3.

GDP are negatively associated with average growth rates, although this is based on a coefficient with a *t*-statistic of 1.2 (1994, table 8). There are indeed a number of objections to such a cross-country analysis of aggregate welfare spending and economic performance which might be cited by the counsel for the defence. Of the general approach, Solow has said that:

I do not find this a confidence-inspiring project. It seems altogether too vulnerable to bias from omitted variables, to reverse causation, and above all to the recurrent suspicion that the experiences of very different national economies cannot be explained as if they represented different 'points' on some well-defined surface. (1994, p. 51)

In the specific case of the Welfare State as an explanatory variable, the fine structure of spending programmes may be crucial to their economic impact. To take one example, unemployment *insurance* may have quite different implications for the working of the labour market than unemployment *assistance* (Atkinson and Micklewright, 1991).

Formulating the question in this way does, however, serve to identify a further important question about the nature of the hypothesis being tested. Does the appropriate specification have on the right-hand side of the growth rate equation

(I) the growth in Welfare State benefits, or
(II) the level of Welfare State benefits?

In other words, does a high level of spending lower the *level* of the growth path or reduce the *rate of growth* itself? Are we saying that Sweden grew slower than Germany because its benefits became more generous over the 1970s, or that the two countries had similar growth experience because they had similar levels of spending? It is the latter hypothesis (II) that is tested by Persson and Tabellini (1994), but it is the former which follows more directly from the incentives literature, as may be seen when we turn in the next section to the deductive arguments.

6.2 Deductive arguments: growth theory

The *a posteriori* argument examined in the previous section does not reveal the underlying mechanism by which the Welfare State is supposed to affect economic performance. If there is a negative correlation between the rate of growth and the level of social security benefits, how is this supposed to come about? I turn now to deductive arguments, drawing on the theory of economic growth, in which there has been a resurgence of interest in the past decade. This choice of theoretical framework means that I am, as indicated earlier, concentrating on the long-run determination of potential output, rather than on the failure of the economy to achieve its potential.

Let us suppose that aggregate output, Y, is governed by a production function with arguments capital, K, and effective labour, AL. A denotes the productivity of labour, although with the Cobb–Douglas form assumed here for purposes of exposition, it is purely a semantic issue that I regard all changes in productivity as being labour augmenting. With an exponent β for effective labour, we have

$$Y = K^{1-\beta} (AL)^{\beta} \tag{6.1}$$

In growth rate form, assuming that there is no growth in the labour force, we have

$$g_Y = (1-\beta)\, g_K + \beta\, g_A \tag{6.2}$$

where g_x denotes the proportionate growth rate of the variable X.

Of the two types of indictment, I and II, distinguished earlier, the first charges that transfer payments reduce the productivity of labour and level of output. For example, the existence of a social safety net may reduce the incentive to supply effort, as in some efficiency wage models, reducing A, and hence Y. We would then expect that a country which chose a higher level of safety net benefits would have a lower level of output. Equivalently, if benefits became more generous, then there would be a reduction in the rate of growth during the period of increase. The long-run growth rate would not however be affected once the size of the Welfare State had been stabilised. Put another way, a move to a 'leaner' Welfare State could be expected to produce a once-and-for-all rise in output level, if it raised A in equation (6.1).[1]

The first indictment has been extensively discussed (see, for example, Danziger *et al.*, 1981, Moffitt, 1992 and Atkinson and Mogensen, 1993), and here attention is centred on the second: that today's Welfare State reduces the growth rate, and hence output at all future dates. In terms of equation (6.2), this means that transfers affect g_K or g_A. Three mechanisms suggest themselves:

savings and capital accumulation,
investment and firm growth,
human capital formation.

These are considered in turn. The discussion involves a number of different models, reflecting the fact that there are a variety of relevant features to social security programmes which need to be considered. Even so, only some of these features are covered in the treatment here, which focuses particularly on retirement pensions and the financing of education.

6.3 Savings and capital accumulation

State pension schemes have accounted for much of the increase over time in Welfare State spending, and ever since they were introduced it has been argued that they discourage private savings. Does this reduce growth? The answer given in the context of the Solow neo-classical growth model is that such a reduction in saving would lower the level of output, but not affect the steady-state rate of growth. The steady-state growth rate is equal to the rate of population growth (here assumed zero) plus the rate of technical progress, g_A, assumed exogenous in the Solow model. In the long run (and the speed of convergence may be slow), any decline in savings induced by the introduction of state pensions does not affect the growth rate.

If however the rate of technical progress is treated as endogenous, rather than exogenous, then the transfer system may affect the long-run growth rate. Here I take for purposes of exposition the simple version of the Arrow (1962) learning-by-doing model which has been widely used, where productivity A depends on experience, which is proportional to cumulated past investment, or K. This gives a production function

$$Y = aK \tag{6.3}$$

and the economy is in instantaneous steady growth at rate

$$g_Y = g_K = S/K \tag{6.4}$$

where S denote net savings. The competitive market return to capital is equal to

$$r = a\,(1-\beta) \tag{6.5}$$

The consequences of state pensions depend on the determinants of savings. Much of recent growth theory assumes that this can be modelled in terms of a representative agent maximising the integral of discounted utility over an infinite horizon. This 'Ramsey' formulation requires that the rate of growth of consumption, and hence the steady-state growth rate of capital (under certain conditions), equals

$$(r-\rho)\,\sigma \tag{6.6}$$

where ρ is the rate of discount and σ the rate of intertemporal substitution in the utility function. It follows that a payment of a state pension, which does not affect r, has no impact on the growth rate. The same is true taking account of the financing (argument (b)) if the pension is financed purely by a tax on wages, as is typically the case. This reflects the fact, pointed out by Bertola (1993), that none of the income of non-accumulated factors is saved in steady growth. In this respect, it resembles the extreme Kaldorian model (Kaldor, 1956) where savings are proportionate to capital income. If savings equal $s_c\, r\, K$ then the rate of growth is simply

$$s_c\, r \tag{6.6a}$$

and is again unaffected by a state pension.

Neither the Ramsey nor the extreme Kaldorian models seem particularly appealing as explanations of savings in modern economies. More commonly used in studies of the impact of pensions have been models of life-cycle savings with a finite lifetime and no bequests (so that there is no Ricardian equivalence). One such model is that of Diamond (1965), where people live for two periods working during the first and living off their savings in the second.[2] In this model, the existence of a state pension (leaving aside the way in which it is financed) reduces the level of private savings and hence the rate of growth. (Savings are reduced still further by the taxes necessary to finance the pension on a pay-as-you-go basis.)

However, the effect of scaling down the state pension depends on what would be the alternative. If the state pension were simply to disappear, then this may affect not just savings but also retirement decisions. If people stay at work longer, this reduces the need for life-cycle savings: 'this reduction in working years and the resulting increase in the period of retirement induce additional saving. The net effect of social security on the saving of the non-aged is indeterminate' (Feldstein, 1976a, p. 78). Feldstein himself feels that the matter is settled by the empirical evidence, and argues that state pensions have a pronounced negative impact on capital accumulation. My own reading of the literature is that there is a lack of robustness in the reported effects and that there are grounds for remaining agnostic (Danziger *et al.*, 1981 and Atkinson, 1987b).

Complete abolition of state pensions is not typically proposed. In the UK, it is argued that universal pensions should be replaced by 'targeted' income-tested benefits.[3] Such a policy move, while it would reduce total spending, would be liable to create a 'savings trap'. Suppose that in the two-period model the universal pension is replaced by a guaranteed income in the second period, reduced by 100 per cent of any private resources available to the person. This causes the budget constraint to be horizontal. The individual savings decision compares the maximum level of utility on the no-pension budget constraint with that attainable consuming all net earnings in the first period and the assistance pension in the second period. It is then quite possible that the switch in the form of transfer causes savings to fall to zero. People realising that they derive no marginal benefit from saving may choose to depend entirely on state provision. In this situation, the universal pension leads to a higher growth rate than does the means-tested system.

Alternatively, state pensions may be replaced by mandatory private pension schemes. Before analysing the implications of this change, I need to elaborate the model.

6.4 Investment and the capital market

To this point, it has been assumed that changes in savings are automatically translated into changes in investment. It is assumed that investment can be carried out of an amount equal to the level of savings, without consideration of the underlying mechanism. As noted by Hahn and Matthews (1964, pp. 11–15), we need to distinguish between the rate of interest, here noted i, and the rate of profit, denoted by r as before.

Consideration of the nature of the investment function leads naturally to the introduction of the corporate sector. As suggested in Atkinson (1994), it may be useful to view the investment rate in an endogenous growth model as being governed by the choice of growth rate by firms which face costs of adjustment. This draws on the early literature on the growth of the firm (Penrose, 1959, Marris, 1964) and follows the work of Uzawa (1969) on the Penrose effect and of Odagiri (1981) on corporate growth.

The key element in the growth theory of the firm is the stock market valuation, V, which is assumed to equal the present value of future dividend payments, where the discount rate is equal to the interest rate i (possibly plus a risk premium, although uncertainty is not treated explicitly). Assuming that all investment is financed out of retained earnings, dividends are equal to profit less the cost of expansion at rate g, given by $c(g)K$, so that

$$V=[r\,K-c(g)K]\,/\,(i-g) \tag{6.7}$$

since dividends grow at rate g.

The firm may maximise its stock market value, in which case the desired growth rate depends on i and on the internal costs of expansion. Equilibrium of savings, which depend also on i, and investment is achieved by variation in the rate of interest. Alternatively, in the managerial version, firms maximise the rate of growth subject to a takeover constraint. The constraint may take the form of limiting the stock market value to some fraction of the 'break-up' value of the assets

$$V\geq m\,K \tag{6.8}$$

In this case, managers choose the highest rate of growth consistent with this constraint, which yields a different, higher equilibrium rate of growth (and interest rate).

In such a model, a reduction in savings due to the existence of a state pension scheme again leads to a reduction in the rate of growth. But it is also the case that a more detailed examination of the fine structure may lead to caution about the reforms proposed. Suppose that the state pension is replaced in part by private pension provision through funded schemes, as proposed by the Swedish Commission and by the World Bank. This undoubtedly has implications for the capital market, since it increases the role of institutional investors. Such a development is welcomed by Lindbeck *et al.*: 'It is also important to stimulate the emergence of a larger number of institutions that not only hold shares, but are also willing to play an active ownership role' (1994, p. 96).

The model of the capital market has not been spelt out, but there are good reasons to expect that the larger the fraction of shares owned by pension funds, the tighter is likely to be the takeover constraint. (An argument may be developed along the lines of the shirking models in the labour market.) If this is the case, then a switch in pension from unfunded state to funded private may lead to a rise in the savings rate but a fall in the desired growth rate of firms. The net effect may be to either raise or lower the rate of growth, or to leave it the same.

6.5 Human capital and growth

The role of human capital in economic growth has long been recognised. In his 1961 Presidential Address, Schultz stated that 'increases in national output have been large compared with the increases in land, man-hours, and physical reproducible capital. Investment in human capital is probably the major explanation for this difference' (1961, p. 1). With the notable exception of Uzawa (1965), human capital was not treated formally in the growth theory of the 1960s. It has however received renewed attention in the recent literature emanating from Lucas (1988), and this provides a starting point for an investigation of the impact of social security (and the direct effects of education spending not considered here).

Returning to the production function (6.1) and dropping the learning-by-doing assumption, the simplest way of introducing human capital, H, is to replace A by H. The empirical study of Mankiw *et al.* (1992) finds some evidence for such a production function with an estimated value for β of 0.3. Lucas (1988) uses a similar form, but allows for an additional term H^{γ} for the external effects arising from human capital (not taken into account below).

Investment in human capital is assumed to take the form of spending in education part, $(1-u)$, of the working period, thus reducing the effective labour supply to a fraction, u. The decision by individuals regarding u may be affected by the transfer system (as well as by the available places in educational institutions, not considered here). If people are only concerned with current-period income, then they maximise

$$u\ w\ h[1-u]\ (1-t)+(1-u)\ b \tag{6.9}$$

where w is the wage rate per efficiency unit of labour, h [] is the number of efficiency units of a person who has spent a period $(1-u)$ in education, t is the tax rate on earnings and b is the tax-free transfer payment made during education.

As formulated above, the impact of transfer payments (and taxes) is on the *level* of human capital, and hence the *level* of national income. The effect is of the type I identified above. It is in these terms that the role of education has been discussed: for example, Denison noted that 'what is required to maintain the contribution of more education to the growth *rate* is maintenance of the *percentage* increase in the amount of education received' (1962, p. 76). The formulation of Lucas, on the other hand, is that the current level of education *adds* to an existing stock of human capital, and hence determines its rate of growth

$$g_H=\delta\ (1-u) \tag{6.10}$$

In other words, the growth rate can be sustained by maintaining a constant level of education.

It is not clear to me that this specification is necessarily appropriately applied to formal education, and, as noted by Solow (1992, p. 21), it assumes strongly increasing returns to scale in the production of human capital. It does however mean that the rate of growth may be affected by the existence of transfer payments. For a steady state, we require that physical and human capital grow at the same rate (assuming there to be no external effects to human capital). The implications depend on the savings function assumed and on the determination of u. The treatment by Lucas can be interpreted in the present context as assuming that individuals take full account of the future value of the human capital. At the other extreme, if we assume that people act quite myopically, then u is determined as before, and this governs the overall growth rate, the rate of growth of consumption being brought into equilibrium via variation in the rate of return to capital. If transfer payments subsidise education, then they raise the rate of growth.

Conclusions

The procedure adopted in this chapter is the reverse of that in criminal law, where it is for the prosecution to establish that there is a *prime facie* case to answer, that there is sufficient evidence for the case to go to trial. In view of the widespread presumption that the Welfare State is a hindrance to growth, I have concentrated on showing that there is a plausible case that can be entered for the defence. I have not tried to provide a balanced presentation. I have not discussed all the ways in which the Welfare State may be a disincentive, nor have I considered the ways in which the Welfare State has failed to achieve its distributional objectives. My aim has simply been to clarify the nature of the charge, which is not always made transparent by the prosecution, and to suggest that there are arguments for the defence. It is for these reasons that I said at the outset that I was not seeking to provide a definitive answer. All that I am arguing is that the jury should stay out.

7 A national minimum? A history of ambiguity in the determination of benefit scales in Britain

The objective of securing a national minimum is a major consideration in the determination of benefit scales. In a social security system dominated by flat-rate benefits, as in Britain, this relation is particularly close. From the choices made about the level of benefits, it may be possible to make deductions about the objectives which lay behind them – a revealed preference argument – and it may be possible to learn from the expressed intentions of governments. The first half of this chapter provides a review of the considerations which appear to have influenced the determination of benefit scales at a national level in Britain. It covers pensions and National Insurance benefits since 1908 and the scales applied in a succession of national means-tested schemes dating from the Unemployment Assistance Board established in 1934.

From this review of the historical record, it is evident that the determination of benefit scales has been characterised more by ambiguity than by clarity. Empson (1953) distinguished *Seven Types of Ambiguity*; in the treatment in the second half of this chapter I limit myself to three types. First, the decisions made by governments may reflect not just a concern to establish a national minimum but also a balancing of this objective against others, including the reduction of the cost of social security programmes and the avoidance of disincentives. There may be a compromise between different objectives. This compromise is often left implicit rather than made explicit, governments hoping that a blurring of the goal (a national minimum) with the instrument (a level of benefit) would leave the impression that the objective had in fact been fully achieved, without any need to compromise with other policy concerns. The first type of ambiguity therefore concerns the relation between the target and the constraints.

The second type of ambiguity concerns the degree of responsibility accepted by the government for the achievement of the goal of a national minimum. Are benefits to be a *contribution* to securing such a minimum, with the recipient dependent on self-help or support from relatives to make up the balance? Where state benefits are seen as the principal source of income, is the provision of a minimum *conditional* on the other resources of the claimant by means of a means test, so that state help is the last resort? Or is there an *entitlement* to benefit irrespective of means, as under an analogy with private insurance? At any one time there has been a variety of conceptions, giving rise to ambiguity in the way in which benefits have been viewed, particularly the extent to which *insurance* benefits should provide an acceptable minimum without recourse to means-tested *assistance*, and the degree to which individuals in a family are liable to support one another.

Thirdly, there is ambiguity about the justification given for the provision of a national minimum. Much of the early discussion focuses on *well-being*, with the objective being to ensure that no one falls below some specified standard of living. Benefits have been related explicitly to studies of 'subsistence needs', such as those of Seebohm Rowntree and Sir Arthur Bowley. More recently, there has been reference to notions concerned with minimum *rights*, or the capacity of people to participate effectively in society. The abolition of poverty is a precondition of securing positive freedom. By revealed preference, and from their expressed intentions, governments appear to have had in mind elements of both well-being and rights when making decisions about benefit levels.

The significance of these ambiguities becomes particularly clear when we consider the uprating of benefits over time, and this is taken as a case study to illustrate the earlier analysis. Uprating poses questions of major long-term significance for the Welfare State, but ones which are often lost from sight in discussion of more short-term policy. At this point, I refer not just to historical evidence from this century but also to the policy issues that are likely to arise over the first part of the twenty-first century.

Clarification of the ambiguities surrounding the achievement of a national minimum is a key contribution of social policy analysis, but it must be recognised that such ambiguities have a role to play in political discourse. This is the subject of the concluding section.

7.1 A national minimum? Benefits in Britain since 1908

The aim of this section is not to provide an exhaustive review of the history of social security in Britain over the twentieth century but to highlight some of the key episodes when the form and level of benefits have been determined. I concentrate on *national* benefit scales, starting in 1908 when state old age pensions were introduced by the Asquith government. It should also be noted that I do not consider housing benefits and the related question of the treatment of housing costs under social assistance.

Old age pensions 1908

The first state old age pension was paid at the rate of 5 shillings (5s.)[1] per person per week. The pension was non-contributory and available to all aged 70 or over, subject to an income test which reduced the amount payable to those with incomes between 8s. and 12s. a week (Clarke, 1939, p. 630). No pension was paid when income exceeded 12s. For a couple, the pension was double, as were the parameters of the income test (applied to their joint income). Whereas the government had originally proposed that a couple should receive only 1.5 times the single pension, this was defeated by back-bench opposition (Fraser, 1984, p. 153). The payment of the old age pension had moralistic overtones, in that a claimant had to satisfy the authorities that he was not guilty of failing 'to work according to his ability, opportunity, and need, for the maintenance of himself and those legally dependent on him' (Clarke, 1948, p. 167), but the income test was applied quite separately from the Poor Law (pension officers were in the service of Customs and Excise) and, unlike the Poor Law, there was no obligation on relatives to contribute.

The introduction of state old age pensions had been the subject of debate for several decades. In this debate, one of the principal concerns had been the possible cost of the new pensions. The pensions proved in fact to be very popular, and by 1909 half a million old persons were in receipt. The resulting rise in public expenditure was one of the factors which led to the 1908 'People's Budget', which Lloyd George described as:

> a War Budget. It is for raising money to wage implacable warfare against poverty and squalidness. I cannot help hoping and believing that before this generation has passed away we shall have advanced a step towards that good time when poverty and wretchedness ... will be as remote to the people of this country as the wolves which once infested its forests. (Hansard, HC Debates, 29 April 1909)

There can be little doubt that the cost was a crucial factor in determining the level of the pension. As a result, it fell short of being adequate on its own to guarantee a national minimum. Of the rate of 5s. per person, Booth had earlier written:

> It does not pretend to be 'an adequate provision' but is the contribution of the State towards it, being about the sum (and less rather than more) which the bare maintenance of a destitute person actually costs. (Booth, 1892, p. 236)

That this was less rather than more is borne out by the estimates of Rowntree (1901) in his study of poverty in York of the minimum expenditure for the 'bare necessaries', which came to 7s. per person (including an allowance for rent). It does not appear that the architects of the scheme saw it as providing more than a contribution to a minimum level of income. Lloyd George, for example, 'claimed that the pension was not intended to give full subsistence, merely an addition' (Thane, 1982, p. 336). According to Clarke:

> Pensions, at 5s. a week, were meant to be supplementary to the resources of the righteous man. They were to be the reward of virtuous living rather than any token of communal responsibility for the well-being of the enfeebled citizens. (Clarke, 1948, pp. 167–8)

The figure of 5s. per week may also be compared with the average earnings of manual workers in the 1906 earnings inquiry, which for adult males ranged from 26s. 4d. to 34s. 4d. (Department of Employment, 1971, table 37). On this basis, the single pension was around one-sixth of average earnings of adult male manual workers.

This first major departure from the Poor Law was followed in 1911 by the introduction of contributory National Insurance. Part I of the Act provided sick pay for insured workers, at a rate of 10s. a week for male workers and 7s. 6d. for female workers, together with medical benefits; Part II provided for unemployment benefit in selected industries at a rate of 7s. per week. Relative to the average earnings figures just quoted, the sickness benefit was around one-third, and the unemployment benefit was around one-quarter. It may be noted that these rates of benefit are different from that paid to pensioners, and that (for sickness) the rates are different for men and women. Both of these points are taken up below.

Up-rating of benefits after the First World War

After the First World War, the level of state benefits was discussed against a background of a price level which had approximately doubled and of expectations that, as a result of the war, living standards would have to be reduced. The Secretary to the Treasury, Sir John Bradbury, described the position in 1919 with regard to the level of old age pensions as follows:

> I doubt whether the active working classes short of a social revolution will be content with a lower standard of comfort. You must therefore make economy elsewhere, and I want to make the economy principally at the expense of the wealthier classes. I want to prevent people riding in motor cars; I want to prevent people wearing expensive furs; I want to prevent people buying unnecessary clothing, and very soon the Income Tax will have that effect. [But] I think it quite impossible to restore people like Old Age Pensioners who are not part of the industrial machine to as favourable a position as they occupied before the war. (Thane, 1982, p. 336)

This is taken from a statement to the Adkins Committee, which also heard evidence about the living standards of pensioners. As a result of its recommendations, the state pension was set at 10s. a week in December 1919. The purchasing power of the pension increased in subsequent years as prices fell, but nonetheless the subsistence calculations by Bowley and Hogg (1925) suggested that a rate of 10s. allowed very little margin to cover housing costs once allowance had been made for food, clothing and fuel. The level of the pension was again lower than the unemployment benefit set in 1920, which was 15s. a week for men and 12s. a week for women.

Unemployment Assistance Board 1934

The provision of income support for the unemployed was one of the major political and economic problems of the inter-war years. In 1934 the government carried out a large-scale reconstruction of unemployment insurance and unemployment assistance. In the latter case, the newly created Unemployment Assistance Board (UAB) took over the functions of Public Assistance, which had itself replaced the Poor Law in 1929. For the first time in Britain there was, for one category of claimants, a national system of means-tested relief operated on a uniform basis. This immediately raised the acute problem of setting the national scale, in view of the previous variation across local Public Assistance Committees in the amounts of benefit which they paid.

As Veit-Wilson has argued, one of 'the principal considerations in the minds of members and officials' of the UAB when determining the new scale was:

> to implement the traditional Poor Law principle of 'less eligibility', that is, to pay benefits below the level of wages which the manual workers would in general earn if they were in full time work. (1989, p. 27)

Similarly, Lynes concluded that:

> It will be apparent from this account of the Board's deliberations that throughout the period from July to October 1934 the relationship between the scale rates and the wages of unskilled workers was a dominant consideration. (1977, p. 42)

The rates originally set for single persons were 15s. for men and 14s. for women (raised to 15s. in 1936). Compared with average earnings of 69s. for adult male manual workers in October 1938 (Department of Employment, 1971, table 40), from which we have to deduct 1s. 10d. contributions to old age pensions, health and unemployment insurance (Beveridge, 1942, p. 217), the benefit of 15s. represented some 22 per cent of net earnings. For a couple, the rate was 24s. a week, and there were additions for children, ranging from 3s. to 6s. depending on their age.

Lynes goes on to say that calculations of subsistence needs played a relatively minor role in the determination of the benefit scales:

> From the start, the Board tended to be sceptical of the scientific approach to the problem of establishing a minimum income scale for the unemployed and their families. (1977, p. 43)

The relationship between the benefit scales and subsistence calculations may be illustrated by reference to Rowntree's *The Human Needs of Labour*, published in 1937. For a family consisting of a couple plus three children (of average age), with rent of 9s. 6d. he estimated the minimum needed to be 53s. a week (or 49s. 11d. if travel-to-work expenses and other costs of working were deducted). The UAB scale would have given this family 37s. 6d. a week if the children were aged 11 to 13. The benefit level was significantly below the level which Rowntree described as that 'below which no section of the community should be compelled to live' (Rowntree, 1937, p. 159). Later he contrasted the human needs scale with his earlier 'primary poverty line', this being 'a standard of bare *subsistence* rather than *living*' (Rowntree, 1941, p. 102, author's italics). This would have been 38s. 6d., so that the benefit scale was nearer to this primary poverty line.

The impact of the UAB scales was also affected by the rigorous way in which the Board attempted to enforce the household means test, taking account of all income coming into the household and in effect transferring responsibility for support of a claimant to parents, children and other relatives. This is discussed further below.

Beveridge Report 1942

The work of Rowntree, Bowley and others received greater prominence in the Beveridge Report, and both served on the Sub-Committee which advised on benefit rates. The Report stated in an apparently uncompromising fashion that 'social insurance should aim at guaranteeing the minimum income needed for subsistence' (Beveridge, 1942, p. 14). It went on at once to recognise that 'what is required for reasonable human subsistence is to some extent a matter of judgement', and it is in the translation of the concept into actual levels of benefit that the objective ceased to be unambiguous. Beveridge himself, in a memorandum for the Committee, drew attention to the difference between Rowntree's human needs scale and his lower primary poverty scale.

The motives underlying the choice of benefit scales in the Beveridge Report are the subject of controversy. Beveridge's biographer has argued that he came down on the side of the more generous Rowntree human needs scale, quoting from the Memorandum a statement by Beveridge that the more stringent scale would 'be rejected decisively by public opinion today' (Harris, 1977, p. 394). Some grounds for believing that this was the case is provided by the fact that the recommended scale for a couple with three children including rent is identical to Rowntree's 53s. Veit-Wilson (1989b) on the other hand has drawn attention to the much larger proportion of this amount which is assumed to be allocated to food (Beveridge adopted the higher League of Nations dietary) and the lower amounts for other items. As a result the scales for other family types differ quite significantly. In broad terms, Beveridge allocated less to single adults and couples without children and more to families with more than three children. Veit-Wilson argues that, as a result of minimising the amount allocated to 'social expenditures', Beveridge was returning to the bare subsistence notion, rather than allowing for the costs of social participation.

Certainly there is evidence that concerns other than that of securing a national minimum played an important role in the determination of the scales recommended by Beveridge. A memorandum by the Committee's Secretary (D. N. Chester) discussed the relation between the benefit standard and the level of wages:

> If this standard is attacked for being too low, it would raise the much wider question of minimum wages and the raising of the standard of living of the working classes. (quoted in Veit-Wilson, 1989a, p. 14)

Consideration of the cost of benefit provision was indicated in Beveridge's use of evidence from the 1930s poverty surveys. He noted that the total surplus income of working-class families above the poverty line was eight times as great as the total deficit of those below, concluding that poverty could be abolished 'by a re-distribution of income within the working classes' (Harris, 1977, p. 393).

National Insurance and National Assistance 1946 and 1948

The legislation of 1946 established the present system of flat-rate National Insurance benefits covering major contingencies and retirement, and that of 1948 set up National Assistance as a unified means-tested safety net. As has been described by Thane:

> The Labour legislation together with the wartime introduction of family allowances came closer to the introduction of a national minimum than any previous government action. (1982, p. 254)

There were however several reasons why this celebrated legislation fell short of providing an unambiguous national minimum.

The first shortcoming lay in the departure from the key Beveridge principle that the national minimum should be guaranteed by social insurance, with social assistance playing a residual and diminishing role. As was explained by Ernest Bevin (then Foreign Secretary), the government

> rejected Sir William Beveridge's argument that benefit rates under the insurance scheme should be related to the cost of maintenance . . . applicants who proved need would be entitled to obtain higher rates of assistance from the Assistance Board. (quoted in Fraser, 1984, p. 231)

The National Assistance scale for a single person was set at 24s. a week, in addition to which housing costs were met, whereas the National Insurance retirement pension was 26s. a week. This meant that a single person with housing costs of more than 2s. would have been below the National Assistance level if he or she had no other income. The minimum was a conditional one.

The second controversial issue is the extent to which the benefit levels matched those proposed by Beveridge when allowance was made for the inflation that had taken place during the war. In the case of the National Assistance scale, the official description of its determination indicates that it was considered to be more generous:

> they constructed a new dietary, the cost of which was much higher than that used by Beveridge (some staple items in pre-war diets were then rationed or unobtainable), and allowed a bigger margin for non-essential expenditure. (Department of Health and Social Security, 1977, p. 8)

On the other hand, Veit-Wilson (1989) has argued that the unpublished memoranda of the Board in 1948 reveal it to be concerned about the inadequacy of the provision and that it 'presupposed only short-term dependence on assistance'. Outside Whitehall, there was contemporary concern about the level of benefits:

> The rates of that benefit payable under the National Insurance Act are not alone sufficient to maintain a family above the poverty line even if other welfare measures are taken into account. (Rowntree and Lavers, 1951, p. 45)

As far as the comparison with Beveridge is concerned, the official Cost of Living Index shows the rise in prices for all items between 1938 and 1948 (linking with the Interim Index) to be 44 per cent. According to this, the National Insurance pension of 26s. for a single person introduced in 1948 corresponded more or less in real terms to Beveridge's recommendation of 17s. 6d. in 1938 prices. However, the London and Cambridge Economic Service estimates (Feinstein, 1976, table 65) show the increase in prices as 75 per cent. This is clearly a major difference, and would mean that the National Insurance scale was some 15 per cent lower in purchasing power.

There is of course a difference between *prices* and *earnings* as a basis for comparison. In the latter case, allowance has to be made for the increased burden of contributions and income tax. In terms of the net earnings of an adult male worker at the average, the Beveridge recommendation for the single pension had amounted to 26 per cent in 1938; the actual benefit level of 26s. in 1948 was 23 per cent of the April 1948 figure.[2] This suggests that in terms of net earnings the scale was more comparable to the pre-war proportion.

Finally we should note that the unification of National Insurance involved not only a unified administration but also the payment of benefits which were largely uniform in amount. The earlier separate systems had paid a level of benefit to pensioners which was typically lower than that paid to those below pension age. This could have been rationalised in terms of the lower food and other requirements of the elderly, as assessed in the studies of Rowntree (1941) and others. There are also issues concerned with the length of time for which a person is dependent on benefit. A government spokesman explained in 1948 that:

> The existing differences in the scales for unemployment and the aged are considered to be no longer justified in conditions of full employment, when the great majority of persons who may be expected to require assistance will be either right outside the employment field or ... only on the fringe of it, and will be likely ... to need it for a long period. (Hansard, HC Debates, 16 June 1948, col. 559)

It should be noted that this argument is inconsistent with the presupposition, referred to earlier, that people would only be dependent on assistance for a short period. It reveals ambiguity as to whether the scales are intended to cover short-run or long-run needs.

The uprating of insurance and assistance benefits

In the uprating of benefit levels over the post-war period, there was a distinct shift of emphasis at the end of the 1950s, as was indicated in the announcement in the White Paper *Improvements in National Assistance* that the government had been

> considering the position of those on National Assistance and have reached the conclusion that the time has come when it is right to move to a higher standard, so giving them a share in increasing national prosperity. (Ministry of Pensions and National Insurance, 1959, p. 3)

Whereas the earlier upratings had been broadly in line with price changes, this introduced a commitment to raise benefits in line with rising standards in the community as a whole. As an objective, it lacked precision, as was later noted by an Opposition spokesman (D. Houghton): 'There is no index for a share in increasing national prosperity. It could be a full share or a proportionate share. It could be something less' (Hansard, HC Debates, 14 November 1962, col. 18). What was agreed was that it represented a real improvement in the scales, a change of policy which has been interpreted as signifying a shift in the way that the role of benefits has been viewed:

> While the conventional idiom was that of the pseudo-absolute poverty line, and class cultural stratification was taken for granted ... from the 1950s one detects a decline in the use of this language. Citizenship rather than class increasingly seemed to become the status criterion of adequacy. (Veit-Wilson, 1989, p. 34)

Or, to quote a contemporary account:

> While the Webbs were concerned to use social security to make the working classes less poor by singling them out for State grants, now it is planned to treat the working classes like the middle classes treat themselves. (Abel-Smith, 1959, p. 363)

In considering the uprating of benefits in more recent years, account has to be taken of the distinction introduced in 1973 between 'long-term and 'short-term' benefits. The ambiguity concerning the function of the benefits has been noted earlier, but it was not resolved by this distinction, since the unemployed were classified as 'short-term' recipients irrespective of the duration of their unemployment. The basis for the distinction appeared to lie in the principles thought appropriate for uprating over time. The long-term benefits between 1975 and 1980 enjoyed statutory indexation to whichever was the faster rising of earnings and prices, and since 1980 have been guaranteed indexation to prices. In practice, the same principle has often been applied to the two types of benefit; none the less a gap has opened up between the Retirement Pension and short-term benefits such as unemployment. Whereas these benefits were aligned in 1948, an unemployed person now receives only 80 per cent of the National Insurance for a single pensioner. Differentiation in the treatment of pensioners to that of those of working age has been reintroduced – in the reverse direction from that which existed before the Second World War.

The principles to govern benefit uprating were discussed in an unusually explicit manner in the 1978 *Annual Report* of the Supplementary Benefits Commission:

> It is right that society should determine through Parliament and the elected Government what level of support should be afforded to pensioners, the unemployed, the sick, and others. That level should be decided by sensitive use of the subjective test that beneficiaries must have an income which enables them to participate in the life of the community. *That means a standard which rises in line with any rise in the general standard of life in the community.* We do not believe it is

sufficient to increase benefits in line with the movement of prices. (Supplementary Benefits Commission, 1979, p. 20, italics in original)

This principle was endorsed by the incoming Conservative government, but in recent years the policy has been different. (Hansard, HC Debates, 6 November 1979, cols. 167–8). The policy has been that of indexation of benefits to prices. For example, in his statement about the 1990 uprating, the Secretary of State made mention of the increase in retail prices (Hansard, HC Debates, 25 October 1989), but there was no reference to shares in rising national prosperity.

Examination of the actual movements in benefit levels relative to earnings over the past two decades shows that for long-term benefits there was a discrete upward shift in 1975 (Social Security Statistics, 1988, table 46.15). This was maintained for the best part of ten years, but since 1985 the pension has fallen relatively as net earnings have increased in real terms while benefits have been indexed to prices (see figure 1.5). For short-term benefits, upratings in the 1970s broadly maintained their relation with net earnings, but they too have fallen since the mid 1980s.

7.2 Ambiguities in the determination of benefit scales

What can be learned from government decisions on benefit levels about the motives which lie behind social policy? In effect, this represents a 'revealed preference' approach to government objectives, seeking to draw conclusions about the nature of social objectives from the policy choices made. The main point which I wish to stress here is the need to come to terms with the ambiguities which characterise government policy in this area.

Ambiguity I: the scales as a compromise between different objectives?

The first source of ambiguity concerns the extent to which the policies chosen reflect a compromise between different objectives. The government, however well intentioned, pursues the objective of a national minimum *subject to constraints*. The resultant benefit policy may be attributable as much to constraints as to goals and there may be ambiguity as to which is the determining factor.

On this view, it would be quite consistent for the government to have as a target a national minimum level of income, Y^*, but to face a trade-off between the level of benefit B, and the contribution rate required to finance the transfer scheme. Increases in the contribution rate reduce the net income of those in work, as indicated by the downward-sloping line in figure 7.1 (for a person with average earnings). Suppose that the govern-

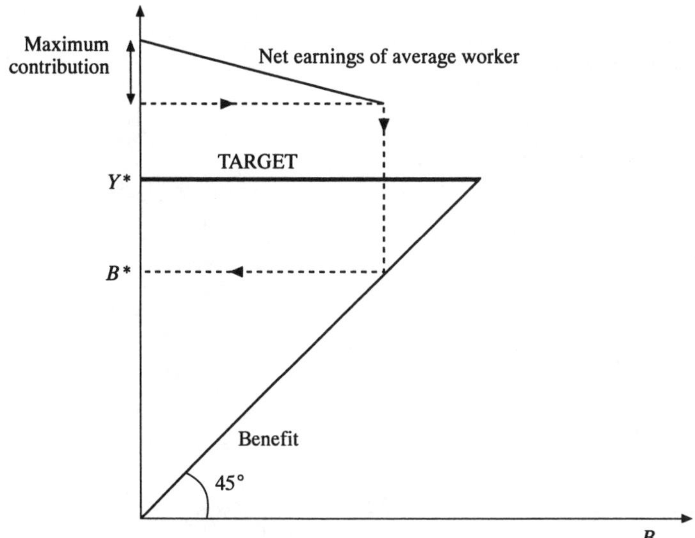

Figure 7.1 Choice of benefit constrained by the maximum acceptable contribution rate

ment has a view of the maximum acceptable contribution, as in figure 7.1. This determines the maximum level of benefit, B^*. If, as shown in the diagram, this is less than the target Y^*, then there is indeed a compromise. The government is in effect setting the level of benefit with an eye to the resources available – which is one interpretation of how the old age pension was determined in 1908. A variation on this is illustrated by the belief of Sir John Bradbury that in 1919 net earnings could not be reduced, so that any increase in the pension would have to be financed by other sources of revenue, effectively limiting the extent to which the value of the pension could be restored after the war.

The constraint in figure 7.1 arises from the total burden of financing. A second important constraint is that arising from considerations of less eligibility. Here the comparison is made not with average earnings but with the position of the low paid. As shown in figure 7.2, there is a required margin between benefit levels and the take-home pay of the low paid, and this may introduce a second upper bound on the permissible benefit level. We have seen the role played by such factors in the determination of the 1934 UAB scales.

How can we interpret the observed policy choices? In some cases it is assumed that the benefit level in fact corresponds to the target national minimum, neither the less eligibility nor the financing constraints being

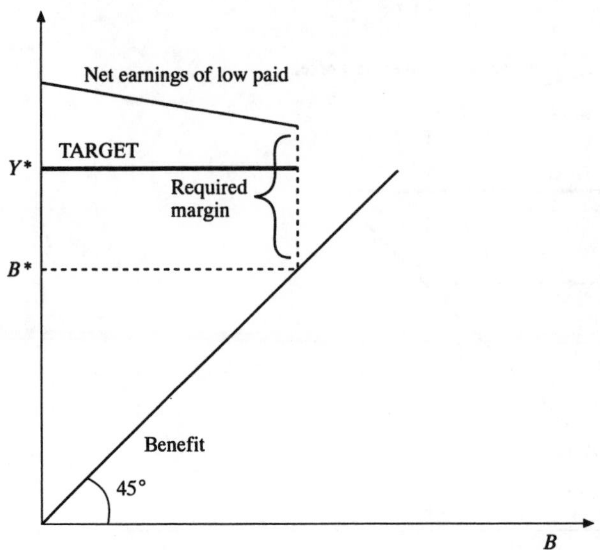

Figure 7.2 Choice of benefit constrained by the less eligibility criterion (required margin between benefit and income in work)

binding. This appears to be the interpretation where the benefit level is used as a poverty line, as in studies of low incomes based on the Supplementary Benefit level. (The fact that some people fall below is an indication that the benefit system is not being fully effective.) It appears to be the case where benefit scales are justified by reference to estimates of subsistence needs, as with Beveridge's use of the work of Rowntree, Bowley and others. On this interpretation, the Beveridge Report is seen as arguing that the attainment of a national minimum was 'affordable'; the benefit level Y^* could feasibly be financed (as in Beveridge's discussion of the surplus of working-class incomes relative to the poverty deficit quoted earlier).

However, in general, the level of benefit chosen is the smaller of Y^* and B^*, and we are not able to deduce simply from the observed policy which is the determining variable. The maximum acceptable contribution may cause B to be set below Y^*, as shown in figure 7.1. Considerations of less eligibility may be a binding constraint, as in figure 7.2. Both of these have been referred to in a recent official statement:

Even if it were possible to arrive at some general consensus on a minimum acceptable income, this would not necessarily provide a determination of the level of benefits to be paid . . . rates are not set in isolation: the Government gives due regard to the relationship between benefit levels and the rewards available to those in work, and to the total resources available for public spending. (House of Commons Social Services Committee, 1989, p. 5)

In such a situation, to use the benefit scale as a poverty line would be quite misleading. A new government, say, which took the view that the acceptable level of contribution was higher than in the past would allow the benefit scale to rise relative to earnings. This would tend to reduce the number with incomes below the desired national minimum, but measured taking the benefit scale as a poverty line, poverty might increase – a fact that successive governments have emphasised.

Ambiguity II: what degree of responsibility?

Recognition that the level of benefits falls short of an adequate minimum is implied where the government describes the role of state support as only a 'contribution' to securing that minimum. The old age pensions of 1908 were seen in that light by the government of the day. The benefit level was governed by the cost of the scheme and calculations of subsistence needs did not enter the picture.

The move to the idea of benefits providing a subsistence minimum represented a major shift in responsibility, but the state has always appeared ambivalent as to the degree to which this minimum has been accepted. Two aspects in particular stand out. The first is the extent to which others have a prior responsibility for the support of individual claimants. There is a marked contrast between social insurance, providing a benefit which is conditional on the efforts of the individual (for example to find work) but which does not demand any contribution from other family members, and the successive versions of means-tested assistance. Under the Poor Law, there had since 1601 been a liability to contribute to support poor relatives unable to work (not the able-bodied unemployed) imposed on parents, grandparents and children. This was taken over by Public Assistance in 1930 and then by Unemployment Assistance. The household means test was one of the most unpopular features of social security in the 1930s, and its scope was considerably narrowed in the 1941 Determination of Needs Act. There remains however the liability to support within the inner family of husband, wife and dependent children.

The lack of certainty with regard to support from relatives arises on account of the fact that this support may not in reality be provided. The situation in the 1930s was described by Bowley as follows:

The process of comparing the aggregate of incomes of members of the family with the family needs assumes that the whole income is pooled if necessary. Where family ties are strong, or where additional earnings come from the wife or young workers, the assumption is justified; but when the income is that of elder brothers or sisters, they may not be willing to hand over all surplus above their special needs to the support of an employed parent or other children. (1937, p. 63)

In more recent times, it has come to be questioned how far incomes are shared between husbands and wives. Pahl (1983) reports that a sizeable proportion of women who have left their husbands report being 'better off' living alone on benefit than living with their husbands, the figures ranging from 18 per cent to one-third. This has to be interpreted with caution, not least because the personal circumstances may colour recollection, but there is clearly no guarantee that obligations of support are met. We have a situation where the state is appearing to offer a safety-net level of income but is leaving the claimant exposed to the risk that others will not contribute their share. There is of course a great deal of difference between a social security system where the state assumes that others contribute, deducting the assumed contribution or denying eligibility, and one where the benefit is paid in full and the state seeks reimbursement from those deemed liable.

The degree of responsibility is also relevant to the time period for which benefit is paid, and this is the second aspect considered here. If the responsibility of the state is to tide people over short periods of low income, then the levels of benefit can be set such that claimants draw down their reserves. These reserves may be monetary assets, and because most means tests reduce benefit by an amount which exceeds the interest on savings, capital must be used up. (The means test applied to the 1908 old age pension took 10 per cent of capital above a certain level, when interest rates were about 2.5 per cent.) Or the reserves may be stocks of goods, whether stores of food or clothing being worn out and not replaced. Or the reserves may be less tangible, as with postponing social obligations (such as presents), or presuming on the help of neighbours/relatives. There is ambiguity as to whether the state is accepting responsibility for long-term support or whether the safety net is meant as a stop-gap measure. This ambiguity is to be observed in the discussion of the adequacy of benefit levels, as we have seen, and in the changing policy with regard to one-off provisions to allow the replacement of durables.

Ambiguity III: standard of living or minimum rights?

The third ambiguity concerns the justification for a national minimum. Much of the early discussion was in terms of a subsistence minimum, or the standard of living. More recently, there has been the shift to a vocabulary of 'citizenship' or 'participation', where considerations of minimum rights enter the picture.

This may appear a rather theoretical distinction, but it has important implications for the benefit scales and their structure. Take for example the benefits for men and women. A minimum rights approach would suggest that they should be identical for men and women, as a matter of principle, and that a couple should receive the same as two individuals. This was indeed the case with the old age pension of 1908, which was paid at the same rate to both men and women, and a couple received twice the amount for a single person. Notions of a subsistence minimum, on the other hand, pointed to lower benefits for women than for men and to a couple receiving less than twice the scale for a single person. Rowntree's scale of 1936 for pensioners allowed 15s. 3d. to a single man but only 12s. 6d. for a woman. For a couple, the Rowntree scale was 22s. 4d. Differential treatment of men and women may also be justified on the grounds of the difference in pay rates, whether on account of the earnings-replacement motive or because of less eligibility constraints. The 'low paid' line in figure 7.2 may be lower for a woman than for a man. The rates of unemployment insurance benefit were indeed different up to 1948; and Beveridge, far from starting from any presumption that the rates of men and women should be the same, only came down against making a distinction on the grounds that the calculated subsistence amounts were relatively close (1942, p. 89). Beveridge set the rate for a couple two-thirds higher than that for a single person, a relativity which has remained very little changed since that time.

The difference between a standard of living approach and one based on minimum rights also becomes evident when we consider the uprating of benefits.

7.3 A case study: the adjustment of benefit scales over time

The systematic comparison of benefit scales at different dates requires more space than I have here, but from section 7.1 it appears that there has been a tendency over the century for benefits to rise at least as fast as average net earnings. Those on benefits have shared in rising national prosperity. In the case of the unemployed, National Insurance benefit has declined relative to net average earnings since the mid 1980s, but it is still the case that in April 1989 it represented 22 per cent of net earnings for a person at the average for *manual workers* (not *all* workers), or virtually the same as in 1948 – and also in 1911 when unemployment insurance was introduced. In the case of the retirement pension, there has been a distinct improvement over the century. Since the basic pension before the First World War was below the benefits paid for sickness or unemployment, and is now above, it is apparent that it has risen more than proportionately. The single pension began at around one-sixth of average net earnings for male manual workers and is now about one-quarter. However, present policy is to link benefits to prices and this is likely to mean that people entirely dependent on state benefit will find their incomes falling progressively further and further behind those of the working population. If real net earnings rise at the rate of 2 per cent per annum but pensions remain unchanged in real terms, then the retirement pension will be back to one-sixth in the second decade of the next century.

How can these different policies with regard to the uprating of benefits be related to the earlier analysis? Suppose first that the actual level of benefits represents a compromise between the desired national minimum and the constraints of either financing or less eligibility. It then seems quite possible that these constraints are eased as incomes rise, allowing benefits to rise. If for example the benefit is limited to some percentage of the take-home pay of the low paid, then a rise in pay would allow the benefit to rise proportionately. Or, if National Insurance contribution revenue rises on account of rising total incomes, then the pensions can be raised proportionately. (In the case of the 1980s, the revenue from National Insurance contributions has indeed risen in real terms, but it has not in general been used to pay higher basic pensions. The increased revenue has in large part been used to reduce the Treasury Supplement and hence to finance tax cuts elsewhere.)

The dynamics of this process may be such that, as the economy becomes richer, the constraints cease to bite, and the target level of benefits becomes attainable. On this optimistic view, we may indeed reach a situation where the poor become as rare as Lloyd George's wolves. This means that the principles governing benefit uprating may change. During the constrained period, benefits rise in line with the easing of constraints, but then are governed by the target national minimum. If the latter is taken to be a fixed standard of living, we may then see earnings indexation during the constrained phase followed by price indexation once the target is attained.

Can this provide a justification for the observed change in policy in Britain with regard to uprating? This is not at all evident. To begin with, the relation between the desired national minimum and rising incomes depends on whether one adopts a standard of living approach or one based on minimum rights. If benefits are justified on a minimum rights basis, then this may lead to the prescription that benefits increase with rising incomes. In the United States, for example, Fuchs (1965) proposed that the poverty line should be set at half the family median income. The Supplementary Benefits Commission in 1979 argued that the standard should rise *in line* with the general level of incomes; this would be Mr Houghton's 'proportionate share' in rising national prosperity referred to earlier.

It may be that current policy represents a return to a standard of living approach. However, it is not evident that this implies that the target level of income should be fixed in real terms, taking a fixed bundle of goods adjusted only for the change in prices of these goods. First of all, in applying the standard of living approach there is the question of the *availability* of these goods. Reference was made earlier to rationing after the war and the fact that certain goods could not be purchased. In the longer term, goods which were once widely available may cease to be so as new goods are introduced. The range of goods may depend on the general level of incomes. As the community becomes better off, the cheaper goods may be taken off the market; the poor may not be able to buy cheap cuts of meat or to buy small quantities of perishable goods. Rowntree noted in 1937 that 'Unfortunately, fresh skimmed milk, which was largely consumed by the lower paid workers in 1918, cannot easily be bought today' (1937, p. 85).

The interdependence between the living standards of different income groups becomes even more important when we consider what consumption involves and the implications of recent theories of household production. We have been talking in terms of 'goods', whereas the literature on household production has rightly pointed to the need to see goods as inputs into household activities, with the level of such activities being our concern, not the purchase of goods as such. On this basis, the objective has to be rewritten as a target level of *activities*, for which the required goods inputs may vary over time. The significance of this approach is that even when we take a fixed set of activities, the required goods may be changing because of changes in the input matrix, and this in turn may be influenced by the general standards of living. This point has been expressed by Sen as follows:

> in West Europe or North America a child might not to able to follow his school programme unless the child happens to have access to a television. If this is in fact the case, then the child without a television in Britain or Ireland would be clearly worse off – have a lower standard of living – in this respect than a child, say, in Tanzania without television. It is not so much that the British or the Irish child has a brand new need, but that to meet the same need as the Tanzanian child – the need to be educated – the British or the Irish child must have more commodities. (1983, p. 162)

Applied to changes in benefit scales over time, the same argument means that – even on a standard of living basis – there may be a case for a rising real standard. In 1970 it would not have been a handicap to a child that his or her family could not afford a home computer; in 1990 the child will find it more difficult to follow lessons than his or her classmates with their computers.

To sum up, the current policy of price indexation of benefits may be seen as a return to a standard of living basis for the national minimum, rather than some notion of minimum rights, but even in these terms it is not evident that increases in the real value of benefits are ruled out. To take account of the changing range of goods available, and of the changing requirements of household activities, a rise in the real value of benefits may be justified. And to the extent that present benefits represent a compromise between the target national minimum and economic constraints, increased real earnings may be expected to ease these constraints and to permit those on benefit to share in rising national prosperity.

Concluding comments: the place of ambiguity

The central theme of this chapter has been the ambiguity surrounding the determination of benefit scales in twentieth-century Britain and their relation to the notion of a national minimum. It might be thought that this ambiguity could readily be dispelled. However, we have to recognise that *within* individuals there is often ambivalence about the objectives to be pursued and that *between* individuals there are considerable disagreements about the ends and means of policy. There is both plurality and diversity of individual judgements. In this situation, it is scarcely surprising that ambiguity is characteristic of political discourse.

The plurality of objectives which any one individual would like to see pursued is not typically taken into account in welfare economics, but it seems very much present in reality. People feel that the state should take responsibility for securing a national minimum and at the same time see how considerations of self-help point to the state only making a contribution. Their conception of the national minimum is based on elements both of well-being and of rights. There may be conflicts between the elimination of poverty and the reduction of inequality; and the relation between these two objectives is far from transparent (Atkinson, 1989, chapter 2). The objectives of an individual may not be reducible to a simple welfare function; nor is there necessarily an internal 'umpire', as supposed by John Stuart Mill (1843), adjudicating between conflicting concerns, such as justice and freedom.

The differences between people are evident. There are those who reject any concern with poverty – either because they feel that any state intervention is unjustified or because they feel that it distracts attention from more fundamental distributional goals. But even among those who are concerned about poverty, there may be disagreement about the weight to be placed on poverty as against inequality. There may for example be different views about the desirability of an anti-poverty programme if the cost falls on those with incomes above the line but below the average, thus accentuating the gap between this group and the wealthy. This is likely to be an issue if there is a 'redistribution of income within the working classes', as referred to by Beveridge.

Those making a case for social policies to secure a national minimum have naturally sought to appeal to the widest possible audience and to give each person the widest possible range of reasons to support their proposals. It is scarcely surprising therefore that this appeal contains elements of ambiguity. The definition of the minimum income has had to be made with an eye to its acceptability as much as to its statistical foundations. To talk, as the Macmillan government did, of giving those on National Assistance a share in rising national prosperity conveys a general intent, while leaving open the precise extent to which there would be real increase in benefits. That the Beveridge plan was based on firm numbers did not mean that it was not capable of different interpretations. Beveridge was writing for a variety of audiences (not least within Whitehall itself) and to meet a variety of concerns. The art lay in the way in which they were interwoven. As Empson has argued, 'if an ambiguity is to be unitary there must be "forces" holding its elements together' (1953, p. 234). As far as British social policy over the course of this century is concerned, this has been achieved with varying degrees of success.

In identifying ambiguity in attitude towards benefits in Britain, I am not therefore seeking to be critical. There is a key role for ambiguity in the presentation of political argument. But, equally, such ambiguity has no place in the scientific analysis of social policy, and one aim of this chapter has been to indicate the dimensions along which clarification is necessary.

8 The development of state pensions in the United Kingdom

The subject of this chapter is the past and future development of state pensions in the United Kingdom (UK). It is concerned with the relation between the basic flat-rate pension and the second tier of earnings-related pensions, provided either by the state, in the form of the State Earnings Related Pension, or by employers in the form of an occupational pension, or (now) by individuals via personal pensions. The analysis is especially directed at those aspects relevant to debate about post-1992 developments in the European Community.

The Community Charter of the Fundamental Social Rights of Workers requires in the case of elderly persons that:[1]

> Every worker of the European Community must, at the time of retirement, be able to enjoy resources affording him or her a decent standard of living (para. 24).
>
> Any person who has reached retirement age but who is not entitled to a pension or who does not have other means of subsistence, must be entitled to sufficient resources and to medical and social assistance specifically suited to his needs (para. 25).

The translation of these principles into more concrete form will doubtless be much debated, but it does not seem unreasonable to suppose that the first refers to the pension system guaranteeing a reasonable rate of replacement of individual earnings on retirement (for example, that workers can retire with a pension of at least a certain percentage of their final net earnings) and that the second ensures an overall minimum level of resources.

The pension system in the United Kingdom may be seen as seeking to meet these twin objectives as follows:

Everyone with a full-employment record (including the self-employed) is eligible for the flat-rate basic pension, payable at essentially the same rate to all who qualify. This has been the main social insurance (in Britain called 'National Insurance') benefit for the retired since 1948.

The second tier of state pension provision is the State Earnings Related Pension introduced from 1978, which provides a pension related to each individual's lifetime earnings. At the same time, many people are covered by occupational pensions, operated by employers or groups of employers, and those in approved occupational schemes are allowed to opt out of the additional state provision. This dual structure, with around half of the population 'contracted out' of the state pension scheme, is an important feature of the British pension system. In addition, the recent reforms in the Social Security Act 1986 allow individuals to contract out if they make sufficient contributions to a personal pension plan. There is now therefore a three-way split, with people either belonging to the state earnings-related scheme, or to an approved occupational scheme, or to a personal pension plan.

In addition to the National Insurance provisions, there is a system of social assistance, which is intended to guarantee a minimum level of income and which is administered via a means test. This general means-tested assistance, the modern-day version of the Poor Law, is now called 'Income Support'.

These different features of the UK system are successful to varying degrees in meeting the objectives of earnings replacement and of guaranteeing a minimum level of resources. Some of the central policy issues for the future development of state pensions in the UK are the subject of section 8.2. But the current situation and the future problems can only be properly understood in their historical context, and section 8.1 gives a summary of the historical development.

8.1 An historical review of state pensions in the United Kingdom

First state old age pension and the growth of occupational pensions

Concern about financial provision for old age has been a long-standing issue in Britain. In the nineteenth century, expressions of this concern took the form of encouragement to thrift, including the introduction of income tax reliefs, and the establishment of friendly society or trade union pension schemes. Employers too began to introduce pensions, such as a non-contributory civil service scheme, paying pensions of one sixtieth of final salary for each year of service. However, provisions of this type provided only limited financial help to the aged in nineteenth-century Britain, and most of those who reached old age had to rely either on continuing to work or on receiving help from their relatives, or else they had to seek relief under the Poor Law. The evidence from the social surveys of Charles Booth and others revealed the extent of poverty in old age and gave momentum to the campaign for state old age pensions.

As described in chapter 7, the first state old age pension was introduced in 1908 at the rate of 5 shillings (5s.) per person per week. (There were 20 shillings in a pre-decimal pound.) The pension was non-contributory and available to all aged 70 or over, subject to an income test. The income test was applied quite separately from the Poor Law and, unlike the Poor Law, there was no obligation on relatives to contribute.

This first major departure from the Poor Law was followed in 1911 by the creation of National Insurance, influenced very much by the German experience, and this provided contributory cash benefits for sickness, unemployment, disability and maternity, coupled with medical benefits. The introduction of National Insurance naturally raised in turn the question of insurable pension benefits, and the 1925 legislation brought in contributory pensions payable when a person reached the age of 65. This scheme applied only to those covered under National Insurance, excluding not just better-off non-manual workers but also the self-employed; nevertheless in the 1940s Beveridge estimated the coverage at some 19 millions out of some 22 million potential contributors (Beveridge, 1942, p. 195).

Alongside the improvement in state pensions in the inter-war period came significant developments in occupational pensions, as employers 'saw welfare benefits as an encouragement to workers to show the goodwill essential if the capitalists system were to run smoothly' (Hannah, 1986, p. 18). The schemes were in many cases self-administered, but the insurance industry entered the business of setting up group pension schemes for employers, which they managed on their behalf.

The level of state pensions was not particularly generous, and for many of the elderly, particularly those without occupational pensions, introduction of old age pensions did not in fact eliminate the dependence of the elderly on the Poor Law administered by local authorities. In 1940 this form of government provision was reformed, with responsibility for the elderly being transferred from the local Public Assistance Committees to a National Assistance Board. Supplementary Pensions were paid as an addition to other benefits in the case of need, subject to the operation of a means test.

Beveridge Report and post-war legislation

As far as state pension provision is concerned, the Beveridge Report of 1942 is an important landmark. Its goal was to complete the transformation of state provision for retirement into a universal system of National Insurance, providing, on a contributory basis, adequate benefits at a flat rate, without a means test. Beveridge saw 'social insurance' as 'a new type of human institution, differing both from the former methods of preventing or alleviating distress and from voluntary insurance' (Beveridge, 1942, p. 13).

It differs from private insurance in being compulsory and involving as such an element of redistribution on an *ex ante* as well as an *ex post* basis. The new National Insurance scheme was designed as a unified one covering all classes of society, appealing to a principle of social solidarity. It differed from the Poor Law in that the insurance benefits would be provided as a right, without a means test, and Beveridge attached considerable importance to the 'strength of popular objection to any kind of means test' (Beveridge, 1942, p. 12). Public assistance would remain, but would be unified on a national basis, as with the Supplementary Pensions introduced in 1940; and Beveridge envisaged that the need for assistance would diminish over time, in that the National Insurance benefits would on their own be adequate to meet subsistence needs.

The Beveridge Plan was received with great popular enthusiasm, and the Labour government elected in 1945 proceeded rapidly to legislation, the key components being the 1946 National Insurance Act and the 1948 National Assistance Act. The former established the flat-rate National Insurance retirement pension, at a rate of 26 shillings a week, financed as part of the overall scheme with flat-rate contributions. The latter set up the National Assistance Board which operated the post-war means-tested scheme. The National Insurance scheme was based firmly on the Beveridge principle of universality, which had met with general acceptance. The Coalition Government White Paper had stated clearly that 'in a matter so fundamental it is right for all citizens to stand in together, without exclusions based upon difference of status, function or wealth' (Minister of Reconstruction, 1944).

But in the relation between National Insurance and National Assistance there was a major departure from the Beveridge principles, as we have seen in chapter 7. The National Insurance pension was not enough to guarantee on its own that people were independent of means-tested assistance. The consequence was that the need for means-tested assistance did not die away, and the number of elderly persons receiving National Assistance rose rather than decreased.

The post-war period also saw the growth of occupational pensions, and the percentage of the work force covered by occupational pension schemes rose from 13 per cent in 1936 to 33 per cent in 1956 (Hannah, 1986, p. 67). But the fact that coverage was still seriously incomplete, coupled with the low level of the flat-rate pension, led to increasing concern. Titmuss (1955) contrasted 'the two nations in old-age' – those with and those without occupational pensions. Those without occupational pensions could have recourse to National Assistance, but it became apparent that a sizeable proportion of those eligible to claim this means-tested assistance were failing to do so. There was incomplete 'take-up'. Receipt of assistance was seen to be stigmatising and a sizeable minority of the elderly sought to manage without. The safety net was not functioning effectively.

State earnings-related pensions and contracting-out

These concerns led to plans for a state earnings-related pension scheme. Proposals to provide state pensions similar to those found in other European countries, although with a redistributive formula favouring the less well paid, were formulated by the Labour Party. These proposals, and the much less extensive scheme actually enacted by the Conservative government in 1959 (the graduated pension scheme), did however allow the 'contracting-out' of those covered by satisfactory occupational pension schemes, and this remains a central element of the current state second-tier scheme.

The graduated pension scheme provided only limited benefits, and an effective second tier of state pensions dates only from the 1975 Social Security Pensions Act, when the Labour government was finally successful in introducing the State Earnings Related Pension Scheme (SERPS), which is now in force in modified form. The SERPS pension is related to the earnings history of an individual worker and builds up progressively over time. Under the 1975 legislation, full pensions were to be paid from 1998, calculated on the basis of the best 20 years of lifetime earnings. The earnings taken into account in the calculation are those lying between a lower earnings limit (the point at which contributions become due) and the upper earnings limit (which determine the maximum contribution). The lower earnings limit is broadly equal to the basic pension, and the upper earnings limit is set at approximately $7\frac{1}{2}$ times the basic pension. As a result, for those retiring between April 1978 and April 1998 (those retiring before April 1978 derive no benefit from the scheme) pension is calculated as: '25% of 1/20th of the sum of (earnings on which contributions are paid – lower earnings limit) since April 1978 revalued to the date of retirement' unless the earnings exceed the upper earnings limit, in which case this becomes the relevant amount. Under the 1975 provisions, widows and widowers inherited their spouse's pension in full.

The factor of 1/20th corresponds to the 20-year transition period, so that full entitlement was to be built up by 1998. The revaluation of earnings is carried out using a factor which reflects the average increase in general earnings, so that the formula is in principle equivalent to expressing earnings in each year as a proportion of the national average (as in the West German system). SERPS pensions in payment, on the other hand, were indexed in line with prices (Government Actuary, 1990, p. 19).

The SERPS continued to allow contracting out. Contracted-out schemes had to provide at retirement a guaranteed minimum pension, but responsibility for the indexation of this element was accepted by the state scheme. Overall, the Labour government can be said to have reached an accommodation with the private pension interests.

1984 review of social security and 1986 Social Security Act

In 1979 the Thatcher government was elected with a commitment to the reduction of public spending and with an ideological opposition to state provision. In 1984, the Secretary of State for Social Services, Mr Fowler, launched a series of reviews of the social security system which led to the 1986 Social Security Act. In the field of pensions a major motive was concern about rising cost as the scheme matured and as the population aged. This led initially to the proposal that the State Earnings Related Pension Scheme be abolished and replaced by a 'new partnership' between the basic state pension and private provision. This met strong opposition, not just from the expected lobbies but also from the employers' organisations, from the National Association of Pension Funds (the private pension organisation) and from the major life assurance companies. In the face of this opposition, the government decided instead to scale down the SERPS, changing the formula from 25 per cent of the best 20 years of earnings to 20 per cent of the lifetime average. As a result, for those retiring in April 2009 or later the formula becomes

> 1/number of years since 1978[2]
> times the total of
> 20% of the sum of (earnings on which contributions are paid – lower earnings limit) since April 1988 revalued to the date of retirement
> plus
> 25% of the sum of (earnings on which contributions are paid – lower earnings limit) between 1978/9 and 1987/8 revalued to the date of retirement

(Again the relevant earnings are those up to the upper-earnings limit.) For those retiring between 1999 and 2009 there are transitional provisions. The 1986 Act also reduced to a half the pension inherited by the spouse.

The scaling down of SERPS was accompanied by measures to increase the number who contract out of the state scheme. These offered rebates on contributions and reduced the requirements imposed on occupational schemes in order for them to be approved. A major departure was to allow money purchase occupational schemes to contract out: i.e., for the conditions to be defined in terms of specified minimum contributions rather than specified minimum benefits. The minimum contributions will generate a pension which depends on the investment return achieved rather than one based on a pre-determined formula.

The move to allow contracting out by money purchase occupational schemes in the 1986 legislation ran parallel to the introduction of personal pensions. Since July 1988 it has been possible to contract out by taking out a personal pension plan – in place of either SERPS or an occupational scheme. In other words, membership of employers' schemes is now voluntary. Personal pensions must be based on one of the following: (i) insurance policy or annuity contract, (ii) unit trust, (iii) deposit with bank or building society.

The personal pension provisions cover the self-employed, replacing earlier provisions which allowed them to take out retirement annuities with tax relief on the premia paid (subject to certain limits).

Conclusion

As a result of this succession of policy choices, the UK approaches the twenty-first century with a pension system where there is a universal basic flat-rate pension, coupled with a second tier where a person may belong to an approved occupational scheme, may belong to the state SERPS, or may have taken out a personal pension. There are however a number of key policy issues to be resolved and it is far from clear that policy with regard to pensions in the UK has reached a steady state.

8.2 Key issues with regard to future development of state pensions

Earnings replacement

The writing of Anglo-Saxon economists has tended to leave on one side the essential function of pensions providing earnings replacement on retirement. As Bodie (1990) has emphasised, pensions have been analysed in terms of their labour market implications, their tax consequences, and of their impact on savings and the capital market, whereas:

> the perspective of pensions as providing retirement income security to plan participants ... is the conventional view of pensions expressed by most pension professionals ... virtually all public debate on policy matters relating to pensions adopts this view. (Bodie, 1990, pp. 28–9)

The effectiveness of pensions in providing replacement income *ex post* would best be assessed by reference to micro-data on individual pension entitlements and receipt. In the United Kingdom such data are not readily accessible. In view of this, I adopt here an *ex ante* approach, considering the pension entitlements in various hypothetical situations.[3]

Let us consider first the position of a person covered solely by the state pension system. He or she will receive at retirement, after 2009, a pension made up of the flat-rate component, written as NI, plus a SERPS additional pension equal to 20 per cent of the lifetime average earnings in excess of the lower earnings limit (taken to be equal to NI). If the lifetime average earnings are a times the final salary, Y^f, then the total pension is

$$NI+0.2[aY^f-NI]=0.8\ NI+0.2\ aY^f \tag{8.1}$$

subject to a maximum of

$$0.8\ NI+0.2\times 7.5\ NI=2.3\ NI \tag{8.2}$$

which is attained if and only if earnings in every year of the working life exceed the upper earnings limit (taken as 7.5 NI). In 1990 the NI flat-rate pension was 16 per cent of the average earnings of male full-time employees (Government Actuary, 1990, p. 18). From (8.1) it may be calculated that a person with lifetime average earnings equal to the national average for males at the date of retirement receives a state pension of around 33 per cent of final gross earnings (taking NI at its current value of 16 per cent of average earnings). The gross replacement rate (ratio of gross pension to gross final earnings) is higher at lower levels of earnings: around 45 per cent for a person averaging half the national average male earnings. (Few men, but more women, are likely to be in this position.) For those with earnings $1\frac{1}{2}$ times the average, the gross replacement rate is 28.5 per cent.

The amounts given above are gross of tax and it is important to take account of the effect of income taxation. This depends on the amount of taxable other income. If there is no other taxable income, then the pension is taxable if it exceeds the personal tax allowance, which for those aged 65–79 is currently around 24 per cent of gross average earnings for men (I assume in what follows that this relationship with gross earnings will be maintained in the future.) From equation (8.1) it may be calculated that tax becomes payable when lifetime average earnings exceed 56 per cent of average male earnings. The net pension where tax is payable at the current basic rate of 25 per cent is given by

$$0.75\ [0.8\ NI+0.2\ aY^f]+0.06\ Y^{av} \tag{8.3}$$

where Y^{av} denotes average male earnings. The net pension for a person with lifetime average earnings equal to the national average for males may be calculated as 30.6 per cent of final gross earnings. Since earnings in work would be reduced to 72 per cent of their gross amount, the net replacement rate rises to 42.5 per cent.[4]

By international standards, the current SERPS pension does not appear particularly generous. The figures of Schmähl for a sample of West German pensioners retiring in 1973 or 1974 show the median gross replacement rates for men retiring at the age of 63 of 55.8 per cent (Schmähl, 1983, table 4). This corresponds to a net replacement rate of at least 65 per cent (Schmähl, 1983, figure 18). In the case of France, the study by CERC (1983) shows gross replacement rates of 59–67 per cent for a 'cadre moyen' in the private sector, 70–1 per cent for a 'non cadre', and 61 per cent for a comparable post in the public sector.[5]

Nor does the SERPS seem generous when compared with occupational pensions. The amount paid under such schemes varies considerably and it is only possible to give some illustrative examples. Suppose for example that the formula is 1/60 of final salary for each year of service (a quite common fraction – see Government Actuary, 1981, table 8.10 – when account is taken of lump-sum payments). If the person has served the maximum of 40 years, contracted out for the entire working life, then the second-tier pension is two-thirds of the final salary. If the flat-rate pension is assumed to have been integrated (the occupational payment being reduced £ for £ with the NI flat-rate pension), then this leads to a net replacement rate for a person with lifetime average earnings equal to the national average for males of some 78 per cent. An alternative formula leading to the same outcome for a person on average earnings would be 1/80 of final salary for 40 years of service with the flat-rate NI pension being paid in addition.

The cases described above refer to hypothetical situations. In practice, the position of any actual person is likely to be more complicated. The person may have spent part of the working life in an occupational scheme, part covered by SERPS. A widow or widower may benefit from the pension provision of their deceased husband or wife. For a person in an occupational scheme which has contracted out on a defined contribution basis, or a person with a personal pension, it is impossible to make such calculations since the outcome depends on the investment performance.

Up-rating the basic state pension

One of the central issues of UK pension policy over the next 25 years is whether the basic NI pension is going to be indexed to prices or to net average earnings. When the National Insurance scheme was introduced in 1946 there was no automatic machinery to adjust benefits, but the need for periodic increases was increasingly recognised, and over the 1950s there came to be a general acceptance of the principle that benefits should be adjusted with the rising real incomes of the working population. This meant that the retirement pension rose broadly in line with the general level of earnings. In the 1970s this practice was formalised, with pensions being increased in line with the higher of earnings or prices, a rather curious ratchet which could have caused pensions to rise as a percentage of average earnings if real average earnings fell.

The indexation of the basic flat-rate pension with earnings was abolished by the Thatcher government and replaced by a requirement that the pension be adjusted in line with the increase in retail prices, although the government has the power to vary the amount 'having regard to the national economic situation'. In practice, this has meant that the NI pension has fallen behind net average earnings over the 1980s – see figure 1.5 in chapter 1 – particularly since 1985.

If real earnings continue to grow, then the policy of price indexation will mean that the NI pension becomes a decreasing proportion of average earnings. The Government Actuary shows how a rate of growth of 1.5 per cent per annum in real earnings would mean that the basic pension falls from 16 per cent of average earnings in 1990 to 8 per cent in the year 2040 (Government Actuary, 1990, p. 18). With a growth rate of 2.5 per cent per annum, it would fall to 8 per cent by 2018. The effect of this fall depends on individual circumstances. A person in an integrated occupational scheme may simply receive a correspondingly larger private pension. On the other hand, for a person receiving no occupational pension, and not subject to tax, formula (8.1) would apply and the amount received on retirement would fall by an amount equal to 6.4 per cent of average earnings. For a lower-paid worker, with a lifetime average equal to 55 per cent of the national male average (the low average possibly reflecting spells of interruption of employment), the gross replacement rate at retirement would fall from 43 per cent to 32 per cent. For a better-paid worker, the effect would be less since the effect of income tax reduces the difference, but it is still sizeable, and the flat-rate pension would become increasingly less important. The consequence of current policy is that 'the decline would continue until the total pension was largely composed of the earnings-related component' (Department of Health and Social Security, 1984, p. 6).

To this point, I have focused on the pension at retirement. Just as, or more, important is the effect of different policies on pensions after retirement. Here the price indexation embodied in the National Insurance scheme is matched only by better occupational schemes. Members of occupational schemes may as a result find their pensions falling back towards the SERPS level. But even with price indexation, the standard of living of pensioners falls behind that of the working population if real

Table 8.1. *Projected contribution rates 1990/1 to 2050/1 on different assumptions about indexation (per cent of relevant earnings)*

	linked to prices	linked to earnings
1990/1	19.1	19.1
1995/6	18.1	19.2
2000/1	17.8	19.9
2010/1	17.4	21.3
2020/1	17.8	23.5
2030/1	18.4	26.4
2040/1	16.4	25.8
2050/1	14.1	24.5

Note: These are combined employee and employer Class 1 contributions for National Insurance (i.e., excluding the NHS contribution). The calculations assume a constant 5 per cent level of unemployment.
Source: Government Actuary, 1990, p. 31.

earnings are rising. The effect is quite marked. Consider for example the case of an occupational pension equal to 50 per cent of final salary, with the NI pension paid in addition, making a gross replacement rate of 66 per cent for a person with earnings equal to the male average. With only price indexation of the pension, and real earnings growth of 2.5 per cent per annum, if the person lives for 20 years after retirement the pension will have fallen to 40 per cent of the then current average earnings. On the other hand, if the NI element had been increased in line with earnings, then the fall would have been less marked (to 46.5 per cent), and the person would have enjoyed some real increase in living standards. Indexation of the basic pension with earnings would moreover benefit those people who retired before the SERPS was introduced and who were not covered by adequate occupational schemes. After all, the government has promised that 'As the economy improves, elderly people will share in that improvement' (Department of Health and Social Security, 1981, p. iii).

The gains from a return to the earlier policy of indexing the pension to earnings, or more precisely net average earnings, are evident. The cost of such a policy has however been a major concern for the government. The papers prepared for the 1984 Review of Social Security showed a predicted rise in the contribution rate, whereas this could be contained if the pensions were linked only to prices, and the same is shown by the estimates of the Government Actuary – see table 8.1. Until 2010/1 the demographic influences (in terms of the projected ratio of pensioners to contributors) are relatively modest. If benefits are linked only to prices, then the projected contribution rate would fall. Over this period it would be possible to increase the real value of the NI pension without an increase in the contribution percentage. And full earnings relation could be achieved with a rise in the contribution rate of about 2 percentage points.

After 2010/1, the demographic factors, plus the growing cost of SERPS, would mean an increase in the contribution rate even with only price indexation. This is only projected to be reversed after 2030/1 when the cutbacks in the 1986 Social Security Act come to have full effect. These are discussed further in the next section.

The calculations just quoted are the gross cost of state pensions. A proper accounting has to allow for the income tax payable on pensions and for the repercussions for means-tested benefits (discussed further below). Quite a sizeable proportion of pensioners are subject to income tax at a current marginal rate of 25 per cent; and of those below the tax threshold a large proportion are in receipt of means-tested Income Support, which is increased £1 for £1 with any reduction in the pension, or of housing benefit, where the rebates increase by 80p. if the pension is reduced by £1. I have estimated using the TAXMOD model (Atkinson and Sutherland, 1988) that, in 1989 terms, the gross saving from £1 reduction in the single basic pension, and an equivalent reduction in that for a couple, would be reduced by 23 per cent when account is taken of the saving on means-tested benefits and by a further 7 per cent when allowance is made for income taxation. The net saving is therefore some 70 per cent of the gross. Or, put in terms of an increase in the SERPS pension, the net cost comes to 74 per cent of the gross. This means that the effective increase in the burden on the working population is significantly less than indicated by the calculations in table 8.1.

Second-tier pensions: two causes for concern

The rationale for the cutbacks in the state second-tier pension was the concern expressed by the government about rising contribution rates; however the government has paid less attention to concerns about the inadequacy of the present system.

First, there is the position of those belonging to the state SERPS without any occupational or personal pension provision. We have seen that the replacement rates under SERPS compare unfavourably with those in occupational schemes and with those in other countries. The measures taken in the 1986 Social Security Act have seriously reduced its adequacy. The earlier formula provided a rate of pension of 25 per cent rather than

20 per cent and took an average over the best 20 years rather than over the complete lifetime. Such averaging is typical of the better occupational schemes. For example, in the Universities Superannuation Scheme, the final salary is calculated as the higher of (i) the best 12-month average of earnings in the last three years and (ii) the best three-year average over consecutive years in the last 13, where in all cases earnings are indexed by the retail prices index. The 'best 20 years average' applied in the 1975 version of SERPS has been estimated by Creedy (1982, p. 36) to give average pensionable earnings about 20 per cent higher than average lifetime earnings (revalued using an earnings index).

The effect of this cutback on a person with average earnings at retirement may be seen as follows. If his lifetime average were 1.2 times the national male average, then his gross pension would have been under the original formula 42 per cent of final gross earnings, compared with 33 per cent under the reformed formula. In terms of the net replacement rate, calculated in the same manner as before, the original formula gives 52 per cent compared with 42.5 per cent with the reformed formula.

The effect may be seen another way. The original scheme ensured (with $a = 1.2$) that the total state pension would be half final gross salary for all those with earnings up to 60 per cent of the male average. As a result of the cutbacks, a pension of at least half final salary is now confined to those earning less than 43 per cent of the male average. If adequacy is judged by this simple 'half' criterion, then SERPS is only effective for the very lowest-paid workers.

Coupled with the fall in the basic pension, relative to average earnings, the changes made in the 1986 Act must cast serious doubt on the capacity of SERPS to meet its intended objectives – a concern to which I return below.

The second major source for concern is the other leg of the tripod – personal pensions. For people who have opted to follow this route, the only guaranteed pension is the basic NI pension. With personal pensions, as with defined contribution occupational schemes, there is no guaranteed pension at retirement. As it has been put by one actuary: 'There will be no comeback if an employee chooses a personal pension plan that performs badly. The individual will have to bear the consequential reduction in benefits' (Campbell, 1988, pp. 20–1).

There must be concern about those who are unlucky in their choice of investments: there is no redistribution between those whose investments have performed well and those whose turn out to be less well chosen. A guarantee is replaced by a lottery. The uncertainty surrounds both the capital sum which will be available at retirement and the rate of annuity which it will purchase. One guide to personal pensions points out that 'Annuity rates are ... extremely volatile as they relate directly to interest

Table 8.2. *Take-up of supplementary pension 1985*

Pensioners receiving Supplementary Pension	1,450,000
Pensioners eligible for Supplementary Pension but not receiving	380,000
% take-up	79%

Source: Department of Social Security (1985).

rates and also on the desire of an insurance company to come in or out of the annuity market' (Reardon, 1988, p. 47).

It is not at all clear that a system of personal pensions of the defined contribution type meets the first objective set out in the Community Charter of ensuring that every worker can enjoy resources affording a decent standard of living.

Means-tested assistance and minimum incomes

The second requirement of the Community Charter is that of a minimum sufficient level of resources. The form by which this is to be provided is very much open to debate, and the development of policy in Britain is in this respect instructive. Britain has a long history of the provision of a universal income floor on a means-tested basis. Originating in the Elizabethan Poor Law, the last 50 years have seen in turn, Supplementary Pensions, National Assistance, Supplementary Pensions (again), and now Income Support. None of these has however succeeded in providing a fully adequate safety net – in that a significant proportion of those entitled to benefits have failed to claim them. They have therefore fallen through the safety net.

The extent of non-take-up of means-tested assistance is demonstrated by official statistics. Making use of information from the Family Expenditure Survey, government statisticians have estimated that in 1985 the position was as shown in table 8.2.

One in five was not claiming. Expressed in terms of expenditure, the take-up was 87 per cent, reflecting the fact that those claiming were in general entitled to above-average amounts, but it still means that nearly £100 million was going unclaimed. As a measure of performance this is not very satisfactory. Moreover, detailed studies have shown that it is not simply a matter of a lack of information. Advertising and publicity campaigns may have increased take-up but they have failed to eliminate the substantive problem. The reasons for non-claiming appear to be deep-seated and to have continued from generation to generation (see Atkinson, 1969, for early evidence).

The failure of the means-tested safety net shows up in the official statistics

Table 8.3. *Number of people in families over pension age with incomes below the Supplementary Benefit level 1972–85*

	thousands	%
1972	980	n/a
1973	850	10.5
1974	550	6.5
1975	740	8.9
1976	870	10.4
1977	760	9.0
1979	1,100	12.7
1981	950	10.8
1983	1,080	12.0
1985	960	10.6

Note: n/a not available.
Sources: 1972–7, see Atkinson (1983), p. 235; 1979–85 from Department of Health and Social Security (1986) and (1988a).

for the number of low-income families. For a number of years the government has produced statistics of the numbers living on incomes below the Supplementry Benefit level. This series has now been discontinued, but there exist figures covering the period 1972 to 1985 – see table 8.3. There have been a number of changes in the methods applied, so that the figures are not entirely consistent from year to year, but they provide a reasonably reliable picture. They show that there has throughout been a sizeable minority – around 10 per cent – of people living in pensioner families who have incomes below the Supplementary Benefit level.

The problem of incomplete take-up was one of the principal reasons why the Labour governments sought to introduce the second tier of state pensions, and the Conservative government in 1981 welcomed the fact that

> Under the [SERPS] scheme, as entitlement builds up, these people will be able to retire with incomes which more and more reflect their earnings from work, and far fewer will need to have recourse to supplementary benefit in retirement. (Department of Health and Social Security, 1981, p. 7)

It has been estimated (Altmann and Atkinson, 1982) that the SERPS in its original form would have substantially reduced the number of pensioners dependent on means-tested assistance (Supplementary Benefit). On pessimistic assumptions about the earnings record of those with low incomes, the predicted number below the Supplementary Benefit level in 2016 would have been reduced from 2.7 million to 1 million; on alternative, more optimistic, assumptions it would have been reduced to 0.2 million. These calculations are only approximate, but they bring out the important contribution which SERPS would have made. In its current scaled-down version, it will be less effective, and low incomes among a minority of the elderly are likely to be a continuing problem in the next century.

Conclusions: UK pensions policy and Europe

I began with a reference to the requirements of the Community Charter. In the case of the first objective – that of guaranteeing a reasonable rate of replacement – I believe that the UK has to learn from the experience of France, Germany and other Continental countries. The policy pursued in the UK in recent years does not seem well directed to meeting the goals of the Charter. It is very doubtful whether personal pensions can be relied on to ensure an adequate pension for all those who choose this option – there are bound to be losers. The down-grading of SERPS means that the degree of replacement will be low by international standards and by comparison with occupational schemes. There is an urgent need to reconsider UK policy in this regard (see chapter 16 below).

On the other hand, I believe that the Community can learn from British experience about the guarantee of minimum resources. A succession of attempts have been made to achieve an effective safety net through means-tested assistance but these have failed to ensure that all those entitled do in fact receive the assistance to which they are entitled. Non-take-up may be much influenced by culture and social attitudes, but there is evidence that it is not a peculiarly British problem (see chapters 12–14 below).

The failure of means-tested assistance to provide a fully satisfactory safety net may be contrasted with the success of the basic pension, which does not suffer from the problem of incomplete take-up. This leads me to the conclusion, based on British experience, that a minimum income for the elderly can only be guaranteed in a fully effective way via a minimum social insurance pension or a minimum basic income for those above a certain age. Given the crucial role of such a minimum, there is a strong case for this being indexed in line with net average earnings and not just prices. This is especially important for existing pensioners. It is easy to concentrate on the future and to neglect the needs of the existing – and ageing – pensioner population.

9 Income maintenance for the unemployed in Britain and the response to high unemployment

In principle, the modern Welfare State provides income support for the unemployed, guaranteeing a certain level of income. This is no doubt one of the reasons why the high unemployment rates in Britain in the late 1970s and 1980s have met with so little public and electoral response. Many people believe that there is an effective system of social insurance, coupled with an income-tested safety net. In practice, income maintenance for the unemployed in Britain is incomplete and inadequate, and in the face of unemployment measured in millions, the reaction of the government was to make the scheme less, rather than more, generous. As described in section 9.1, the majority of the measures taken in Britain over the past decade have been to limit the extent and coverage of National Insurance unemployment benefit and to reduce the effectiveness of the safety net. In the same way, in the United States, Burtless (1987) has shown how there has been a tightening of eligibility requirements, and reduction in the extended benefit programme, which has been associated with a 25 per cent drop in the number of recipients of unemployment insurance relative to the number of job losers.

Section 9.2 examines some of the motives for providing unemployment benefit and how far they can explain why the response to rising unemployment was not to remedy the inadequacies of benefit but to make the system less generous. Was this the response chosen by the majority of the electorate? Has there been a shift in the attitudes of the employed majority? Section 9.3 develops the analysis further in considering the influences on the administration of the scheme and the conditions of entitlement. Is the tightening of eligibility requirements a response to electoral pressures? How far are the wishes of the electorate subordinated to the interests and concerns of those administering the benefit programme or to the dictates of the Treasury?

9.1 Unemployment benefit and unemployment in Britain

The system of income support for the unemployed in force in Britain involves a dual tier structure of benefits. Entitlement to the top tier – flat-rate unemployment insurance paid by the National Insurance Fund – is based on contributions, is limited in duration, and is subject to other conditions but is not means tested. The second tier – means-tested Income Support – is in principle a safety net designed to rescue those whose entitlement to insurance benefit is exhausted or incomplete.

The original intention of the 1942 Beveridge Plan had been to reduce the second tier to only a residual role: 'The scheme of social insurance is designed of itself when in full operation to guarantee the income needed for subsistence in all normal cases' (Beveridge, 1942, para. 23). Not the least of the reasons for this was the 'strength of popular objection to any kind of means test' (para. 21), an objection which reveals itself in the incomplete take-up of these benefits, a substantial minority of those eligible not claiming the benefit to which they are entitled. However, the actual system introduced in 1948 set the National Insurance scale at such a level that for a sizeable number of people the second tier was a necessary supplement to the insurance benefit. As a result, the role of means testing did not decrease. Since the take-up was considerably less than 100 per cent, the system of income maintenance for the unemployed was crucially flawed, as was indeed recognised from the outset. James Griffiths, Minister of National Insurance, said in 1946 that 'if we were – God forbid that we should – to allow ourselves to drift back to the mass unemployment of the inter-war years, this scheme would be sunk' (Hansard, 6 February 1946, col. 1751).

The system was not really put to the test on a large scale until the high unemployment rates of the late 1970s and 1980s, when the response was not to remedy the defects of the safety net, by improving the coverage of unemployment insurance, but to make the scheme less generous. Atkinson and Micklewright (1989) have listed 38 significant changes which have been made in the period 1979–88 affecting National Insurance unemployment benefit and the income-tested benefits relevant to the unemployed. Some of these have been favourable, but the great majority have reduced the effectiveness of unemployment insurance, and this has not been compensated for by the income-tested benefits, which have themselves been curtailed. Not only has the indexation of benefits been limited to price increases, so that they have fallen behind average earnings, but the scope and coverage of benefits have been reduced.

The main changes affecting unemployment insurance in Britain over the 1980s are summarised in the appendix. In two cases the measures introduced have improved the position of the unemployed. The equal treatment provisions, imposed by the European Community, mean that husbands and wives are now treated symmetrically, and extend the range of choice open to unemployed couples. The redefinition of voluntary redundancy in 1985 was designed to ensure that workers are not regarded as having left their job voluntarily even when they agree to be made redundant. The majority of the measures, however, were unfavourable to the unemployed. The abolition of the Earnings Related Supplement (introduced in 1966 to provide an earnings-related element in addition to the basic flat-rate insurance benefit) involved a substantial reduction in the total sum transferred to the unemployed. The amount of benefit paid has been reduced by the abolition of child additions, by the exclusion of students, and by the abatement for occupational pensions. The abolition of the reduced rates of benefit mean that those with incomplete contribution records now receive no insurance benefit at all rather than a fraction of the benefit. Entitlement may also be lost as a result of the extended disqualification period, applicable, for example, where there is deemed to have been voluntary job quitting or refusal of work. The period of six weeks, unchanged since the original 1911 act, has been increased to 13 weeks and then, only 18 months later, to 26 weeks. The new contribution conditions in the 1988 Social Security Act meant that an estimated 350,000 lost benefit entitlement, including people with lengthy contribution records. A man may have been employed for thirty years and still not qualify for insurance benefit during a second spell of unemployment, since the crediting of contributions during the first spell will not now count towards the relevant condition.

The combined effect of these measures has been to reduce substantially in real terms the amount of National Insurance benefit paid per head to the unemployed (even when account is taken of the increase in long-term unemployment). This reduction has not been shared uniformly. This is particularly true of measures which eliminated entitlement to National Insurance benefits altogether and which mean that now only a minority of those in the relevant duration receive unemployment insurance.

Nor is it the case that the curtailment of insurance benefit is simply offset by a corresponding increase in the payments under the second tier of means-tested Income Support:

(a) In some cases the cuts in the insurance benefit have been complemented in Income Support: for example, where a person is disqualified from National Insurance benefit, there is a 40 per cent voluntary unemployment deduction from Income Support.
(b) Income Support is assessed on a family basis rather than an individual

basis, and the total family income may be such that the person is not eligible.

(c) As stressed earlier, a sizeable fraction of those entitled do not claim their entitlement. The official figure is that the take-up rate for the unemployed in 1983 was 81 per cent. [1] This means that some one in five persons are not receiving their entitlement, and, even though take-up measured in value terms may be higher, the safety net evidently has holes.

Changes have also been made to the means-tested tier over the period 1979–88. The effects of the major reforms in 1980 and 1988 are not easily summarised, in that there were many different changes, some of which operated in different directions as far as the unemployed are concerned. The reduction in 1980 in the number of scales for children, for instance, represented a real improvement for younger children in the new ranges. On the other hand, the introduction of an absolute capital cut-off meant that a number of the unemployed lost their entitlement, and in 1988 the new Income Support scales did not compensate in all cases for the limitation of rates assistance to 80 per cent, for the loss of help with water rates, for the fact that payments for special needs have been abolished, and for the repayment of loans to the social fund.

In general, there have been a number of measures that represent a continuing attempt to administer the receipt of both benefits more stringently. In this the government's response to high unemployment has been similar in nature to that in the interwar period (see Deacon, 1976). The 1988 white paper, *Training for Employment*, highlights the government's view that 'significant numbers of benefit claimants are not genuinely available for work' (Department of Employment, 1988, p. 4), and this is regarded as one of the 'three major problems' to be faced if unemployment is to be reduced. While there is controversy about the quantitative extent, there can be little doubt that more stringent administration not only reduces the number of ineligibles who claim but also increases the number of eligible claimants who do not receive benefit. As has been pointed out by Goodin (1985), there is a reduction in Type II errors (false positives) but an increase in Type I errors (false negatives). Policy in Britain has moved in the direction of erring on the side of harshness.

9.2 Unemployment benefit: motives, votes and administration

The post-war unemployment benefit system in Britain has never been such that it could cope adequately with mass unemployment, and when put to the test, with unemployment rising to record post-war levels in the 1980s, the response was to restrict benefit generosity and entitlement, rather than to make good the deficiencies of unemployment insurance. Why is this so? What is the reason that we have tended to err on the side of meanness? Why have measures been taken to exclude some people totally from benefits rather than sharing reductions uniformly?

The answers to these questions depend on the motives which lie behind the provision of income support and on the mechanisms – political and administrative – by which these motives are translated into action. Here I give particular prominence to the interests and concerns of the electorate but recognise that these may be influenced by the ideological views of politicians and by the goals of the civil servants administering income support.

Suppose first that policy towards unemployment benefit reflects the wishes of the majority of the electorate who are in employment. The employed have some degree of concern about the level of welfare of the unemployed – whether from the self-protection motive or on the basis of more enlightened considerations.[2] A typical employed person (for simplicity, differences in the distribution of income among those in work are ignored, all being assumed to have the same level of earnings w and to have no unearned income) is willing to pay some contribution c towards unemployment benefit, reducing his or her own utility from $u(w)$ to $u(w-c)$, because of concern about the level of utility of a person out of work, assumed to have only unemployment benefit b. This concern is assumed here to take the form of putting oneself in the shoes of the unemployed person, assessing their utility as $u(b)$, but discounting this by a factor r, lying between 0 and 1, which limits the altruism of the employed. The employed person is further assumed to weight the utility of the unemployed according to their relative size in the population, $p/(1-p)$, where p is the unemployment rate. The objective of the typical employed person is therefore to maximise

$$(1-p)u(w-c)+pru\,(b) \tag{9.1}$$

This objective is assumed to guide voting behaviour, and (unless unemployment were to exceed 50 per cent) there would be a majority in favour of the policy which maximised (9.1).

The contributions required depend on the size of the unemployed population relative to the working population and on the costs associated with the transfer, where these may be administrative or may arise from distortions of work decisions. These are simply represented here by a proportionate cost, h, so that the budget constraint for the unemployment benefit scheme is

$$c(1-p)(1-h)=bp \tag{9.2}$$

A straightforward choice of b to maximise (9.1) subject to (9.2) yields the following first-order condition for an interior solution (i.e., where some level of benefit is provided)

$$u'(w-c)=u'(b)\ r\ (1-h) \tag{9.3}$$

If the utility function is concave ($u''\leqslant 0$), it follows that any change in the parameter p must lead b and c to move in opposite directions; from (9.2) it may be deduced that if the rate of unemployment rises then the level of benefit chosen falls, and at the same time contribution rates are raised.[3] The onset of a recession may indeed cause benefit generosity to be reduced, but the employed majority would be willing to pay higher contributions to lessen the cut in benefit. If, for example, the utility function is iso-elastic, so that

$$u(x)=x^{1-\epsilon}\ /\ (1-\epsilon) \text{ and } u'(x)=x^{-\epsilon} \tag{9.4}$$

(where $\epsilon\geqslant 0$), then (9.3) implies

$$(w-c)[(1-h)r]^{1/\epsilon}=b \tag{9.5}$$

so that the net replacement rate, $R\equiv b/(w-c)$, depends only on h and r. A rise in the proportion unemployed leads to equal proportional reductions in benefits and net earned incomes, so that in relative terms the generosity of policy towards the unemployed is unchanged.[4] This may be contrasted with what happened in Britain in the 1980s when the level of benefit fell relative to average net earnings. Although contribution rates have increased since 1979, this has been attributable to a shift in the method of financing (the phasing out of the contribution to the National Insurance Fund from general revenue) rather than to the rise in unemployment. With the fall in the number unemployed there has been no corresponding reduction in contribution rates.

This representation of the motives for redistribution is essentially concerned with individual interests. Another may be given in terms of 'ethical preferences', or those which would apply if a voter chooses as 'if he did not know what his personal position would be – but rather had an equal chance of obtaining any of the social positions' (Harsanyi, 1955). Behaviour in such a situation, acting behind a 'veil of ignorance', is represented by the objective function (9.1) if r takes the value unity, since this corresponds to expected utility. The preceding analysis therefore applies. It may be noted that this model is consistent with high degrees of risk aversion, and that, if the utility function is iso-elastic, we approach the Rawlsian position by letting ϵ tend to infinity. In this case, it may be seen from (9.5) that the replacement rate R approaches unity.

Electoral support for unemployment insurance based on such ethical preferences may be seen in terms of voters giving priority to their 'higher selves' when making decisions, in contrast to the 'lower selves' which would consult only narrow self-interest. It is possible to interpret the ungenerous reaction to higher unemployment as a reversion to self-interest. When the commitment to unemployment insurance had a relatively low cost, ethical preferences governed electoral opinion, but when it came to the test people failed to view the problem as though through a veil of ignorance. This would yield a 'reversion to self-interest' explanation, in that r, and hence from (9.5) the replacement rate, shifts downward.

A third representation of the motives for redistribution is one based on genuine uncertainty. In the contractarian theory of justice described above, the uncertainty is of an 'as if' kind: we are supposing that moral judgements are made as if people did not know their true position. Suppose, however, that we assume that the uncertainty is in fact genuine, an assumption recently explored by Goodin and Dryzek (1987) in their analysis of the development of the post-war Welfare State: 'The pervasive uncertainty of war-time led to new popular demand for risk-spreading and broke down old barriers to it, and [this] provides a powerful (if only a partial) explanation for the dramatic postwar upsurge in welfare states.' They also cite the uncertainty generated by the Depression of the 1930s, particularly relevant to unemployment insurance.

Applied to the recession of the late 1970s and the 1980s, this analysis would on the face of it lead us to expect an increase in the support for unemployment insurance, particularly as the inadequacies of the second means-tested tier became apparent. The rise in unemployment to levels unprecedented in the post-war period may be expected to increase the degree of uncertainty and make people more concerned about the level of support. They are more likely to behave as if behind a veil. This would not, however, provide an explanation of the observed policy changes.

On the other hand, it is possible to imagine another interpretation. *Ex ante* people were uncertain whether they would be affected if unemployment returned to the levels of the 1930s. The British unemployment rates of the 1950s and 1960s were not sufficient to provide information about the likely incidence of a major recession. By the time that the rise in unemployment in the 1980s had levelled off, however, people had a much better idea what it was like in reality and, in particular, whether they themselves were likely to lose their jobs. The majority found that they were not at risk, and their preferences ceased to give as much weight to the state of being unemployed. Not only did the rate of unemployment rise, but also the utility of the unemployed became subject to the discount factor, r. Looking at equation (9.5), we can then see that the net replacement rate in the case of the iso-elastic function is reduced by a factor $r^{1/\epsilon}$, and we do not have an equiproportionate sharing of the burden of the recession. This provides a 'lifting of the veil' explanation of the reactions to high unemployment – especially those that took place after unemployment appeared to have peaked.

The two explanations of 'reversion to self-interest' and 'lifting of the veil' in effect make the preferences of the electorate endogenous. It is of course difficult to distinguish these empirically from the explanation that preferences have shifted in an exogenous fashion; indeed it has been an explicit objective of the Thatcher Conservative government to shift dominant political values. The coincidence of the tightening of policy towards the unemployed with the rise in unemployment may have arisen because both were consequences of a shift in political ideology. This is referred to below as the 'changing political climate' explanation.[5]

There is also a rather different political explanation. Whether or not the preferences of the electorate are translated into policy depends on the degree of 'slack' in the political process.[6] Policy is not governed by binding referenda: rather, it is made by politicians elected on broad platforms for terms of office of several years and who may therefore have considerable freedom to impose their own values. It is quite possible, for example, that the shift in policy is simply a reflection of a shift in political ideology. The government has reduced income support to the unemployed without regard to the preferences of the electorate.

According to a 'political slack' explanation of this kind, the Conservative government was elected with a mandate to cut the size of the public sector and to reduce taxation, but the form of such cuts was not specified in detail. The government had a degree of freedom to act according to its own criteria. These criteria may be ones that reflect the individual interests and concerns of politicians, and the circumstances of the unemployed are unlikely to receive priority. The criteria include the sensitivity of different areas of spending to lobbying. It seems reasonable to suppose that the unemployed are a relatively underorganised lobbying group. The 'middle class capture' theory of Le Grand (1984) suggests that those parts of the Welfare State protected from cuts are the ones for which the middle classes are users and/or suppliers of services. In their statistical analysis, Le Grand and Winter (1987) assign unemployment benefit to the category of 'low proportion of middle-class beneficiaries/low proportion of middle-class suppliers' (since the professions such as doctors and social workers are not involved in the payment of unemployment benefit).

9.3 Identification of entitlement: erring in which direction?

To this point we have considered the generosity of the unemployment insurance system simply in terms of the level of benefit; however, some of the major changes in Britain have affected the entitlement to benefit. The tightening of the eligibility conditions and of the administration of the scheme may have meant that the government has been more successful in excluding those who do in fact have a job, or via the abatement for occupational pensioners those with substantial alternative forms of income, but it has also increased the number who do not receive benefit and who do not have another source of income. It is easy to see how this may have come about on the political slack explanation. Politicians may have found it easier to take selective measures affecting only what they consider to be the 'less deserving' of the unemployed. Changes in complicated contribution or other conditions are less likely than the level of benefit to form the basis for lobbying campaigns.

How far though are such measures likely to have resulted from electoral preferences? In order to incorporate these considerations into the earlier analytical discussion, we need to allow for the imperfect identification of those entitled to unemployment benefit. Suppose that of the proportion of the population p who are genuinely unemployed, the Department of Social Security (DSS) successfully identifies a fraction θ ($0 \leqslant \theta \leqslant 1$) as eligible, the remaining $(1-\theta)p$ not receiving benefit and having a zero income. These are Type I errors, or 'false negtives'. The administration also awards benefit to a fraction $\delta\theta$ (where $0 \leqslant \delta \leqslant 1$) of those who are in employment, δ being a property of the system of administration. These are Type II errors, or 'false positives'. The position in terms of proportions in the total population may be summarised as follows:

	Unemployed	Not unemployed
Receiving benefit	$\theta\, p$	$\delta\theta\,(1-p)$
Not receiving benefit	$(1-\theta)p$	$(1-\delta\theta)(1-p)$

This model is based on that of Goodin (1985), but the treatment is rather different. Whereas he assumes that the aim is to maintain a desired ratio of false negatives to false positives, we are here looking at the reasons for concern about such errors. Suppose that a majority of the population are in employment and not simultaneously receiving benefit. Their preferred policy depends on the weight that they attach to the different groups. As before, we suppose that they are concerned about the welfare of the unemployed, applying a discount factor r. We now introduce a discount factor ρ for those who receive benefit illegitimately; the weight attached by voters to this group could well be negative. They therefore maximise

$$\Omega \equiv (1-p)(1-\delta\theta)u(w-c) + pr[\theta u(b) + (1-\theta)u(0)] \\ + (1-p)\delta\theta\rho u(w+b-c) \tag{9.6}$$

The budget constraint for the unemployment benefit scheme is

$$c(1-p)(1-h)=b[\theta p+\delta\theta(1-p)] \tag{9.7}$$

where it is assumed that contributions are collected from those both receiving benefit and working. The choice of the benefit level is governed by the first-order condition for an interior solution. Suppose, for example, that $\rho=0$, so that the employed majority attach no weight to the utility of those who simultaneously work and claim benefit. The first-order condition where $\rho=0$ is

$$u'(w-c)=u'(b)r(1-h)\;/\;[(1+\delta(1-p)/p)(1-\delta\theta)] \tag{9.8}$$

The square bracket is equal to 1 if $\delta=0$ and is an increasing function of δ.[7] Comparing (9.8) with (9.3), we can see that the administrative error operates just like other sources of loss captured by h. It affects the level of the replacement rate, and in the case where u is iso-elastic with $\in<1$, we have

$$R^{\epsilon}=r(1-h)\;/\;\{[1+\delta(1-p)/p](1-\delta\theta)\} \tag{9.9}$$

In contrast to the earlier finding, the replacement rate now varies with p, but it increases with p, so that policy is predicted to become more generous (because the ratio of genuine to total recipients increases). This conclusion is parallel to that by Goodin that 'in hard times when the demand for welfare benefits is legitimately high, we should be more generous' (1985, p. 151).

The choice of θ raises other issues. By increasing this parameter the coverage of the scheme can be improved, at the cost of a greater outlay. The effect may be seen by differentiating with respect to θ and making use of the budget constraint

$$\begin{aligned}\partial\Omega/\partial\theta = {} & pr[u(b)-u(0)-bu'(b)]+(1-p)\delta\rho[u(w+b-c)\\ & -u(w-c)-bu'(w+b-c)]-(1-p)\delta(1-\rho)u(w-c)\end{aligned} \tag{9.10}$$

The concavity of the function u ensures that the terms in square brackets are positive. It therefore follows that if $\rho=1$ (so that the third term is zero), or if δ is sufficiently small (so that the first term dominates), then the expression is positive. The objective function is increased by a rise in θ which is paid for by reducing b. This reduces the inequality among the unemployed and between those in work who claim benefit and those who do not (where $\delta>0$), and is strictly preferred. Under the assumptions made, the policy should minimise false negatives (which leave penniless people without benefit). False positives are tolerated in the sense that they lead to a lower level of the overall benefit.

In order for there to be pressure from the employed electorate for the tightening of the administration of the scheme, they must attach a smaller, or negative, weight to the utility of those who illegimately claim benefits. If, for example, $\rho=0$, and u is iso-elastic with $\in<1$, we can calculate that the right-hand side of (9.10) is negative where

$$R^{1-\in}<\delta(1-p)\,/\,pr\in \tag{9.11}$$

It is possible that δ is sufficiently large that this is satisfied and a more restrictive administration preferred. On the other hand, if we examine the implications of a rise in the unemployment rate, p, we have already seen that it leads to an increase in the chosen R. Since the right-hand side of (9.11) is a decreasing function of p, it follows that higher unemployment does not lead to pressure to tighten the administration of the scheme.

If the objective function is assumed to be derived from expected utility viewed behind the veil of ignorance, then $\rho=1$ may appear at first sight the most reasonable assumption to make: however, the state of claiming benefit while working is a choice that the person makes after the veil is lifted. For a person who knows that he will be honest but does not know if he will be poor, the expected utility is

$$(1-p)u(w-c)+[\theta u(b)+(1-\theta)u(0)] \tag{9.12}$$

The condition for the choice of the replacement rate is then the same as (9.8) (since it is equivalent to $\rho=0$), with $r=(1-\delta\theta)$. The derivative with respect to θ is given by

$$pr[u(b)-u(0)-bu'(b)] \tag{9.13}$$

and it is unambiguously the case that an increase in θ financed by a reduction in b is preferred. It is therefore possible that if the arrival of the recession reduced uncertainty (a 'lifting of the veil'), then there would have been a switch in the preferred policy from increasing θ to reducing it. This would be the case where the policy chosen on the basis of (9.10), with $\rho<1$, favoured a tightened administration. This may also be consistent with a 'reversion to self-interest' explanation.

The administration of the scheme has been discussed as though it were a decision to be made by politicians in response to the pressures of the electorate. But in addition to the political slack referred to earlier, there may also be 'administrative slack' which permits the civil service some degree of discretion in the operation of the scheme. It is self-evident that the operation of the scheme allows individual officers discretion in the interpretation of the regulations, in adjudicating claims, in the decision as to which cases to investigate, and in the efforts made to advise claimants of their entitlements. What is less clear is how far discretion may be exercised in the formulation of higher-level policy of the kind described in section 9.2. In view of its political visibility, it seems unlikely that the level of benefit is the subject of decisions by civil servants, even the most senior. On the other hand, in the case of other measures of a more technical nature, ministers may well rely heavily on the advice of their civil servants and the options presented to ministers may involve a significant degree of pre-selection. It may have been a political decision to tax unemployment benefit or to tighten the contribution conditions, but the precise form in which these emerged may have owed a great deal to the administrators.

If this is the case, we have to investigate the objectives of the civil servants and how they may have been expected to respond to rising unemployment. It may, for example, be argued that they are likely to act as a conservative force, minimising the impact of any change. For example, they may have resisted any suggestion that tax could be collected on current benefit, the scheme devised being one that remained close to existing practice (collecting tax due in an end-of-year assessment). They may also have resisted cuts in spending on the basis of the 'budget maximization' motive stressed in the US literature on bureaucracy. These considerations do not, however, explain the observed pattern of policy response. If, on the other hand, we turn the US explanation on its head and suppose that civil servants are predominantly accounting officers whose concern is with the limitation and control of expenditure, then a rise in unemployment is likely to lead to increased concern to reduce spending per unemployed person in order to ease the budgetary pressure. Civil servants believe that increased spending, resulting from the higher unemployment, leaves the Department of Social Security exposed in budgetary negotiations.[8] This becomes of greater importance when we recognise that the civil service is not monolithic. Departments compete to appropriate the administrative slack, with the traditional conflict being that between spending departments such as the DSS and the Treasury. It is possible that there has been a shift in power away from the DSS towards the Treasury which accounts in part for the observed policy changes.

Concluding comments

The analysis of policy towards the unemployed in Britain, and the response to the high unemployment of the late 1970s and 1980s, has shown that there has been a significant change in the extent and form of income support. With little public debate, the role of insurance benefits has been eroded by such measures as the tightening of the contribution conditions, the extension of the disqualification period, and the abolition of the lower-rate benefits: their value has been reduced by the taxation of benefits: and the abandonment of statutory indexation has made the position of recipients insecure. These measures add up to a substantial reduction in the amount and extent of National Insurance benefit paid to the unemployed. At the same time, income-tested assistance has been reduced.

In seeking to explain why the response has been to restrict benefit generosity and entitlement, rather than to make good the deficiencies of unemployment insurance, I have considered explanations based on electoral preferences, on the behaviour of politicians, and on the behaviour of the civil service. These were: (i) a reversion to self-interest explanation, as *ex ante* policies based on the 'higher selves' of the electorate gave way to *ex post* self-interest; (ii) a lifting of the veil explanation, according to which the majority, whose jobs were not in the event threatened, began to give less weight to the needs of the unemployed; (iii) a shift in political ideology, or changing political climate explanation; and two theories based on the fact that policy may reflect (iv) the interests and objectives of politicians (the political slack explanation) or (v) the balance of different objectives within the civil service (the administrative slack explanation).

In the analysis, considerable attention was devoted to the electoral preferences since these are relevant not only to explaining the form policy took but also to the issue whether the response of policy should have been more generous. If, as with the changing political climate explanation, the less generous policy simply reflects a shift in opinion away from redistributive objectives, induced by the ideology of the incumbent government, then it can be argued that there is no case for intervention. The resulting harshness towards the unemployed is a consequence of a democratic decision-making process, which in itself offers no safeguards to minorities.[9] On the other hand, if the shift in policy towards the unemployed results from political or administrative slack, then there is a *prima facie* case for intervention to prevent this happening. If the outcome reflects the objectives of policy makers or administrators, rather than of voters, there are grounds for limiting the freedom of maneouvre of the government or civil service.

The position with the reversion to self-interest and lifting of the veil explanations is less straightforward. In both cases, the policy pursued does indeed correspond to the judgements of the majority made *ex post*: it must however be questioned whether we should judge the outcome by these preferences. Which of our different selves we wish to be when making this decision seems an open question. It seems perfectly possible that we would like to protect ourselves against the consequences of our actions once the veil is lifted.[10] Or, we may have a contemporaneous plurality of judgements. As discussed by Sen (1977a) there may be meta-preferences governing the choice between different preference orderings, as expressed by such statements as 'I wish I liked vegetarian foods more'. People may prefer that they acted according to their 'higher selves'. Concretely, if allowed to pursue their own interests, in which the welfare of the unemployed enters only with a heavy discount, people may support a harsh policy but at the same time prefer not to be offered this choice.

Appendix: changes in National Insurance (NI) Unemployment Benefit (UB) in Britain, 1979–88[11]

Measures favourable to the unemployed

Equal treatment provisions – In accordance with a 1978 European Community directive, in November 1983 regulations were introduced to ensure 'equal treatment' of men and women. These allow married women to claim NI dependency additions.

Definition of voluntary redundancy – The Social Security Act 1985 amended the disqualification provisions to ensure that they are not applied to those who volunteer or agree to be made redundant within the meaning of the Employment Protection (Consolidation Act, 1978).

Measures whose effect may be positive or negative

Linked spell rule – As of 14 September 1980, the linked spell period was reduced from 13 weeks to eight weeks if there is unexhausted entitlement to National Insurance benefit (if entitlement has been exhausted then the period remains at 13 weeks). The significance of the linking is that a person does not have to wait a further three waiting days, but the total period of receipt in the linked spells is limited to 52 weeks.

Earnings rule – As of 8 March 1982, the regulations were amended to increase from 75p. to £2 the amount that an unemployed person could earn per day without losing UB providing that he or she is still available for full-time work on the day.

Measures unfavourable to the unemployed

End of earnings related supplement (ERS) – The Social Security (no. 2) Act 1980 abolished ERS. The 15 per cent rate of ERS was reduced to 10 per cent in January 1981, and as of January 1982 no new claims could be made for ERS. As a result, no ERS was payable after June 1982.

Taxation of NI unemployment benefit – The income tax treatment of the unemployed has been changed in two respects: tax refunds are not paid until after the resumption of work, or the end of the tax year if that is sooner, and UB and Supplementary Benefits have become taxable. On the termination of the benefit claim, or the end of the tax year if that comes sooner, the claimant's tax position is calculated, taking account of the benefit received, and any net refund due is made. Where there is a net liability, this would normally be collected by an adjustment of the PAYE code. In the case of a breadwinner wife, the tax office will only transfer the balance of the married man's allowance after subtracting UB at the standard rate for the rest of the tax year.

Suspension of statutory indexation – The Social Security (No. 2) Act 1980 suspended for three years the duty of the Secretary of State to index link short-term NI benefits, giving power to increase them by up to five percentage points less than the rate of inflation. In 1980 there was a 5 per cent withholding of UB pending taxation of UB, which was restored in November 1983. The Social Security Act 1986 provides for the Secretary of State to vary the amount of any increase 'if he considers it appropriate, having regard to the national economic situation and any other matters which he considers relevant'.

Abolition of child additions – This addition was abolished as of 26 November 1984, except for claimants over pensionable age.

Abolition of lower rate benefits – The $\frac{3}{4}$ and $\frac{1}{2}$ rates of NI benefit for those not meeting the full contribution conditions were abolished under the Social Security Act 1986 as of 5 October 1986.

Abatement for occupational pensioners – As of 6 April 1981, a person over the age of 60 and receiving an occupational pension of more than £35 has NI Unemployment Benefit reduced by 10p. for every 10p. above this level (Social Security [No. 2] Act 1980). The Social Security Act 1988 reduced the age from 60 to 55 (introduced in January 1989).

More stringent administration – The operations of Unemployment Review Officers (UROs), responsible for finding out what the claimant is doing to get a job, traditionally based on the Supplementary Benefits (SB) side, were extended to cover those receiving NI Unemployment Benefit supplemented by SB in 1980. As of 18 October 1982, registration for work at a Job Centre became voluntary for unemployed people aged 18 and over. At the same time, unemployment benefit offices took over from Job Centres the task of testing 'availability for work'. In August 1983 the Department of Employment set up Regional Benefit Investigation Teams. In 1984 the Department of Health and Social Security (DHSS) ordered a major drive in

59 areas into social security abuse. The Restart scheme was introduced nationally in July 1986 with a benefit-monitoring function. More stringent availability to work test was introduced in October 1986, involving a new questionnaire for new claimants. A revised questionnaire for new claimants and a new questionnaire for claimants called to Restart interviews were introduced as of April 1988.

Disqualification period – The Social Security Act 1986 extended the maximum period of benefit disqualification from six to 13 weeks, with effect from October 1986. This applies where there is quitting without just cause, or loss of job through industrial misconduct, or refusal to take suitable work or training offers. The act gave the Secretary of State the power to alter this period and as of 11 April 1988, there was a further increase to 26 weeks. The act also allows the Secretary to make regulations which will provide that days of disqualification count towards the entitlement to a total of 312 days of benefit.

Students – As of 1 September 1986, regulations were made to remove entitlement by full-time students to UB and SB during the 'grant-aided period', effectively removing entitlement for most students in the short vacations.

Full extent normal rule – This rule prevents those who do not normally work on every working day in the week from claiming UB on their 'off' days. This has caused particular difficulties with part-time Community Programme (CP) workers. Regulations were introduced with effects from 4 March 1987, preventing such people from claiming UB for days on which they are not employed on a CP scheme.

Contribution conditions – The Social Security Act 1988 tightened the contribution conditions for NI benefit, with the change taking effect as of October 1988. The entitlement will depend on the contribution record for the two tax years before the start of the benefit year, as opposed to the previous one tax year. Class 1 contributions on earnings of at least 50 times the lower weekly earnings limit must have been paid or credited in both tax years: and, for unemployment benefit, Class 1 contributions must have been paid (i.e., not credited) on earnings of at least 25 times the weekly lower earnings limit in one of the two tax years (as opposed to any tax year). Moreover, the rule permitting the aggregation of contributions paid in more than one tax year in order to satisfy the second condition is abolished.

10 Institutional features of unemployment insurance and the working of the labour market

The principal theme of this chapter is that much of the theoretical literature dealing with the relationship between benefit and unemployment fails to capture the essential institutional features of unemployment insurance. The literature – with some notable exceptions – has ignored important aspects of how benefits actually operate in the real world. As a result, the conclusions reached may be misleading. It is not adequate to treat unemployment insurance as simply wages received when not in work. One has to consider the conditions under which benefits are paid, their link to labour market decisions, the contributory basis of unemployment insurance, and the limited duration of insurance benefit.

The first section (10.1) describes certain key institutional features of unemployment insurance, distinguishing it from unemployment assistance and from general welfare benefits. Among the most important aspects are that claimants may be disqualified from unemployment insurance if they have quit voluntarily or been dismissed for industrial misconduct, that entitlement to benefit depends on the past record of insured employment, and that there is a limited duration of benefit. These features are illustrated by reference to the social security systems of the United States and the United Kingdom. Section 10.2 considers how far these institutional features have been modelled in a selection of contributions to the theoretical literature on unemployment benefits and the labour market. The third section concentrates on a model of a dual labour market model with efficiency wages related to the need to induce workers to apply effort, and imperfect matching of unemployed workers and vacancies, coupled with queue unemployment.

This model, used in Atkinson (1988), has evident limitations, but it serves to illustrate some of the key features of unemployment insurance. These are the subject of section 10.4. Among the most important considerations is that the existence of unemployment insurance does not directly affect the incentive of workers to supply effort, in contrast to what has been assumed in earlier literature, if in the case of dismissal for shirking they are disqualified from benefit. At the same time, unemployment insurance affects the level of wages, since it increases the attractiveness of employment in a sector in which there is an external risk of job termination. The main conclusions are summarised at the end of the chapter.

10.1 Institutional features of unemployment insurance

In much of the literature on unemployment benefit, it is assumed that the benefit operates just like a wage for the unemployed: for example, 'the wage when working is w, and is b when not working' (Oswald, 1986, p. 369). Probing more deeply, one finds that it is assumed, as far as the recipient is concerned, that

(a) the benefit is paid irrespective of the reasons for entry into unemployment,
(b) there are no contribution conditions related to past employment,
(c) the benefit is not related to past earnings in employment, and is usually assumed to be a constant flat-rate amount,
(d) the benefit is paid independently of the recipient's efforts to search for new work, or of availability for work,
(e) the benefit is paid for an unlimited duration.

On this basis, all of those out of work are assumed to be in receipt of unemployment compensation. Yet in reality, this is not the case. This is because real-world benefits do not satisfy these assumptions.

If one looks at *unemployment insurance* (UI), which is the principal focus in this chapter, then its features are better described by the following assumptions:

(a*) the benefit is refused, or there is a period of disqualification, where the claimant has quit employment voluntarily or has been dismissed for industrial misconduct,
(b*) entitlement to UI depends on the past record of insured employment, typically requiring a minimum earnings level for eligibility and a minimum contribution period,
(c*) the UI benefit may be a flat-rate amount, but is more typically related to past earnings,
(d*) continued receipt of benefit is conditional on the recipient making demonstrable efforts to search for new employment, on being available for employment and on accepting suitable job offers,
(e*) there is limited duration of entitlement, after which UI benefit ceases to be paid.

As a result of these conditions, there may be a sizeable proportion of the unemployed who do not receive UI benefit. There are those who have been refused benefit, or disqualified for a period, on grounds of voluntary quitting, dismissal for industrial misconduct, for failing to carry out job search, or for refusing suitable job offers. There are those who do not satisfy the contribution conditions: for example new entrants to the labour force may not be eligible. There are those who have received UI earlier in their unemployment spell but whose entitlement is now exhausted.

In listing these features, I have referred explicitly to unemployment insurance, and it is important to distinguish this from *unemployment assistance* (UA). In some countries, UA is closer to the hypothetical 'wage when not working' in that there may be no contribution conditions (condition (b)), and that it may be paid for an unlimited duration (condition (e)). However, the assumptions (a) and (d) are not typically valid. People may be disqualified from UA in the case of voluntary quitting or dismissal for industrial misconduct; and benefit may be withdrawn if they are not considered to be actively seeking employment or refuse suitable job offers.

In what follows, I concentrate on unemployment insurance. Much of the literature has referred to UI, doubtless because in the United States this is the principal social security scheme for the unemployed. In the US there is no specific unemployment assistance scheme and the role played by General Assistance is limited. The US unemployment insurance system is a state programme, and therefore varies from state to state, but it typically has features similar to those listed under (a*)–(e*). The method of job separation may disqualify an applicant from UI:

> The purpose of such qualifications is to restrict benefits to those who become unemployed through no fault of their own; that is, it is generally held that an employee who 'voluntarily' leaves his job should take the consequences. The series of disqualifying reasons include voluntary separation from work, discharge for misconduct, refusal of suitable work, and unemployment due to a labor dispute. (Williams, Turnbull and Cheit, 1982, p. 394)

Eligibility for UI depends on the applicant having earned qualifying wages in covered employment during the 'base year' (for example, the first four of the last five calendar quarters completed prior to filing a claim), generally requiring wages to have been earned in more than one quarter of that year. The benefit formula takes the form in many states of a fraction, for example the weekly benefit is 1/26 of the wages in the quarter for which wages were the highest, subject to a minimum and a maximum. Applicants must demonstrate continuing attachment to the labour force by registration for work at an employment office and are subject to disqualification if they refuse suitable work. Some states pay benefits up to a stated maximum period, but most limit the maximum total dollar payments to a fraction (usually one third) of their base year wages. In periods of 'high unemployment', the maximum duration may be extended. The benefits are financed by employer contributions, with experience rating of employers (the contribution rate is related to the history of claims). There are some private unemployment insurance plans, negotiated between unions and employers, known as *supplementary unemployment benefits*, but the coverage of these plans is largely restricted to manufacturing (Oswald, 1986). (Private unemployment insurance is discussed in Barr, 1988.)

The UI system in the US departs therefore in significant ways from the hypothetical 'wage when not working'. The same is true of National Insurance unemployment benefit in the United Kingdom. Where a claimant left his previous job voluntarily, he may be disqualified from benefit unless there was good cause for leaving. Disqualification may also ensue in the case of dismissal for industrial misconduct, which 'can cover a wide range of disruptive behaviour and bad work, which is causally connected with the loss of employment, and where there is evidence of fault' (Fenn, 1980, p. 243).

There are complex contribution conditions for NI benefit, which were significantly tightened in 1988 (see appendix to chapter 9). They require that the person should (in effect) have been in the labour force for the two tax years preceding the start of the benefit year and that total contributions should have been paid of at least 25 times the lower limit for weekly earnings in at least one of those years. Contributions are paid by both employers and employees as part of the general National Insurance system which covers retirement pensions, invalidity benefits, widows' benefits and other contingencies apart from unemployment (there is no ear-marking within the scheme). The UK unemployment insurance benefit is now flat rate (it is the only European Community country not to have an earnings-related system) but an earnings-related supplement was in force from 1966 to 1982. Benefit may be withdrawn if a claimant fails to make use of a reasonable opportunity of suitable employment, refuses to apply for a vacancy, or fails to follow advice intended to assist the claimant in finding a job. National Insurance unemployment benefit is paid for a maximum of one year in any spell of interruption of employment, and two periods of unemployment separated by less than eight weeks constitute a single spell. Once benefit is exhausted, the person must work at least 13 weeks before any further eligibility is possible (in addition to satisfying the contribution conditions).

In the UK the unemployed may also receive assistance. Historically, this has been quite separate. Unemployment insurance was introduced in

Britain by Lloyd George in the National Insurance Act of 1911, which drew on the German social insurance system initiated by Bismarck and on the existing trade union schemes for insurance against unemployment. Unemployment assistance, on the other hand, had its origins in the Poor Law and now forms part of the general means-tested system of Income Support.

10.2 Treatment of unemployment compensation in the theoretical literature: a selective review

It is commonly believed that an increase in unemployment benefit leads to a rise in equilibrium unemployment, either directly or else indirectly via an increase in wages. Examination of the theoretical literature provides grounds for this belief (the empirical literature is not considered here, for a recent survey, see Atkinson and Micklewright, 1991).

The *Handbook of Labor Economics* seems an appropriate place to commence this selective review of the theoretical writing on unemployment benefit. In their chapter entitled 'The natural rate of unemployment: explanation and policy', Johnson and Layard summarise the findings from their first supply and demand model: 'The model yields some immediate policy insights. It shows, for example, that, if the market clears, unemployment insurance will increase unemployment, as in all our models' (1986, p. 923). In this model, individuals may choose a fraction of the year to be unemployed; in their words 'unemployment is the annual holiday'. During this period they receive a benefit, b, in place of wages, so that annual consumption is given by

$$c = (1-u)w + ub \tag{10.1}$$

where u is the fraction of the year spent unemployed. The individual's utility depends on c and leisure (u), and it is assumed that leisure is a normal good. For those choosing an interior value of u, a rise in b reduces the effective labour supply at any given wage on account of both income and substitution effects. If the rise in b is assumed to be financed by a tax on wages in work, then there is purely a substitution effect. The supply curve shifts upward; and there is an increase in 'voluntary' unemployment.

The other models considered by Johnson and Layard include those where the firms set wages and those where wages are set by trade unions. In the former case, they consider versions of the efficiency wage model. Suppose that firm i is concerned about the rate at which workers quit, this depending on the variable x which is the ratio of the wage offered by firm i, w_i, to the expected income on quitting, given by the right-hand side of (10.1), where w is the average wage paid in the rest of the economy. In other words, the quit rate faced by firm i is assumed to be $q(x)$ where

$$x = w_i/((1-u)w + ub) \qquad (10.2)$$

There is a cost-minimising level of quitting and hence x, denoted by x^*. It follows that

$$w_i/w = x^* \, [(1-u) + u \, \rho] \qquad (10.3)$$

where ρ is the replacement rate, b/w. In equilibrium all firms pay the same wage, so that (10.3) determines the equilibrium relationship between the replacement rate and the level of unemployment: 'If the replacement rate is higher, quitting becomes more attractive and, to offset this, unemployment has to be higher' (Johnson and Layard, 1986, p. 961). Johnson and Layard then consider a model of 'matching', where there are frictions in matching workers to jobs and a cost of unfilled vacancies. The probability of filling a vacancy depends on the proportion of the unemployed who search, and this latter proportion is assumed to be a declining function of the replacement rate, leading again to a positive relationship between benefits and unemployment.

In the union wage-setting model, it is assumed in the simplest version that workers are either employed at the union wage or unemployed receiving b. The conclusion is straightforward: 'the higher the replacement ratio the less union members will suffer if the union pushes up wages and reduces employment. Thus a higher replacement ratio will lead to lower employment' (1986, p. 974). In a more realistic dual labour market model, with a unionised sector and a non-unionised (competitive) sector, they assume that there is a queue of unemployed people waiting for union jobs, there being no direct recruitment from the non-unionised sector. There is a union wage differential so that people in that sector earn $(1+\mu)$ times the competitive wage. From the condition that the expected present value of waiting should equal that of working in the competitive sector Johnson and Layard derive an equilibrium relationship between the unemployment rate (u) and the replacement rate (ρ, defined relative to the competitive wage), the rate of interest (r), the rate of job termination in the union sector (δ), the proportion of employment in the union sector (v), and the union mark-up (μ)

$$1/u = 1 + r(1-\rho)/[\delta \; \mu \; v] \qquad (10.4)$$

(see Johnson and Layard, 1986, pp. 976–7, where it should be noted that they assume that the present value of a union job is not affected by the probability of termination). Once more a rise in the benefit rate is associated with a rise in the equilibrium unemployment rate.

In this range of models, therefore, it appears to be the case that a rise in unemployment benefit leads to a rise in equilibrium unemployment.

However, it is also clear that the specification of the benefit corresponds to our hypothetical 'wage when not working' rather than to the institutional features of UI identified in the previous section. The model of quitting was based on the assumption that benefit would be received, but we have seen that UI in principle disqualifies claimants who have entered unemployment voluntarily. No role is played in any of these models by contribution conditions. All of the unemployed are assumed to receive benefit. No distinction is made between those who have entered unemployment after losing their job and those who are new entrants to the labour force (and have no rights to UI). In the model of matching, the unemployed person is assumed to be able to choose whether or not to search for a vacancy, whereas UI legislation embodies job search requirements and in the UK considerable administrative resources are devoted to enforcing this condition. The benefit is assumed in the theoretical models to be of unlimited duration, so that none of the unemployed have exhausted their entitlement. So whatever conclusions may be drawn from these models, they cannot be assumed to apply to unemployment insurance with the institutional features identified in section 10.1.

If we turn to other reviews of the theoretical literature, then the findings are in some cases different. Stiglitz, for example, has argued that the policy conclusions drawn may vary in efficiency wage models:

> The policy consequences may differ markedly depending on the explanation of the dependence of productivity on wages. Consider, for instance, an increase in the unemployment compensation. In the 'shirking' version of the efficiency wage model, this results in firms having to raise their wages in order to induce workers not to shirk (the penalty for being caught is smaller at any fixed wage and unemployed level). This in turn results in a higher equilibrium unemployment rate and a higher real wage. (1986, p. 188)

He goes on to say that:

> on the other hand, in the quality–efficiency wage model, an increase in unemployment compensation may have a differential effect on the search intensities of individuals of different abilities and thus shift the wage–productivity curve facing different firms. If low productivity workers' search is reduced relative to the high productivity workers, then the applicant productivity–wage curve may shift up ... with a consequent change in the wage (which may either increase or decrease) and increase in the demand for labor. (1986, p. 188)

But despite the different conclusions, the treatment of unemployment compensation is again of the 'wage when not working' variety. If we look at the shirking model of Shapiro and Stiglitz (1984), then the central feature is the choice between supplying the required level of effort and 'shirking' in which case there is a probability that the worker will be caught and fired by his employer. It is assumed that workers who are fired receive unemployment compensation. Yet we have seen that UI legislation specifically excludes those who are discharged for misconduct (and the same applies to UA). In the real world the condition may not be fully enforced, but the worker has to allow for the possibility that benefit would be denied. The same objection applies to the dual labour market model of Bulow and Summers (1986).

The real-world features of UI have not been totally neglected in the theoretical literature. As noted at the outset, there are notable exceptions to the criticism made here. Mortensen (1977) and Burdett (1979) have examined the implications of the fact that UI is paid for a limited duration and that entitlement depends on the past earnings record. Burdett and Mortensen (1980) have analysed the consequences of the fact that UI benefits are paid only to laid-off workers and not to new entrants. The fact that benefits are related to past earnings is the focus of the model of Hey and Mavromaras (1981). Lippman and McCall (1980) have considered the differences between UI and welfare assistance. Hamermesh (1979) has drawn attention to the fact that the possibility of qualifying for UI may induce people to supply more labour. (For further references to the theoretical literature, see Atkinson and Micklewright, 1991.)

From these articles, it is clear that the effects of UI may be rather different from those of a benefit paid simply as a 'wage when not working'. But this warning has not been heeded and much of the literature on unemployment continues to treat UI in an oversimplified way. The aim of this chapter is to show the effect of introducing into an equilibrium model of unemployment the five features of UI identified earlier. The representation is necessarily stylised but it goes beyond earlier research in attempting to introduce all of the features, rather than just some of them.

The final point to be noted from this brief review of earlier work is that the comparative static analysis of unemployment compensation has in part treated a rise in benefits with no change in taxes or contributions and in part considered a balanced budget change, with both benefits and contributions being increased. The latter is illustrated by the first model of Johnson and Layard, where the cost of the benefit is assumed to be met out of a tax on wages in work, but their discussion of the quitting and wage-setting models considers only a rise in benefits with no change in taxes. Shapiro and Stiglitz refer to both benefit and contribution sides of the budget, arguing that the two effects re-inforce each other:

> Increases in unemployment benefits have the same impact on the No-Shirking Condition [the wage has to rise at any level of employment], but they also reduce labor demand as workers become more expensive [on account of increased contributions], so they cause unemployment to rise for two reasons. (1984, p. 439)

In the analysis of unemployment insurance in section 10.4, both comparative static exercises are considered. It seems interesting both to ask how the unemployment compensation system as a whole affects the working of the labour market and to examine the impact of changes in benefit levels with no change in contributions (it being assumed that the deficit on the UI scheme is met by lump-sum taxes). The latter is for example the relevant question when considering policy changes in the UK over the past decade, since benefits have been cut with no corresponding adjustment in contributions.

10.3 A dual labour market model

The model described in this section draws on a number of sources. The matching of workers and vacancies in a search framework builds on Diamond (1981 and 1982), Mortensen (1988) and Pissarides (1979, 1984 and 1985). The shirking version of the efficiency wage is discussed by, among others, Bowles (1985), Calvo and Wellisz (1979), Foster and Wan (1984) and Shapiro and Stiglitz (1984). The dual labour market formulation is influenced by Doeringer and Piore (1971), Bulow and Summers (1986), McDonald and Solow (1985) and van de Klundert (1988). As in a number of these articles, the model is dynamic (in continuous time), but the analysis is simplified by concentrating on a stationary state.

The economy is assumed to consist of a primary sector, in which L_p workers are employed each earning a wage w_p, and a less favoured secondary sector, in which L_s workers are employed each earning a wage w_s. The features distinguishing the two sectors are described below. The total labour force is fixed at N, and the level of unemployment is U

$$U = N - L_p - L_s \tag{10.5}$$

In the primary sector, firms are unable to monitor effort precisely and, as in the model of Shapiro and Stiglitz (1984), a worker can choose between supplying effort, at cost ε, and facing a risk λ of being monitored, in which case the worker is fired. Both ε and λ are assumed constant over time. Firms find it profitable to pay a wage premium such that a worker is indifferent between putting in effort and shirking

$$\varepsilon = \lambda\,[\Omega_p - \Omega_u] \tag{10.6}$$

where Ω_p denotes the expected present value of holding a primary-sector job and Ω_u denotes the expected present value of being unemployed. Workers evaluate alternatives in terms solely of the expected present value of a continuous stream of returns, discounted at a constant interest rate r over an infinite horizon. (For a fuller discussion of the contract between firm and worker, including a treatment of 'good behaviour bonds', see Macleod and Malcomson, 1993.)

The present value of a primary-sector job depends on the probability of involuntary job loss. Job losses are assumed to take place at a constant rate, δ, and this is taken to be the probability faced by any individual worker in the primary sector. In a stationary state, with constant wages, the present value is stationary, and we can write

$$r\,\Omega_p = w_p - \varepsilon - \delta\,[\Omega_p - \Omega_u] = w_p - \varepsilon - \delta\,\varepsilon/\lambda \tag{10.7}$$

Workers are recruited into the primary sector from the stock of unemployed. There is no recruitment directly from secondary-sector employment. This assumption is parallel to that made in the Harris–Todaro (1970) model of migration – see McDonald and Solow (1985). (A more realistic assumption is that there is a lower, but non-zero, probability of moving from the secondary to the primary sector.) There is assumed to be no problem of monitoring work effort in the secondary sector. (This sector may be thought of as small-scale enterprises or as home production.) This means that the present value of a secondary-sector position is, in a stationary equilibrium, simply

$$\Omega_s = (w_s - \varepsilon)/r \tag{10.8}$$

There is free movement between the secondary sector and unemployment, so that

$$\Omega_s = \Omega_u \tag{10.9}$$

The present value of being unemployed depends on the probability of getting a job in the primary sector. If at any time there are M matches of job vacancies with unemployed workers, and all unemployed face an equal chance of being recruited, then the probability of getting a job is M/U, and we have, in a stationary equilibrium

$$r\,\Omega_u = (M/U)\,[\Omega_p - \Omega_u] \tag{10.10}$$

From (10.7), (10.8) and (10.9) we can solve for

$$w_p - w_s = (r + \delta)\,\varepsilon/\lambda \tag{10.11}$$

The wage differential between the two sectors is proportional to the cost of effort; it is not affected by changes in the levels of employment. Using (10.6), (10.8), (10.9) and (10.10), we obtain

$$w_s = \varepsilon + (M/U)\,\varepsilon/\lambda \tag{10.12}$$

and hence

$$w_p = \varepsilon + [M/U + r + \delta]\,\varepsilon/\lambda \tag{10.13}$$

The wage paid in the secondary sector exceeds the cost of effort since the supply price is determined by the option of being unemployed and seeking a job in the primary sector. The level of wages depends on M/U, which depends on the matching process.

In the conditions described above, a primary-sector job is always accepted by an unemployed worker; however, there is imperfect matching of unemployed workers to vacant primary-sector jobs, so that not all vacancies are filled instantaneously. I work with the special form of the matching function such that, if there are U unemployed and V vacancies, then the instantaneous rate of matching is

$$M = m\sqrt{(UV)} \tag{10.14}$$

In that case

$$M/U = m\sqrt{(V/U)} \text{ and } M/V = m\sqrt{(U/V)} \tag{10.15}$$

The ratio V/U determines the probability of getting a primary job offer (M/U) and of a vacancy being filled (M/V).

How is the number of vacancies in the primary sector determined? It is assumed that there is a fixed cost, c, of advertising a vacancy which is incurred whether or not the position is filled. There is assumed to be free entry of firms and all vacancies are equally likely to be filled. Firms maximise the expected present value of profits. We have therefore a condition equating the cost to the expected return

$$c = (M/V)\, J \tag{10.16}$$

where J denotes the value to a firm of a filled position. It is assumed that product prices are governed by world prices. The value of the output produced by a worker, net of monitoring costs, is y, so that in equilibrium with constant w_p and J, the value of J must satisfy

$$rJ = y - w_p - \delta J \tag{10.17}$$

The last term appears because each job is assumed to be subject to the same probability of involuntary termination. In equilibrium the level of employment is constant, so that new matches must equal the involuntary job terminations

$$M = \delta L_p \tag{10.18}$$

Finally, in the secondary sector there is assumed to be a downward-sloping demand function for labour

$$L_s = S\{w_s\} \text{ where } S' \leq 0 \tag{10.19}$$

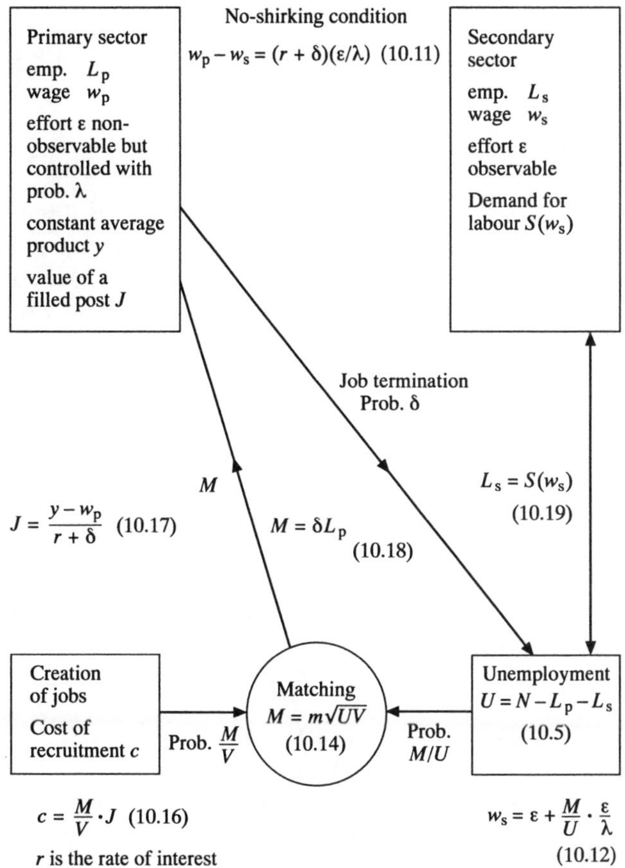

Figure 10.1 Structure of dual labour market model with efficiency wages and imperfect matching

and it is assumed that $S(\varepsilon) < N$, so that in the absence of the primary sector there would be no full-employment wage in excess of the cost of effort.

The different elements of the model are summarised in figure 10.1. The stationary equilibrium is described as follows. From (10.15) and the free-entry condition (10.16)

$$M/V = m\sqrt{(U/V)} = c/J \tag{10.20}$$

and

$$M/U = m\sqrt{(V/U)} = m^2 J/c \tag{10.21}$$

Using (10.13) and (10.17)

$$(r+\delta)\, J = y - w_p = y - \varepsilon - [M/U + r + \delta]\, \varepsilon/\lambda \tag{10.22}$$

Hence, using (10.21)

$$(r+\delta+m^2\, \varepsilon/c\, \lambda)J = y - \varepsilon - (r+\delta)\, \varepsilon/\lambda \tag{10.23}$$

(It is assumed y is sufficiently large that the right-hand side is strictly positive). The equilibrium value of a job is an increasing function of c and a decreasing function of m. These are indicators of the extent to which the frictions in filling vacancies create an entry barrier protecting firms with workers in post. The equilibrium vacancy/unemployment ratio is given by

$$\sqrt{(V/U)} = mJ/c \tag{10.24}$$

From (10.12) and (10.21)

$$w_s = \varepsilon + m^2 J\, \varepsilon/c\, \lambda \tag{10.25}$$

$$w_p = w_s + (r+\delta)\, \varepsilon/\lambda \tag{10.26}$$

The level of employment in the primary sector is governed by the fact that in equilibrium the number of involuntary job terminations is equal to the number of matches (10.18)

$$L_p = m^2 JU/c\, \delta \tag{10.27}$$

Employment in the secondary sector is determined by (10.19) and (10.25). The level of unemployment follows from (10.5)

$$U = N - m^2 JU/c\, \delta - S\{w_s\} \tag{10.28}$$

(A positive value follows from the assumption that $S(\varepsilon) < N$.)

In this model, unemployment arises because people 'queue' for jobs in the primary sector and on account of the frictions in matching the unemployed to vacancies. These effects may be seen if we consider the impact of a rise in the productivity of a worker, y. The equilibrium value of a job, J, rises (equation (10.23)). The equilibrium V/U ratio rises as firms create more vacancies (equation (10.21)). Primary-sector employment rises with J, at any level of unemployment, and the ratio of primary-sector jobs to unemployment certainly rises (equation (10.27)). This makes queueing for a primary-sector job more attractive and the equilibrium secondary-sector wage rises (equation (10.25)), so secondary-sector employment falls (equation (10.19)). The effect on total employment depends on whether this is outweighed by expansion of the primary sector. In what follows it is assumed that the elasticity of demand for labour in the secondary sector is sufficiently small that total employment rises if the value of J increases.

Differentiating (10.28) and (10.25), we may see that this requires, after some rearrangement

$$[-S'\{w_s\}\cdot w_s/S\{w_s\}] < [1+\lambda/(M/U)]L_p/L_s \qquad (10.29)$$

If the primary sector accounts for more than half of total employment, then a sufficient condition is that the elasticity of S be less than unity.

Given the assumptions made, unemployment is an equilibrium phenomenon. There is no demand deficiency in this economy; the output of both sectors is assumed to be sold on world markets. I do not regard the model as fully adequate to explain observed unemployment, but it provides a sufficient framework for the points I want to make about unemployment insurance.

10.4 The impact of unemployment insurance in a dual labour market model

The first important feature (a*) of unemployment insurance is that benefit is paid in the case of involuntary job termination but not where the worker is dismissed for industrial misconduct or quits voluntarily. I assume that in the case of dismissal for shirking there is permanent disqualification. (A more realistic treatment would allow for a probability of disqualification less than unity and for a finite period of disqualification.) This means that we have to distinguish between the state of *insured* unemployment, in which benefit is received, and *uninsured* unemployment. It is the latter which enters the worker's calculation about shirking, since in the event of being monitored and dismissed no UI is received. Equation (10.6) remains applicable, where Ω_u is the present value of being in uninsured unemployment. This is clearly different from the analysis in Stiglitz (1986) quoted in section 10.2, and one of the central points of the analysis is that the existence of UI does not affect the incentive to shirk in terms of the present value of a primary-sector job. At the same time, the level of wages is affected since UI makes primary-sector employment more attractive – see below.

UI is restricted to covered employment (feature b*), and there is typically a minimum qualifying period of employment and a minimum qualifying level of earnings. I represent the effect of these restrictions by assuming that employment in the primary sector is fully covered, whereas that in the secondary sector is not covered by UI. This could be because the secondary sector is composed of home production; it could be because paid jobs in that sector do not last long enough for workers to acquire rights to UI; it could be because the secondary-sector wage is below the qualifying minimum. A worker leaving the secondary sector enters therefore uninsured unemployment. We have the conditions (10.8) and (10.9) as before.

Those eligible for UI are workers whose primary-sector jobs are terminated. This means that

$$r\,\Omega_p = w_p - \varepsilon - \delta\,[\Omega_p - \Omega_i] \tag{10.7'}$$

where Ω_i denotes the present value of being in insured unemployment.

The level of UI payment (feature c*) is denoted by b, where this allows for both a flat-rate benefit as in the UK or an earnings-related benefit, in which case b is assumed to be a proportion ρ of the primary-sector wage.

Receipt of UI is conditional on making efforts to search for new employment and on accepting suitable job offers (feature d*). This is incorporated in two ways. First, the UI administration is assumed to require that a claimant puts in effort in job search at cost $\eta\,\varepsilon$, where $0 \leq \eta < 1$. Less effort is involved than in working but nonetheless it is not pure holiday, as typically assumed. Secondly, it is assumed that refusal of a job offer in the primary sector leads to immediate termination of UI benefit (for example because UI is administered by the state employment agency through which job matches take place). Of course, an unemployed person could always take a job in the secondary sector. Whether this is regarded as a 'suitable' job offer is a matter of interpretation. Here I assume that there is a constant probability, γ (≥ 0), that a UI recipient is monitored and benefit terminated on the grounds that suitable employment is available in the secondary sector.

Finally, UI benefit is of limited duration (feature e*). Rather than take a fixed benefit period, for analytical convenience I assume that at any date a constant proportion, θ (>0), of UI recipients have their benefit terminated, and that the probability of benefit termination is the same for all insured unemployed. (Treatment of a fixed benefit period would be more realistic, particularly when examining the full dynamics of the model.)

Taking these features together, the present value of insured unemployment must satisfy in a stationary equilibrium

$$r\,\Omega_i = b - \eta\,\varepsilon + (\gamma + \theta)\,[\Omega_u - \Omega_i] + M/U\,[\Omega_p - \Omega_i] \tag{10.30}$$

There are two possible exits – to uninsured unemployment (secondary employment) or to primary-sector employment. It is assumed that the probability of receiving a job offer in the primary sector is the same for all the unemployed, regardless of their UI status (this assumption could readily be relaxed to allow those in receipt of UI to have a higher probability of a job offer as a result of the effort devoted to job search). For uninsured unemployment, equation (10.10) continues to apply. Comparing these, it is clear that the condition that the state of insured unemployment be preferred is that

$$b' \equiv b - \eta\,\varepsilon > 0 \tag{10.31}$$

In other words, the net benefit allowing for the cost of the job search requirement must be strictly positive.

The number of insured unemployed is denoted by U_i and the total number of unemployed by U. In stationary equilibrium, the inflow into insured unemployment equals the outflow to jobs in the primary sector or to uninsured unemployment

$$\delta L_p = (M/U)\, U_i + (\gamma + \theta)\, U_i \tag{10.32}$$

The level of uninsured unemployment is determined as a residual. From (10.18), we may note that the proportion of the total unemployed who are in receipt of UI is given by

$$U_i/U = (M/U)/[\gamma + \theta + M/U] \tag{10.33}$$

The UI scheme is financed by contributions paid at the rate of τ_e by employees in the primary sector and a rate of τ_r by employers in that sector, so that

$$r\,\Omega_p = (1 - \tau_e)\, w_p - \varepsilon - \delta\,[\Omega_p - \Omega_i] \tag{10.7''}$$

and

$$rJ = y - (1 + \tau_r)\, w_p - \delta\, J \tag{10.17'}$$

The budget balance for the UI fund requires that

$$bU_i = (\tau_e + \tau_r)\, w_p L_p = (1 - \tau_e)\, w_p L_p \left[\frac{1 + \tau_r}{1 - \tau_e} - 1\right] \tag{10.34}$$

Defining

$$\frac{1 + \tau_r}{1 - \tau_e} - 1$$

as the total 'wedge' between net wage and cost to the employer, we can see from (10.7″), (10.17′) and (10.34) that it is only the net wage and the total wedge which are relevant. We may therefore set $\tau_e = 0$ without loss of generality, and this is done in what follows, with τ_r capturing the wedge. It may also be noted that the assumption that the rate of job terminations, δ, is exogenous precludes consideration of the decision to lay off worker and the fact that δ is assumed the same for all jobs means that experience rating would yield the same contribution rate.

The modifications involved in introducing UI into the model are summarised in figure 10.2. As already noted, the introduction of UI does not affect the relation between Ω_p and Ω_s; on the other hand, it does affect

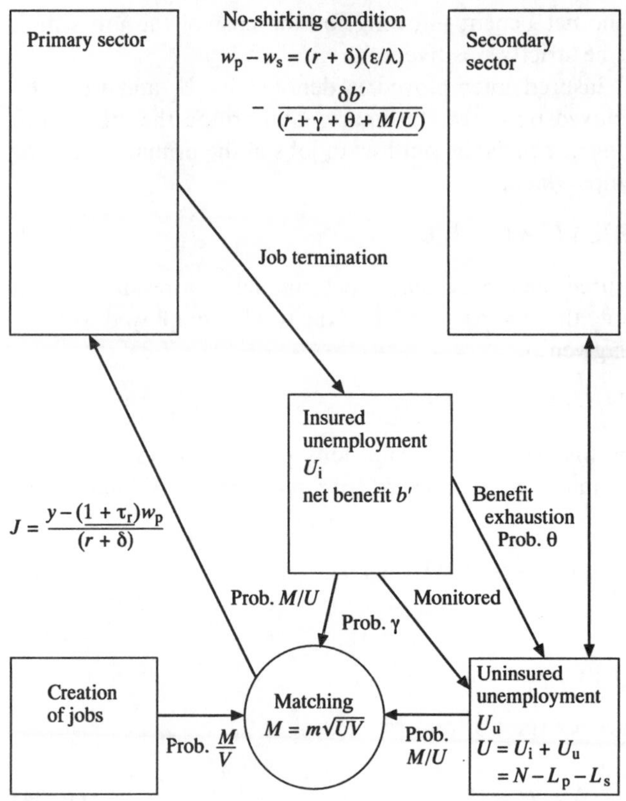

Figure 10.2 Effect of introducing unemployment insurance

the level of wages in the primary sector. This may be seen as follows. We can use (10.6), (10.8), (10.9) and (10.10) as before to obtain

$$w_s = \varepsilon + M/U \ \varepsilon/\lambda \tag{10.12}$$

In order to calculate w_p, we can solve for $(\Omega_p - \Omega_i)$ from equations (10.7″) and (10.30), using (10.6) to replace $(\Omega_p - \Omega_u)$

$$(\Omega_p - \Omega_i)\ [r + \delta + \gamma + \theta + M/U] = w_p - \varepsilon - b' + (\gamma + \theta)\ \varepsilon/\lambda \tag{10.35}$$

It may be noted that even if the net benefit, b', is equal to the net wage, allowing for the cost of effort, there will still be a positive incentive to leave unemployment and accept a primary-sector job $(\Omega_p > \Omega_i)$ providing that $(\gamma + \theta)$ is strictly positive. This brings out the importance of the conditions under which UI is administered. If there is a positive probability that benefit will be terminated, either because entitlement is exhausted or on the grounds that secondary employment is considered a 'suitable' alternative, then there is no disincentive even with 100 per cent replacement of net earnings. Substituting (10.35) into (10.7″), we can solve, using (10.6), (10.8), (10.9) and (10.12) to obtain

$$w_p = \varepsilon + [M/U + r + \delta]\ \varepsilon/\lambda - \delta b'/[r + \gamma + \theta + M/U] \tag{10.36}$$

where b' has been left on the right-hand side, but it must be remembered that it may depend on w_p (where the benefit is earnings related). It is the difference between (10.36) and (10.12) that is shown in figure 10.2.

Comparing (10.36) and (10.13), it may be seen that, at any given M/U, the net wage in the primary sector is lower when the UI scheme is in effect (and this is true of both flat-rate and earnings-related schemes). (The net wage is shown in the left-hand side of (10.36); the first two terms on the right-hand side are the same as those on the right-hand side of (10.13.) UI is in this sense *complementary* to employment in the primary sector: the existence of UI makes employment in the primary sector more attractive, since it reduces the cost if the primary-sector job is terminated. In the case of a flat-rate benefit, a rise in b reduces the primary-sector wage, and with an earnings-related system a rise in the replacement rate ρ has the same effect (the right-hand side of (10.3) is a declining function of w_p). The wage also falls with an increase in the expected duration of receipt of UI (a low value of θ) and a reduction in the risk of benefit being terminated (lower γ).

The effect of UI on the value of a filled job is

$$(r + \delta)J = y - (1 + \tau_r)\ w_p \tag{10.37}$$

Hence, using (10.21) and (10.36)

$$\begin{aligned}[r + \delta + (m^2\ \varepsilon/c\ \lambda)\ (1 + \tau_r)]J = y - [\varepsilon + (r + \delta)\ \varepsilon/\lambda](1 + \tau_r)\\ + \delta b'\ (1 + \tau_r)/[r + \gamma + \theta + m^2 J/c]\end{aligned} \tag{10.38}$$

(It is again assumed that the values of the parameters are such that the right-hand side is positive.) If b' were zero, then the difference between (10.38) and the situation in the absence of UI (given by equation (10.23)) would be in the terms $(1 + \tau_r)$. These increase the left-hand side and reduce the right-hand side, so that, not very surprisingly, the value of a filled post is reduced by the obligation to pay UI contributions. On the other hand, if we consider the impact of the UI benefits, leaving aside the contributions ($\tau_r = 0$), then it can be seen that J rises (the right-hand side is larger for all J). The existence of UI means that primary-sector firms can offer lower wages, and this increases the value of a filled job position.

If J is reduced, then it follows that V/U falls, from equation (10.21), and hence M/U. This means that the secondary-sector wage falls (see equation (10.12)). It follows that employment in the secondary sector rises. On the assumption (10.29) about the elasticity of labour demand in the secondary sector, this is not enough to outweigh the fall in primary-sector employment, and total unemployment rises. It may also be noted from equation (10.33) that the proportion of insured unemployment falls, irrespective of the effect on total unemployment.

From these results, we can see the effect of variation in the parameters of the UI system ignoring first of all the budget balance requirement (assuming that the deficit on the UI fund, or the surplus, is allocated in some way that does not affect the equilibrium conditions). A rise in the contribution rate, whether employee or employer, reduces J and has the effects just described. The same applies to a rise in the job search requirement (η), which reduces the net value of the benefit (of course, the impact may be different if it raised the probability of a job matching: i.e. the search was 'productive'). It also applies to the rate of termination (γ). If benefits are administered more stringently so that more people are disqualified for failing to accept secondary-sector jobs, then the value of J falls. It may appear paradoxical that more stringent administration leads to a lower J, and hence higher unemployment, but this greater stringency reduces the effective value of UI.

On the other hand, as we have seen, a rise in the rate of benefit, b, has the effect of raising J and this has the reverse effects of those just described. There is a switch in employment towards the primary sector, and, on assumption (10.29), a rise in total employment. The same applies if benefit duration is increased (θ is smaller). UI operates in effect as a subsidy on the uncertain employment in the primary sector. The effect is different from that described by Shapiro and Stiglitz (1984) because those dismissed for industrial misconduct are assumed not to be eligible for UI and hence the benefit does not enter the No-Shirking Condition (10.6). Of course, if monitoring of this condition by the UI authorities is imperfect, then the results will be modified.

If we now consider a balanced budget UI programme, then – in contrast to the situation described by Shapiro and Stiglitz where the effects of benefits and contributions reinforced one another – the effects in the model described here operate in opposite directions. As far as J is concerned, it does indeed seem possible that the gain to the employer from lower primary-sector net wages may be exactly offset by the contributions payable. Suppose that there is no job search requirement ($\eta = 0$), so that the net benefit is b. We may write

$$w_p = \varepsilon + [M/U + r + \delta]\ \varepsilon/\lambda - \delta b/[r + \gamma + \theta + M/U] \tag{10.39}$$

or

$$w_p \equiv w_p^0 - \delta b/[r + \gamma + \theta + M/U] \tag{10.40}$$

where w_p^0 denotes the value in the absence of UI (at any given values of M/U), and

$$(r+\delta)\,J = y-(1+\tau_r)\,w_p \tag{10.41}$$

and, from (10.32) and (10.34)

$$\tau_r w_p\,[\gamma+\theta+M/U] = \delta b \tag{10.42}$$

Combining these we can see that

$$(r+\delta)\,J = y-(1+\tau_r)\,w_p^0/(1+\tau_r\{[\gamma+\theta+M/U]/[r+\gamma+\theta+M/U]\}) \tag{10.43}$$

From which it is clear that the value of J falls with the introduction of UI where $r>0$. If there were no discounting, then the benefit in terms of lower wage would exactly equal the contribution paid. The scheme would be purely redistributive – the wage rate in the primary sector would fall, but there would be UI benefit for those whose jobs had been terminated. It does not matter which compensation scheme (wages and UI) is adopted if they have the same actuarial value. The reason that $r>0$ causes the UI scheme to be no longer neutral is that the scheme considered here is pay-as-you-go, so that a current job has to pay for those currently unemployed, rather than for the expected present value of future unemployment associated with that job (as is assumed by Shapiro and Stiglitz, 1984, n. 12). With a positive interest rate, and no growth in the earnings base, this is unfavourable. (The analysis could be extended to allow for a funded UI scheme.) In this situation, the over all effect on employment may be negative (we have described the consequences of a fall in J), but it is the result of both negative and positive influences – not a purely negative effect.

Conclusions

The main purpose of this analysis has been to draw attention to the role played by certain institutional features of unemployment insurance in countries such as the United Kingdom and the United States. Unemployment insurance is not simply a 'wage when not working'. There is not typically an entitlement to benefit when the person has quit employment voluntarily or has been dismissed for industrial misconduct. Entitlement depends on the past record of covered employment and on contribution conditions. The continued receipt of benefit is dependent on job search and on accepting suitable job offers. There is a limited duration of entitlement. As a result, a sizeable proportion of the unemployed at any one time are not in receipt of UI benefit. Others are in receipt of unemployment *assistance*, but this scheme too may disqualify those quitting voluntarily or dismissed for misconduct and may terminate payments to those refusing suitable job offers.

The aim of the simple dual labour market model set out here has been to provide a framework within which we could examine the impact of UI taking account of these institutional features. The UI scheme treated is necessarily stylised, but it allows for covered and uncovered employment, for those dismissed for 'shirking' being disqualified from UI benefit, for a job search requirement, for the possibility of benefit termination for refusing employment, and for a limited duration of benefit. In the model only a proportion of the unemployed (the 'insured unemployed') receive benefit; this differs from much of the theoretical literature which takes it for granted that all of the unemployed are in receipt of benefit.

In this model the effects of a UI programme, taking both benefits and contributions together, are different from those that have been described in much of the earlier theoretical analyses. In particular, it is necessary to take account of the benefit provided to workers by the existence of insurance against involuntary job loss, and the way in which this reduces the equilibrium level of wages paid in the covered sector. There is a positive as well as a negative dimension to UI as far as employers, and employment, is concerned.

The total effect of a UI scheme is made up of an unfavourable effect on employment arising from the contributions side and a favourable effect arising from the benefit side. This means that, if a government reduces benefits while leaving contributions unchanged, we would expect this to have an adverse effect on employment. Such a comparative static analysis appears especially relevant to situations such as that in the UK in the 1980s when National Insurance unemployment benefit was cut in several different ways with no off-setting reduction in contributions. The earnings-related supplement was abolished; the contributions conditions were tightened; the period of disqualification was increased; the administration became more stringent (for details, see appendix to chapter 9). According to the analysis presented here, such a cut-back in benefits and tighter administration may have been expected to make primary-sector employment less attractive, putting upward pressure on wages in that sector. The number of vacancies in the primary sector per unemployed worker is reduced. There is a shift towards secondary-sector employment; in effect a transfer from 'good jobs' to 'bad jobs'. For a government seeking to encourage the development of the economy this can scarcely be seen as progress.

11 Social insurance

'Social insurance' is a term which I have been using for many years without being entirely clear about its essential economic features. When asked about its economic consequences, or the effects of reforms to social insurance, I have been increasingly unsure as to the appropriate framework within which to attempt to answer the question. The existing economic models do not seem to capture fully what is at the heart of social insurance.

Social insurance is one of those comfortable short-hand expressions which people tend to use without close examination of its precise content. When I began writing this chapter, I looked at a variety of sources for definitions of 'social insurance'. The *International Encyclopedia of the Social Sciences* contains no entry under this heading, nor does it refer the reader to another entry. The *New Palgrave Dictionary of Economics* contains an entry on 'Social Security', but does not tackle the definition of social insurance. And those reference books which do provide information are not always very enlightening: for example the *Penguin Dictionary of Economics*, under the heading of 'Insurance' says that 'there are also many other kinds of insurance, including sickness and unemployment insurance, some of which ... are not carried out by the traditional insurance companies' (Bannock *et al.*, 1979, p. 240).

There is indeed a lot of the proverbial elephant about social insurance: we may not be able to define an elephant, but we recognise one when we see it. We know what programmes people have in mind in Britain when they speak of National Insurance: for example, retirement pensions, widows' pensions, invalidity benefit and unemployment benefit. We know that it means these benefits rather than means-tested Income Support. We know that in Germany it refers to Rentenversicherung and Arbeitslosengeld rather than to Sozialhilfe. We know that in the US it refers to OASDI and not to AFDC or SSI.

From these examples, it appears that key elements in social insurance are that it is compulsory and that it does not involve, as such, a test of means.

But it is not the sole income maintenance programme to have these features, as illustrated by the proposals for a basic income scheme. (In its pure form, a basic income would replace all social security transfers and personal tax allowances by a single basic income paid unconditionally to everyone – see Parker, 1989.) What, beyond compulsion and the absence of a test of means, are the essential elements of social insurance and how can we best model its economic consequences?

You may feel that this is a rather scholastic exercise. However, I believe that a clear understanding of the role of social insurance is particularly important at the present juncture. In Britain we have seen the fiftieth anniversary of the Beveridge Report (1942), regarded by many as the essential embodiment of the idea of social insurance. It is therefore a good point at which to ask whether the principles which guided post-war legislation are appropriate for the next half century. In the context of the European Community, the move to a common internal market is bound to bring to the fore discussion of different social security systems and their underlying principles. The economic and social transformation of Eastern Europe raises the question of the role of social insurance in these new market economies. These policy issues will not be my primary concern, but I return to them in my concluding comments.

11.1 Understanding social insurance

In what follows, I am going to focus particularly on unemployment insurance and retirement pensions, two rather different programmes which illustrate a variety of considerations. I am also going to concentrate on the experience of Britain, which is a major qualification, since the development of National Insurance in Britain has undoubtedly reflected its political, social and economic circumstances, and these differ from country to country.[1] At the same time, this was an area of policymaking where the influence of foreign experience was strong (see, for example, Hennock, 1987), and there are important common elements. As it was put rather colourfully by an American commentator in 1913:

> From the frozen shores of Norway down to the sunny clime of Italy, from the furthest East and up to Spain, all Europe, whether Germanic, Saxon, Latin or Slav, follows the same path. Some countries have made greater advance than others, but none have remained outside of the procession, unless it be a few of the more insignificant principalities of the Balkan peninsula. The movement for social insurance is one of the most important world movements of our times. (Rubinow, 1913, p. 26)

It may be helpful if I indicate at the outset my main conclusion – that it is essential in understanding the role of social insurance to take account of its close relation with the functioning of the labour market. The role of social insurance is only comprehensible in the light of the development of the modern labour market. I should say at once that I claim no originality in highlighting this aspect, which one finds to varying degrees in the literature from the early days to the present. But it does differ from that emphasised in the recent economic writing on social insurance, in which the main focus has been the market for insurance, not the labour market. Drawing on the research of the last fifteen years on the economics of imperfect information, social insurance has been portrayed as arising from the incompleteness of private insurance markets. The 'failure' of the insurance market is seen by some to provide an *explanation* for the historical origins of social insurance; by others it is seen as providing the *justification* for state intervention in this form. To quote from the work of my colleague, N. Barr, 'the key role of social insurance [is] in coping with risks which would be covered inefficiently or not at all by private insurance' (1990, Abstract) and 'information failures provide both a theoretical justification of and an explanation for a Welfare State which is much more than a safety net' (1992, p. 754).

In my judgement, this is only part of the story, and it would be misleading to base an economic analysis of social insurance solely on this aspect. This applies to both the *explanation* and the *justification* of social insurance. While failure of the insurance market may play some role in explaining the origins of social insurance, there are other considerations, notably the development of the modern employment relation. Most importantly, this helps us understand how the contingencies arise against which social insurance offers protection. We have to explain not just why insurance was not available on the market but also why the insurance was needed. Nor, in terms of justification, is the analysis sufficient. Not only is there the well-recognised fact that moral hazard remains a problem for governments as well as private insurers (Stiglitz, 1983), but there are other, indirect, routes by which insurance may be provided.

These criticisms are elaborated in the next two sections.

11.2 Social insurance and market failure

The potential problems with insurance under imperfect information have been well rehearsed. Borch (1981) discussed how asymmetric information, where the insured are better informed about the risks than the insurer, leads to a problem of adverse selection, and the possible non-existence of a competitive equilibrium. The problem of moral hazard, where the actions of those who purchase insurance cannot be perfectly monitored, and the possible non-existence of a competitive equilibrium, was discussed by Stiglitz (1983).

These findings have entered the literature on the Welfare State. To quote from the public economics textbook of Stiglitz, 'the market failures that give rise to the government provision of social insurance include the failure to provide insurance for many of the most important risks facing individuals' (1988, p. 344). And the story of market failure has been used to argue that the Welfare State has a justification on efficiency grounds: 'Information problems of this sort greatly strengthen the case for a welfare state.... We need a welfare state of some sort for efficiency reasons, and would continue to do so even if all distributional problems had been solved' (Barr, 1987a, p. 421).

In order to set out the underlying economics more explicitly, I take the simple model of adverse selection described by Rothschild and Stiglitz (1976). People face a probability that they become incapable of work (on grounds either of ill-health or of the absence of employment opportunities). The probability is fixed: there is no problem of moral hazard. The standard assumptions are that people are expected utility maximisers, and that they are risk averse, so that if offered actuarially fair insurance, with no transaction costs, they will choose full insurance.

The problems with insurance arise when there are different risks in the population, and insurers cannot distinguish between them (information about the risk is known by the person seeking insurance but not by the insurer). Suppose that there is a high-risk group and a low-risk group. Then there cannot be a stable equilibrium with a single contract pooling different types of individuals, since there are unexploited profitable opportunities.[2] On the other hand, suppose that the insurance companies seek to get people to reveal their personal risk by offering full insurance at the less favourable rate (i.e., assuming that everyone is high risk), but only a limited amount of insurance on the favourable terms. (It is assumed that such price/quantity contracts are enforceable.) By appropriate choice of the contract, the population may be separated into its two constituent groups, one purchasing one type of contract and the other a second contract. However, to make sure that only the low-risk group purchase insurance on the favourable terms (necessary for this policy to break even), the amount of insurance at such a separating equilibrium must be strictly limited. If such a separating equilibrium exists, it means that the low-risk group can only secure a limited amount of insurance. Whether such an equilibrium exists depends on the relative numbers in the two groups (also on the difference in the probabilities and degree of risk aversion – see Rothschild and Stiglitz, 1976). If there are relatively few high-risk people, there may be no perfectly competitive equilibrium, in that at any point an insurance company can see an unexploited profitable opportunity.

The model just outlined is one that I have used myself to explore the implications of proposals for reliance on private provision of insurance (Atkinson, 1989, chapter 7), arguing that the market is unlikely to remain perfectly competitive. Nonetheless, there are several reasons why I feel uncomfortable about the application of this analysis either as a positive explanation of the emergence of social insurance or as a normative justification.

In saying this, I am not asserting the irrelevance of informational considerations and adverse selection. As Goodin (1988, p. 158) has pointed out, in the House of Commons debate on the introduction of National Insurance in 1911, Winston Churchill clearly had the problem of adverse selection in mind: 'Voluntary schemes of unemployment insurance . . . have always failed because those men likely to be unemployed resorted to them, and, consequently, there was a preponderance of bad risks . . . which must be fatal to the success of the scheme' (Hansard, 1911, vol. 26, col. 495). And, while the problem of moral hazard may be as great with state as with private insurance, the compulsion entailed in social insurance may be expected to overcome adverse selection.

The difficulty which I have is with relating the economic analysis to the policy issue. To begin with, suppose that in the case of unemployment insurance there are a large number of people with a high risk and that a competitive separating equilibrium exists. If so, then a feature of the account just given is that the group unable to obtain full insurance cover is the low-risk group – just as in the original 'lemons' analogy of Akerlof (1970), it is the sellers of *good* used cars who lose out from the absence of full information, not those who own wrecks. In the insurance context, 'ce sont les bons risques qui sont pénalisés par l'asymétrie d'information' (Laffont, 1981, p. 40). Yet, it is the high-risk group that has generated most of the concern about the shortcomings of market insurance: the problems they face in obtaining *any* insurance. The adverse selection model, as set out above, does not explain these problems.

On the other hand, suppose that no competitive equilibrium exists, as may happen where there are a small number of people with a high risk, a situation which may apply to retirement pensions (the 'risk' being longevity). It does not then follow that there will be no insurance. Indeed, as Hellwig (1983) pointed out, no insurance is also not an equilibrium, since a single firm as a monopolist will find it profitable to enter the market. We have therefore to consider the characteristics of a monopolistic or monopolistically competitive equilibrium. As has been shown by Jaynes (1978), and by Hellwig (1983) in the case of moral hazard, the conclusions are highly sensitive to the assumptions made about the information held by firms.

This illustrates the more general difficulty that the conclusions drawn from this kind of model depend sensitively on the precise formulation. This applies to the concept of equilibrium, where alternative definitions to those of Rothschild and Stiglitz (1976) have been proposed by Wilson (1977) and Riley (1979) or where there may be an equilibrium in mixed strategies (Dasgupta and Maskin, 1986). It applies to the structure of moves in the market, where Hellwig (1987) has contrasted a 'two-stage game', where insurance companies make binding offers of contracts and then individuals select among them, with a 'three-stage game', where the company can subsequently reject the application for insurance. He goes on to say that:

> the discrepancy between the predictions of the different game-theoretic models presents a fundamental dilemma. On the one hand, it is important [to] determine which of the different models is appropriate for the market at hand. On the other hand, this may be impossible to determine because matters like the order in which people make moves, which make all the difference for the game-theoretic specification, may not be observable and may not even be fixed in a given market. (Hellwig, 1987, p. 325)

In other words, the actual outcome may depend a great deal on the way in which the market operates. More institutional structure needs to be provided, and it is not evident that firm predictions can be made on the basis of the existing theory.

My third criticism of the analysis is that it is concerned with actuarial risk, rather than what is called *uncertainty* in the sense of Knight (1921).[3] It misses the important function of social insurance in providing for contingencies which are not foreseen, or to allay fears about events which we cannot forecast. As Giarini and Stahel have argued, 'The development of social security can be attributed mainly to changes in social philosophy, which in turn is conditioned by the changing levels and characteristics of risks and vulnerability produced by the modern environment' (1989, p. 38). The set of contingencies over which people formed probabilities years ago may have excluded the breakdown of the extended family, or the development of modern medicine, simply because they were inconceivable. This is not an aspect that I shall seek to develop here, except to note the interesting work of Bewley (1988 and 1989) on Knightian decision theory involving uncertainty aversion and inertia, which makes reference to unemployment insurance.

Finally, before drawing any conclusions about the explanation of, or justification for, social insurance, one has to ask whether there are other transactions which may play an equivalent role, and this is the subject of the next section.

11.3 The equivalence of transactions

The view of social insurance criticised in the previous section may appear to non-economists as a peculiarly inward-looking approach to the subject, seeking to define a problem in relation to a reference point (a complete set of insurance markets) which has little intrinsic interest. It may be another case of economists looking for an object under the lamp-post rather than where it was lost. There are however respects in which the economic literature may offer insights, in particular the *equivalence of transactions*. As Barro (1974) articulated in the case of inter-generational transfers, where people are linked through a series of transactions, a change in one type of transfer (or tax) may simply cause offsetting changes elsewhere. Where for instance people are already saving for old age, the introduction of a compulsory government pension scheme on the same terms may simply displace the private saving.

In the present context, we have therefore to ask not simply why private insurance does not exist, but also why there are no equivalent transactions. This insight is not of course limited to economists. Briggs asks in his essay on 'The Welfare State in Historical Perspective', 'Why not rely for "welfare" on the family, the church, "charity", "self help", "mutual aid" (gild, trade union, friendly society) or "fringe benefits" (business itself)?' (1961, p. 229).

The answer depends on the nature of the contingency, but there appear to be cases where equivalent transactions may exist. Suppose that people experience spells of both employment and unemployment. Why can they not even-out consumption by borrowing and lending on the capital market? The same question arises even more obviously in the case of pensions, where private provision for retirement is at the heart of the life-cycle savings theory and if people are forward-looking, there appears no need for social insurance (see the discussion in Kessler, 1989).

The typical response is that capital markets are imperfect, and in particular that there are limited possibilities for borrowing: 'What makes unemployment so painful ... is not the loss in lifetime income, but the inability of individuals to borrow to meet current needs. Thus the true problem was not a problem of insurance, but a problem of capital markets' (Stiglitz, 1989, p. 65). Flemming (1978) has emphasised the importance of the capital market assumptions in the optimal design of unemployment insurance; Diamond (1977) has drawn attention to the problem of securing a safe real return for the smaller investor seeking to accumulate funds for retirement. These considerations suggest in turn a further set of questions about the explanation for the emergence of social insurance and about its justification. Why are capital markets imperfect? It may be that the answer involves the same considerations of informational asymmetry, as in the literature on credit rationing (Stiglitz and Weiss, 1981), but the argument needs to be made – it cannot be taken for granted.

It is not however the capital market on which I focus here but the labour market, on the grounds that it is necessary to understand the contingencies against which social insurance provides protection. I therefore want to go back a stage and consider briefly the origins of first unemployment, and then retirement, as labour market phenomena.

11.4 Historical evolution of unemployment insurance

The first point to be made is that unemployment is a relatively recent concept. According to the *Oxford English Dictionary* (1989), the word came into common use in Britain around 1895.[4] Its recent origins are well captured in the title of the book by Salais *et al.* (1986) about unemployment in France called *L'invention du chômage*, in which they see the emergence of unemployment as associated with a particular form of labour market situation. As described by Piore in his review, the view of Salais *et al.* is that:

> the modern concept of unemployment derives from one particular employment relationship, that of the large, permanent manufacturing establishment. Employment in such institutions involves a radical separation in time and space from family and leisure time activity . . . When employment ties . . . are severed, there is an empty space in the worker's life which is sharply defined and that space is what is meant by unemployment. (1987, p. 1836)

On this view, as the economy industrialised and became urbanised, employment became all or nothing. A depression could leave industrial workers totally without resources, unable to fall back on home production or on the mixture of part-time employment and self-employment which might be found in rural society. At the same time, it would be misleading to draw a completely sharp distinction between industrial and rural employment. In the case of Britain, at least, the enclosure of common land, and the decline of cottage industry, may have left the landless agricultural labourer equally exposed to variations in the demand for labour. Rather than thinking simply in terms of a transition from agriculture to industry, there may be 'an intermediate phase of development in which the dependence on the market [of agricultural labourers] increases sharply (given the breakdown of the traditional peasant economy) and in which guaranteed entitlements in the form of social security benefits have yet to emerge' (Sen, 1977, p. 56).

The key element is that of wage labour. According to Garraty:

> Historically, unemployment has been distinctively associated with free-enterprise capitalism . . . because under capitalism labor is free (neither employer nor employee

is permanently obligated one to the other) and because, on the other hand, the system has increased the dependence of labor by separating workers from the ownership of the means of production. (1978, p. 5)

While the insecurity of wage employment was not confined to the industrialised, urbanised ('modern') sector, growth in this latter employment posed particular problems for the traditional forms of income support: 'methods of dealing with poverty and unemployment devised for pre-industrial societies broke down under the new conditions' (Garraty, 1978, p. 86). In Britain, while the Poor Law did provide some relief to the able-bodied in the textile areas of Lancashire and the West Riding in the middle of the last century (Boyer, 1990, chapter 8), its role was limited and, according to Harris, 'at least since 1870, the Poor Law had never been a major source of relief to the unemployed' (1972, p. 148). Rose similarly refers to 'the failure of the nineteenth-century poor law to cope with the problem of large-scale industrial unemployment' (1972, p. 40). Nor did private institutions succeed in filling the bill. It is true that there were, and indeed still are, trade union unemployment insurance schemes (Beenstock and Brasse, 1986), but the proportion of trade union members in the nineteenth century was small and the schemes had considerable difficulties.[5] In the present day, Oswald has examined the existence of negotiated private unemployment benefit plans in the US, concluding that the coverage of such plans 'is rather greater in manufacturing industry than may well be realized (although about half the workers still do not have such a scheme), but that [such plans] are almost nonexistent in the nonmanufacturing sector' (1986, p. 366). He goes on to ask why there is not more private unemployment insurance, a point to which I shall return.

11.5 The invention of retirement and retirement pensions

Retirement pensions are different from unemployment insurance and in Britain the first state pension explicitly rejected the insurance approach. Nevertheless, the relation with the new wage labour market is again central, as is brought out by Hannah (1986), who, at the same time that Salais was writing on the invention of unemployment, produced his study of the development of occupational pensions entitled *Inventing Retirement*. The parallel extends beyond the title, Hannah emphasises that 'for a proper understanding of this largely new phenomenon, we have to look to the employment relationship' (Hannah, 1986, p. 21).

Retirement, like unemployment, became a discrete event, in contrast to the earlier more gradual diminution of productivity. In 1913, Rubinow described how:

> the economic conditions of the wage-contract accentuate the economic disability of old age. Under normal physiological conditions, old age, unless preceded by a definite ailment, should lead to a gradual failing of the productive powers. As the medieval independent worker became old, he worked less and produced less, but he went on working as long as he could produce something. (1913, p. 304)

whereas under a wage system:

> the condition is altogether different. The economic disability of old age may arise suddenly while the aging worker is still fit for productive activity, but finds himself below the minimum level of productivity set by the employer ... Industrial efficiency, scientific management, Taylor system – these are all forces ... to use up human energy at greater speed ... and to dispense with it immediately its high degree of efficiency begins to decline. (Rubinow, 1913, pp. 304–5)

In this respect there is a close similarity with unemployment; there is however an important difference, which is that along with compulsory retirement came also the provision of occupational pensions.[6] As has been described by Hannah:

> Mandatory retirement, legitimised by more generous pensioning, conveniently allowed bureaucracies to buy themselves out of the expensive bias towards overpaying older workers implicit in their reward systems. In the twentieth century, such motives were commonly behind the expansion of existing pension schemes or the founding of new ones. (Hannah, 1986, pp. 135–6)

The coverage was not of course universal, being concentrated on the 'employees of "core" firms with internal labour markets and bureaucratic employment features' (Hannah, 1986, p. 29).

But, even if only benefiting a minority of workers, the private provision of retirement pensions was more developed than employer protection against unemployment. This difference in response to these two contingencies – unemployment and retirement – is one of the aspects that has to be incorporated into the analysis.

11.6 Social insurance and the labour market

The brief historical account suggests that, in order to understand the origins of social insurance, we have to consider the development of the economy. In chapter 10, I have used for this purpose a two-sector model of the economy, where unemployment is associated with one of the two sectors (the 'primary sector' in the terminology of Doeringer and Piore (1971), the other sector being referred to as the 'secondary sector'). In the primary sector, the problem of monitoring work effort causes employers to pay a wage premium, and this leads in turn to a 'queue' of unemployed workers seeking such jobs. There is in addition a continual process of job separations and imperfect matching of unemployed workers to vacancies. In the secondary sector, a job can always be found; although there may be underemployment or seasonal unemployment, workers are not solely dependent on wage labour. In this way, the move from the traditional agricultural sector to modern industry may be characterised as that from a lower level of income to one where the wage was higher but subject to the 'catastrophic' hazard of total unemployment. Unemployment emerges as part of the 'modernisation' of the economy. This is of course an oversimplification, not least because it leaves out of consideration the dualism within the traditional sector, where some people have entered the intermediate stage of pure wage labour.

In such a context, the introduction of state unemployment insurance benefits can (depending on the method of finance) act to subsidise employment in the industrial sector. It is quite possible that the British Poor Law performed a similar function with respect to agricultural employment (Boyer, 1990), but National Insurance was particularly relevant to the modern industrial sector. Not only was the original 1911 legislation specifically limited to certain industries, but the institutional provisions – the importance of which is often understated (see Atkinson and Micklewright, 1991) – restricted its effective coverage. Contribution conditions mean that new entrants to the labour force are not eligible and that those with irregular or short-term employment are excluded. Groups such as the self-employed or part-time workers may also be without cover. These exclusions are particularly relevant to the traditional sector, and there is a sense in which the institution of unemployment insurance should be seen, not as providing universal income maintenance, but as being functional in the development of the modern sector.

But we have to ask why such private insurance does not emerge spontaneously as part of the labour market contract. The role of employer-provided unemployment insurance has indeed been studied in the literature on implicit contracts. In certain cases, the payment of unemployment compensation, or severance payments, is an integral part of the analysis (for example, Grossman and Hart, 1981). In other cases, the payment of unemployment compensation is assumed to be ruled out (as in Azariadis, 1975). The latter is closer to what empirically is the case, but leaves open the question as to why employer transfers are not typically paid. We have also to ask why employer transfers at retirement are more prevalent. Occupational pensions, while far from universal, are of much greater significance; and this asymmetry requires explanation.

Several possible lines of explanation suggest themselves. The first is in terms of seniority, and trade union negotiations based on majority voting, as discussed by Oswald (1986). If layoffs are on the basis of last-in-first-out, then it is easy to see why a majority of union members may feel themselves less at risk from unemployment and hence not favour explicit or implicit provision of insurance through the labour contract. At the same time, they may well have a strong interest in the payment of pensions.

The second is in terms of efficiency wages and the need for a reward structure which elicits effort. Whereas severance payments may undermine the effectiveness of a wage premium paid to induce effort, delayed payment in the form of a retirement pension may form part of an efficient pay structure. Lazear (1981) argues that the need to ensure industrial discipline and loyalty may lead to a pay structure where earnings are not necessarily directly related to productivity at a particular date, with wages initially below and later above the value marginal product. Hence the need for compulsory retirement. Although Akerlof and Katz (1989) show that a simple labour discipline story does not necessarily lead to this result, their analysis does indicate the role of deferred pay, and without a determinate date of retirement, such a contract may well not be credible.

Thirdly, there is the effect of bankruptcy and the risk that the benefit may not be paid. Drèze (1979) suggested that this may be one explanation for the provision of social rather than private unemployment insurance. The same consideration is also likely to reduce the value of the pension promise, but it may have a much larger impact on the desirability of unemployment pay, since the two contingencies (unemployment of the worker and bankruptcy of the firm) are likely to be more highly correlated.

These aspects are suggestive; here, however, I would like to emphasise another aspect, which is that the role of social insurance has to be seen in terms of the *segmentation* of the labour force. By this I mean taking a richer view of segmentation, which goes beyond the dualism of industrial and non-industrial sectors described above, to consider dualism *within* the industrial sector. Within industry, and even within enterprises, there is differentiation of the labour contract. As an illustration, I refer to the finding in a French study of:

> duality *within* mining in France, an industry previously taken as the paradigm of a stable, fixed labour force. The division in the mines lay between a permanent labour force composed of skilled adult men and an unskilled, variable labor force composed of women, youth who had not yet completed their military service, part-time peasant workers, and foreign workers. (Work of Cornu, reported in Berger and Piore, 1980, pp. 26–7)

The differentiation within enterprises may apply to particular groups of staff, such as cleaners or catering staff, or to people doing the same job but on a contract or temporary basis. There has undoubtedly been considerable growth in 'flexible' contracts in recent years in a number of OECD countries.

This differentiation may go together with the elements just discussed. With collective bargaining in which permanent workers dominate the union side, one can see that there will be no pressure for unemployment benefit, but that there will be interest in negotiating private pensions with qualifying periods which exclude all but permanent workers.

11.7 Towards a richer model

This suggests that in seeking a theoretical framework to analyse the role of social insurance we should consider a richer model, which allows not just two sectors but for different types of employment in the two sectors. I have already noted the need to allow for the distinction in the secondary sector between pure wage labour and those who have access to other resources. It is however on the primary sector that I focus here, sketching a model based on the recent work of Saint-Paul (1990) and Bentolila and Saint-Paul (1992).[7]

There are in the primary (industrial) sector 'permanent' workers who have continuing employment, subject to only a bankruptcy risk. They are paid an efficiency wage premium, in part via a retirement pension. On the other hand, industrial firms also employ 'contract' workers on a short-term contract, which may be terminated without severance pay, and where no pension rights accrue. Contract workers are employed using a technology which requires no monitoring, so that no efficiency wage is paid, but is less productive and the unit labour costs are higher. The employer faces a firm-specific risk, which leads them to maintain a mix of permanent and contract workers (if there were no risk, then they would employ only permanent workers). (Alternatively, concern about uncertainty leads firms to maintain the flexibility of having a proportion of contract workers.) In response to a downturn in demand, the firm lays off contract workers and does not recruit new permanent workers. Other than in cases of bankruptcy, permanent workers are not laid off, the adjustment being achieved by natural wastage (which may include early retirement). Taken together with the distinction between wage labour and other workers in the agricultural sector, we have a *dual-squared model*, with two sectors and dualism within each sector.

In this situation, no private unemployment benefit is paid and private pensions are paid only to permanent workers. The introduction of social insurance may be seen as a response to this partial coverage, and the framework just sketched may be used to examine the likely effects. This may produce some unexpected conclusions. For example, it is conventionally argued, following Feldstein (1976), that state unemployment benefit without full experience rating increases the incidence of layoff unemployment. On the other hand, the existence of unemployment insurance may act as a subsidy to permanent employment in that it reduces the financial costs of bankruptcy to workers, and hence reduces wages. This may cause employers to switch from contract to permanent workers and hence reduce the incidence of layoffs.

This positive effect on permanent employment may be reinforced when we take account of the institutional features of unemployment insurance, such as contribution conditions. These may serve to exclude from unemployment insurance not just those outside the industrial sector but also those in contract jobs. Unemployed contract workers may be forced to become wage labour in the secondary sector, or to fall back on means-tested assistance. As Disney has argued, the institutions of social insurance are related to the segmentation of the economy. We have a kind of duality in benefit receipt. In advantaged employment, a worker 'is less frequently unemployed, is eligible for a range of lump sum and non-means-tested social security benefits and is primarily located in the National Insurance sector' (1982, p. 45), whereas a worker in less-favoured employment 'when unemployed, generally has insufficient contributions ... is subject to the various work-disciplining exclusions covering payment of national insurance benefit and is therefore primarily located in the means-tested subsistence sector' (1982, p. 45). Examination of the institutional details does indeed suggest a rather different side to social insurance, one which reflects, and reinforces, the pattern of labour market advantage and disadvantage rather than perform radical redistribution.

Conclusions: the future of social insurance

I should like to finish by drawing out briefly some of the implications of my analysis for the three areas of future policy to which I referred at the outset. Before doing so, I should emphasise once again that my coverage has been only partial. Just to give one instance, I have not considered the macro-economic aspects of social insurance which played an important part in its history, notably in the 1940s, when the Beveridge Plan was discussed with an eye not just to income distribution consequences, but also to the role of social insurance as automatic stabiliser.[8] I should similarly stress that the economic model outlined in section 2 is not enough on its own either to *explain* or to *justify* the introduction of social insurance. I am not espousing a purely functional explanation. In order to understand the reasons for its enactment at different dates, in different forms, in different countries, we have to examine the political economy of transfers. In order to make any statements about its desirability, the welfare economic basis needs to be articulated.

My aim has been to provide a framework within which the economic role of social insurance may be understood, and I hope that it provides some insights. First, and perhaps most important, it must be recognised that social insurance arose with a particular form of labour market situation and that this may change with the evolution of the economy. It is no accident that the proponents of the main alternative to social insurance – a universal basic income – have paid a great deal of attention to the labour market context (Parker, 1991). They have been well aware of the origins of social insurance in the industrialisation of the economy and the case for a basic income has been related specifically to the changing and more 'flexible' nature of employment, including greater reliance on contract labour, increased part-time employment and job sharing, increased labour market participation by married women, growth of self-employment, and earlier retirement. In a sense, the process of economic change may be seen as a reversal of the earlier transition to an industrial economy, with the secondary, notably service, economy now gaining at the expense of industrial employment. In this context, the dualism within the secondary sector, touched on earlier, acquires particular significance.

Secondly, the idea that social insurance is 'functional' in improving the working of the industrial labour market is likely to play a role in European Community negotiations similar to that played earlier this century at a national level. Labour and production remain the key area of Community activity, and it is primarily in this form that it will impinge on social policy, as witnessed by the replacement of the word 'citizen' by 'worker' in the final version of the Social Charter. Any reform at the national level must recognise that it is the interface with the labour market that will receive priority at the level of the European Community.

Thirdly, for countries in transition, it has to be remembered that while social insurance was a response to the inadequacies of the traditional safety net (the Poor Law), it did not itself provide a fully comprehensive income guarantee, not least because it was tied to participation in the modern labour force. There are limits to what can be achieved by this form of redistribution. While it is too strong to say with Keir Hardie that social insurance is simply 'a porous plaster to cover the disease that poverty causes' (quoted by Fulbrook, 1978, p. 129), I have indicated some of the reasons why I agree with Beveridge that 'social insurance should be treated as one part only of a comprehensive policy of social progress' (1942, p. 6).

In particular, the institutions of the labour market are not immutable. The existence of unemployment is not inevitable, nor must employment be an all-or-nothing phenomenon, as has been highlighted in work on the 'Fourth Pillar' (Kessler, 1990).

Part III

Targeting and the future of social security policy

12 On targeting and family benefits

Targeting is an attractive idea. The concentration of benefits on those in need is an objective which commands wide support. According to the Green Paper outlining the approach of the United Kingdom government to social security reform, 'the Government believe that resources must be directed more effectively to the areas of greatest need. . . . We must target the resources we have more effectively' (Department of Health and Social Security, 1985, p. 18). In policy terms, this is taken to mean a shift towards income-related transfers and away from universal benefits paid without a test of means.

For policy makers, there is much appeal in the idea that the existing total of transfers can be reallocated to increase their effectiveness in combating poverty. And simple arithmetic appears to support this view. In the United States:

> in 1983 outlays on means-tested cash assistance totalled $31 billion. . . . In that same year, the poverty gap, measured before the receipt of any means-tested transfers, was $63 billion. If all the money had been effectively targeted on the poor, it should have reduced the poverty gap to $32 billion, essentially cutting it in half. (Sawhill, 1988, p. 1101)

But in fact 'the poverty gap measured after the receipt of transfers was still $47 billion, implying that only $16 billion actually reached the poor' (Sawhill, 1988, p. 1101). Among the reasons for this apparent 'inefficiency' are that transfers were more than sufficient to raise people to the poverty line and that transfers were made to people already above the poverty line. Seen in terms of poverty alleviation, there appears to be scope for better targeting, particularly in the field of family policy which is the particular concern of this chapter.

However, although politically fashionable, calls for greater targeting need to be treated with caution. The argument in favour has to be made explicit and critically examined. Behind such policy recommendations lie views with regard to (a) the objectives of policy, (b) the range of instruments available to attain those objectives, and (c) the constraints under which policy has to operate (economic, political and social).

All too often policy debate is based on implicit assumptions about the nature of objectives. It is tacitly assumed that the sole objective of policy is the reduction of poverty, whereas the typical social security programme in Western countries has a multiplicity of objectives. Even if the alleviation of poverty were the over-riding concern, the relative efficiency of different policies would depend on the precise way in which poverty is measured and on the 'sharpness' with which the poverty objective is defined.

The range of policy options may be wider than commonly supposed. Whereas the choice of policy is frequently represented in gladiatorial terms, with 'universal' benefits opposed to 'targeted' benefits, in reality most transfers involve a degree of conditionality. The choices to be made are more subtle. Conditional transfers can take a variety of forms and offer scope for 'fine-tuning'. Consideration has to be given to the relation between social security and other areas of government policy, most obviously the personal income tax.

The case for greater targeting is typically based on the assumption of a fixed total budget for the social security ministry. The constraints on policy choice may however be more complex. The capacity of the government to target benefits depends on the information available to it and the extent to which it can verify information supplied by others. The constraints may be administrative, an aspect all too often ignored by economists. Account has to be taken of changes in the behaviour of recipients, and the limits to targeting may arise from the adverse incentives created. Targeting may affect the degree of political support for the programme and hence the funds available for poverty alleviation.

One of the aims of this chapter is therefore to caution against drawing oversimplified conclusions. As such, its role is negative, and practical implementation has indeed suggested that targeting is less straightforward than may appear at first sight. But there are also positive conclusions to be drawn. Instead of viewing the issue as an either/or choice ('uniform' versus 'targeted'), we can ask what are the appropriate conditions under which transfers should be made. The population is differentiated along many dimensions, and we have to ask which are the appropriate ones to take into account when determining benefit eligibility. How far can we allow for a range of objectives? How can we balance disincentive effects against effectiveness in meeting the redistributional goals. Taking account of the method of administration of benefits, we may be able to understand why certain policies are successful and others fail to reach their target. Two benefit systems with identical effects on the family budget constraint may have different implications depending whether the benefit administration identifies the recipient or whether there is self-selection by the participants.

This chapter examines the theoretical case for targeting and illustrates the analysis by reference to the experience of Western industrialised countries in targeting social security benefits for families with dependent children. This review of Western experience makes no pretence of being comprehensive, either in terms of schemes within one country or in terms of the countries covered. The focus is on programmes specifically directed at families with children, rather than on general programmes of cash transfers which benefit families with children. A country may for example have a general social assistance scheme, where the amounts paid increase with the number of child dependants, but this is not explicitly considered. In terms of countries, the United Kingdom receives particular attention, with reference also being made to other members of the European Community and the United States. Nor does the review aim to be up to date in terms of describing the policies of different countries; when a particular scheme is cited, it should not be inferred that it is currently in operation.

This chapter is particularly concerned with the relation between targeting and the reduction of poverty. However, as is stressed elsewhere in the book, social security has other important functions besides poverty alleviation. These include:

(a) smoothing of income over the life cycle in relation to people's needs,
(b) provision of security against events, such as sickness, disability, unemployment or bereavement (where these involve a loss of income but not necessarily poverty),
(c) redistribution towards those with dependants such as children (where this may reflect pro-natalist objectives),
(d) redistribution according to gender, and securing individual independence.

These objectives are not discussed here, but evidently must be taken into account in any assessment of the overall 'efficiency' of the social security system. Expenditure which is considered poorly 'targeted' when judged solely by the objective of alleviating poverty may well be directed at other objectives of the social security system. This might hardly seem worth saying, but much of recent debate seems to have lost sight of the fact that the relief of poverty is only one of the objectives of the transfer system. Indeed, historically in a number of Western countries it was not even the most important motive for the introduction of transfers: for example, in France 'social security was never primarily conceived as a tool to fight poverty. Security, in terms of protection against the risks and hazards of life, was its first, paramount objective' (Jallade, 1988, p. 248). The objective was seen less in individualistic terms and more in terms of solidarity:

> when statutory social insurance and family allowances were first introduced in the 1930s, their purpose was not to combat poverty but to establish a form of mutual support, *solidarité*, first between wage-earners, then between wage-earners' families and eventually among all categories of worker and family. (Ameline and Walker, 1984, p. 193)

The existence of wider objectives to social security may in turn have implications for the ability of the government to finance transfer programmes, the size of the poverty alleviation budget being dependent on the form of the transfer. There are those who suggest that highly targeted benefits to a minority of the population lack political support. The ILO report *Into the Twenty-First Century* commented that the argument that 'more generous provision could be made for the poor on an income-tested basis – seems at first sight to have a compelling logic' (International Labour Office, 1984, p. 23), but went on to say that 'people are more willing to contribute to a fund from which they derive benefit than to a fund going exclusively to the poor. The poor gain more from universal than from income-tested benefits' (1984, p. 23). The 'political economy' of targeting is not considered in this chapter, but is evidently important.

12.1 Targeting and the objectives of social security

Efficiency in alleviating income poverty

The objective of alleviating poverty is taken for present purposes to mean raising people to a specified 'poverty line', expressed in terms of income per equivalent adult using an appropriate equivalence scale. I refer to this poverty line as z and to the corresponding income variable as y, so that a person i with income y_i is in poverty where $y_i < z$.

The specification of the level and structure of the poverty line raises many difficult questions (some of which are considered later in this section,[1] but even when these issues of identifying the poverty population have been resolved there remains the problem of arriving at an aggregate measure of poverty. Among the aggregate measures in common use are the proportion of families with incomes below z (referred to as the headcount ratio, and denoted here by H) and the extent of the short-fall as measured by the poverty gap (denoted here by G), which is the total amount by which the incomes of the poor fall short of z, expressed per head of the total population.

The approach commonly taken to the measurement of efficiency may be

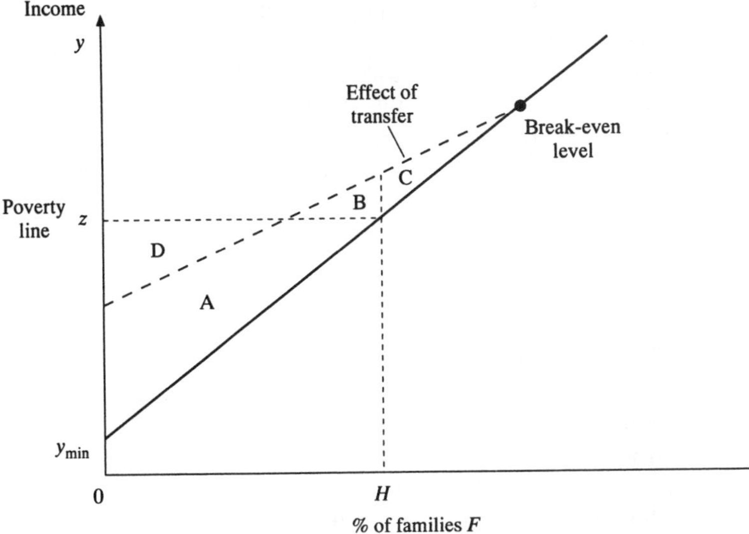

Figure 12.1 Measuring target efficiency: hypothetical example

illustrated by reference to figure 12.1, which is the inverse of the more usual cumulative distribution. All families are ranked in increasing order of income along the horizontal axis, and the solid line shows the income corresponding to a given percentile point in the distribution, so that for each proportion of the population, F, we can read off the highest income, y, found among the bottom F per cent. The lowest observed income is denoted by y_{min}. The diagram is drawn for the special case where the density function is uniform for y greater than or equal to y_{min}, so that the cumulative distribution, shown by the solid line, is a linear function of y. The distance between the solid line and the dotted line where $y = z$ measures the extent of shortfall from the poverty line, or the individual family's poverty gap. The aggregate gap, G, is measured by the total area between these lines.[2]

Figure 12.1 is based on the diagram given by Beckerman (1979 and 1979a), who defines the 'poverty reduction efficiency' of transfers as the extent to which they reduce the poverty gap. Suppose that the solid line in figure 12.1 represents the situation before transfers and the dashed line the cumulative distribution after transfers. Everyone is better off up to the break-even level of income (no account is taken here of the financing of the transfers). The reduction in the poverty gap is then indicated by the area A, and the poverty reduction efficiency of the transfers is measured by Beckerman by the ratio of the area A to the total transfers (A + B + C). The efficiency is less than 100 per cent to the extent that there are payments to the non-poor (C) and that there are 'excess' payments to the poor (B).

In these terms, the figures quoted earlier for the United States indicate that only $16 billion of the $31 billion means-tested cash assistance contributed to reducing the poverty gap, or a poverty reduction efficiency of 52 per cent. The estimates of Beckerman for four countries in the 1970s show the following results for total social security spending: Australia 56 per cent, Great Britain 49 per cent, Norway 44 per cent and Belgium 8 per cent (1979a, table 19).

Vertical and horizontal efficiency

A programme could score well on poverty reduction efficiency but still leave a high level of poverty. The dashed line in figure 12.1 could be shifted vertically downwards until the break-even point coincided with the poverty line, eliminating the areas B and C. But the poverty gap would still remain substantial. Alternatively, a relief programme could fill the poverty gap, but only for a fraction of those below the poverty line.

It was this consideration which led Weisbrod (1970) to introduce the distinction between *vertical* and *horizontal* efficiency: 'Two issues are involved, having to do with the accuracy of the program in assisting *only* the "target" group, and the comprehensiveness of the program in assisting *all* of that group' (1970, p. 125). The former – vertical efficiency – is that already discussed. The latter – horizontal efficiency – is defined by Weisbrod as 'the ratio of benefits going to the target group to the total benefits "needed" by that group' (1970, p. 125). In terms of figure 12.1, horizontal efficiency is measured by the ratio of the area A to (A + D). For the four countries studied by Beckerman (1979a, table 19), the horizontal efficiency of the social security programme was 74 per cent in Australia, 92 per cent in Norway, 96 per cent in Great Britain and 99 per cent in Belgium. This gives a rather different picture, in part because of differences in the total level of spending, from the measures of vertical efficiency cited in the previous section, where Australia scored best and Belgium worst.

The vertical and horizontal efficiency indicators above have been based on the poverty gap. Alternatively, they could be defined on the basis of the headcount measure of poverty. As Weisbrod noted, the indicator of horizontal efficiency is then 'the ratio of the number of beneficiaries in the target group to the total number of persons in the target group' (1970, p. 125). This indicator will lead to different answers. The programme represented by the dashed line in figure 12.1 achieves 100 per cent horizontal efficiency measured in this way, since all those below the poverty line benefit, and the same would be true if the dashed line were to be shifted vertically downwards until the break-even point coincided with the poverty line. Notions of 'efficiency' are not independent of the way in which we choose to measure poverty.

Explicit formulation of the poverty alleviation problem

Vertical and horizontal efficiency are therefore valuable indicators, but they are not on their own sufficient to guide policy formation. After all, a high level of horizontal efficiency may be achieved at great total cost; and we have seen that the value taken by the indicators depends on the choice of poverty measure. The indicators need to be related to the overall policy problem, with an explicit formulation of the objective and constraints. The statement that a particular programme has x per cent efficiency can only be interpreted in the context of such an explicit formulation.

Suppose that the government aims to maximise the poverty reduction achieved with a given budget,[3] and that, initially, the degree of poverty is measured by the poverty gap, which is given algebraically by

$$G/z = (1/n)\ \Sigma_i\ [(z - y_i)/z] \qquad (12.1)$$

where the sum is taken over those people with incomes below z, n denotes the total number of people, and the poverty gap has been normalised by dividing by the poverty line.

The policy aim is to minimise G subject to a government budget constraint. In general, this constraint has to take account of changes in behaviour by the recipients of transfers. Recipients may spend part of the transfer on taxed goods, generating additional indirect tax revenue, or on those subsidised by the government, increasing public spending. The beneficiaries may adjust their labour supply behaviour, affecting the receipts from income and other taxation. For the present, these second-round effects are not taken into account, it being assumed that the cost of a transfer is measured simply by the difference between pre-transfer and post-transfer incomes. (Possible changes in labour supply are considered in section 12.4.)

In this context, let us consider the class of transfer programmes represented by the dashed line in figure 12.1. If y denotes pre-transfer income, then net income is equal to a guaranteed income, b, minus a tax rate, t, times the pre-transfer income, with a break-even level at b/t. The intercept on the vertical axis shows the net income received by a family with the lowest pre-transfer income (equal to y_{min}). Three special cases are shown in figure 12.2: (i) $t = 0$, (ii) where the break-even level is set at the poverty line, so that $b = t\ z$, and (iii) $t = 1$. The special case where $t = 0$ is often described as a 'uniform' benefit, since it pays an equal amount, say b^*, to all

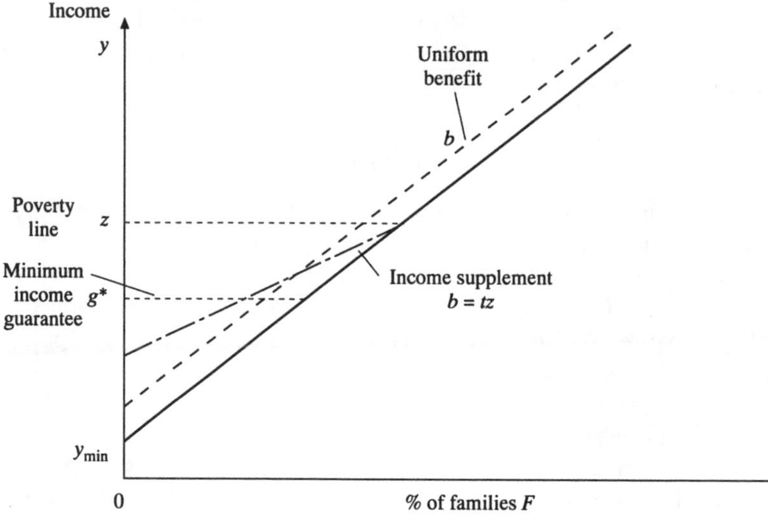

Figure 12.2 Three special cases of transfer programmes

families. Where t is positive, then the benefit may be said to be 'income-targeted'. In the special case where the break-even level is set at the poverty line, referred to as an 'income supplement', the poverty reduction inefficiency associated with the areas B and C in figure 12.1 is eliminated, since transfers are limited to those below the poverty line, and the transfer is less than the individual poverty gap. The same is true of the case shown where $t=1$, which provides a 'minimum income guarantee', g^*, which concentrates the transfer on the poorest, with net income becoming g^* for all y less than or equal to g^*.

How do these transfer programmes fare when compared according to the explicit poverty alleviation problem? The answer obviously depends on whether the total budget is sufficient to eliminate all poverty. If the budget allowed the poverty gap to be completely filled by a guaranteed income equal to z, then this policy could not be bettered. In what follows, it is assumed that the available budget is less than the total poverty gap.

To illustrate the comparison, let us take a numerical example which is used at several points in this chapter. While artificial, it provides a useful laboratory within which to explore the quantitative magnitudes. The example takes a poverty line of half average family income. It assumes a uniform distribution of incomes over the relevant range upwards from zero income (i.e., $y_{min}=0$). Taking the headcount as 30 per cent, the poverty gap is then $7\frac{1}{2}$ per cent of total income.[4] Suppose that the total budget is $2\frac{1}{2}$ per cent of total income, allowing an income supplement of $33\frac{1}{3}$ per cent, a

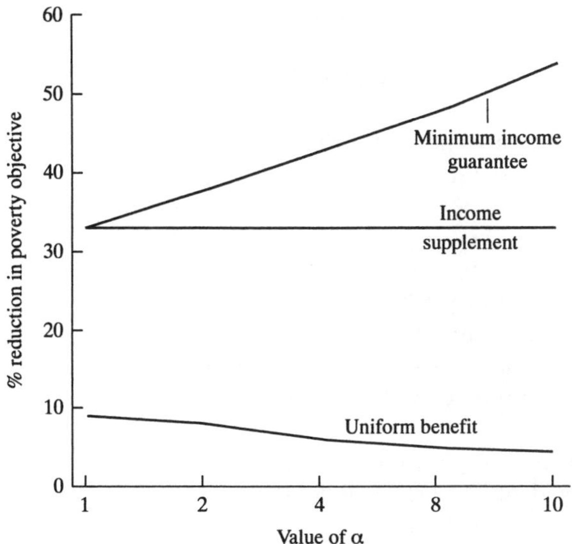

Figure 12.3 Effect of variation in poverty objective on relative efficiency of different types of transfer programmes

uniform payment equal to 5 per cent of the poverty line, and a minimum income guarantee of 57.7 per cent of the poverty line.[5]

Where the poverty measure takes the form of the poverty gap, the income supplement, or any other transfer limited to those below the poverty line, such as the minimum income guarantee, achieves the maximum reduction in poverty subject to the budget constraint. The value of the objective function is reduced to $(1-t)$ of its previous value, or by $33\frac{1}{3}$ per cent with our numerical example. The reduction achieved by the uniform transfer is considerably less: the gap falls by a factor $(1-b^*/(z-y_{\min}))^2$. In our numerical example, the value of the objective function is reduced by some 10 per cent – see the left hand of figure 12.3. Where the problem of poverty is that of a minority, the universal transfer does not score well on this measure of efficiency.

As has been brought out in the literature on poverty measurement,[6] success in reaching the anti-poverty objective may be measured in a variety of ways. There are not only the headcount and the poverty gap measures of poverty reduction, but objectives which give more weight to people who are a long way below the poverty line. A severe poverty gap may be of greater concern, £1 for £1, than a smaller poverty gap. Following Foster *et al.* (1984), we may introduce a parameter, α, that generates different forms[7]

$$(P_\alpha)^\alpha = (1/n)\ \Sigma_i\ [(z-y_i)/z]^\alpha \quad \text{where } \alpha \geq 1 \tag{12.2}$$

where values of α above 1 give more weight to larger individual poverty gaps.

If the objective function attaches more weight to larger poverty gaps, then the relative advantage of the income supplement rises. The reduction in the objective function continues to be a factor of $(1-t)$, but that from the uniform transfer is $(1-b^*/(z-y_{\min}))^{1+1/\alpha}$, which falls with α. The consequence in our numerical example is illustrated in figure 12.3. Where α equals 2, the reduction in poverty achieved by the uniform transfer falls to 7.5 per cent. In the limit, as α approaches infinity, all weight is attached to the poverty gap of the poorest person, which is reduced by $33\frac{1}{3}$ per cent in our numerical example, compared to a reduction of 5 per cent with the uniform payment.

It is also clear that, where the government attaches more weight to larger poverty gaps, the targeted income subsidy is not the most effective means of poverty reduction. A greater reduction in the objective function can be achieved by the minimum income guarantee, as is illustrated in figure 12.3. As α rises towards infinity, approaching a Rawlsian concern with only the least advantaged, the remaining level of poverty reduction reaches 57.7 per cent, compared with $33\frac{1}{3}$ per cent with the income supplement.

The formulation used to date does not include the headcount measure of poverty. As is well known, the largest reduction in the headcount is attained by concentrating transfers on those closest to the poverty line, since their poverty is the 'cheapest' to alleviate. The same applies with forms of the objective (12.2) with α positive but less than 1 (Bourguignon and Fields, 1990). In our numerical example, it would mean raising to the poverty line all those with incomes above $(1-\sqrt{t})z$ but transferring nothing to those below this level. The headcount would be reduced by 57.7 per cent. In contrast, the income supplement would fill only part of the poverty gap and hence would not reduce the headcount at all; in this respect, it would perform *less* well than the uniform payment, which in the numerical example reduces H by 5 per cent. The ordering of the two policies is reversed. The same is true of the comparison of the uniform payment with the minimum income guarantee.

The headcount may continue to be popular in broad statistical analyses of the extent of poverty, but it seems of limited applicability in the present context. A policy calculated to reduce the poverty score by concentrating help on the *better off* of the poor, while denying it to those most in need, is not what most people appear to have in mind when they talk of targeting.

The 'sharpness' of objectives

The crucial role played by the form of social objectives in this field may lead us to be more questioning about their formulation. The efficiency advantage of the income supplement arises because we are agreed that the poverty line is z. A marginal \$1 received by a person below z is valued in full but a marginal \$1 to a person above z is valued at zero.

Such a 'sharp' representation of social objectives may not however be universally accepted. There may well be disagreement about the location of the poverty line. What one person may see as 'wasteful' expenditure on the non-poor, another may regard as contributing to the reduction of poverty. We have then to consider a range of possible poverty lines (see Atkinson, 1987). Alternatively, there may be agreement about the location of z, but concern for the 'near-poor', or the group above but close to the poverty line.

A wider distributional objective – while still concerned with poverty – may give some weight to transfers received within a range of the poverty line. Following the procedure of Ribich (1968), we may set a higher level so that transfers within a certain distance of the poverty line receive a positive weight (although less than that below the poverty line). Another approach, that explored here, is to combine a 'high' value of the poverty line with a form of the objective function (12.2) with values of the parameter α greater than 1, 'shading' the poverty objective, allowing differential weights to be attached to different poverty gaps.

With such a less 'sharp' objective, the relative efficiency of the different transfer schemes is changed. We have seen that with the adoption of a value of the parameter α greater than 1, the minimum income guarantee (and the income supplement) become more efficient. The raising of the poverty line, on the other hand, has the opposite impact. From figure 12.2, we may see that a rise in the poverty line brings with it a rise in the number of beneficiaries from the uniform transfer who are 'deserving' according to the poverty criterion, but that there is no increase in the case of the minimum income guarantee, which remains fixed at g^* (the total budget being held constant). In relative terms, the poverty reduction falls for both transfer programmes, but the fall is much larger for the minimum income guarantee.

Suppose for example that we take α equal to 2, a value commonly used in empirical work. The minimum income remains at the same level as before in our example, which is 28.9 per cent of average income; the uniform transfer is 2.5 per cent of average income. With the poverty line set at 50 per cent of average income, the efficiency of the minimum income guarantee is such that it reduces the poverty measure by 38 per cent, compared with 7.5 per

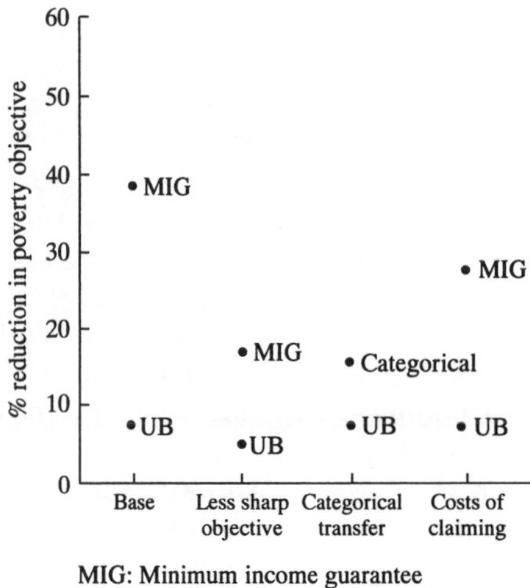

Figure 12.4 Relative efficiency of uniform benefit and minimum income guarantee in different situations ($\alpha=2$)

cent for the uniform transfer, as shown in figure 12.3. On the other hand, if we take a 'high' poverty line of 75 per cent of average income, then the reduction achieved by the minimum income guarantee becomes 18 per cent, compared with 5 per cent with the uniform transfer. The relative superiority of the minimum income guarantee is less when we adopt this less 'sharp' objective, as illustrated in figure 12.4. (The other points in figure 12.4 are discussed later.)

Evaluation of individual welfare

Lack of sharpness in objectives does not simply affect the aggregate poverty measure; it may also apply to the assessment of individual welfare.

As a first example, we may refer to the relative poverty rates for different-sized families, which are sensitive to the choice of equivalence scale used to put their incomes on a comparable basis. The potential room for disagreement may be illustrated if, as in chapter 4, we approximate the family equivalence scale by N^{γ}, where N is the number of members of the family.[8] Then, according to Buhmann *et al.* (1988), scales based on subjective evaluation of family needs tend to give relatively low values of γ (around 0.25), whereas those based on observed consumer spending behaviour (and identifying restrictions) tend to be rather higher (say 0.36), those based on expert assessment of consumption baskets tend to be higher still (around 0.55), and finally the scales applied in official statistics tend to be associated with values of around 0.72. Adopting a high value of γ, such as that applied in official statistical practice, would give a higher proportion in poverty among large families, whereas the low values of γ, such as those found in subjective evaluations, would give a smaller proportion.

The extent to which variation in the equivalence scales for different types of family can produce significantly different impressions is illustrated by figure 12.5, based on the results of Buhmann *et al.* (1988). This shows the relative rates of poverty, defined as 50 per cent of the median income, with the four different equivalence scales identified above, for the overall population and for the sub-group of couples with two or more children (it also shows the position for single mothers, which is discussed below). In the US, the overall poverty rate is much the same for all four scales, but that for couples with two or more children rises from under half the overall rate to nearly the same level, as we move from the subjective scale to those based on official statistical practice. A minimum income guarantee calculated on the basis of a subjective equivalence scale would provide less help, relatively, to families with children and its performance in targeting help would appear less impressive when judged by the statistical scale. The same is true in Australia and Canada, where the poverty rate for couples with two or more children in fact rises above the overall average when we move to the scale based on official statistical practice. In the UK the poverty rate for couples with two or more children is around a quarter of the overall rate with the subjective scale, suggesting that this group are less of a priority, but the rate rises to the national average with the statistical scale. (In this case the overall poverty rate falls as we move to the right.)

A second example of potential disagreement about objectives concerns the treatment of earned incomes. As has been emphasised in the recent contributions of Kanbur, Keen and Tuomala (1990) and Besley and Coate (1992), there is a difference between evaluating the position of individuals in terms of their *consumption* and evaluating their *utility*, where the latter takes account of the disutility of work. To make the point, we may note that corresponding to a constant elasticity labour supply function with elasticity β (used later in section 12.4)

$$l = w^{\beta} \tag{12.3}$$

where w is the wage rate, the indirect utility function can be written as

$$v = wl/(1+\beta) + m \tag{12.4}$$

where m denotes benefit and other (unearned) income. It is the level of indirect utility that would enter a 'welfare' measure of poverty, with labour income being discounted by a factor $(1+\beta)$ which allows for the cost of

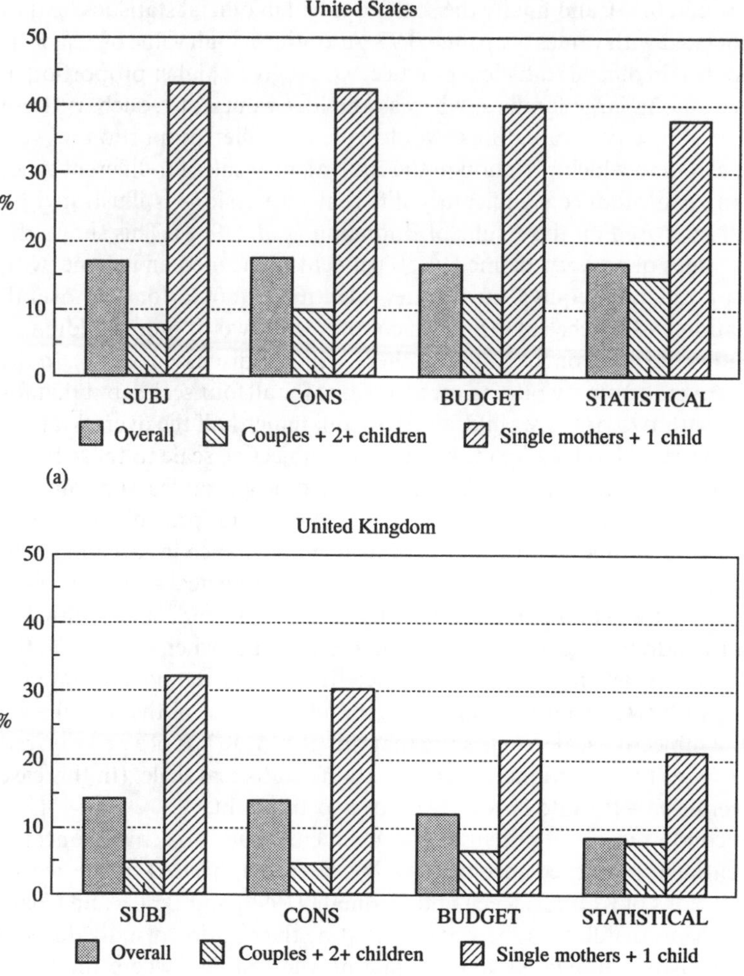

Figure 12.5 Proportions in poverty with different equivalence scales
Source: Buhmann *et al.*, 1988, tables 10 and 12.

working. In contrast, as Kanbur, Keen and Tuomala point out, the policy debate gives no weight to the disutility of effort, and the individual situation is evaluated in terms of $wl + m$. The difference between these two valuations can affect the conclusions drawn regarding working families: the group identified as below a specified poverty line is different.

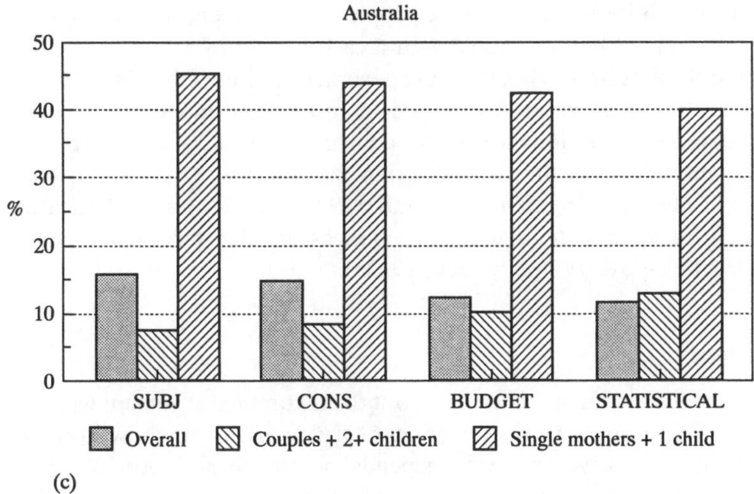

(c)

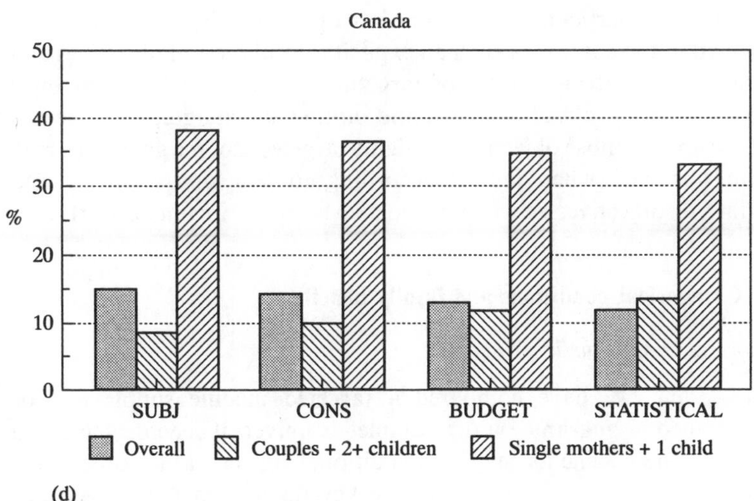

(d)

Figure 12.5 (*cont.*)

A third, related, example is that the claiming of benefits may involve costs for the recipient, either of time or money. There is then a question as to whether these costs should be deducted. Individuals may evaluate their welfare, and base their decision whether or not to claim, on the net position, but the government may determine their poverty status according to their gross income, if only because the cost may be difficult to measure. Again, the 'policy' definition excludes some people who consider their own welfare level to be below that attainable with a cash benefit of z.

Behind these examples lies the more general question of the dimension of poverty with which we are concerned. A move from income poverty to measures based on notions of utility is controversial; and the evaluation of poverty may be based on non-utilitarian foundations, as in the capacity approach advocated by Sen (1985 and 1992). The adoption of such an approach may lead to significant changes in the recommendations regarding anti-poverty policy (Sen, 1992a).

Conclusion

The aim of this section has been to set out the theoretical argument which is implicit in many of the calls for greater targeting, and to show how the assessment of relative efficiency depends on the formulation of social objectives and the constraints under which they can be achieved. The statement that a particular programme has x per cent efficiency can only be interpreted in the context of such an explicit formulation of objectives and constraints. The attractiveness of targeting depends on how narrowly defined are the objectives of policy, and on how much agreement there is about the form of those objectives. A highly targeted income guarantee may perform less well when judged according to less sharp criteria and according to objectives other than the alleviation of income poverty.

12.2 Categorical conditions and family benefits

Categorical conditions in principle

To this point, we have compared a targeted income supplement or minimum income guarantee with a completely universal benefit, whereas in practice all these benefits may be conditional on indicators other than income. As Barr (1987) brings out, the key distinction is that between conditioning on income and conditioning on other variables. For instance, child allowances, often cited as an 'inefficient' use of the transfer budget, are focused on families with children, and their relative efficiency depends on the incidence of poverty among this group.

The use of indicators other than income, referred to here as 'categorical conditions', may be seen in the context of the earlier formulation. With the poverty measure (12.2), Kanbur (1987) shows that the effect of a marginal universal transfer to a group i on the measure P^{α}_{α} is proportionate to the value of $P^{\alpha-1}_{\alpha-1}$ for the group i. The marginal reduction in the poverty gap (α equal to 1) achieved by a universal payment to group i is proportionate to the proportion in poverty in that group. This provides justification for the policy which appears often to be implicitly adopted of giving priority to groups with a high poverty count. On the other hand, it depends on the choice of poverty measure. If we were to take a value of α equal to 2, then the marginal reduction would be indicated by the poverty gap for group 1, rather than the headcount. This may well give a different order of priority for the allocation of a marginal increase in transfers.

In terms of an explicit minimisation exercise, where the objective function takes the form of the poverty gap, the universal transfers would be allocated so as to equalise the poverty proportions. If there is a requirement that the transfers be non-negative, then this may involve no transfer being made to certain groups with a low poverty headcount. With α equal to 2, the first-order conditions for optimal allocation of a given budget require that the poverty gap be equalised across groups.

The potential gain from the use of categorical conditions may be seen from the earlier illustrative example. Suppose that the overall poverty rate of 30 per cent (with a poverty line of half average income) is the average of that for two equal-sized groups, with poverty rates of 10 per cent and 50 per cent, where the distribution is uniform over the range from zero to the poverty line (but the density is five times in the latter case). Where the transfers are constrained to be non-negative, the maximum reduction in poverty is obtained by concentrating the universal transfer on the group with the highest poverty rate for all values of α less than 15. The reduction in the poverty gap that can be achieved in this way is 16 per cent, compared with some 10 per cent with an unconditional universal transfer.

Policy towards families with children

In practice, one of the main groups singled out in anti-poverty policy is that of families with children. Family poverty is an important issue on the agenda of many industrialised countries. In the United States, it became evident during the 1980s that, while poverty among the elderly was declining, that among families with children was on the increase (Preston, 1984 and Palmer *et al.*, 1988). If the situation is less dramatic in other countries, there are nonetheless similar concerns about the growth of child poverty – see Smeeding, Torrey and Rein (1988) and Cornia (1990), for an international comparison. In the UK, the Green Paper on the *Reform of Social Security* stated that:

> In the 1930s working-age families were seen as the main group in poverty: the main causes being unemployment and low earnings among men with large families. By the 1950s and 1960s pensioners were the major cause for concern. Now the position

has changed again and in 1985 it is families with children who face the most difficult problems. (Department of Health and Social Security, 1985, p. 2)

At the same time, the identification of high priority groups depends on the nature of social objectives. The choice of a poverty line of 40 per cent of median income may lead to a quite different picture of composition of the poverty population from the choice of a 60 per cent cutoff. Moreover, as emphasised earlier, the sharpness of the objective concerns not just the level of the poverty line but also its structure. As is apparent from figure 12.5, the poverty rate for couples with children, relative to that of the overall population, depends on the choice of equivalence scale.

This brings out how a lack of sharpness with regard to social objectives may limit the scope for targeting, not just by income testing, but also by categorical criteria. There may be differences in view with regard to the treatment of different categories of the population, and hence to the desirability of differentiating transfers on this basis. At the same time, the findings in figure 12.5 for single mothers with one child show that there may nevertheless be categorical conditions which allow priority groups to be unambiguously identified. The poverty rate for single mothers is considerably above the overall rate for all equivalence scales shown.

As the example of single mothers illustrates, there are in fact many possible dimensions along which transfers to families could be differentiated in addition to the number of children. The range of possibilities include:

(a) payment of lump sums at birth, possibly with special provisions for multiple births (a further distinction is between payments during pregnancy versus childbirth benefits),
(b) relating cash payments, or paid leave, at birth to labour market status, as in the provision to employees of maternity leave (a further distinction is that between maternity and parental leave),
(c) in the case of continuing child benefits, the amount per child may be varied with the number of children, rising less than proportionately with the family size (for example, where there is an additional family premium), or more than proportionately (for example where no child benefit is paid for the first child),
(d) child benefit may be varied with the age of the child,
(e) the amount of child benefit may be varied with the labour market status of the parents, including extra payments where there is a single wage earner, or where one parent remains at home to take care of the child,
(f) payments for child care costs of those in work,
(g) there may be special payments for single-parent families,
(h) the definition of a 'child' is open to a number of interpretations and may

be related to age, to educational status, labour market status, residence, or other criteria,

(i) the payments may vary geographically, as between rural and urban areas.

As this (incomplete) list indicates, there is considerable scope for the variation of transfers in order to achieve a greater reduction in poverty. Once again, this has to be qualified by the need to reach agreement about the nature of objectives. This is well illustrated by (d) above, where the direction of the differential with age is less than evident. Increased needs with age for food and clothing point to an allowance which increases with age; on the other hand, there are those who argue for a higher allowance for children below school age in view of the greater child care costs.

It should also be noted that benefits with respect to children may take the form of tax allowances rather than cash payments. Insofar as the amount of tax paid depends on variables such as the number of children, there are 'tax expenditures' which have an effect equivalent to the provision of family benefits, and we may ask about the efficiency with which they are targeted in just the same way as for cash benefits.

Evolution of child benefit in the UK

How far in practice has targeting by categorical criteria been applied in family policy? The pattern of family benefits varies a great deal across countries – even among those at a similar level of development. This is demonstrated by the contrast between the United States, which has no universal child benefit, and almost all other major industrialised countries, which do provide such a benefit. And among the latter group, there are large differences in the structure and operation of the benefit.

In this section, we describe the situation in the United Kingdom, taking this as a case study. After a long campaign before the Second World War, it was accepted that help for children should form part of the state social security system and a crucial assumption underlying the Beveridge Plan for Social Security was that family allowances would be paid. The case for the introduction of family allowances was based by Beveridge on two main grounds. The first was that 'social surveys of Britain between the two wars show . . . that the want which remained was almost wholly due to two causes – interruption or loss of earning power and large families' (1942, p. 154). The second was a concern with maintaining a gap between incomes in and out of work. If adequate support was to be given to those who were unemployed or sick, then this required 'giving allowances for children in time of earning or not-earning alike' (1942, p. 154). (He also referred to pro-natalist arguments.) The provision of child benefit in this way contributes to both incentive and anti-poverty objectives. Family allowances, in the form of a cash payment to the mother, were introduced in 1944.

In the 1970s, family allowances were amalgamated with the (much older) income tax allowances for children. By eliminating the child income tax allowances, which increased in value with the marginal rate of income tax and hence with taxable income, the government was able to pay a more generous child benefit. This is an illustration of the government taking a wider view of policy instruments, planning social policy and fiscal policy in conjunction rather than in isolation.

The UK child benefit was designed as a universal payment equal per child. However, along with this apparent simplicity there has in fact been considerable differentiation along the lines described earlier. To take the same lettering as above:

(a) until it was abolished in 1987, a lump-sum maternity grant per child was paid for all confinements,
(b) maternity pay is provided for those in employment prior to the birth,
(c) when family allowances were introduced in 1944, they were paid for all children except the first in the family, the exclusion of the first child being justified by the assertion that even low wages were sufficient to support a family of this size. From 1956, the differentiation was taken further, with a higher rate being paid for the third and subsequent children. The introduction of child benefit led to uniformity of payments, until 1991 when a higher rate was introduced for the first child,
(d) child benefit has not varied with the age of the child, but the income tax allowances for children did vary with age,
(g) a uniform payment is made to all one-parent families (One-Parent Benefit).

Experience in a range of countries

The possibilities for a greater degree of targeting by a richer categorisation are illustrated by the experience of other Western countries.

In many countries, child benefits are differentiated according to family size and the age of the children. In table 12.1, the pattern of variation is summarised for countries in the European Community (except Italy). In two countries benefit is uniform; in three it increases with family size; and in four it increases both with family size and age. So that, in France, the analogous benefit to the UK child benefit, the *allocation familiale*, makes no payment for the first child and a smaller payment for the second child than

Table 12.1. *Variation of child benefit with age of child and family size in European Community* 1990

		AGE OF CHILD Same benefit per child	Increases with age	Decreases with age
FAMILY	Same benefit per child	United Kingdom (pre-1991) Spain Portugal		Denmark
	Benefit increases with size	Germany Greece Ireland	Belgium France Luxembourg (up to 3 children) Netherlands	
	Benefit decreases with size	United Kingdom (post- 1991)		

for the third and subsequent children. There are age premia for older children. Whereas the amount for a two-child family is broadly similar in France and the UK, there is a strong 'tilt' in France in favour of larger families and older children (Atkinson, 1987a). The Dutch structure has three age bands (increasing with age up to 16, but with a lower rate above that age), and is graded more finely with the number of children, including benefit for the first child. The German benefit is paid for the first child and increases with the number of children, although not with age. In Denmark, in contrast to Benelux and France, a higher amount of child benefit is paid to younger children.

In Norway and Sweden the amount per child increases with the number of children: for example, in Sweden in 1990 the amount received by a family with six children was 12 times that received by a family with one child (NOSOSO, 1993, p. 59). In Finland and Iceland a higher rate is paid for younger children. In Canada, the Federal Family Allowance is uniform per child, but the Family Allowance Act 1973 allowed provincial governments to vary the allowance with the age of the child and the number in the family. Quebec and Alberta have availed themselves of this provision.

Any comparison of benefits has to take account of the relation with the tax system. The restructuring of child benefit in the Netherlands in 1980 was similar to that in the UK in that income tax allowances were abolished (Holmans, 1987) and the same applies in Denmark. However, in Germany tax allowances were re-introduced after their earlier abolition, and there is a supplement to the family benefit for those families whose income is too low to take advantage of the tax allowance (European Commission, 1990, p. 154). In France the income tax offers significant benefits to tax payers with children. Under the French *quotient familial*, the tax charged depends on income divided by the number of 'parts'. Each adult receives one part, and each child a half part, with a whole part for the third and subsequent children. This means that a couple with three children pay the same average tax rates as a single person earning a quarter of their income. Although there is an upper limit to the relief that may be given for children by the quotient system, for any given family size the system is of greatest benefit to those with the highest marginal tax rates (Atkinson, Bourguignon and Chiappori, 1988 and Glaude, 1991).

In addition to age and family size, there are a number of other dimensions which may be varied within the universal child benefit programme. For instance, the definition of an eligible child may differ. The normal age limit varies within the European Community from 14 in Portugal, 16 in the UK, Ireland and Germany, 17 in France and Netherlands, to 18 in Belgium, Denmark, Greece, Spain, Italy and Luxembourg (European Commission, 1990). Above this normal age limit, there is further variation in qualifying conditions. In the United Kingdom, a child for the purposes of child benefit can be aged 16–18 if in full-time school education. Those studying in higher education, for professional qualifications, or taking an apprenticeship are excluded. In contrast, the German benefit is payable with respect to those aged 16–27 who are students or trainees with educational scholarships of less than a specified amount. In France, benefit is payable with respect to children aged up to 20 where they are apprentices, undergoing professional education or students, providing that their income does not exceed 55 per cent of the minimum wage.

A second example as to how the targeting of the benefit may be refined concerns the definition of the recipient. In the UK, the payment of the child benefit to the mother has played an important role, and reflects concern with the distribution of income within the family. Even if the family or household is taken as the unit, the question as to *who* actually receives the transfer may affect the outcome.

Income-testing and categorical conditions

The use of categorical conditions may be an alternative to income testing, or it may be complementary. Almost all means-tested social security schemes are in practice conditional not just on income but also on satisfying criteria and many are limited to sub-groups of the population.

A number of countries have attempted to target child benefits by relating them to family income, but this has taken different forms. First, the child benefit itself could be related to income. In Germany, the benefit for the second and subsequent children is reduced to approximately half its value if the parental annual income exceeds a specified figure. In Australia, the previously universal family allowance became subject to an income test in 1987; according to the estimates of Saunders (1991, figure 4), in 1989 this reduced the expenditure by some 12 per cent compared with the level without an income test. A more thorough-going income-relation is to be found in Italy, where since 1988 the family allowance is paid in inverse relation to the family income and in direct relation to the number of family members (European Commission, 1990). As a result, the benefit is scaled progressively down as income rises, until it is extinguished.

A second approach is to operate alongside child benefit a separate income-tested scheme for families with children. In the UK, in 1970, when the Conservative government was elected with a pledge to 'tackle the problem of family poverty', they rejected an across-the-board increase in family allowances and introduced an income-tested Family Income Supplement (FIS). This benefit combined being both income tested and categorical, being limited to families with children and to those headed by a full-time worker. The amount paid fell progressively with family income and was extinguished at a relatively low level of income. Although benefiting only a small proportion of families, the scheme has since then formed a significant part of government policy, and in the 1988 social security reforms it was revised and extended as Family Credit. In 1990–1 there were on average 320,000 families in receipt, or some 5 per cent of families receiving child benefit. A rather similar history has been followed in Australia, where a Family Income Supplement Scheme for working families with children was introduced in 1982–3, and then substantially extended in 1988, when the scheme was re-named Family Allowance Supplement.

The French income-tested Complément Familial presents an interesting contrast to the UK Family Credit, in that it is not restricted to those in work, but is restricted to families with three or more children, or with one child aged under three. Moreover, it is less sharply tapered with income, the ceiling for payment extending considerably further up the income scale. This latter feature means that the proportion of all families in receipt is

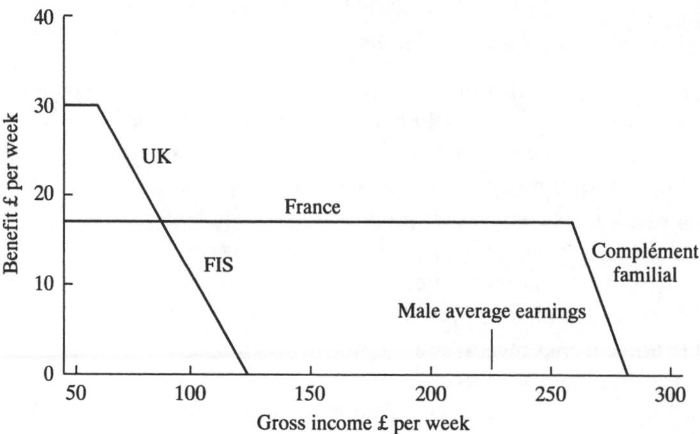

Figure 12.6 Income-related benefits in France and the UK (couple and three children aged under 11)

considerably higher in France. Despite the categorical restrictions, in 1988 the number of recipients was over 700,000 (Ministère des Affaires Sociales, 1990, p. 159), or some 10 per cent of all families, including those with one child. The transfers in France and the UK in 1987 are compared in figure 12.6 for a couple with three children (the amounts have been converted at an exchange rate of 9.5 francs to £1). Whereas FIS in the UK was tapered out at a relatively low level of earnings (at that time the average male earnings were about £225 a week), the Complément Familial continued to be paid until well above average earnings.

The experience of France and the UK shows the scope for choice between tapering at modest levels of income, confining the benefit to low-income families, and tapering at a relatively high level, excluding the upper-income groups. An upper taper can also be achieved by subjecting family benefits to income tax. In the latter case, the income tax operates like a test of means, reducing (although not eliminating) the value of the payment to families with higher incomes. The extent of tapering of the net benefit depends on the structure of marginal rates of tax. With a flat-rate tax, the only differentiation is between tax payers and non-tax payers; with a graduated rate structure, going up say by 5 per cent steps, the net benefit can be quite finely tuned. There may in this regard be gains from the co-ordination of fiscal and transfer policy.

The taxation of benefit may however differ from an income test in the unit of assessment. Income tests are typically applied to the family unit, or to a wider household definition. Income tax is more commonly applied to a narrow family unit or to the individual. Where there is independent taxation of husbands and wives, the tapering achieved by taxation depends on whether the benefit is taxed in the hands of the husband or the wife.

Conclusion

The choice of family benefits is considerably richer than is suggested by a simple opposition of uniform and income-tested transfers. In principle family benefits can be differentiated in a variety of ways, which may be combined with income relation; income testing may take different forms. The experience of Western countries indicates that a wide variety of types of family benefit have been implemented in practice.

12.3 Problems in targeting: imperfect information and administration

Imperfect targeting

The scope for governments to target benefits effectively is limited not just by the budgetary cost, which has been the sole constraint taken into account above, but also by administrative considerations and by the impact on economic incentives. In this section, we examine the problems of imperfect information and administration.

Imperfect targeting may arise on account of errors in administration. The conditions for receipt of a transfer such as child benefit may be perfectly aligned with social objectives, but the existence of the programme may not be known to all those potentially eligible, or people may make false claims which are not detected. Imperfect targeting may also arise because the conditions of benefit are only imperfectly correlated with the objectives. A reduced rate of Value Added Tax on clothes below a certain size, intended to benefit families with children, will exclude some families whose children are larger (and have to buy adult sizes) and falsely include some adults who are small enough to buy child-size clothes. Restriction of an income-related family benefit to those not in full-time work will mean that the families of low-paid workers may still be in poverty.

Where the correlation is less than perfect, or where there are errors in the identification of the categories, then this may lead to type I errors, or 'false negatives', where eligible families are not awarded benefit, and to type II errors, or 'false positives', where benefits are awarded to those not eligible.[9] The awarding of benefits to those not eligible (type II errors) reduces the vertical efficiency of the programme; the exclusion of eligible families (type I errors) leads to horizontal inefficiency in that the programme becomes less effective in covering the poor. Seen in terms of poverty minimisation, type II errors add to the cost with no benefit (just as with the universal transfers paid to the non-poverty population), and type I errors reduce both costs and benefits.

Administration of benefits

This brings us to the question of the administration of the benefits and the role of information. One of the most important advances in recent years in the theory of markets has been the exploration of the consequences of imperfect information. In many situations there is an asymmetry, with one participant in the market being better informed than the other. The purchaser of life assurance, for example, may have information not available to the potential insurer. This recognition has radically changed the views held by economic theorists about the working and efficiency of competitive markets. The same considerations have however received less attention in the administration of government programmes. In the operation of a transfer programme, there is often an asymmetry of information in that the needs of the individual are known to him or her but not to the administering agency. There may also be third parties, like employers, who have the necessary information. There is then a 'principal-agent' problem in the design of transfers, where the aim of the government is to induce all of those eligible to claim and to ensure that all of those who claim are in fact eligible.

If we begin with a purely categorical programme, like child benefit, then it may be possible for the government to make use of information already available or collected for other purposes. If there are birth (and death) records, then these will provide a basis for establishing the eligible population for a child benefit, and would allow payments to be made which varied with age. At the same time, the birth records would not necessarily allow the present location of the family to be determined. To make the payment requires a file of current addresses. There may well be problems here in that those with low incomes are particularly mobile and that they may be less anxious to publicise their whereabouts. For example, a battered wife who has left her husband may not register her new address so as to avoid the risk that he will find her.

Even the simplest form of categorical benefit – a uniform child benefit – may therefore pose administrative problems. These are likely to become greater if the transfer payment is differentiated in the way described in the previous section. To take in turn some of the different dimensions (following the same lettering as before):

(b) and (e) a payment related to labour market status requires that this be identified, and adjusted for changing circumstances, and low-income families may exhibit higher rates of employment turnover,

(c) birth records may not allow the benefit administration to identify the present composition of families, necessary to allow the payment to vary with the number of other children in the family or the position in the family,
(f) payments for child care costs may be made at source, as with the free or subsidised provision of care, but this would not allow a transfer related to private child care expenditure,
(g) birth records would not typically allow the administration to identify single-parent families; if a higher child benefit is to be paid to single parents, then it seems likely that they would have to initiate a claim,
(h) where the definition of a 'child' depends on their labour market or educational status, then this information would have to be collected.

There are limits, therefore, to the extent to which categorical benefits can be paid automatically. In many cases, the payment will require action on the part of the claimant. There are then two important stages: the decision by the potential beneficiary to make a claim, and the verification by the government of the claim.

The first of these may be considered purely as a problem of information, but in fact people may be aware of their entitlement but not make a claim, as where they regard the status of recipient as stigmatising. This problem of incomplete 'take-up' is particularly associated with income-tested benefits, and is discussed below, but may arise with categorical benefits such as those for single-parent families. Officially, take-up of One Parent Benefit in the UK for 1984 was estimated at 93 per cent, and it was noted that 'no significant increases in take-up are expected' (HM Treasury, 1988, p. 273).

The verification stage of the administrative process depends on the nature of the categorical distinction. Some criteria, such as age, may give rise to dispute, but are intrinsically straightforward. Others, such as labour market status, are more complex. An example is provided by Family Credit in the UK, currently paid to those families where the head or partner is engaged in at least 24 hours of remunerative work per week. 'Work' is defined to exclude training courses, or education, charitable work where the person is paid only expenses, and to include work paid in kind and self-employment (where the hours include preparation time). Hours may be aggregated for more than one job, and there are provisions for fluctuating weekly hours.

Administration of an income-tested transfer

If we turn to a targeted income-related scheme, then it is possible to imagine circumstances in which there is no problem of information. *If* the government operates a personal income tax, *if* everyone files a tax return, and *if* this information is deemed sufficient to determine the payment, then in theory it would be possible for the agency to identify from the income tax records those people with low incomes, calculate the necessary benefit amount, and *if* the administrative machinery exists, to mail a payment to the beneficiary. In the United States, the earned income tax credit for families with dependants operates by making payments to those whose income tax returns reveal that their earned income is below a certain level (and satisfy a condition on total income). In this situation, one could operate an 'automatic' income-related programme.

However, these conditions are highly unlikely to be satisfied, even in developed countries. The obligation to file a tax return may not be enforced among those who are likely to have incomes below the tax threshold. In the case of the United States earned income credit, this means that a number of those potentially eligible do not benefit (Seidman, 1990, p. 92 and Scholz, 1994). As we have seen, the typical transfer programme depends on categorical criteria as well as income eligibility. Information necessary to verify these categorical conditions may not be contained on the income tax return: for example, that in the UK does not include details of the number of children. Information on income in the past tax year, the basis for paying the US earned income credit, will not allow urgent current needs to be met. The US scheme does include provisions for the credit to be claimed in advance, but this has to be initiated by the recipient.

It seems likely therefore that any actual income-related transfer programme will not be automatic and we have again the two stages of claiming and verification. As far as verification is concerned, the problem faced by the government in the case of income testing is similar to that with tax evasion. As has been extensively discussed in the literature on evasion (see, for example, Cowell, 1990), the government has to decide on an audit policy (the proportion of claims investigated, the extent of the investigation, etc.) and on the structure of penalties imposed in the event of income being understated. The factors limiting the enforcement activity will obviously include its cost, but may also include the impact on the probability of claiming.

The problems of administration are illustrated by the UK Family Income Supplement (FIS), the introduction of which involved devising new administrative procedures to collect relatively current income information (and Family Credit requires in addition information on capital assets). The benefit must be claimed and would-be recipients have to supply information on income in the past five weeks or two months. This has imposed burdens on employers and potential claimants may have been deterred by the need to ask their employers for documentation. Special procedures are necessary for the self-employed. An important simplification has been that,

Table 12.2. *Administrative costs of family benefits*

	Child benefit/ one parent benefit	Family Credit
Administration cost as % benefit expenditure	2.2	5.3
Average weekly administrative cost per family in receipt	£0.30	£1.80

Source: Department of Social Security (1993), p. 20.

once the benefit has been assessed, no change in the payment is made for a specified period (which has been six months or one year). This means that the benefit paid is not necessarily appropriate to the current income, but reduces the administrative costs. Nonetheless, the administrative costs are significantly higher than those for the universal child benefit. In 1991–2 the position was as shown in table 12.2. The figure for Family Credit includes increased capital investment for information technology and publicity costs, but the latter arises from the problem of securing take-up.

The calculation of benefits on the basis of past income is a device widely used in the administration of income-tested benefits. In France, certain benefits are based on net taxable income in the preceding tax year, so that applicants must make an annual declaration to the fiscal authorities, including those below the tax threshold who can obtain a certificate that they are not liable for income taxation. This considerably simplifies the administrative procedure. It does however entail adopting the income tax definitions in assessing benefit eligibility, and these may not be considered appropriate. The use of a past earnings period also means that there are inevitably people currently in receipt who are not eligible on the basis of current circumstances. An interview study in the UK by the Department of Health and Social Security (1975) found that over half of FIS recipients would have been entitled to less benefit if assessed at the date of interview and that 20 per cent would have had no entitlement. With an assessment based on income tax declarations, as in France, the problem is that receipt may be delayed far beyond the period of current need. A person whose income falls below the level of eligibility in tax year t may not be eligible in year $(t+1)$, since the total annual income may exceed the ceiling, and have to wait until well into year $(t+2)$. In the case of the Australian Family Allowance Supplement, payments are made for the calendar year on the basis of taxable income in the preceding tax year, ending 30 June.

The problem of take-up

At the heart of the administrative problem is that the government has no machinery for identifying potential recipients and its operation depends on claims being made. This may be purely a problem of information, as discussed above. People may be unaware of the existence of a benefit. They may be aware of its existence, but not believe that they are entitled, as may happen where they have previously applied and have (correctly) been deemed ineligible but where there has been a subsequent change in the programme, or in their circumstances, which make them eligible. Informational deficiencies may apply to both categorical and income-tested programmes, but the latter, with their inherently greater complexity, may be more difficult to communicate. In order to overcome these problems of information, substantial advertising and other costs may be entailed.

It is also possible that advertising alone is not sufficient. The potential beneficiaries may lack the necessary skills of literacy or numeracy required to assimilate the information provided. It may in such cases be possible to make use of third parties, such as social workers or employers. In the latter case, there may or may not be an incentive to convey information. If the employers believe that offering a package including government benefits allows labour costs to be reduced, then they may co-operate, but this may not happen if they believe that the effect on labour supply is unfavourable or if claiming the benefit involves them in additional paperwork.

People may not claim even where perfectly informed: imperfect information is not the only reason for non-take-up. The simplest is the time required to file a claim. Where families face a time constraint as well as a budget constraint, non-claiming may be a quite rational response. Where there is some degree of uncertainty about the answers to be given to certain questions on the application forms, and penalties are imposed on those making incorrect returns, then a potential applicant may consider it more prudent not to apply. Non-take-up may be associated with preferences. People may be aware of their eligibility but not claim on the grounds that they regard receipt as demeaning or stigmatising. They may be deterred by the way in which the benefit is administered and the treatment they receive from officials. They may not wish to reveal information to their employer: for example that they have a child. These kind of considerations take us outside those usually discussed by economists, and we may need to draw on psychology and other disciplines (see, for example, the review of recipient reactions to aid by Fisher *et al.*, 1982).

The importance of the different reasons for non-take-up is likely to vary across groups of the population and across countries. Matters such as stigma clearly depend on the particular culture and are influenced by historical experience. For example, in the case of Australia, it is noted that:

> Other countries are said to regard the means test as an abhorrent affront to social justice. It does not seem to be so regarded in Australia. ... the means test as it is operated in Australia is not only fairly liberal, but also the 'poor-house' and 'work-house' connotations, which attach to the concept of the means test in some other countries, do not exist in Australia which had no experience of such institutions. (Henderson *et al.*, 1970, pp. 10–11)

It is also the case that attitudes towards take-up depend on the *form* of the programme. Taking again the case of Australia, 'The wide coverage among the categorically eligible populations and the absence of a test on assets also mean that stigma does not appear to be a major problem and take-up is generally considered to be high' (McAlister *et al.*, 1981, p. 27). However, the Australian experience with Family Income Supplement is less reassuring. According to Whiteford and Doyle (1991), the estimated take-up in 1986 among wage and salary earners was 24 per cent, and on an expenditure basis it was 36 per cent. Replacement by the new Family Allowance Supplement, based on tax returns for the previous year, appears to have led to a substantial increase in receipt, but the extent of eligibility also increased.

There is indeed evidence from a range of countries that incomplete take-up is a serious problem and that it is not readily overcome. A survey of European experience, while stressing the limited knowledge about this subject in many countries, concluded that 'Research that has been carried out in Britain, West Germany and the Netherlands invariably shows high to very high non-take-up of means-tested benefits' (van Oorschot, 1991, p. 19). Much of the evidence relates to the UK. When the Family Income Supplement was introduced in the UK, concern was expressed at the outset about the problem of incomplete take-up and the government set a target take-up rate of 85 per cent. The early numbers claiming did not suggest that this had been attained and examination of the time-series of numbers in receipt indicated no trend towards improved take-up (Atkinson and Champion, 1989). There is no evidence that advertising campaigns had any appreciable lasting effect on take-up. The official estimates (Department of Social Security, 1989, table 48.02) for 1985–6 show that 48 per cent of those eligible were claiming. This corresponds to a 'headcount' measure; seen in terms of expenditure, which corresponds to the poverty gap, the take-up rate was rather higher at 54 per cent. Those with larger entitlements were more likely to claim.

One of the aims of Family Credit, which replaced FIS in the United Kingdom in 1988, was to improve take-up. At the same time, the new scheme widened the field of eligibility, so that nothing can be deduced from the rise in the number of families in receipt, which went from 220,000 families receiving Family Income Supplement in 1987/8 to 280,000 families receiving Family Credit in 1988/9 (Department of Social Security, 1993a, p. 45). The official estimate of take-up of Family Credit in 1988/9 is that 57 per cent of families were claiming and that the amount of benefit claimed was 67 per cent (Department of Social Security, 1993a, p. 7). The same source quotes an estimate for 1991 by the Policy Studies Institute that 64 per cent of families were claiming and that 70 per cent of the benefit was claimed. It appears that non-take-up remains a serious problem with this means-tested benefit, whereas the government comments that for the main non-income-tested benefits 'take-up is thought to be close to 100 per cent' (Department of Social Security, 1993, p. 10).

The different reasons for the non-take-up of income-tested benefits have different implications for the design of programmes. The natural policy response to lack of information is to seek to improve communication, through advertising and other campaigns, or to seek to identify potential beneficiaries through administrative records. On the other hand, the obstacles to claiming may be seen as a form of screening. Nichols and Zeckhauser argue that a role can be played by purely deadweight costs. 'The demeaning qualification tests and tedious administrative procedures involved in many transfer programs *may* serve such a sorting function' (1982, pp. 376–7). It has similarly been argued that the time costs of claiming may be seen as a rationing device, limiting claims to those for whom time has a lower opportunity cost (Nichols *et al.*, 1971 and Alderman, 1987). However, the poor may also be poorly endowed with time and they may also find interaction with benefit agencies more time-consuming (for example where they have a low level of literacy) than do the non-poor.

These considerations are also relevant to the evaluation of individual welfare, and whether the value of a benefit is net of the cost of claiming or the gross amount. If the cost of claiming is foregoing an income-generating activity which is not observed by the benefit authorities, then the position of the individual may reasonably be assessed in terms of the gross transfer (the cost of claiming cancelling with the unobserved income). On the other hand, where the cost is that of travel to the benefit office, stamps, etc., then there are good grounds for subtracting them from the gross transfer.

In the analysis by Besley (1990) of the implications of the cost of claiming for the comparison of a minimum income guarantee, g^*, and a universal benefit, he treats the cost as a fixed deduction from gross income, written here as cz. This cost deters from claiming those whose potential benefit, g^*-y, is less than cz; and, if we measure their net position, it leaves recipients below the poverty line by an amount cz. Making the same assumptions as in the numerical example of section 12.1, we can show how this affects the relative efficiency of the minimum income guarantee compared with the universal benefit.[10] With a cost of claiming equal to 10 per cent of the poverty line, the gross guarantee that can be financed rises to 59 per cent of the poverty line.[11] The take-up rate is 83 per cent. Deducting the costs of claiming, the net guarantee is 49 per cent of the poverty line; and the proportionate reduction in measured poverty is 24 per cent with the poverty gap and 28 per cent with a value of α equal to 2. The latter compares with 38 per cent in the absence of claiming costs – see figure 12.4. While the higher costs of claiming may not on their own reverse the choice between a minimum income guarantee and a uniform benefit, they may materially reduce the attractiveness of the highly targeted benefit.

Conclusion

The problem of administration is often disregarded by economists, who concentrate solely on the benefit schedule. However, even purely categorical benefits may involve a decision by potential beneficiaries to make a claim and the verification by the government of their eligibility. In the case of income-tested transfers, it is very unlikely that the necessary information is available automatically to the government. Imperfect information may mean that some people receive benefits who are not entitled and that some of those entitled do not claim. Experience of a number of OECD countries suggests that the latter, take-up, problem can be serious for income-tested benefits, with a third or more of potential benefit going unclaimed. This reduces the effectiveness of the income targeted transfer relative to a uniform benefit.

12.4 Problems in targeting: work incentives

Income testing and work incentives

Income testing and categorical restrictions both raise important questions of work incentives. It is evident that the minimum income guarantee, involving a 100 per cent marginal tax rate, is likely to affect work decisions. High rates of withdrawal of a targeted transfer may create a 'poverty trap', such that people have little inducement to increase their gross income. Similarly, the restriction of entitlement to people meeting certain conditions regarding family or labour market status may lead them to change their behaviour in order to qualify. A system of family benefits payable, say, to single parents not in work may discourage them from seeking employment. We have to consider the trade-off between the efficiency of targeting and the possibly adverse effect on incentives.

The conventional utility-maximising model of labour supply predicts that a minimum income guarantee of amount g, with 100 per cent marginal tax rate, causes those with incomes below g to cease to supply labour, and also affects a range of families whose incomes were previously above g. The size of the pre-transfer poverty population is increased. As a result, the cost of the transfer rises above the earlier calculation (although it may still be considerably less than that of a universal benefit). This is illustrated by the indirect utility function (12.4) considered earlier, according to which a person chooses not to work, but to live on the guaranteed income, g, where his previous income (assumed to be all earned) was less than $(1+\beta)$ times g. Since β is the elasticity of labour supply, we can see that the recipient population increases, other things equal, with the elasticity. A value of 0.5 means that the income-tested scheme brings in those whose incomes would otherwise be up to 50 per cent above the minimum income. In addition, the fact that recipients reduce their gross income to zero raises still further the cost of the transfer.

In order to see the implications of labour supply adjustments, let us take the earlier numerical example, but now assume that the wage rate (rather than income) is uniformly distributed over the relevant range upwards from zero. The proportion considered to be in poverty in the absence of transfers depends on whether we evaluate the position of individuals according to gross income or utility, as discussed in section 12.1. Suppose that we take gross income, so that those with

$$y = wl = w^{1+\beta} \leq z \qquad (12.5)$$

are in poverty. With the poverty line at 50 per cent of average income, and $H=30$ per cent as before, the poverty gap where $\beta=0.5$ is equal to 9 per cent of total income.[12] If the available budget is a third of this gap, as before, then the transfer which can be financed is 32 per cent of the poverty line.[13] The reduction in the poverty gap is 13 per cent, compared with 10 per cent with a uniform transfer costing the same amount. The targeting advantage of the minimum income relative to a universal benefit is much reduced when we take account of the work disincentive. Of course, the comparison depends on the value of β and on the particular labour supply function,[14] but the calculation provides an indication of the possible importance.

Concern about the poverty trap generated by high marginal tax rates has led governments to taper the withdrawal of benefits, the reduction being less than £1 for £1. A typical formula would pay a benefit g to people with income less than or equal to y_e, and then reduce the benefit by \$t for each \$1 of income in excess of y_e. The universal benefit then emerges as the limiting case of $t=0$. Choice of the withdrawal rate t subject to a budget constraint involves balancing the gains of increased concentration of benefit as t increases against the induced reductions in gross income (and welfare). The benefit may also be distinguished according to categorical conditions.[15]

The poverty trap in practice in the UK

In practice, the tapering of benefits with earnings is more complex. To begin with, many people on low income face the cumulation of several marginal tax rates. In the United Kingdom, a person increasing his or her gross earnings, for example by working additional hours, may pay higher income tax and National Insurance contributions. In 1992/3, the marginal tax rate over the relevant earnings range was 34 per cent, so that there remained in net terms a proportion (1–0.34). For the low-paid family receiving Family Credit (FC) there would in addition be the withdrawal of means-tested benefits when these are reassessed,[16] so that the net gain became

$$(1-0.34)(1-0.7)=0.20 \qquad \text{if FC received}$$

But the person may also be eligible for Community Charge Benefit (CCB), which is also means tested, so that the net gain becomes

$$(1-0.34)(1-0.7)(1-0.15)=0.17 \qquad \text{if FC and CCB received}$$

Finally, the person may be eligible for Housing Benefit (HB), so that the net gain is

$$(1-0.34)(1-0.7)(1-0.15-0.65)=0.04 \text{ if FC, CCB and HB received}$$

(the calculations have been rounded to two figures). This structure of means tests, applied to net income and taking into account benefits earlier in the chain, ensures that the overall marginal tax rate cannot exceed 100 per cent, but it reaches 96 per cent where all three benefits are received. As a result, the budget line relating net income to gross income is virtually flat for a wide band of earnings.

The position is further complicated by the aggregation of family earnings. The calculation in the previous paragraph assumes that there is only a single earner in the family, an assumption which does not apply in many cases and which fails to draw attention to the implications of means-tested benefits for family decisions. Since the test is applied to the joint earnings of husband and wife, they in effect face the same composite marginal tax rate as far as benefits are concerned. The situation is in this respect different from that which applies to income tax and National Insurance contributions, which are essentially operated on an individual basis. Therefore, a married woman considering taking a part-time job which pays less than the income tax and contribution thresholds will face a marginal tax rate which depends on the Family Credit and other benefit withdrawal rates, but can be between 70 per cent and 91 per cent. The poverty trap affects not just the main breadwinner but also his or her partner.

How many people are in fact affected by high marginal tax rates depends on the joint distribution of earnings and family characteristics. The latter include, in the UK for example, the level of rent, which determines the range over which there is eligibility to Housing Benefit, and the level of family savings which may disqualify them from benefits via the assets test. Estimates based on sample survey information suggest that the number of families facing marginal tax rates higher than 70 per cent is some half a million (Department of Social Security, 1993, p. 11). Overall, the numbers are small in relation to the total number of tax units in the UK of some 30 million. At the same time, it has to be remembered that people may have been led by the existence of the poverty trap to choose a level of work effort outside the range where the marginal rate is high.

Marginal tax rates and work incentives

Recent years have seen a great deal of research on the empirical magnitude of labour supply responses. In the reviews of this research there appears to be broad agreement that, to the extent that disincentive effects exist, they are modest in size.

In terms of hours of work, the value of 0.5 for the labour supply elasticity assumed in the numerical calculations is to the high end of the range typically estimated. The significance of labour supply adjustment may therefore be less than indicated. At the same time, labour supply has many dimensions. The main variations in annual hours may be attributable to periods out of the labour force (non-participation) or unemployment. While at work, people may be able to vary their effort, intensity of work, or the degree to which they are willing to take risks or responsibility. The working career has to be seen a a whole, labour supply reductions taking the form of later entry or earlier retirement.

These dimensions of labour supply other than hours of work are important, because much less is known about how they are affected by transfer programmes. Even in principle the direction of the effect may be different. An income guarantee may give a positive incentive for people to make risky career decisions. Suppose that people are deciding whether or not to become self-employed, with all the attendant risks, rather than continue with a certain salary. The existence of an income supplement, payable in the event of low self-employment earnings, may induce them to take the plunge when they would not otherwise have been willing to do so.

This would be further reinforced if the benefit served to finance an initial period of unprofitable operation before the business became successful.

The analysis of work incentives is further complicated by the fact that labour supply may not be purely the result of the decisions of individual workers. Choice of matters such as standard hours, or annual holiday, may be the result of collective bargaining. A transfer received by a minority of trade union members may have no impact on the collective choice. An individual worker is constrained by the labour market opportunities faced; the annual hours worked may be rationed where there is unemployment.

There are therefore grounds for being cautious about the conclusions which can be drawn regarding the relation between work incentive and the design of transfers. We have also to recognise that concern about incentives may arise less from the quantitative effect on labour supply as from a notion of 'desert'. It may not be regarded as 'fair' that a person is unable to improve his or her position by working more. If this is the case, then 'desert', rather than an equity–efficiency trade-off, may determine the maximum rate of withdrawal and hence the acceptable level of targeting.

Categorical conditions and work incentives

The discussion of work incentives to date has focused on the role of the benefit withdrawal rate under an income-tested scheme, but categorical conditions may also affect labour supply. Indeed, one important mechanism for reducing the possible disincentive effects of targeted transfers is through making the transfer conditional on a minimum level of work. Family Credit in the UK is only available to families where the head is working for at least a specified number of hours per week.

An income-tested transfer with a minimum hours requirement has both positive and negative incentive effects. It may still cause people previously working more than the minimum to reduce their work effort or to take a less-demanding job, but it may also induce people to enter the labour force or increase their hours to the minimum.

The categorical restriction described above has a positive role as far as incentives are concerned, but these restrictions may also have adverse effects on incentives. The reverse restriction – where benefits are limited to those not in work – is an obvious example. Categorical unemployment benefit may induce people to quit voluntarily or to delay return to work, although in practice this is typically accompanied by sanctions on voluntary quitting, on the refusal of suitable job offers, and the benefit may be accompanied by job search or training requirements. These administrative elements of the benefit system may seriously moderate the disincentive which appears if one simply considers the budget constraint in isolation.

Categorical transfers may have other labour supply effects. Just to take one example, the provision of child benefit to those in full-time education may provide an incentive for young people to stay on at school; the extension of the definition of a 'child' to include those above the age of majority but attending higher education may influence the achievement of university-level qualifications.

Overall conclusions

Greater income testing of social security payments, as with a targeted minimum income guarantee, appears at first sight attractive, since it promises to concentrate benefit on those in need. The intention of this chapter however has been to caution against drawing oversimplified conclusions.

The first aim has been to set out the theoretical argument which is implicit in many of the calls for greater targeting, and to show how the assessment of relative efficiency depends on the formulation of social objectives. The statement that a particular transfer scheme is more efficient than another can only be interpreted in the context of such an explicit formulation of objectives and constraints. The attractiveness of targeting depends on how narrowly defined are the objectives of policy, and on how much agreement there is about the form of those objectives. Objectives may not be sharply defined, with differences of view about the weighting of different poverty gaps, about the location of the poverty line, and about the equivalence scale to be applied. A highly targeted income guarantee may perform less well when judged according to less sharp criteria and according to objectives other than poverty alleviation. The existence of wider objectives may in turn affect the level of benefits which can be financed.

The second main point of the chapter is that the choice of benefits is considerably richer than is suggested by a simple opposition of uniform and income-tested transfers, a point which has been illustrated with reference to family benefits. In principle family benefits can be differentiated in many ways, which may be combined with income relation; income testing itself may take different forms. The experience of Western countries indicates that a wide variety of types of family benefit have been implemented in practice.

Thirdly, the design of effective targeting faces the problems of imperfect information and of work incentives. These arise with both income testing and categorical conditions, but there are some reasons to suppose that they are more serious in the former case. Translating a scheme into practice in the face of imperfect information on the part of both administrators and potential recipients is particularly demanding for transfers that require evidence of current income. The experience of Western countries indicates that there is a major problem of securing adequate take-up of income-tested benefits. Concerns about work incentives, whether based on empirical findings or notions of desert, may limit the acceptable degree of income targeting.

13 The Western experience with social safety nets

This is a time of historic changes in Russia and Eastern Europe. These changes offer great prospects and there will be greater freedom and opportunities for individual action. There is a desire to learn from the Western experience, but in the West too changes are under way: we have just [in 1992] seen the signing of the North American Free Trade Agreement; in Western Europe, the European Community is about to complete the common internal market and is in the process of enlargement.

These changes offer great prospects but are also a source of insecurity. There will be losers as well as gainers from economic reform. Anxiety is understandably felt by the elderly, by the unskilled, by those with little education, and by those in peripheral areas. Uncertainty is greatest for those without family or friends to help in the event of adversity. These concerns are not confined to countries in transition to market economies. In the European Community, too, there are fears that greater internal competition will weaken the position of marginal regions and that the constraints on macro-economic policy will lead to a continuation of high levels of unemployment. There has indeed been concern for a number of years about those left behind by rising prosperity. The Commission's estimates for 1985 identified some 50 million of the Community's 320 million population as being in poverty (Eurostat, 1990). This figure is, interestingly, much the same proportion of the population as the 40 million figure given by the former USSR government for poverty in 1989 in the Soviet Union (Atkinson and Micklewright, 1992, p. 178).

Such concern raises the question of the protection which can be offered against insecurity. How far can help be provided to those who are the losers from economic change?

The need for a social safety net is widely recognised in international discussion of economic problems. Michel Camdessus, the IMF Managing Director, has emphasised the need for a social policy accompanying economic change. To quote from his address to the UN Economic and

Social Council: 'the essential missing element... is a sufficient regard for the short-term human costs involved during adjustment or transition to a market economy' (1992, p. 255). To avoid such costs he argues for the installation of social safety nets. The study of the Soviet economy by the IMF, World Bank, OECD and EBRD in 1991 noted that the move to a market economy and removal of existing government intervention 'will impose substantial hardship on many groups of the population during the transition' (IMF *et al.*, 1991, p. 331) and went on to say that 'to minimize this hardship and to assure political support for economic restructuring, it is necessary to design policies that cushion the less well-off from excessive burdens' (ibid., p. 331). The Stand-By Arrangement agreed between the IMF and the Russian Federation in August 1992 included the statement that 'The Russian authorities are committed to protecting the most vulnerable groups of the population during the economic transformation process, while ensuring that social safety net expenditures are consistent with macroeconomic stabilization' (IMF, 1992, p. 267).

I take it as agreed that there *should be* a social safety net, and I shall not examine the justifications that may be given (see Atkinson, 1991, for discussion of the different motives that may lie behind support for a safety net). What I want to do is to make three points about such a safety net, based on the experience of Western countries.

1 That a safety net can have very different meanings, and that major decisions have to be made about its form and mode of operation.
2 That it is not easy to set in place an effective safety net, and its effectiveness depends on the policy choices made.
3 The design of a safety net should be an integral part of economic policy making, which must recognise the limitations to the protection that can be provided.

The first two of these points are dealt with in the substance of the chapter; the third is treated in the concluding section.

In making these points, I refer to Western experience, notably that of Europe and of the United States. This means that I should enter two important qualifications. The first is that I am concerned with medium-term assistance rather than emergency relief to meet imminent risk of starvation or the consequences of natural disasters. I am not addressing the problem of famine, our understanding of which Sen (1981) has done so much to increase. Secondly I should make clear at the outset that I do not believe that the experience of Western economies can be carried over unmodified to other countries – indeed this is evident from the diversity of practice among Western countries themselves – but I do believe that the experience of these countries raises questions which have to be answered in the design of policy in the successor states of the USSR and other countries in the process of moving to a market economy.

13.1 What is the meaning of a safety net?

The need for a safety net is widely recognised. What is less widely appreciated is that a safety net can take many different forms. The choice of the form that such a safety net should take is an important question: it is not just a detail which can be left to be settled by junior policy makers.

Mechanism

The first issue concerns the *mechanism* by which the safety net is provided. It may be conceived very broadly, covering not just the whole range of cash transfers, but non-cash provision, such as food, health care, education, retraining or public employment for the unemployed, subsidies for housing, fuel and other essentials.

Here, I am going to focus on cash transfers. It is evident, however, that the importance of cash transfers depends on the extent of non-cash provision and of subsidy programmes. The role of cash assistance is less in an economy where there is state-provided health care and education, where housing is provided at low rents, where food is heavily subsidised, and where children are fed free at school. (The significance of such non-cash provision is documented in Saunders *et al.*, 1993.)

I am concentrating on cash transfers because it is clear that there has been a trend towards the reduction in non-cash provision. In many countries, food subsidies are being reduced or eliminated, the rents of state-owned property are being increased, often in association with the privatisation of the housing stock, charges are being introduced for health care and education, and private position is *de facto* or *de jure* replacing state provision. These changes reflect the exigencies of macro-economic and budgetary policy, as well as the shift in both East and West towards a market ideology. In this way the form of the social safety net depends on other decisions made about the economic system. The provision of cash assistance is acquiring greater significance as other forms of intervention are curtailed.

Within the category of cash assistance, too, there are important distinctions to be drawn. Some people regard all cash transfers as forming part of the safety net including retirement pensions, unemployment insurance, disability insurance and so on. These programmes, however, have much wider functions than that of poverty relief. For this reason, when people talk of a 'safety net' in the West they typically have in mind transfers that are 'targeted' to those with low incomes via a test of means. Such means-tested,[1] or social assistance, programmes are operated in the USA as Aid for Families with Dependent Children (AFDC) or as the Supplemental Security Income (SSI) for the aged, blind and disabled, in the United Kingdom as Income Support and Family Credit, and in France as the Revenu Minimum d'Insertion (RMI). Some of the key features of these social assistance schemes are summarised in table 13.1. It is on this type of social assistance that attention is focused here.

Level

If a means-tested programme aims to bring people to a specified minimum level of resources, then the choice of that level is clearly crucial. The European Community poverty estimates quoted earlier were based on a poverty line set at 50 per cent of average disposable income for each country. Such a 50 per cent target was the result of a political judgement, and it can clearly be debated whether this is the right percentage. Should, for example, the percentage be higher or lower in countries with a lower level of average income? One can imagine arguments which go in different directions, but it is interesting to note that the poverty line (of 81 roubles) used in the former USSR in 1989 was almost exactly 50 per cent of average household per-capita income (Atkinson and Micklewright, 1992, statistical appendix, tables UI1 and UP2).

The appropriateness of a particular level depends on whether we are concerned with a *partial* safety net, which assumes that people can supplement the payment from other sources, or whether we are aiming for a *total* safety net, adequate for people to survive without additional sources. In assessing the adequacy of the safety net to achieve the latter goal, one approach is to ask what can be bought with a particular amount of income. We can seek a foundation for the level of the safety net in a minimum basket of goods, or what has come to be known in the development literature as 'basic needs'. This has of course a long history, including the work carried out in the early days of the Russian Republic in 1918, when minimum budgets were worked out by town departments of the Labour Department and by trade unions (Matthews, 1986, p. 15). More recently, under Khrushchev, calculations were made by Sarkisyan and Kuznetsova (1967) and colleagues of 'current', 'prospective' and 'rational' minima, the latter two providing a dynamic to the policy objective.

In the constitution of such budgets, the scope of the safety net is made concrete and it takes account of non-cash forms of support. The Khrushchev budgets for 1965 reflected, for example, the subsidies to rents, with housing accounting for only 5 per cent of the total (Matthews, 1986, p. 20),

Table 13.1. *Examples of Western means-tested cash safety net programmes*[a]

Programme	Brief description	Number of recipients
United States		
Aid for Families with Dependent Children (AFDC)	Primarily for single-parent families with children. Income and assets tests. Participation required in Job Opportunities and Basic Skills (JOBS) programme.	12.4 million in 1991
Supplemental Security Income (SSI)	Aged, blind and disabled. Income and assets tests.	4.8 million in 1990
United Kingdom		
Income Support (IS) (previously Supplementary Benefit)	Those not in full-time work. Income and assets tests. Availability for work and job search requirements (not single parents).	4.8 million in 1991
Family Credit (previously Family Income Supplement)	Families with children, where at least one parent in full-time work. Income and assets tests.	0.4 million in 1991
France		
Revenu Minimum d'Insertion (RMI), introduced 1988	All aged 25 and over, or with family responsibilities. Income test. Associated with contract of 'insertion'.	0.6 million in December 1991

Note: [a] The above brief account of the different transfer programmes does not take into account all of their complex features.

compared with a figure of 12 per cent for actual budgets at that time in the United Kingdom. Little provision was required in the Khrushchev budgets for education and medical care. In the work which is no doubt being done today, the composition of the minimum budget is likely to look rather different. If subsidies are being removed, and if provision in kind is being reduced, then the amount of cash provision has to be correspondingly higher.

Structure of minimum scale

The minimum budget must also reflect the composition of the spending unit. Suppose, for example, that a household consists of a couple, their son aged 14, their daughter aged 20, a friend of the daughter who is lodging with the family and the wife's mother. There are six people in the household and the simplest procedure is to take a safety net which is six times that for a single person: in other words, to apply a per-capita scale. This has indeed been the standard way of presenting income distribution data in the former USSR or in Czechoslovakia, Hungary or Poland. On the other hand, it has been less common in the West. Such a distribution is not officially published for the United Kingdom and, indeed, the main long-term series of income distribution data in the United Kingdom treats all families in the same way, making no allowance at all for differences in their size.[2]

If one has to choose between these extreme ways of allowing for family size, then it seems to me that there is a lot to recommend a per-capita calculation. There is little apparent justification for ignoring family size: the needs of the family of six *are* greater than those of a single person. It may be more attractive, however, to make an intermediate calculation, as has been the common practice in many countries which apply an 'equivalence scale'. According to such a scale, a couple are rated as more than one but less than two, children receive a weight less than adults, and so on. The derivation of such an equivalence scale raises many issues, and any choice must be governed by the ultimate objectives of the safety net. Here I want simply to emphasise that the decision regarding the equivalence scale can make a major difference as to which families qualify for the safety net. In figure 13.1 are shown calculations made for the former USSR in 1989 for the population of worker families with children with income below 75 roubles a month. For this purpose I take a simple equivalence scale, where the needs of a family of size N are given by N to the power s where s is a constant. A value of $s=1$ corresponds to the per-capita figure, treating a family of six as the same as six single people. This is shown at the right-hand end of the diagram. At the other extreme, at the left-hand end, is the value of $s=0$, which treats all families as having the same needs. In the middle are cases like N to the power of a half, where a family of six is equivalent to 2.45 single people. One can see how the composition of the low-income families changes with different values of s.[3] With no allowance for the differences in family size, families with one child account for over 40 per cent of the total number of low-income families, and large families (four or more children)

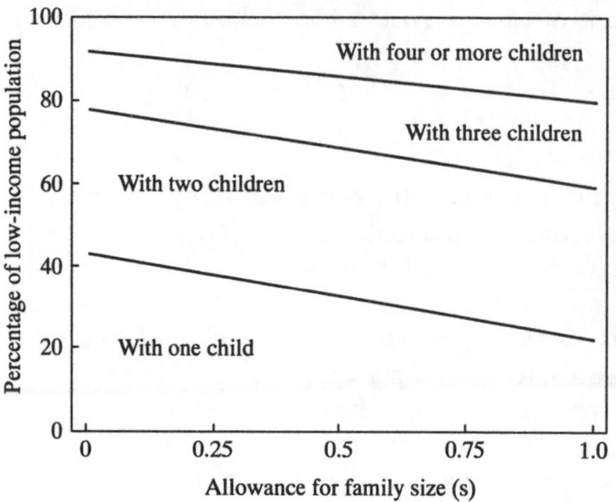

Figure 13.1 Composition of low-income families[a] in former USSR 1989
Note: [a] Less than 75 roubles a month.
Sources: The figures are calculated from table U15 in Atkinson and Micklewright (1992), using the proportions in different family size groups taken from the report of the 310 000 March Household Survey (Goskomstat, 1990, p. 175): one child (49.9 per cent), two children (37.7 per cent), three children (8.1 per cent), four children (2.5 per cent), and five or more children (1.8 per cent). The figures relate to worker and employee families.

are only about 8 per cent. With $s = 0.5$, one-child families are about twice as important as large families; and with $s = 1$ they are about equally important. It is evident that the conclusions drawn with respect, for instance, to the structure of the safety net for families of different sizes may be quite different.

Conditionality

There are many more elements that enter the design of a safety net, but here I want to refer to only one other – the conditions, other than income, which have to be fulfilled in order to qualify. Economists tend to assume that a minimum income guarantee simply depends on income, but in reality it is rare to find safety net schemes that involve *only* a test of means; the typical scheme also involves categorical conditions. The claimant has to satisfy conditions other than lack of resources, as is illustrated in table 13.1.

Categorical conditions are particularly relevant to the labour market. First, there is an important distinction between safety net schemes that cover the whole population and schemes that exclude people in work. The latter is the case in the United Kingdom, where Income Support covers all families *except* those supported by a person in full-time work. (It is complemented by the Family Credit scheme which provides assistance to low earners, but this covers only people with dependent children.) A person in full-time work, and without children, is categorically excluded from assistance, irrespective of the level of earnings, whch may be below the safety net level.

Second, categorical conditions may limit the coverage of those not in work: for those of working age, and capable of work, assistance may be conditional on labour market participation. This condition may require registration at a public employment agency; it may require evidence of job search; assistance may be terminated if the claimant refuses to accept suitable employment. The French Revenu Minimum d'Insertion, introduced in 1988, gives a central role to such conditions, payment beyond the first three months normally being linked to the condition that a contract for 'insertion' in the labour market has been negotiated with the recipient and that the terms of this contract are respected. In the United States, AFDC recipients may be required to take part in the Job Opportunities and Basic Skills (JOBS) training programme. Where these conditions are not satisfied, the safety net protection may be withdrawn.

It is important to stress these categorical elements of safety net schemes, since a *conditional* safety net cannot be guaranteed to be fully effective. There is always the possibility that a person is unable, or unwilling, to satisfy the conditions; if those in work do not qualify, then the scheme does not resolve the problem of the working poor. People will fall through the safety net, which brings me to the question of Western experience regarding its effectiveness.

13.2 How successful have safety nets been in Western economies?

In considering the role of means-tested safety net programmes in Western economies, one should first underline their quantitative importance. Whereas one might have expected their significance to decline with the development of modern forms of cash transfer programmes, such as social insurance, this has not been the case. In the United Kingdom, for example, it was envisaged in the Beveridge Plan of 1942 that social insurance benefits, paid as of right on the basis of contribution and not subject to a means test, would progressively replace the traditional social assistance:

> the scope of assistance will be narrowed from the beginning and will diminish ... the scheme of social insurance is designed of itself when in full operation to guarantee the income needed for subsistence in all normal cases. (Beveridge, 1942, p. 12)

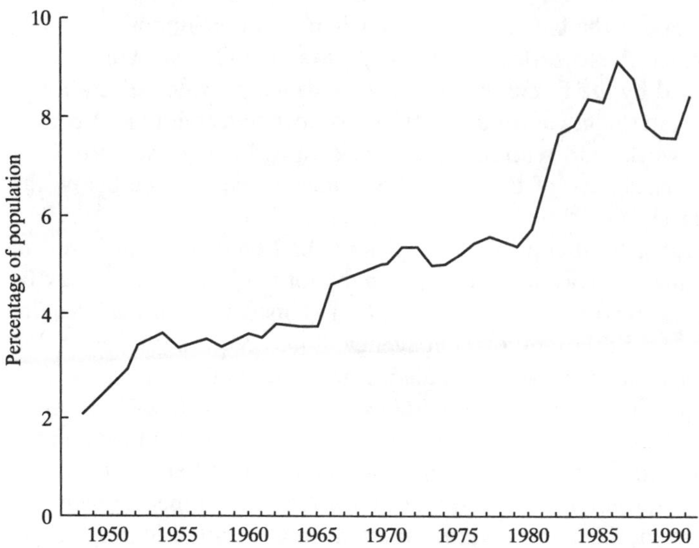

Figure 13.2 Receipt of social assistance in Great Britain 1948–91
Sources: 1948–65 (National Assistance) from National Assistance Board, *Report for the Year Ended 31 December 1965*, p. 54, figures for December of each year; 1966–87 (Supplementary Benefit) from Department of Health and Social Security, *Social Security Statistics*, 1980, table 34.30, and Department of Social Security, *Social Security Statistics*, 1989, table 34.29, figures for November or December; 1988–91 (Income Support) from Department of Social Security, *Social Security – The Government's Expenditure Plans 1992–93 to 1994–95*, p. 41.

The population figures are the mid-year estimates from Central Statistical Office, *Annual Abstract of Statistics 1992* (no. 128), table 2.1 *1961* (no. 98), table 6 *1938–1950* (no. 88), table 6.

This has not in fact happened. In 1948 the number of recipients of National Assistance was around 1 million; in 1991–2 Income Support was paid to 4.8 million. The growth in the role of the safety net is illustrated in figure 13.2, which shows how the proportion of the population receiving cash assistance rose steadily over the post-war period and then jumped in the 1980s. Recipients may have others dependent on them, so that the total proportion of the population living in families in receipt of assistance (adding in those provided for by Family Credit) is about one in six of the population.

Indeed in quite a few OECD countries there has been a growth in the number receiving benefits under safety net programmes. In the USA, the number of recipients of AFDC rose from around 2 million in 1950 to 7.5

million in 1970 and, despite the Reagan cuts, was 12.5 million in 1991. The number receiving SSI (or earlier Old Age Assistance) grew from 3.1 million in 1970 to some 5 million in 1990 (US House of Representatives, Committee on Ways and Means, 1992, p. 813). While social insurance grew faster, social assistance did not die away (Burtless, 1986). In West Germany, the total receiving Sozialhilfe in 1964 was 1.4 million; by 1986 it had risen to 3.0 million (Hauser, 1990, p. 25).

The spending on safety net programmes is substantial. In the United Kingdom in 1990–1 spending included (£ million):

Income Support	9,310
Family Credit	494
Housing rebates	5,279
Total	15,083

(HM Treasury, 1992, table 2.5).

This amounted to 2.7 per cent of GDP. In the USA in 1990 the total spending of federal and state governments combined on the major means-tested programmes was as follows ($ billion):

Medicaid	72.5
Food stamps	17.7
Family Support (AFDC)	21.2
SSI	16.6
Earned income tax credit	6.9
Federal housing assistance	15.7
Other	12.1
Total	162.7

(US House of Representatives, Committee on Ways and Means, 1992).[4]

This is a slightly higher percentage of GDP (3.0 per cent) than in the United Kingdom. It may be noted that a relatively small part (0.7 per cent of GDP) was in the form of cash transfers (AFDC and SSI).

The extent of poverty

The expansion of these programmes, costing substantial sums, has however coincided with continuing concern about the extent of poverty. In the United States, according to the official poverty line, the poverty rate fell in the 1960s from over 20 per cent to around 12 per cent, but in 1990 was still 13.5 per cent – corresponding to some 34 million people (US House of Representatives, Committee on Ways and Means, 1992, pp. 1274–5). Despite the safety net programmes, a sizeable minority of Americans are considered to be in poverty. This could be because:

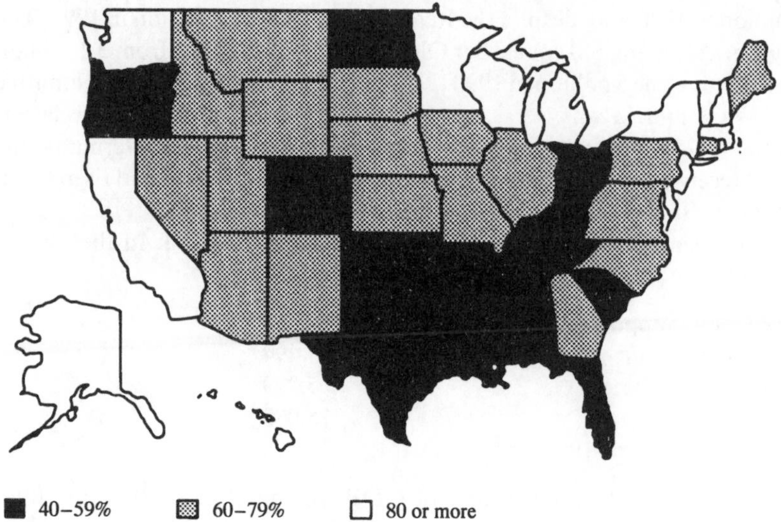

Figure 13.3 Maximum AFDC/Food stamp benefit[a] as a percentage of official poverty line, USA 1992
Note: [a] For a one-parent family of three.
Source: US House of Representatives, Committee on Ways and Means, 1992, p. 635.

the programmes are not targeted on the poor, or
the amounts paid are insufficient to raise people above the poverty line, or
not all of the poor are covered.

As far as the first is concerned, Weinberg (1987, table 2) identified for 1984 those people whose incomes, apart from all cash transfers, were below the poverty line (the 'pre-transfer poor') and shows that 86 per cent of all spending on income-conditioned programmes went to this group. In terms of *vertical target efficiency* (that is, accuracy in assisting only the poor), the US programmes appear relatively well targeted.[5] Nevertheless, a substantial proportion of the population remain below the official poverty line. The most obvious reason for this is that the income cutoffs for the safety net programmes are below the official poverty line. As a result, families may receive less than the amount required to reach the poverty line; or they may be in poverty but be disqualified on income grounds from AFDC or food stamps.[6] This is illustrated by figure 13.3, which shows the maximum AFDC and food stamp benefit as a percentage of the poverty line by state in the USA. For only those states unshaded was the percentage 80 or more.

The median state offered 72 per cent. For those states shown in black the percentage was below 60 per cent, the lowest being Mississippi, with 46 per cent.

That the government safety net level should be set below the official poverty line may appear like a lack of co-ordination; however, as discussed in chapter 7, it is perfectly consistent if the government is seen as pursuing this objective subject to constraints. These constraints may be those of budgetary cost, or they may be concerned with the possible effect of safety net provision on work or other incentives. If, in terms of the Tinbergen (1952) theory of economic policy, the poverty target is 'flexible', rather than 'fixed', then it may not be fully achieved. The operation of a safety net is then a compromise between aspirations, on the one hand, and constraints, or competing objectives, on the other.

This is not however the only reason why safety net programmes fail to be fully effective, as is shown by evidence from those countries that judge effectiveness in relation to the standard set in the safety net programme itself. In the United Kingdom, the effectiveness of the safety net in meeting its own objectives was the subject of official reports on 'Low Income Families', which estimated the proportion of families (benefit units) with incomes below the level at which they would become entitled to Income Support (then called Supplementary Benefit). In 1985, 5.6 per cent of all families had incomes (net of housing costs) which were below the entitlement level, containing 4.5 per cent of the population (Department of Health and Social Security, 1988a). The limited success of safety net programmes is reported in a variety of other countries. In the case of West Germany, the social assistance level has been used in a definition of 'combated poverty' (those in receipt of assistance) and 'concealed poverty' (those eligible on the basis of income, but not in receipt). The results of Hauser and Semrau (1990, p. 37) show that, in 1983, 2.6 per cent of the population were in receipt of social assistance, but that 1.3 per cent of the population were in concealed poverty. On this basis the safety net had left a third of the problem unsolved.

Failure of safety net coverage

There are several reasons why coverage may be incomplete. First, there are the categorical conditions for entitlement. Where the programme excludes certain categories, or requires claimants to meet certain conditions, then it is by definition incomplete. Of those below the social assistance level in the United Kingdom, a sizeable fraction are not eligible for the safety net because they are in full-time work (full-time is defined as 24 hours or more a week). Since there is no minimum wage, there is no guaranteed minimum income for those in work, and low-paid workers may fall below the safety net level.

Second, we have made no allowance so far for the problems of administration: there may be rejection of valid claims by administrative error. The application of the means test is a complicated basis. In contrast to social insurance, where error rates in benefit calculation are typically 1 per cent or less, in the case of Income Support, error rates are now around 6 per cent and they have been over 10 per cent (HM Treasury, 1985, table 3.12.11).

Third, there may be incomplete take-up by those eligible, with people not claiming their entitlement. That this should happen is often regarded with suspicion by economists. Why should people pass up what may be quite sizeable amounts of money or valuable benefits in kind? This behaviour scarcely accords with that assumed in other branches of public finance, such as the expected utility-maximising tax evader. But there are a number of explanations for the non-take-up of transfers which are quite consistent with utility maximisation, as discussed in chapter 12. The simplest is the time required to file a claim. Where there is a time constraint as well as budget constraint, non-claiming may be a quite rational response. Once we allow for imperfect information, a variety of reasons for non-claiming arise. People may be unaware of the benefit, perhaps because they lack the skills of literacy or numeracy required to assimilate the information provided. They may be aware of its existence but not believe that they are entitled. This may happen where they have previously applied and have (correctly) been deemed ineligible but where there has been a subsequent change in the programme, or in their circumstances, which makes them eligible. They may be deterred by the way in which the benefit is administered and the treatment they receive from officials. Certainly there is evidence from a number of countries of incomplete take-up. In the Netherlands, for example, an analysis of administrative records for a means-tested supplement to the basic earnings-related benefit showed that 33 per cent of the unemployed did not claim and there is evidence of incomplete take-up for other benefits (van Oorschot, 1991). In Ireland, Callan *et al.* (1989) found that in 1987 the take-up of Supplementary Welfare Allowance was less than 50 per cent.

Finally it has to be remembered that most of the statistical information relates to the *household population*. Those living in institutions may not be covered by the safety net. The payment of benefit to people without a fixed address is administratively more difficult, and Western societies have seen growing concern about the incidence of homelessness. People sleeping in the streets of cities like London, New York and Paris provide very real evidence of failure in the safety net.

Negative effects of the safety net

We have also to consider the argument that the persistence of poverty in rich countries stems from the existence of the safety net itself. Conservative commentators suggest that people have taken advantage of the safety net, and not sought their own solutions. The proportion of the population with pre-transfer income below the poverty line has been augmented by the disincentive effect of the safety net provisions. People have been discouraged from seeking work and have not made private provision for old age. The effects may be expected to be greatest in the case of means-tested programmes, in view of the fact that any private income – from work or savings – tends to reduce the transfer payment by the same amount. There is typically a 100 per cent marginal tax rate. Where entitlement depends on categorical criteria, people have adapted their behaviour to satisfy these conditions.

That there are situations in which this happens cannot be denied. What can be debated, however, is the quantitative importance of the disincentive effects. This requires careful examination of the evidence about the many different decisions which may be affected. There is not space here to survey this evidence, but a number of such reviews have been undertaken in recent years, and I think that there is broad agreement that, to the extent that disincentive effects exist, they are modest in size. Burtless (1990) summarises the evidence from the US Negative Income Tax (NIT) experiments: 'on average, studies based on the NIT experiments suggest that means-tested transfers have a statistically significant, but quantitatively small, effect on the labour supply of low-income men and women who have children' (p. 73). Moffitt (1992) concludes that there is unequivocal evidence of an effect of the US welfare system on labour supply, but that 'the importance of these effects is limited in many respects' (p. 56).

It should also be remembered that the safety net may have positive as well as negative effects on incentives. To give just one example, it is frequently argued that people are too unwilling to leave wage employment to set up as self-employed entrepreneurs. This decision is likely to be affected at least in part by the costs of failure. The existence of a safety net reduces these costs and may increase the attractiveness of self-employment; it will reduce the probability of success required to take the plunge; this will be further reinforced if the benefit also serves to finance an initial period of unprofitable operation before the business becomes successful.

Conclusions: the integration of economic and social policy

The discussion of incentives is illustrative of the interrelationship between economic and social policy, two areas which are too often treated as independent. This interrelationship has appeared at several stages in the argument. The extent to which cash assistance is necessary depends on the degree of non-cash provision, which in turn is influenced by decisions about price subsidies and public spending which are usually debated in terms of their macro-economic consequences. The categorical criteria for assistance depend on policy in the labour market.

Economic policy, and programmes of economic reform, have implications for the role and scope of the safety net; and it is imperative that these be taken into account in the design of this policy. Most importantly, too much weight should not be placed on the safety net. The experience of Western countries suggests that a safety net is not easy to design and typically has only limited effectiveness. A safety net cannot resolve all problems and it can easily become overloaded. Indeed the term safety net is itself misleading in suggesting a public good which cannot become overcongested. From asking people what image is conjured by this term, I know that most people think naturally of the safety net in the circus – a particularly appropriate response in this city (Moscow) – and in the case of the circus the establishment of the safety net costs the same whether it protects one trapeze artist or ten. It is a public good in that sense. But with a social security safety net the cost goes up with the number protected.

A better analogy may be with a *lifeboat*, which has a definite capacity. When the British liner *Titanic* struck an iceberg in the North Atlantic on her maiden voyage in 1912, the main reason for such a high loss of life was that the lifeboats on board could hold only 1,178, whereas there were nearly twice as many (2,201) people on board. After this disaster ships were required to carry sufficient lifeboats for all persons on board. But we have seen that the effective coverage of social safety nets in Western economies is considerably less than 100 per cent. That is why the avoidance of icebergs is of crucial importance, a factor which should in my view be given more weight in the design of economic reform and macro-economic policymaking.

Finally I have talked about safety nets at a national level, but we must not lose sight of the need at a world level. The sums spent by Western countries on safety net provision to their own citizens are too small to meet their needs, but these sums are much larger than those transferred to those in need outside their boundaries. The safety net spending in Britain represents 2.7 per cent of GNP; official development assistance is 0.27 per cent. There is a ratio of 10 to 1, or, on a per-capita basis, of some 1,000 to 1. As national boundaries come to have less significance, as is happening all over the world, there is less justification for such differences in generosity.

14 Towards a European social safety net?

14.1 Introduction

In this chapter I am going to ask you to suspend any disbelief you may feel about plans to develop the European Community. I ask you to do this because I want to explore the implications for social policy if the pace of change in Europe is maintained post-1992. I quite appreciate that there are good reasons to doubt whether the plans for monetary union will be realised, let alone those for a social dimension to the Community. It is not, however, my intention to try to predict what *will* happen. The question mark in my title does not concern whether or not a European safety net will come about. I am not trying to make a political forecast.

The aim of the chapter is rather to pose the conditional question – *if* a social dimension to the Community is to develop alongside the Common Internal Market, *then* what form is it likely to take? Taking the income protection objectives of the Social Charter seriously, how can they be achieved? What is the role of existing social protection in member countries? How are national programmes likely to be affected by developments post-1992? Should one be thinking of a *European* safety net? Such thoughts may appear far removed from practical politics, but I believe that the subject is an important one, not least because it tells us something about what we are missing if such a safety net does not come into existence. So I ask you for the duration of the chapter to suspend your disbelief.

14.2 The social dimension of the Community

In the early days of the Community, social policy received relatively little attention; it was the narrow economic view that dominated, and the Community's organs were provided with very limited powers in the social field. Social policy was, to a large extent, a means towards achieving other objectives. The restructuring of the coal and steel industries, through the

European Coal and Steel Community, involved social measures in aid of training and to finance adjustment. There was concern with *negative integration*, that is, removing barriers to labour mobility and ensuring that differences in the costs of social protection did not prevent competition in the supply of goods.

In the 1970s the social dimension of the Community began to play a more important role. Some writers (Crijns, 1991) attribute this in part to the debates which took place about the social aspect while the United Kingdom and others were deciding on accession to the Community. The issue was certainly raised by opponents of entry. Within the Community, the 1972 Paris Conference called for measures to reduce social and regional inequalities. In the social field, the Commission produced a Social Action Programme, accepted by the Council in 1974, which recognised that the Community had an independent role to play in the formation of social policy, and among the measures agreed were:

(a) to extend gradually social protection to categories of people not covered or inadequately provided for under existing schemes;
(b) to implement, in co-operation with Member States, specific measures to combat poverty.

In terms of concrete action, the achievements were limited in scale and scope. The Regional Development Fund was put in place. The Social Fund was increased in size, with an emphasis on the education, training and insertion into the labour market of young persons, and on regional redistribution. Policy to combat poverty, on which attention is focused here, led in July 1975 to the first European Action Programme, covering the period 1975–80. In December 1981, the Commission made an evaluation report, containing an estimate of the number of poor people in the Community. Despite the concern generated by these figures, it took several years to agree the Second Action Programme, for the period 1985–9. Finally there has been a third programme in force since July 1989, stressing social exclusion and marginalisation.

At the same time, the social dimension was receiving more attention generally in the Community. In 1989 the Commission put forward a draft of the 'Community Charter of Fundamental Social Rights' and this was adopted in modified form at the Strasbourg European Council in December 1989 by 11 of the 12 Member States (with the United Kingdom dissenting). For our purposes here, the key paragraph is number 10, which states that:

Every worker of the European Community shall have a right to adequate social protection and shall, whatever his status and whatever the size of the undertaking in which he is employed, enjoy an adequate level of social security benefits. Persons who have been unable to enter or re-enter the labour market and have no means of subsistence must be able to receive sufficient resources and social assistance in keeping with their particular situation.

The opposition of the UK at the Maastricht European Council led to the Social Chapter as such being excluded from the final Treaty on European Union, signed on 7 February 1992. But there was an attached Social Protocol, in which the 11 other members expressed their wish to continue along the path laid down in the 1989 Social Charter, and their intention to take decisions outside the Treaty from 1 January 1993.

As far as income maintenance is concerned, it is clear that the Social Charter has in mind in the second part of paragraph 10 a form of income-tested social assistance. Beyond this, what precisely the paragraph means is not entirely clear. A senior official of the Commission described the clauses on social protection in the following terms: 'They are very open-ended and are stated in very general terms, because the concept of "sufficient resources" remains to be determined' (Quintin, 1989, p. 4). If we go back to the Community's Action Programme on Poverty, then the definition accepted by the Council of Ministers in launching the Second Poverty Programme was that the poor are those 'whose resources . . . are so limited as to exclude them from the minimum acceptable way of life in the Member State in which they live' (European Commission, 1991, p. 2). This in turn was translated into the concrete criterion, used by the Commission in measuring poverty, that households are considered poor if their income is below 50 per cent of the average in the Member State in which they live. It is on this criterion that is based the widely quoted estimate that there were some 50 million people living in poverty in Europe in the 1980s, a statistic which played a powerful role in mobilising public and political opinion in favour of extending the social responsibilities of the European Community.

Such an interpretation raises a number of questions. However, whatever one's doubts as to the meaning of the Social Charter, one must recognise the significance attached to the social dimension by most of the mainland members of the Community. The same is true of countries such as Austria and Sweden that have since joined the Community. In my judgement, our European partners *are* serious about the social dimension. As it was put by the Dutch Minister for Social Affairs and Employment (de Koning, 1990, p. 5), 'The pace of its realization [of the single market] might be as slow as that of the French Revolution, but that it will come is as certain as the downfall of Louis XVI. Consequently it is a matter of some urgency to discuss the future of European social policy.'

I should emphasise that I am not here discussing whether they are *right* to insist on the social dimension, and I am not asserting that it is *necessary* for the development of the Internal Market. All that I am saying is that we have to take it seriously, and that is what I am going to do in the rest of this chapter.

14.3 The principle of subsidiarity

Whether or not any concrete action will follow at the European level depends on how far social protection is deemed to be within the competence of the European Community. This brings us to the famous principle of subsidiarity. Article 3b of the Treaty on European Union states that:

> the Community shall take action, in accordance with the principle of subsidiarity, only if and insofar as the objectives of the proposed action cannot be sufficiently achieved by the member states and can therefore, by reason of the scale or effects of the proposed action, be better achieved by the Community.

What, however, exactly does the *principle of subsidiarity* mean? In seeking further illumination, I turned to two sources. The first is the public finance literature on fiscal decentralisation and the economics of multi-level governments. The second is the social teaching of the Catholic Church, which applied this principle long before the Community was invented. (The classic reference is the encyclical *Quadragesimo Anno* (On Reconstructing the Social Order) of Pius XI, published in 1931; see also such documents as the 1986 Letter of the American Catholic Bishops.)

In the public finance literature on decentralisation, there has been analysis of the allocation of functions to different levels of government, particularly between federal (which I take to be the Community in the present context) and local (which I take to be the national governments of the Member States). One of the criteria which has been evoked is that functions should be allocated to local governments where there are marked differences in preferences between local areas. As Meade has put it in his recent paper on 'The building of the new Europe' (1991), this allows freedom for *national diversity*, as opposed to *continental uniformity*.

The criterion of allowing for diversity in local preferences has been applied in the field of redistribution, originally in an article by Pauly (1973) in which he describes redistribution as a local public good. Subsidiarity would then mean that a Member State was free to determine the extent of redistribution on the basis of the expressed preferences of its electorate. Some countries would choose a highly redistributive policy, with associated higher taxes, and another would provide less social protection. As Meade (1991, pp. 27–8) puts it, this would allow country A to adopt 'a wide range of institutions and policies to redistribute income and wealth in an egalitarian direction; but [country B to interfere] very little with the distribution of income and wealth which results from the free play of the competitive markets'.

It seems to me, however, that this is not what is envisaged in Article 3b, which refers explicitly to *the objectives of the proposed action*. In other words, it does not leave the lower-level government free to determine the *objectives* of redistributive policy. While the Social Charter is consistent with country A pursuing more than average egalitarian policies, it presumes that there is agreement on a minimum level of social protection that even country B is required to provide.

This interpretation is supported by reference to the principle of subsidiarity in Catholic social doctrine, which is surely based on assumed agreement about basic objectives. It is not a question of the Catholic Church handing over moral authority to lower levels of organisation. Moreover, two further points emerge. First, the doctrine is concerned not just with the relation between different levels of government, but also with the relation between individuals, their families and associations of individuals, as well as the state. So that while in the recent European debate the principle of subsidiarity has been taken to concern only the relation between the Community and national governments, it has a much wider applicability. This is not an issue which I shall pursue here, but it has obvious implications in terms of the role of voluntary bodies, trade unions and other organisations in the provision of social protection.

Second, and less widely appreciated, is the emphasis placed on the role of the central authority in *supporting* the activities of the lower-level bodies. In accordance with the generally 'corporatist' aims of Pius XI, the central authority was seen to have the role of providing aid to lower levels in a mutual attempt to achieve common goals. As it was put by the American Bishops (cited in Gannon, 1987), 'Government should not replace or destroy smaller communities and individual initiative. Rather it should help them to contribute more effectively to social well-being and supplement their activity when the demands of justice exceed their capacities.'

So that, while subsidiarity undoubtedly means different things to different people, one reasonable interpretation is that the European Community should act to support the social protection activities of Member States and to fill the gaps at the national level. This interpretation of the principle of subsidiarity seems to accord with the origins of the word in the Latin 'subsidium', meaning 'troops stationed behind or in reserve'. It means that we have to ask how well the front-line contingent – the existing social protection in Member States – is performing its function. It is to this that I now turn, beginning with the current situation and then considering how national systems are likely to be affected by future developments.

14.4 Existing social protection in Member States

I have already drawn attention to the widely quoted statistic that there were 50 million people living in poverty in the European Community in the mid 1980s. Is this figure the result of setting an unrealistically high standard for the measurement of poverty, or does it indicate serious deficiencies in social protection in this community of relatively advanced welfare states?

The first point to be made is that poverty, measured in this way, is to be found in all 12 Member States. The definition is a *national* definition, the poverty line being taken as 50 per cent of the average in the Member State in question. According to the official estimates, the 'rich countries' – the original six Community members, Denmark and the United Kingdom – accounted for some three-quarters of the 50 million figure. (The estimates are given by Eurostat, 1990, table 1, and it should be noted that they are based on *expenditure* as an indicator of resources, rather than *income*.) Over 25 million were to be found in just the United Kingdom, France and Germany (even before the accession of East Germany).

Why is this? Why have countries such as Germany, France and the United Kingdom a substantial number of households with low incomes? The first possible explanation is that the 50 per cent of average income criterion is overambitious when compared with the target levels of social protection. However, this does not appear to be the case. For instance, from a historical perspective it is interesting to compare the benefit scales recommended by Beveridge in 1942 with the 50 per cent of average expenditure criterion as it would have operated at that date. In 1937–8 there had been a budget survey of the households of industrial workers (*Ministry of Labour Gazette*, December 1940). This was not a national sample, and understated the average in that it excluded better-off households. On the other hand, it also excluded agricultural workers with a lower level of average expenditure. The average expenditure was 86s. 3d., or £4.31 a week, and the average number of persons was 3.8. This may be compared with the Beveridge calculation (1942, pp. 87 and 89) of the rate of subsistence benefit at 1938 prices for a couple with 1.8 children, which was £2.23, or just over 50 per cent of the recorded average. If, alternatively, we take the national accounts figures for personal expenditure in 1937 (Feinstein, 1976, table 10) and divide by an estimate of the equivalent number of people, applying the same equivalence scale as in the Eurostat calculations,[1] then the Beveridge subsistence minimum for a single man of working age was some 40 per cent of the average.

If we come to the present day, then, in 1985, the year of the European poverty figures, the European Commission poverty line for the UK was some £40 per week. At that time, the Supplementary Benefit scale for a single pensioner was £35.70 prior to the November uprating (and the basic National Insurance retirement pension was virtually the same) and that for a single unemployed person was £28.05 (again the NI unemployment benefit was virtually the same). In addition there was entitlement to housing benefit. On average, net housing expenditure was some 16 per cent of spending on all items (*Employment Gazette*, September 1988, table 7.2). If the European Commission £40 figure is reduced by this percentage to £33.60, then it appears that the 50 per cent target was then somewhat below that implicit in Supplementary Benefit for pensioners, although short-term benefits were more like 40 per cent of the average. These figures refer to 1985 and we may expect the comparison to have worsened since that time, because benefit levels are linked with prices, while average expenditure is rising in real terms. The corresponding figure in 1990 for pensioners is indeed 48 per cent and that for the unemployed 35 per cent.

The comparison is most easily made in the UK, in view of the preponderance of flat-rate social security benefits, but in France, where in 1985 the European Commission poverty line was 25,900 FF per person per year, we may make a comparison with the minimum vieillesse, which was 30,470 FF for a single person in 1985. In Belgium, on 1 January 1980 the minimex scale for a single person was 106,896 francs per year, compared with a European Commission poverty cutoff in 1979 of 113,300 francs. For 1985, the European Commission poverty line was 15,092 francs per month, compared with legal minima of 14,177 for a single elderly person and 16,406 for a single active person (Deleeck, 1989). In the case of Germany, Hauser and Semrau (1989, footnote 4) have compared the scales for Sozialhilfe with average disposable income (rather than expenditure), concluding that they lie broadly in the range 40–50 per cent of the average. According to Kohl (1992, p. 227), the overall value of social assistance for a single pensioner was some 800 DM per month, which is close to the reported figure of 762 DM for 50 per cent of national average expenditure (European Commission, 1991, table A.5).

From this it appears that the criterion being applied by the European Commission, of 50 per cent of average spending, is not far from the level of social protection at which these countries are aiming. The *level* of the benefit scales is, however, only part of the story. The second aspect we have to consider is that of *coverage*. The Welfare State does not in general provide an unconditional guarantee. Safety net benefits are *conditional*, in that recipients have to satisfy conditions with regard to their current and past status. In this respect, there is an important distinction between those countries that have a general safety net (Income Support in the United Kingdom or Sozialhilfe in Germany) and those where there is no general safety net programme, as in the Mediterranean countries and as was true in

France until the introduction of the Revenu Minimum d'Insertion in 1988. Even Income Support is not, of course, universal, in that it excludes those in full-time work. The latter are eligible for Family Credit, if they have children, but there is no comparable provision for those in work without children.

The effectiveness of the safety net is further reduced by a third consideration, which is the *incomplete take-up* of safety net benefits. As has been recognised for more than 25 years in the United Kingdom, a minority, but a sizeable minority, of those entitled to assistance do not claim. The most recent evidence (*Social Security Statistics 1991*, table H5.01) shows that in 1987 out of 5.5 million potentially eligible recipients, in fact 1.1 million were failing to claim. It is true that those with larger entitlements were more likely to claim, so that in cash terms the shortfall in effectiveness was proportionately smaller: 10 per cent of the potential £7.2 billion was not claimed. But this is still quite worrying.

The problem of incomplete take-up appears to be endemic in Britain. This does not mean that it applies to the same extent in other European countries. To the extent that it is due to the stigma attached to income-tested benefits, this may not be found to the same extent in other countries, where attitudes and social expectations may be different. Interestingly, the recent Vanlerenberghe (1992, p. 221) report on the Revenue Minimum d'Insertion in France concluded that the take-up rate of this new benefit is at least 90 per cent. On the other hand, in Germany the estimates of Hauser and Semrau (1990, p. 37) suggest that take-up, while higher than in the past, was only around two-thirds in 1983.

Together, the limits on coverage and incomplete take-up mean that a sizeable number of people fall through the safety net. All of this suggests that the national safety nets have to date enjoyed only partial success; it is also clear that they are going to come under increasing strain post-1992.

14.5 National safety nets after 1992

According to the European Commission (1991, p. 28):

> The completion of the Single European Market guarantees a more dynamic, efficient market likely to create more jobs, but it is also likely to have two further consequences with adverse effects on the fight against poverty.
>
> The first of these is the limitation of margins for manoeuvre traditionally employed by the Member States in their social policies...
>
> There is in the second place ... an increased risk, at least in the short term, of insecurity and marginalisation affecting certain categories.

There are indeed grounds for concern that the development of the European market after 1992 will lead to greater inequality and poverty within the Community. The micro-economic sources of the forecast gain in productivity involve the reallocation of production; the realisation of benefits of scale from the larger internal market require the concentration of production. The opening-up of public purchasing will mean that in some cases, local supply becomes inefficient and there may, at least in a period of adjustment, be increased unemployment. Moreover, poverty is not purely a matter of geography. Within prosperous regions, persistent unemployment, and downward pressure on the wages of the low-skilled, may put at risk many workers and their families.

At the same time as the need for social protection is increased, the capacity of national governments to provide such protection will be restricted. The Maastricht rules on the use of deficit financing, if adopted, will mean that public spending is under considerable pressure in most member countries. In particular, the need for fiscal rectitude is likely to materially constrain the execution of domestic income redistribution, such as that from those in employment to those out of employment. The increased mobility of capital will limit the taxation of capital and mean that the costs of social programmes will be borne disproportionately by workers and consumers. There are therefore likely to be powerful obstacles to domestic governments which wish to offset the tendency to increased inequality and poverty.

There are indeed those who argue that the Welfare State itself is under threat. This argument has been made forcefully by Sinn (1990, pp. 501–2):

> the poor will lose because governments will no longer be able to maintain their current scales of redistribution ... it will be difficult for a single country to extract the required funds from the rich. On the other hand, net benefits being given to the poor in one jurisdiction will attract poor people from everywhere and so make this policy unsustainable. The New York city effect will be the death of Europe's welfare states if the unmitigated competition of tax systems is allowed.
>
> Those who see redistribution as the greed of Leviathan will welcome this outcome. However, redistribution is more than that. It can be seen as an efficiency enhancing government activity which [provides] insurance against the risks of lifetime careers. After all, many young people ... welcome the protection of the insurance state, because they do not know how the dice of destiny will fall. [However,] middle-aged managers who know that the dice have been cast in their favour tend to object to redistribution.
>
> Even if all Europeans ... would prefer government redistribution to *laissez-faire*, competitive and decentralised governments would not be able to satisfy their needs. Any country that tries to establish an insurance state would be driven to bankruptcy because it would face emigration of the lucky who are supposed to give and immigration of the unlucky who are supposed to receive.

This argument sounds persuasive, and suggests that the national governments may indeed be in need of Community assistance in ensuring adequate social protection. There are, however, two aspects which we need to clarify.

The first is that Sinn's argument does not apply equally to all forms of social security provision. If we take a *social insurance* scheme, and if we abstract from problems of asymmetric information, then the provision of actuarially fair unemployment or retirement insurance is valued by risk-averse workers, and will be reflected in the wages demanded. What one has to look at is the *net benefit* from the social insurance scheme, and this may well make countries with high levels of social protection attractive to prospective workers. High social contributions may not be a deterrent if they are matched by more than comparable benefits.

Of course, it is possible that a scheme which is actuarially fair over a person's lifetime nonetheless involves periods when it is advantageous to opt out, as is indicated by Sinn's example of middle-aged managers. It is, however, clear that the main problem arises with the *redistributive* elements of social protection. Since much of social security is not in fact redistributive, at least on a life-cycle perspective, this limits the applicability of his fiscal competition argument. At the same time, the argument applies with particular force to the kind of social assistance protection with which I am concerned in this chapter. National governments will be under pressure to reduce their social assistance provisions.

The second question concerns the mechanism by which this pressure will be exerted on national governments. It is important to distinguish different forms of reaction. Sinn refers principally to the migration of labour, but there are reasons to doubt whether this will be of sufficient quantitative importance, at least in the foreseeable future. The evidence from the US about 'welfare migration' between states with different levels of benefits (for example, Peterson and Rom, 1990) suggests that there is a significant effect, but that its quantitative magnitude is rather small. If we turn to the effect on contributors, rather than beneficiaries, then the evidence for the European Community to date does not suggest that substantial migration has been induced by the significant differences which exist between Member States in net-of-tax wage rates. Ermisch (1991, p. 101), after examining the evidence for different countries, noted 'the failure of the pattern or volume of migration among EC countries to change much after the formation of the EC'.

The mechanism may, however, be a different one from labour migration. It may be the location decisions of firms and investment policies that are affected. The European Commission has warned that there may be what it calls 'social dumping', whereby the countries with the lowest levels of benefits attract businesses, via lower labour costs, and this puts those with more generous welfare provisions at a competitive disadvantage. This argument, as noted above, does not apply where the welfare provisions provide a net benefit, but it may apply to redistributive social assistance. The UK, by not signing the Social Charter and by holding down the level of social assistance, may be seeking to increase domestic employment.

It is not clear that there is a great deal of empirical evidence to support this position, and it is easy to imagine arguments in the reverse direction. If companies are not myopic, but are deciding on a location for the medium term, then they will foresee that such a UK policy may provoke reactions, either along the Sinn lines or through barriers erected against Britain because it has not accepted the social provisions. Moreover, uncertainty about whether Britain will in fact sign the Social Protocol at some future date will itself be a disincentive to investors, which may more than offset the immediate cost advantage.

There remains, however, a further dimension to the argument – and perhaps the most important. This concerns the impact of *potential*, or threatened, movement of labour or capital on the policies of government. Hirschman (1970) distinguished between 'exit' and 'voice' as reactions to economic change. Workers who perceive that taxes are lower in other Member States may not migrate but may seek to exercise political power to achieve lower taxes at home. Comparisons of tax rates with those in other Member Countries will play a role in national election campaigns. I believe that these public choice aspects may be the most important restrictions on the freedom of national governments to carry out social protection.

14.6 A European safety net?

This indicates that there may indeed be a need for intervention at the Community level. National governments may come under pressure, particularly via the expression of political voice, to reduce that part of social spending which is essentially redistributive. And the need for social protection may at the same time be growing with the development of the Internal Market.

This has led to proposals for a kind of social snake, where, by analogy with the monetary snake, social protection would be brought into convergence. This idea, put forward by Dispersyn and Van der Vorst (see Dispersyn *et al.*, 1990), is an interesting one, but there are two ways in which the snake is misleading as a parallel. First, there is no reason to reduce existing levels of social protection in those countries where it is relatively generous. The parallel should be that with environmental protection, where in adopting a water quality standard we are not asking low polluters to *increase* their emissions. Safety net seems to me a better analogy, since we hope that most people will not be in the net.

Second, the parallel with the monetary snake suggests that we are concerned with something that can be readily measured, like an exchange rate. The definition of a social minimum is, however, complex. Unlike an exchange rate, an income-tested social minimum has many dimensions. As anyone will know who has tried to make comparisons across countries, the level of protection is not unambiguously defined. One country may provide a relatively generous allowance for single persons but only a modest amount for other adults or for children. Provisions for children may vary with age and family size. Pensioners may do better or worse than those of working age. Receipt of assistance may provide additional entitlements, acting as a 'passport' to other benefits. In France the Revenu Minimum d'Insertion provides a right to l'assurance maladie and to l'allocation de logement familiale (Milano, 1989, p. 97). Housing benefit is potentially a particularly valuable addition. The total value of the package has to be taken into account. One could therefore get different answers about the degree of social protection in various countries by taking different representative families.

Moreover, as I have already argued, it is not just the level of the minimum but also its coverage which is important. It is rare to find safety net schemes that involve *only* a test of means; the typical scheme also requires that the claimant satisfy conditions other than lack of resources. These are particularly relevant to the labour market. For those of working age, and capable of work, assistance may be conditional on labour market participation. This condition may require registration at a public employment agency; it may require evidence of job search; assistance may be terminated if the claimant refuses to accept suitable employment. More generally, we have to ask whether the safety net is restricted to the *household population*. Are those living in institutions eligible? Is it necessary to have an address in order to be eligible? The extent of the safety net may vary considerably across countries.

Conclusions

The reason I have described some aspects of a safety net scheme in detail is to bring out the complexity involved in translating a safety net into reality. The setting of a minimum standard for social protection – a European safety net – involves many different dimensions, along each of which important decisions have to be taken. If we ask whether a particular Member State is providing the agreed minimum level of social protection, then this is not easily verified. The degree of social protection offered by a Member State will not be highly visible – unlike its exchange rate. It may not be easy to prevent fiscal competition.

Nor is it evident that such a European safety net would overcome the shortcomings of existing national social protection identified earlier. The problem of coverage and incomplete take-up may remain. Even with a set of common standards, a European safety net may have the same holes as the existing national schemes such as that in the UK. This suggests that in considering the form of social protection, we should perhaps look wider than at income-tested social assistance. Although it is the latter which is apparently envisaged in the Social Charter, it is not obvious that the Elizabethan Poor Law provides the best model for Europe of the next century.

I hope that I have convinced you that there are important questions to be asked about the form of a European social safety net. It does therefore seem to me highly regrettable that the British government will not be taking part in the formation of the social dimension of Europe post-1992. I referred earlier to 'exit' and 'voice' as possible reactions. The British government has chosen the former, but I believe that it would be much more valuable at this stage to be exercising voice.

15 Beveridge, the national minimum and its future in a European context

I hesitated for some time as to the subject matter of this chapter. I considered examining the present-day lessons that could be deduced from the Beveridge Report, to see what this remarkable document has to say about the design of social security for the next fifty years. However, this did not seem to me appropriate; and I sense that Beveridge himself would have been impatient with such an exercise. He was a man of his time. He would have recognised that the world has changed, and if he had reported today he would doubtless have written differently.

I considered therefore devoting the chapter to speculation as to what he *might* have written had he been alive today. To seek to extrapolate forward the evolution of his thinking. This too I rejected. Not only can I make no claim to be a Beveridge scholar, but, as Harris (1977) has brought out, his thinking on these issues went through several stages, which would make any attempt at extrapolation a difficult exercise. It also seemed to me presumptuous. In writing his report, Beveridge brought together an unrivalled blend of academic thought and administrative experience, a blend which leaves me simply humble in admiration.

I have therefore decided to do neither of these, but rather to present a personal view as to how we should seek to provide a national minimum – and, more broadly, a European minimum – in the years to come. Beveridge was clearly a person who held strong convictions and who did not conceal them; I have attempted to describe my own perception as to what should be done. We are living in less difficult times than 1942, but the next few years may be equally crucial for the development of social policy. Important decisions have to be made, and if they are not made but evaded that too will have serious implications. It is my impression that there is at present a vacuum regarding the future of social policy – that here, as in other areas of policy, we are drifting rudderless.

15.1 Old problems

The central problem that concerns me is very much the same as that which confronted Beveridge 50 years ago. His Plan began 'from a diagnosis of want'. What he meant by this has been the subject of debate, and what we mean today is undoubtedly different. I do not want here to go into this important topic. I am simply going to state that there *is* concern about the living standards of those at the bottom of the income distribution in Britain today.

These concerns are based in part on the evidence of our eyes and in part on statistical evidence from household surveys. The former should not be neglected. As social scientists, we are trained to be cautious about reliance on personal experience and are aware of the unrepresentativeness of everyday life. But this does not mean that we should close our eyes to what we see, and it should enter our judgements alongside the more representative sources of evidence. In this connection, I remember being very struck when I first began studying this subject by the case studies that the National Assistance Board used to include in its Annual Reports. Such case studies are now less common in official reports, which, for all their stylish production, seem remote from real people.

The household surveys which provide the main evidence are similar in principle to those used by Beveridge, but their operation and their analysis are in a number of respects more sophisticated. Having just criticised official documents, I should in particular pay tribute to the considerable efforts made in recent years by the statisticians and economists at the Department of Social Security. While one can take issue with some aspects of their publication 'Households Below Average Income', such as its focus on the household as a unit, it must be recognised that their work represents a major development in official statistics.

From the Households Below Average Income study (Department of Social Security, 1992, p. 28), one can see that the lowest income groups have failed to share equally in the gains in average real incomes over the past decade. Average real equivalent income rose by around 30 per cent from 1979 to 1988/9, but the income in the middle of the bottom decile (that is, 5 per cent up from the bottom) increased very little (2 per cent before housing costs) or fell (−6 per cent after housing costs). Corresponding figures for the middle of the second decile (15 per cent up from the bottom) are rises of 5 per cent (before housing costs) or 2 per cent (after housing costs).

Looked at a different way, the European Commission yardstick defines low income as having less than 50 per cent of national average income (European Commission, 1991). In 1979 in the United Kingdom, according to the 'Households Below Average Income' study, 4.4 million people had incomes below half the national average; by 1988/9 the number had more than doubled to 10.4 million. The official UK government estimates (Department of Social Security, 1992, pp. 52, 56 and 89) show that 19 per cent of the population, and 22 per cent of children, had low incomes according to this European Commission standard.

In seeking the reasons why the poor are failing to keep up, it is striking how relevant today is the answer given by Beveridge in 1942: 'Of all the want shown by the surveys, from three-quarters to five sixths ... was due to interruption or loss of earning power' (1942, p. 7). Between the 1970s and the 1980s there has been a decline in the contribution of work to family incomes (see chapter 1). In 1975 employment and self-employment accounted for 80 per cent of household income; by 1990 this had fallen to 72 per cent. In 1975, 81 per cent of families were supported by a person in work; ten years later in 1985 this had fallen to 69 per cent. Whereas about one in five families were without work income, the proportion has now risen to nearly one in three.

In turn, the social security system has failed to provide the necessary guarantee against loss of earned incomes. National Insurance has not ensured the effective national minimum which Beveridge envisaged. This is most striking in the case of the unemployed, where it is scarcely an exaggeration to say that post-war unemployment insurance worked in an acceptable manner only as long as there was no significant unemployment. When put to the test in the late 1970s and 1980s, unemployment insurance failed.

Unemployment insurance failed for several reasons. The insurance benefits were not set at a level which ensured that people could live independently of means-tested assistance in all but exceptional cases, as had been Beveridge's intention. (I am distinguishing here between social *insurance* benefits, paid by virtue of contributions, and social *assistance*, paid without regard to contributions but subject to a means test.) The limitation of insurance benefits to a 12 month period means that, with extended periods of unemployment, many people exhaust their entitlement to insurance. There are the often forgotten conditions attached to the receipt of unemployment benefit. Some economists refer to unemployment insurance as the 'wage when not working', but this reveals a lack of knowledge of the many reasons why people may not be eligible for, or may be disqualified from, receipt of the benefit. These include the contribution conditions, which have been significantly tightened in recent years.

An observer from outside our society might naively have expected that the response to high unemployment would have been to make the unemployment insurance system more effective. The reaction of the government has in fact been quite the reverse. John Micklewright and I have listed no fewer than 38 significant changes which were made in the 1980s to benefits for the unemployed in Britain (see chapter 9) and all but a few reduced the extent and effectiveness of income protection (Atkinson and Micklewright, 1989). The final effect is that a small minority of the unemployed now receive unemployment insurance. Whereas in the 1950s and 1960s more than half of the unemployed received insurance benefit, now only about one quarter do so (Micklewright, 1990). In 1989, for example, the number of people receiving National Insurance unemployment benefit in the United Kingdom was almost exactly the same as in 1963 – despite the fact that the recorded level of unemployment was more than three times higher in 1989 (*Annual Abstract of Statistics* 1966, table 43 and 1992, table 3.15).

Other groups have been less affected by reductions in coverage, but there has been pressure on benefit levels. Most important here is the change in policy with regard to the uprating of the basic state retirement pension. Over the 1950s there came to be a general acceptance of the principle that benefits should be adjusted with rising real incomes of the working population. However, the automatic link with earnings was abolished in the 1980s and only price uprating guaranteed. The full implications of this change in policy have yet to be appreciated, but the retirement pension has fallen from being more than 30 per cent of net average male weekly earnings – not itself a particularly generous figure – to some 20 per cent. This goes alongside the down-grading of the State Earnings Related Pension Scheme. As shown in chapter 8, state pensions now provide a degree of income replacement which is low by international standards and by comparison with occupational schemes.

Growth in means testing

The consequence is that there has been increased – rather than reduced – dependence on means-tested assistance. As insurance benefits have been cut back, more of the unemployed have become dependent on Income Support. Many pensioners continue to depend on Income Support, as do one parent families, the disabled and others. Rather than the numbers on assistance falling, as Beveridge hoped, they have grown substantially, as is brought out by figure 13.2. In 1948, about 1 million people were in receipt of National Assistance, or around 2 per cent of the population. By 1966, when the scheme was rechristened Supplementary Benefit, the number had more than doubled. The 1980s saw a big increase, and Income Support is now paid to some 5 million people, or about 9 per cent of the population. Moreover, these figures do not include the members of the families concerned, and if we add those living in families in receipt of Family Credit, then we arrive at a figure of some 16 per cent of the population. About one person in six is dependent on these means-tested benefits. Put another, more tendentious way, there are more than twice as many people in Britain dependent on Income Support or Family Credit as there are people working in manufacturing.

15.2 New dimensions

These problems would have had a depressingly familiar ring to Beveridge, but there are also new dimensions. Everyone has no doubt their own list of the important changes that characterise today as opposed to fifty years ago. Here I shall just highlight three.

Labour market pessimism

The first of these I shall call 'labour market pessimism'. In my view Beveridge was absolutely right to stress that social insurance should be seen as an integrated part of a wider policy of social and economic progress. It is not a separate self-contained area of policy. He was right to base his plan on the assumption that government policy would be directed at maintaining employment.

Today however we are less confident that this objective can be achieved. We are less confident in the capacity of the government to manage the economy, and more aware of the limits on economic policymaking. Among the most important of these limits are those imposed by external considerations. It is also the case that work has become less effective as an anti-poverty guarantee. Over the 1980s, the low paid have fallen systematic-ally further behind average earnings, intensifying the problem of poverty among working families, a problem which Beveridge effectively dismissed with his statement that 'very few men's wages are insufficient to cover at least two adults and one child' (1942, p. 156). (I shall return in a moment to the fact that he referred to 'men'.)

So that while I am definitely not arguing that we should accept the present labour market state and present levels of unemployment, I do believe that social security has to be designed taking a cautious view as to what policy can achieve in this area.

Independence

The second major change has been in social attitudes towards independence and the obligation placed on others to support those in need. In one respect, Beveridge was quite progressive, viewed even from today, endorsing the important change made in the Determination of Needs Act of 1941 regarding the liability of relatives to maintain and the ending of the hated household means test. National Assistance gave a right to support without consideration of the resources of non-dependent children or of parents (other than the contribution of other household members to rent and other common costs).[1] By the standards of other European countries, this allowed a much greater degree of freedom. It allowed young people to establish themselves away from their parents and for the elderly to preserve their independence.

Our conception of independence has now however gone further, as is evidenced by the introduction of separate income taxation for husbands and wives. This may be contrasted with Beveridge's refusal to put married women on the same footing as men for the purposes of social insurance. In his treatment of the position of women, Beveridge was arguably in line with contemporary thinking, and may indeed have been in advance in his recognition of the role of unpaid work. But seen from today's perspective, it is not now acceptable to base a plan for social security on a model of the family supported by male bread-winners and where the principal role of women is to be wives and mothers. The assumption from which I work here is that any social security system for the twenty-first century must be based essentially on the individual, and must permit and support independence. This is relevant particularly to women with the sole care of dependants, including one-parent families, and to women in old age.

European context

The third dimension which is new is that alluded to in my title – the European context. Discussing matters European at the moment is hazardous, since one runs the risk of being overtaken by events. For this reason, I shall take the medium- to long-term perspective which is appropriate for this occasion. I therefore discuss the European dimension on the assumption that the Maastricht Agreement will proceed, that the Social Charter will be adopted, and that Britain will see the error of its ways and sign the Charter.

The social protection provisions of the Charter have a two-tier structure. First, all workers have a right to social security benefits of a sufficient level. Second, all persons excluded from the labour market have the right to a guaranteed level of resources. It is the second tier which represents the European minimum, and on which attention here is largely concentrated.

In asking what is envisaged for the second tier, it is important to see the British situation from a European point of view. As far as social assistance is concerned, Britain has been among the leaders. The product of the 1934 establishment of Unemployment Assistance, of the 1941 Determination of Needs Act, and of the Beveridge Report, was a unified system of national assistance. Assistance was assessed according to a national scale, and covered people out of work for whatever reason. The existence of such a national scheme, unified geographically, and without categorical distinctions, marked Britain out from most other European countries.

This context is important in understanding the reason why the social protection provisions of the Social Charter are being seen on the mainland in terms of a minimum income guarantee – that is of income-tested assistance. Income Support, or the French Revenu Minimum d'Insertion (RMI), introduced in 1988, is being seen as a model for the implementation of second tier of the Social Charter. But this would be a mistake, since Beveridge was right about means testing.

15.3 Beveridge was right about means testing

The conception by Beveridge of the role for means-tested assistance is well known, but deserves re-emphasis at the present time. For Beveridge, national assistance had an essential, but subsidiary role. To quote, 'the scope of assistance will be narrowed from the beginning and will diminish. . . . The scheme of social insurance is designed of itself when in full operation to guarantee the income needed for subsistence in all normal cases' (1942, p. 12). He took this view on account of 'the strength of popular objection to any kind of means test' (1942, p. 12), and of the way in which it penalised individual efforts (through the high marginal tax rate). In fact, we have seen that assistance did not decline but increased in importance.

But Beveridge was right. For several reasons. The means-tested approach necessarily penalises personal effort. Even if the poverty trap no longer involves marginal tax rates in excess of 100 per cent, the marginal rates are still higher than those levied on the rest of the population. Perhaps more importantly it is not just individual efforts that are penalised, but those of the person's family. Unlike individualised social insurance, social assistance discourages the partners of those out of work from earning income. I find it strange that a government so concerned with incentives should not see that reliance on means testing has such a counterproductive effect, an effect which becomes apparent when one compares Britain with other European countries that provide more extensive social insurance for the unemployed and do not rely on the same degree on means testing.

Secondly, the popular objection to which Beveridge referred has been revealed in the recurrent problem of incomplete take-up. A significant minority of those with incomes below the assistance level do not claim the benefits to which they are entitled. The reasons are doubtless manifold, but the failure of successive take-up campaigns indicates that it is not simply a matter of inadequate information. There are deep-seated objections to claiming means-tested benefits. These problems of take-up reflect past history and cultural values. They may therefore be different in other countries, and the French do appear to have achieved a high rate of take-up with the RMI (Vanlerenberghe, 1992). But other countries, such as Germany and the Netherlands, report problems of incomplete take-up (van Oorschot, 1991).

The objections to means testing are further reinforced when we take account of the new dimensions. The means test can only make sense when applied to the family or the household as a unit. As such, it runs counter to the desire to have a social security system which ensures independence. This is particularly important for women. But it also applies to young people, as we have seen with the problems of young adults and Income Support.

Turning to the European context, and looking ahead to the ways in which European policy may be aligned, we have to ask how far means-tested benefits would be amenable to such developments. There have for example been proposals for a kind of 'social snake', as discussed in chapter 14, where by analogy with the monetary snake, social protection would be brought into convergence. The parallel with the monetary snake suggests that national policies can be summarised in a single variable, like an exchange rate, or a relatively small number of variables. It is possible to imagine benefits for which this is possible, such as child benefit, although even in the case of child benefit, there are problems such as defining the age of eligibility.

The definition of a means-tested social minimum is however much more complex. It has many dimensions. How is income to be defined in applying the income test? Is certain income to be disregarded, like gratuities for the Victoria Cross? What is the definition of the recipient unit? What liability is there of other family members to maintain? Over what period is income to be measured? How far are assets to be taken into account? The fact that the administrative costs per £1 of benefit are seven times higher for Income Support than for child benefit is indicative of the greater complexity. The complexity means in turn that the co-ordination of policy across member states would be much more difficult. If we were to ask whether a particular country is providing the agreed minimum level of social protection, then this would not be easily verified. If we are seeking a basis for the second tier which allows a European-wide, and not just a national, minimum to be set in place, then it has, in my judgement, to be based on a benefit which is simpler in structure than means-tested social assistance.

To sum up, Britain has the dubious advantage that it has experimented extensively with a minimum income guarantee, and we have seen its shortcomings. The saying of Santayana, that those who do not remember the past are condemned to repeat it, should perhaps be extended to include those who do not learn from the experience of their neighbours. A means-tested second tier is not the route for Europe to follow.

15.4 Should we go back to Beveridge?

Should we then go back to Beveridge, and see social insurance as the primary basis for income maintenance? In Atkinson (1969), I argued that the Beveridge recommendations had not been tried as proposed and examined the case for a significant increase in social insurance benefits designed to reduce dependence on Income Support. Such a 'Back to Beveridge' policy has been advocated over the years by the Child Poverty Action Group and others.

I am still convinced that social insurance has an important role to play. It enjoys considerable public support, and it provides for a wide range of contingencies. It is independent in construction, so that, with some exceptions, benefits are paid in relation to individual rather than family circumstances. Of course, there are major areas which need reform. Unemployment Insurance should be paid for an unlimited duration. The basic state pension should once again be indexed to net average earnings. The State Earnings Related Pension should be restructured to provide a benefit which is closer to those available in France and Germany. There should be new benefits for carers and the disabled.

The design of a *Modernised* Social Insurance is, I believe, an important task on the agenda. Moreover, the European dimension has reinforced my belief in social insurance. The social security systems of the other EC countries are heavily based on this principle, and it enjoys the confidence of the social partners – that is employers and worker representatives – who under Maastricht enjoy increased authority. Indeed social insurance offers a way of making sense of the principle of subsidiarity. This principle has popularly been interpreted as concerned with relations between Brussels and national governments, whereas in its original usage it clearly refers also to the relation between governments and subsidiary organisations, like those of workers or employers. A social insurance system can be managed at a national, or sub-national, level by quasi-independent institutions, which may be answerable to members or their representatives.

Moreover, social insurance by providing a transparent link between contributions and benefits via the contribution principle is less subject to the downward pressures of fiscal competition. The idea that taxpayers will engineer a reduction in welfare expenditures by threatened or actual migration to countries with lower tax rates becomes less plausible when the migration decision also entails the transparent loss of benefits. The contribution principle is at least a partial defence against competitive pressures to dismantle the welfare state.

Yet the same contribution principle is one of the reasons why reformed social insurance cannot be the whole of the story. The origins of social insurance are to be found in the modern employment relationship (see chapter 11). Social insurance was adopted, at least in part, because it was functional in the working of modern employment. It does not recognise the needs of those outside the formal economy, such as people taking care of dependants. It excludes by the contribution conditions those who have recently entered and those who have interrupted work careers. There are difficulties in providing for part-time employees and for the more flexible working arrangements that are likely to characterise the next century. And, there is the basic difficulty that it does not provide for those in work. Beveridge dismissed the problem with the statement quoted earlier – that wages would cover the needs of at least two adults and one child. Today we cannot do this. Not only have the low paid been left behind, with the widening of earnings inequality in the 1980s. But also we have to look at the wages of women, and the extent to which they can provide for one-parent families, or indeed for the needs of a single adult. Despite some narrowing of the gender differential as a result of Equal Pay legislation, it still remains substantial.

15.5 Basic income rather than social insurance?

The limitations of social insurance are one reason why the idea of a basic income, or social dividend, has been put forward as an alternative. Fifty years ago, this idea was being promoted as an alternative to Beveridge by Lady Juliet Rhys Williams (1943) under the title of 'a new social contract'. It was later taken up by among others her son, Sir Brandon Rhys Williams, and James Meade. As subsequently developed, the basic income would replace all existing social insurance and assistance benefits by a single payment, paid on an individual basis, without any test of means, and paid unconditionally. The benefit would also replace all income tax allowances, and in this sense there would be an integration of taxation and social security, although the tax would be collected in a separate operation. In the simplest form of the scheme, there would be a single tax rate on all income.

In fact, the idea dates back much earlier than 1942, as Van Trier (1990) has shown, going back at least to the State Bonus advocated by Mabel and Dennis Milner in 1918. The review of their pamphlet (Milner and Milner, 1918) in the *Economic Journal* for June 1919 by Clara Collet, who worked as one of Charles Booth's assistants on his Survey of London Life and Labour, has a first paragraph which is perhaps a record in acidity:

> The authors of this pamphlet propound a scheme for an equal distribution of 5s. (pre-war) per head per week for all persons, to be provided from a pool maintained by everyone contributing 20 per cent of their incomes. The demerits of such a proposal are too obvious to need enumeration. (Collet, 1919, p. 241)

She does immediately go on to suggest that the state bonus deserves careful attention. However, despite the attention which has since been given, and despite finding supporters in all political parties, the basic income has not got close to being introduced. It is the demerits that have so far carried the day. If one asks why, then in my judgement there are two serious obstacles. The first is that there remains strong support for social insurance. This is particularly true among the social partners and in a European context this is important. Moreover, this support is not without foundation. The differentiation involved in the typical social insurance scheme is not entirely arbitrary, and the basic income payments would need to retain some categorical elements. The relation of benefits received to contributions paid reduces, as noted earlier, the risk of fiscal competition between governments.

In my view, it is therefore a mistake to see basic income as an *alternative* to social insurance. The historical opposition to Beveridge should be forgotten. It is more productive to see basic income as complementary. For this reason, I am much more persuaded by the approach to basic income adopted by Parker (1989) as the first phase of a move to a basic income. In her BIG Phase 1, she outlines a scheme that would replace tax allowances, although retaining an earned income disregard, but would keep the existing structure of social insurance benefits. However I would see this partnership between social insurance and basic income not just as a transitional compromise, but as an alternative conception of the basic income. The basic income would complement an improved social insurance scheme by reducing dependence on means-tested social assistance and by helping low-wage workers.

But this is not enough to ensure political support. I am sure that a major reason for opposition to basic income lies in its lack of conditionality. One of the legacies of the Thatcher years has been concern about dependency, and these concerns are not limited to Britain. The French Revenu Minimum d'Insertion gives a central role to such conditions, being payable beyond the first three months only on the condition that a contract for 'insertion' in the labour market has been negotiated with the recipient and that the terms of this contract are respected. In this way, there is a link with positive measures of labour market policy.

I believe therefore that, in order to secure political support, it may be necessary for the proponents of basic income to compromise. To compromise not on the principle that there is no test of means, nor on the principle of independence, but on the unconditional payment. To do so would in fact be in line with the original proposal of Lady Rhys Williams, who wrote of a new social contract between the individual: 'and the State, whereby the State would acknowledge the duty to maintain the individual and his children at all times, and to ensure for them the necessities of a healthy life. The individual, in his turn, would acknowledge it to be his duty to devote his best efforts to the production of the wealth whereby alone the welfare of the community can be maintained' (1943, p. 145).

15.6 A participation income?

This leads me then to conclude that the most promising route is to complement Modernised Social Insurance with a scheme which preserves the principles of a basic income, of not being means tested and of being on an individual basis, but which is conditional on *participation.* The way in which this participation would be defined requires detailed consideration. It would no doubt include:

work as an employee or self-employed,
reaching pension age,
inability to work on grounds of disability,
unemployment but available for work,
engaging in approved forms of education or training,
caring for young, elderly or disabled dependants,
undertaking approved forms of voluntary work, etc.

As the last examples make clear, the condition is not *paid* work; it is a wider definition of social contribution. The determination of these conditions would be different from those involved with Income Support at present: for example, an unemployed person who undertook part-time work would be *qualifying* rather than the reverse. But there would undoubtedly be problems, problems which would not arise with the unconditional basic income. And these problems would mean that there were people who failed to secure the basic income. There would undoubtedly also be behavioural responses, as people adjusted their actions in order to qualify, and there may be repercussions for wages.

But such a scheme does offer considerable prospects, particularly in what I conceive to be its main role – the reduction in dependence on means-tested benefits. Moreover, I believe that such a scheme offers the only realistic way in which governments may be persuaded that it offers a better route forward than the dead end of means-tested assistance. This is particularly true at the European level, where the driving forces are very much concerned with the labour market.

For this reason, I believe that the basic income movement may be making a mistake in changing its name to a 'Citizen's Income'. (And I am here leaving on one side the problems which arise if the concept of citizenship is applied to the determination of benefit eligibility.) It could be called an 'Active Citizen's Income', but I rather prefer the term – not my own invention – *participation income*.

What would such a scheme look like in more concrete terms? When it came to the costing of his proposals, Beveridge was helped by Lionel Robbins and others working in the Economic section of the Cabinet Office, as well as the Government Actuary, and, of course, Keynes. Harris refers to Keynes and Beveridge discussing the costing over dinner at the Gargoyle Club (1977, p. 411). Today access to tax-benefit models means that one can operate independently, although perhaps without such gastronomic benefits. The scheme which I have sketched here has indeed been run through the new model POLIMOD which has been produced by Holly Sutherland as part of the Welfare State Programme, and which will be available from the Microsimulation Unit of which she is Director.

The version of the Participation Income considered involved:

complete abolition of tax allowances,
abolition of the upper earnings limit on National Insurance contributions,
abolition of the 20 per cent income tax band, but retention of the present 25 per cent and 40 per cent bands,
taxation of all social insurance benefits.

Indeed all income would be taxed, except for

disregard of the first tranche of earnings £10 a week,

On the benefit side,

payment of a basic income to all children of £12.50 a week, in place of the current child benefit,
payment of a participation income to all those aged 18 and over, who are in work, or self-employment, are away from work on account of sickness or injury, are aged over the minimum pension age, are disabled, are caring for dependent children, are in full-time education, or unemployed and seeking work.

The calculations suggest that the revenue neutral level of adult participation income would be some £18.25 a week. This would cover the great majority of the population. If all others were to change their behaviour in order to qualify, then the amount would be reduced to £17.75 a week.

With such a basic income, the number dependent on means-tested benefits would be reduced by half a million. A third of families would be worse off in cash terms; 10 per cent would be virtually unaffected; and 57 per cent would gain. Among the latter would be many women.

If the tax rate were to be raised from 25 per cent to 35 per cent, and the higher rate to 50 per cent, than the basic income for adults would rise to between £37 and £39 a week. The number receiving means-tested benefits would be reduced by more than $2\frac{1}{4}$ million. This would be a major improvement. In terms of figure 13.2, it would bring us back to about the level of the mid 1960s. However, as this indicates, the participation income would not on its own be enough; there would have to be improvements too in social insurance. The Participation Income would be a complement to Modernised Social Insurance.

Conclusions: a personal view

This, then, is my personal view. The route to providing an effective national minimum for Britain is a combination of improved social insurance, complemented by a participation income. The means-tested route followed by the present government cannot offer an effective solution, as Beveridge was well aware. For all the rhetoric about targeting, means testing has not worked, and a major aim of policy in Britain should be to reduce dependence on means-tested benefits. Income Support should be playing only a subsidiary role, just as Beveridge advocated.

Such a two-tier strategy of Modernised Social Insurance plus Participation Income is, in my view, consistent with developments in Europe. While social insurance can be set according to national preferences (questions of fiscal competition being less likely to arise), it is the Participation Income that should provide the basis for the European safety net. Our European partners should be told that the way to an effective European safety net cannot be found by some modern version of the Poor Law. It is to influence this choice that it is, in my view, essential that Britain take part in the Social Charter.

Finally, in discussing the choices to be made, I have made judgements about political feasibility. In this respect, I have followed the lead of the Beveridge Report, which may be seen as ultimately concerned with such issues of feasibility. Like the Beveridge Report, the proposals sketched here involved redistribution. This cannot be avoided. To achieve an effective national minimum, those above that minimum are going to have to pay higher taxes. If the proportion of families without an income from work has risen from 1 in 5 to 1 in 3, then those in work are going to have to pay higher taxes or contributions. It does public debate no service to suggest that an effective national minimum can be achieved at no cost simply through more efficient targeting.

If political support for change is dependent on journalists paying no more tax, then there is little prospect for progress. Taxation has to be rehabilitated. Progress will only come if sufficient people are willing to say that the present state of affairs is unacceptable and that there has to be redistribution. For my part, I believe that if Beveridge were to join us here today, then we would be ashamed to admit how far we are from achieving the objectives of his Plan.

16 State pensions for today and tomorrow

Pensions are a complicated subject, but my purpose in this chapter is simple. I want to argue that the present pension provisions in Britain cannot guarantee an adequate minimum standard of income in old age, and that, unless there is a change in policy, particularly with regard to state pensions, then the problem of poverty in old age is likely to remain with us. The story line is revealed right at the start, so that when I get into the details of pension schemes, or Income Support, or of my alternative proposals, you know where the discussion is leading.

The future of pensions has, of course, recently been much debated. The newspapers have been full of the subject and there have been a series of television documentaries. In my view, however, the focus of much of this debate has been wrong. The point of departure has been the government budget deficit and the claim that Welfare State spending is out of control. An atmosphere has been created in which pension provision is seen as a burden on the economy and as a threat to our future. This has led to a debate which is overly negative, and which fails to take a balanced view of the role of pensions in a modern society. Politicians appear too often to have lost sight of the purpose of pension provision, which is to assure the living standards of those in retirement.

The aim here is to redress this imbalance, by starting from the function that pensions, whether public or private, are intended to perform. I begin therefore in section 16.1 with the aims of pensions policy.

16.1 Aims of pension policy

My primary concern in this chapter is with the adequacy of incomes in old age, viewed in relation to a socially determined standard. Before considering the implications of such a criterion, I should clarify two points.

Range of objectives

The first is that I am not asserting that the sole function of pensions is the prevention of poverty. Such an assertion appears to underlie the proposals that are made for 'greater targeting' of the social security system. There are frequent calls for a reform of transfers to concentrate help on those 'in need', so as to make them more effective as an anti-poverty policy. This however ignores the other important objectives of pensions and other benefits. (On targeting in general, see chapter 12.)

The objectives of pension policy include both other redistributive goals and non-redistributive purposes. Redistribution has to be seen not just in terms of people above or below a poverty line. Pensions may be designed to offset disadvantages which people have suffered in their working lives, such as low pay or repeated spells of unemployment, or at least to ensure that these disadvantages are not reproduced in retirement. There may be concern about the distribution between men and women, with state pensions redressing some of the gender earnings inequality.

Such redistributional goals may be open to dispute, in that people have different social judgements, but there may also be non-redistributive grounds for policy intervention. As it has been well put, the Welfare State:

> does things which private markets for technical reasons either would not do at all, or would do inefficiently. We need a welfare state of some sort for efficiency reasons, and would continue to do so even if all distributional problems had been solved. (Barr, 1993, p. 433)

In terms of pensions, everyone should have the opportunity to smooth out income over their lifetime. A major rationale for state pensions in the past has been that of aiding people to make their desired provision for later in life in an efficient manner and on terms which offer a reasonable degree of certainty against risks like that of inflation. Looking forward, the aim should be to provide today's workers with a sense of security about their future old age. Looking back, the retired should feel that their current situation bears a reasonable relation to what they have saved.

In what follows, I am going to give priority to the goal of an adequate minimum pension, but these other objectives are an important part of the story and may influence our choice between different approaches to guaranteeing an adequate minimum.

Adequacy as a relative standard

The second point concerns the definition of an 'adequate' standard. Here there is a major departure between the position taken in this chapter and that of the present Conservative government. I say the *present* Conservative government, because earlier governments have held a different view, with which I have much more sympathy. In 1959 the Conservative Minister for Pensions and National Insurance issued a White Paper in which he referred to giving those on National Assistance 'a share in increasing national prosperity' (Ministry of Pensions and National Insurance, 1959, p. 3), as discussed in chapter 7. This became a position of general consensus, and implied that our criterion of adequacy would rise with rising standards of life in the community. Even as recently as 1981, the Conservative government promised that 'as the economy improves, elderly people will share in that improvement' (Department of Health and Social Security, 1981, p. iii). However, since then, as revealed by its policy on up-rating pensions and other benefits, the government's view appears to have become that the minimum should be fixed in real terms. There is no longer a guarantee that the elderly will share in rising real incomes.

In my judgement, a static standard of living, fixed for all time, is quite unacceptable as an objective of pensions policy. People retiring today may well live to 2020 or beyond. Is the only real increase to which they can look forward in this time the 25p. addition at age 80? The reason why a fixed standard is unacceptable was well described by the Supplementary Benefits Commission a few years ago: 'beneficiaries must have an income which enables them to participate in the life of the community' (1979, p. 20). They cannot participate if community activities require new or additional goods and services. Indeed, if the goods they used to buy are no longer available, or only available in more expensive forms, then even with a fixed real income they will be increasingly excluded from the life style they used to enjoy, let alone that of the rest of the community. (The participation approach is well known from the work of Townsend (1979); economists have treated it in terms of 'capabilities', a concept introduced by Sen (1983).)

The concept of participation has in turn been adopted by the European Union in its approach to social exclusion, where it has spoken of the challenge posed by a phenomenon 'which excludes part of the population from economic and social life and from their share of the general prosperity' (European Commission, 1993, p. 7). The Commission has taken as a working definition that people face exclusion if their income is below 50 per cent of the average in the member state in which they live. On the basis of the government's own study, *Households Below Average Income*, average net household income adjusted for household size corresponds to some £80 a week in round terms (Department of Social Security, 1993b, table A2, p. 61, equivalised net income before housing costs at April 1993 prices, expressed for a single adult).

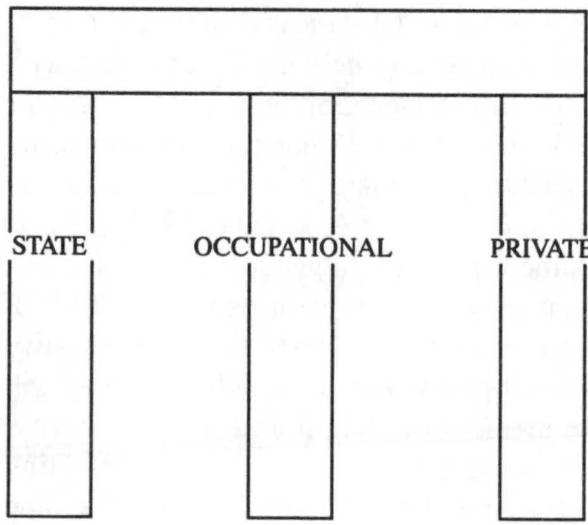

Figure 16.1 The three pillar approach

In what follows, it is assumed that the objective of pensions policy is that of ensuring an adequate minimum determined in relation to the general level of incomes. Where a precise number is needed, particular attention is given to the 50 per cent standard adopted by the European Union, or £80 a week in current terms in the United Kingdom. The simple question I now want to ask is how far existing pension provisions in Britain can meet the test of providing such a guarantee.

16.2 The decline of the basic pension

In discussion of financial provision for retirement in other European countries, reference is often made to the *three pillars* of the state, occupational provision, and private savings – see figure 16.1. This may look like a good example of a redundant graphic, containing no information other than the words, but it is intended to underline the fact that the three pillars are seen as *complementary*. They all combine to provide security in old age: a multi-faceted approach. In the German case, for instance, essentially all workers are covered by the state earnings-related pension scheme, many have complementary occupational provision, and this may be supplemented by private savings.

This philosophy is different from that which now governs pensions policy in Britain. The picture here (figure 16.2) is of a basic flat-rate pension supplemented by a choice of second-tier provision. The second-tier may consist of the state earnings-related pension (SERPS), or of an occupational pension which is contracted out of the additional state provision, or

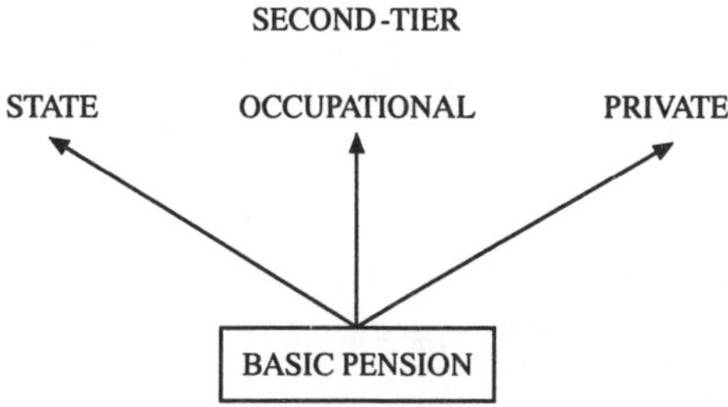

Figure 16.2 The UK pension structure

of a contracted out personal pension plan. At any point in time, an individual has a choice, and that choice may have serious consequences.

Basic pension

The structure set out in figure 16.2 may well appear ideally suited to meet the objective of pensions policy with which I am concerned here, with the basic National Insurance pension ensuring the target adequate minimum and the second-tier allowing individual choice as to additional provision.

This was indeed the Beveridge approach. The only problem is that the Beveridge approach was never implemented as he intended. Twenty-five years ago, in *Poverty in Britain and the Reform of Social Security* (Atkinson, 1969), I examined the implications of the fact that the basic National Insurance pension had never been set at a level sufficient to ensure that the elderly were independent of means-tested social assistance. In this respect, little has changed. Many pensioners have to rely on Income Support to supplement the basic pension, and the objections to this remain (see section 16.5 below). However, the situation *has* changed in that the very *existence* of the National Insurance pension is now under threat. The abolition by the Thatcher government of the earnings indexation of the basic flat-rate pension and its replacement by price indexation has meant that the pension has fallen relative to net average earnings since the early 1980s, as we have seen in chapter 8. There has been a very substantial reduction, and if projected into the future means that the basic pension will become of dwindling significance.

The importance of this development may be seen in terms of the target of adequacy based on the European Union standard. Figure 16.3 shows that in 1979 the basic pension fell short of 50 per cent of average income, but at 42 per cent was within striking distance. (These figures are higher than the percentages of average earnings just quoted since average male earnings are significantly higher than average equivalent incomes.) If the basic pension

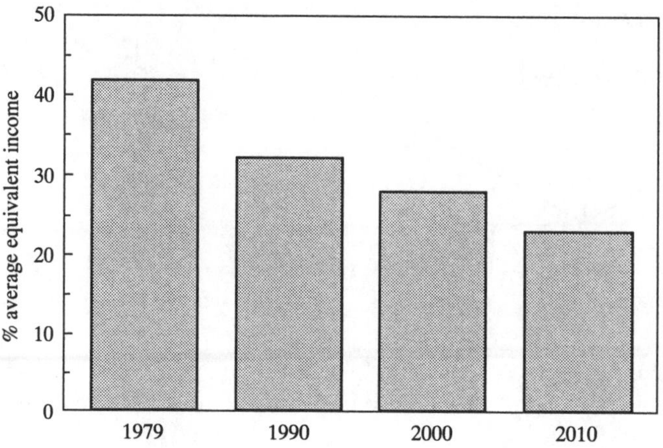

Figure 16.3 Basic National Insurance pension as per cent of average income

for a single person had been increased with the higher of prices and earnings, as in the previous legislation, then in April 1993 it would have been £75.35 a week (Walker, 1993, table 1), which is close to the £80 target. In fact it was £56.10 a week, or some 35 per cent of average income. We have, as demonstrated in figure 16.3, moved away from the target, rather than towards it, and this will continue if real net incomes continue to rise. At a growth rate for real average net income of 2 per cent per year, which is the trend for the past forty years, by the year 2000 the pension will be 28 per cent of average net income and by 2010 it will be down to less than a quarter.

What I am describing here is not news. It is well understood by the government. The basic pension 'is going to be worth a nugatory amount in the coming century, because people's earnings are rising so much faster than prices' (M. Portillo, MP, *Guardian*, 8 December 1993). 'Nugatory' means of 'trifling importance', and we have therefore to ask the question Mr Portillo himself posed – how far does the second-tier replace the basic pension which was supposed to be the foundation of our pension policy?

16.3 Shortcomings of the second-tier

The second-tier offers a three-way split, with people either belonging to the state earnings-related scheme, or to a contracted-out occupational scheme, or to a personal pension plan. In broad proportions, there are about 45 per cent of employees in contracted-out occupational schemes, 35 per cent in SERPS and 20 per cent in personal pensions. Although some people may be following more than one route at once, as with occupational schemes which are not contracted out, and even though a lot of people change from one to another in the course of their lives, people are heavily dependent on the route that they choose or which is chosen for them.

Each of these routes is considered in turn.

The state earnings-related pension (SERPS)

SERPS dates from the 1975 Social Security Pensions Act, which introduced a second-tier state pension (replacing the earlier Graduated Pension) related to the earnings history of an individual worker. It was to have paid full pensions from 1998, calculated on the basis of the best 20 years of lifetime earnings as described in chapter 8.

There can be little doubt that the SERPS scheme, as originally introduced, would when mature have gone a long way towards ensuring an adequate minimum income in old age. Estimates by Altmann and Atkinson (1982) show that, on pessimistic assumptions, the number of pensioners on means-tested assistance would have been reduced to a third, and that on more optimistic assumptions very few would have had to resort to assistance. However, the Fowler Review of the social security system in the mid 1980s made major changes (Department of Health and Social Security, 1985 and 1985a). It was proposed initially that SERPS be abolished. This met strong opposition, not just from the expected lobbies but also from the employers' organisations and from the pension industry. The government decided instead to scale down the SERPS scheme, changing the formula from 25 per cent of the best 20 years of earnings to 20 per cent of the lifetime average, thereby reducing the accrual rate from 1/80th of earnings to 1/245th (taking a working lifetime of 49 years).

The 1986 Act has reduced the efficacy of SERPS, and there are now serious doubts whether, as modified, it can provide an adequate minimum pension. This may be seen from the following arithmetic. In round numbers, average male gross earnings are about twice the average net equivalent income used as the basis for my adequacy criterion. The total state pension has to be some 25 per cent, therefore, of average gross male earnings. If the basic pension has fallen to some $7\frac{1}{2}$ per cent of average gross male earnings, as it may well do by 2030 (Hills, 1993, p. 51), then the additional pension has to be $17\frac{1}{2}$ per cent. Multiplying by 5, and adding the lower earnings limit (assumed equal to the basic pension), we can see that, in order to reach this target, a person has on average to earn 95 per cent of average gross male earnings for the whole of the working lifetime (or the working lifetime reduced by the period covered by home responsibility protection). As is well known, at any one time less than half of male workers earn the male average or more, and only some 20 per cent of women earn more than the male average. (Here I am talking not about replacement rates (ratio of pension to final earnings), which are the usual basis for assessment, but about the actual level of pensions promised for the future.)

Even taking good years with bad years, once the 1986 changes have taken full effect, many people will have SERPS pensions which leave them below the minimum adequacy standard.

Occupational pensions

Occupational schemes as a whole provide more than a fifth of the income of today's pensioners and they will become even more important in the future. At the same time, occupational schemes have their limitations. Some of these are addressed in the recommendations of the Goode Report (1993). The recommendations include appointment of a Pensions Regulator, the introduction of minimum solvency requirements, the right of scheme members to appoint trustees, and a compensation scheme to cover deficits arising from fraud, theft, or other misappropriation. If the recommendations are in large part accepted by the government, then they will go a substantial way towards strengthening the security of the occupational pension promise.

But problems will still remain, and there may continue to be cases where the pension promise is not fulfilled, even in the case of defined benefit schemes. The proposed compensation scheme does not cover cases where the employer is bankrupt, the scheme is in deficit, but there is no presumption of fraud or theft. The employee still shares some of the risk. There is the problem of transfer on changing employment, where the situation has improved, but the terms of transfer do not ensure that a person with *x* years of service in a defined benefit scheme carries a full *x* years eligibility into the new scheme. As noted in the Report of the Goode Committee, a particular problem arises in the case of discretionary benefits, which may not be included in the transfer value. The issue of transfers is related to that of incomplete work careers. An occupational scheme cannot provide for periods of unemployment, and it is unlikely to cover retraining or absence for child care. The existence of an occupational scheme may provide employers with an incentive to terminate the employment of older workers.

Finally, there is the risk faced by the employee that the employer may decide to wind up the scheme. A person may have a reasonable expectation that the scheme will remain in existence until he or she reaches the retirement age, with pension calculated on the basis of final salary, but the employer may terminate the scheme before that date. In such a case, rights must be preserved, but, if this is done via cash equivalents, this in effect converts the pension promise from earnings related to money purchase. This brings me to money purchase schemes and personal pensions.

Money purchase and personal pensions

A further major departure of the 1986 Act was to allow money purchase occupational schemes to contract out (i.e., for the conditions to be defined in terms of specified minimum contributions rather than specified minimum benefits), and for individuals to contract out via a personal pension plan. With personal pensions, as with defined contribution occupational schemes, there are two major anxieties about the final level of pension, even if we assume that people make a fully informed choice. (I am not discussing here the controversial question as to whether people have been correctly advised.)

The first anxiety is the investment risk that is borne by the individual, who may be unlucky in choosing investments. There is no redistribution between those whose investments have performed well and those who turn out to have chosen less well. The second risk relates to the state of the annuity market at the date of retirement. There is considerable uncertainty surrounding the rate of annuity which can be purchased. One guide to personal pensions points out that 'Annuity rates are ... extremely volatile as they relate directly to interest rates and also on the desire of an insurance company to come in or out of the annuity market' (Reardon, 1988, p. 47). There are moreover good reasons, notably adverse selection, why individuals may face less advantageous terms than an employer buying on behalf of an entire labour force, and why insurance companies may be unwilling to quote on indexed annuities.

As a result, there is no guarantee of a specified pension at retirement, and there is no way in which a money purchase arrangement can provide such a guarantee. Concerns about the adequacy of personal pensions are reinforced when we take account of the low level of the contributions being made under such schemes, a large proportion of which have in the past been funded only through the contracted-out rebate and the additional government 'incentive'. A worker would typically have to put in considerably more to provide a pension comparable with good occupational schemes. If, for example, the target is a pension of 1/80th of final salary, with a spouse's pension of 50 per cent on the death of the worker, and 3 per cent indexation in retirement, then the required contribution rate is 11 per cent of earnings at age 45. If the target is a pension of 1/60th of final salary, with a spouse's pension of two-thirds on the death of the worker, and 5 per cent indexation in retirement, then the required contribution rate rises to 18 per cent of earnings at age 45. These figures are very considerably in excess of the amount financed by the rebate plus incentive.

Conclusion

It is not my intention here to discuss the overall performance of the three alternative routes to a second-tier pension. It is possible that future capital market conditions will be such that personal pensions turn out on average to have been a sound choice, and if adequate amounts are saved in this way, then they may become a major part of total pensioners' income. For employees who stay with the same employer, and whose defined benefit scheme remains in full force, the occupational route may well provide a highly satisfactory method of providing for retirement.

My point is a different one – that the second-tier, as presently constituted in Britain, cannot *guarantee* a minimum level of pension in old age. Both occupational and personal pensions involve risks, and there are likely to be people following these routes who end their working life with pensions which are inadequate according to the criterion set out at the beginning of this chapter. SERPS, as modified by the Conservative government, cannot achieve its original objective.

16.4 Pensioners' incomes today

My account has been set in terms of the future, but differences are already becoming apparent. The government has drawn attention to the growth in the average real income of pensioners. In 1989, the Secretary of State stated that 'By 1986, pensioners' net average incomes from all sources had grown by 23% more than prices since 1979 – twice as fast as the income of the population as a whole' (J. Moore, MP, quoted by Falkingham and Victor, 1991). The performance over the decade as a whole was less impressive, but between 1979 and 1990/1, the mean net income adjusted for household size of pensioner couple households grew by 38 per cent, which was slightly faster than the average for the population as a whole (35 per cent). The growth for single pensioner households (32 per cent) was slightly less than the average. (These figures are from Department of Social Security, 1993b, tables A1 and A4, and relate to income before housing costs.)

Improvements in *average* incomes do not however imply that all pensioners have gained equally. As has been demonstrated (for example by Falkingham and Victor, 1991), it is misleading to treat the elderly as a group. The distribution of income did not move up uniformly, as is illustrated by figure 16.4, which shows the growth in real income at different

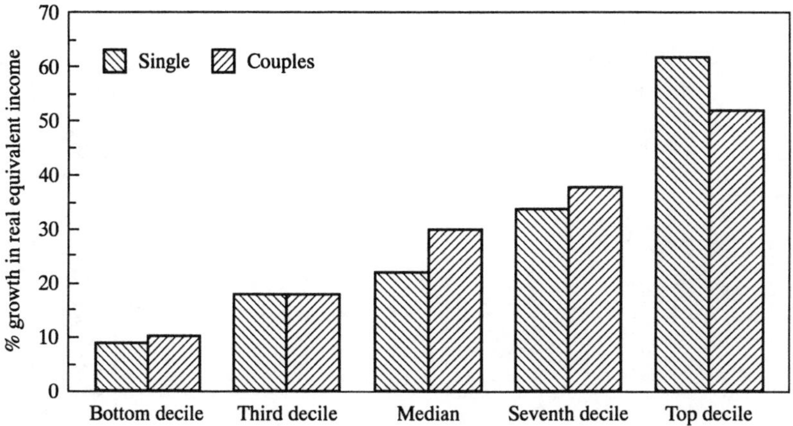

Figure 16.4 Growth in pensioners' real incomes at different points in the distribution 1979–1990/1
Source: *Social Security Statistics*, 1993, table B2.03.

points in the distribution, with separate bars for single persons and married couples. The top decile of single pensioners in 1990/1 had a real income 62 per cent higher than their counterparts in 1979. For those 30 per cent down from the top, the growth was close to the national average. But for the remaining deciles, the growth in real income was well below the national average. For the bottom decile (those a tenth of the way from the bottom), the growth was 10 per cent or less. The gap widened noticeably between the top and the bottom.

The rise in inequality means that, despite the improvement in the average income of pensioners, more pensioners now fall below the standard of adequacy adopted in this chapter. The proportion of pensioners with net equivalent incomes below 50 per cent of the national average (as noted earlier, this corresponds in 1993 terms to some £80 a week for a single person and £130 for a couple) was estimated to be 16 per cent in 1979 for both single persons and couples. This is shown in figure 16.5, where again the two bars correspond to single and pensioner couples. (These figures are taken from the official study, *Households Below Average Income*, table F1, and relate to incomes before housing costs; it should be noted that the estimates are described as 'particularly uncertain'.) The proportion fell in 1981, but after that began to rise, and has now reached 33–4 per cent. In the terms defined by the European Union, a third of British pensioners are in poverty. (See, for further discussion of European comparisons, Walker (1993) and Walker, Alber and Guillemard (1993).)

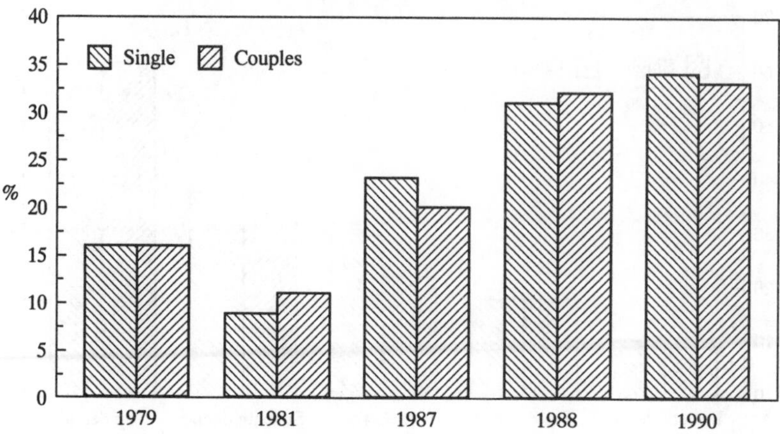

Figure 16.5 Pensioners below 50 per cent of average income 1979–1990/1
Source: See text.

16.5 Why means testing is not the solution

What then can be done? How can an effective minimum be ensured? One solution is to place increased reliance on Income Support. If Income Support levels were to be increased in line with average net earnings, while the basic pension fell behind, then this means-tested strategy would provide a safety net for those who did not benefit sufficiently from the second tier. A variation on this has been proposed by Dilnot and Johnson (1992).

The means-tested route was rejected by Beveridge half a century ago, and his reasons remain valid today, as has been argued in chapter 15. First, Beveridge attached considerable importance to the 'strength of popular objection to any kind of means test' (1942, p. 12), and to the associated problem of incomplete take-up. Evidence of the extent of non-take-up by pensioners of means-tested assistance is provided by the official studies making use of information from the Family Expenditure Survey. The most recent estimates show that in 1989 only 79 per cent of the total Income Support entitlement of pensioners was being claimed, and that the proportion of eligible pensioner units who were claiming was 67 per cent (Department of Social Security, 1993a, tables 5 and 6). The existence of errors in the recording of benefit receipt, and other factors, mean that these figures may understate the degree of take-up (Department of Social Security, 1993a, appendix D), but if the proportion not claiming were one fifth, rather than one third, this would nonetheless be a major source of concern. Even a 90 per cent take-up would still seem unsatisfactory, given the importance of the safety net for the financial security of the elderly if the National Insurance pension is allowed to erode.

The second objection by Beveridge to means testing was that it penalises individual efforts. We have heard a great deal about the 'poverty trap' faced by low-paid workers, in that they lose a great deal of the advantage from earning more, as a result of the withdrawal of means-tested benefits. Much less attention has been paid to the same 'savings trap' faced by pensioners. This applies to both pension income and other sources. Recently, Watsons, the actuaries, published a study (Collins, 1993) of the impact of means-tested benefits on occupational pensions. They contrasted a hypothetical Mr Lilley (their choice of name), who had no occupational pension, with an equally hypothetical Cabinet colleague who had a pension from his previous employer of £6 a week. As a result of the withdrawal of means-tested benefits, the latter was, according to their calculations, only 87p. a week better off. This represents a marginal tax rate of 85.5 per cent. There is in fact little net gain from the occupational pension until it reaches some £50 a week.

For those with private savings, the position is even more serious. People with savings in excess of a specified amount (currently £8,000) are not eligible for Income Support; and those with savings between this amount and a lower figure (£3,000) are assumed to be receiving a weekly 'tariff' income equal to £1 for every £250. This corresponds to an assumed return of over 20 per cent per annum. As a result, it is actually a disadvantage to have income from savings. Figure 16.6 shows the net income of a pensioner couple (paying £30 a week rent and £7.63 Council Tax) with different amounts of income from savings (assuming a 5 per cent rate of return). There is a definite savings trap. This diagram is based on the work of Hills, who comments that 'If people realise that they will face this position in advance, they may decide there is little point in saving or building up pension rights below a threshold' (Hills, 1993, p. 29).

16.6 An alternative way forward

What are the alternatives? The simple answer is an increased basic National Insurance pension linked to net average earnings (subject to its real value being preserved). This is the present day counterpart of the Back-to-Beveridge policy which I have long advocated – see Atkinson (1969). There are two major objections. First, there is the cost, which even in 1969 was large; the scheme then advocated would have meant adding about 9 per cent to the standard rate of income tax (not the reduced rates). Secondly, the second-tier of pensions has evolved, and what people are seeking is different, including an understandable desire for greater individual choice.

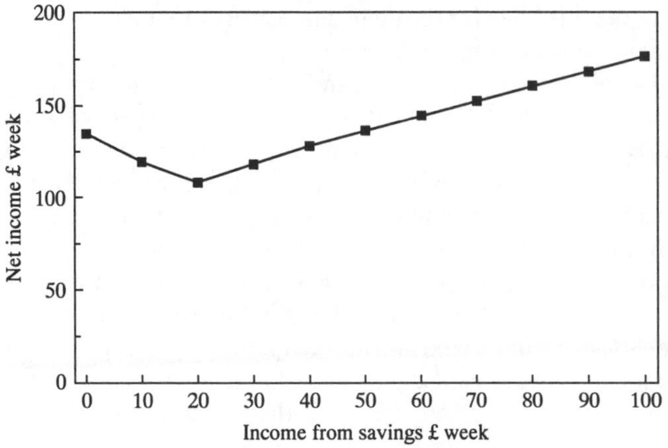

Figure 16.6 The savings trap for pensioners

I do not myself find these objections overwhelming, and I would certainly vote for the proposal to restore the role of the basic National Insurance pension, but I sense that I am in a minority. It may therefore be more helpful to describe an intermediate route, which accepts the decline which has taken place in the value of the basic pension relative to average earnings, and seeks to complement the pension by other second-tier provisions. At the same time, I assume that, if the basic National Insurance pension is to play any significant role at all in the next century, then we have to end its erosion in relation to net earnings. My intermediate route assumes that the basic pension remains at its current level, but is henceforth linked to an index of net average earnings, and regularly uprated in line with this, subject only to the condition that if real net average earnings should fall, the real value of the pension would be preserved until real net average earnings have regained their previous value.

The proposals for the second-tier are based on three main elements. The first is to make membership of a defined benefit pension plan mandatory for all employees and for the self-employed, with benefits satisfying specified minimum conditions. As I have argued, personal pensions and money purchase occupational schemes, whatever their other merits, cannot guarantee an adequate minimum pension. The individual employee would be free to choose his or her defined benefit plan, which could be offered by the employer, by a third party, or could be SERPS (about which I say more below). The entry of third parties would be encouraged, where this might include trade unions and financial insitutions, if they felt able to match the defined benefit promise. It should be stressed that the defined benefit need not be of the final salary form, and could be based for example on an average of the best x years of earnings.

Individual choice, and contracting out, would therefore remain. What would be different would be the terms. Not only would the alternative to state provision have to be a defined benefit promise, but the standard set by SERPS would be raised. The second element in my proposal would be the restoration of SERPS to the original formula, based on 25 per cent of earnings from the best 20 years. This would provide a realistic accrual rate, of particular benefit to manual workers, to those who have to retire early, and to those who work part-time. It would be accompanied by the extension of the crediting of contributions, to include periods such as those spent in education, and would make specific provisions for part-time workers. SERPS would also be extended to the self-employed.

In this way, SERPS would be a serious competitor to private schemes, and the contracting out test, requiring comparable provision, would ensure that future private pension accrual provided an adequate minimum pension. It would however do nothing for today's pensioners. The third element in my proposal is therefore the introduction immediately of a *Minimum Pension Guarantee*, as part of the social security system.

The idea of a Minimum Pension Guarantee grows out of consideration of proposals for tax/benefit integration. It is sometimes suggested that such an integration is unproblematic in the case of pensioners, since their income does not vary very much and benefit could be paid on the basis of an annual income tax return. In my view this understates the difficulties in securing income tax returns from several million pensioners, difficulties which would increase with the age of the pensioner. I do not believe that income maintenance for the elderly can be based on requiring all low-income pensioners to file annual income tax returns. Nor is the test of income applied for income tax purposes necessarily applicable to the income testing of pensions.

The integration of income taxation and benefits may form part of a wider longer-term reform. The introduction of a basic income, or, as I prefer, a Participation Income (chapter 15), may be possible without requiring tax returns from everyone. In the immediate future, however, a Minimum Pension Guarantee provides a more realistic short-run route to reforming income maintenance for pensioners alone, and does not depend on the collecting of regular information from pensioners.

The next section describes the Minimum Pension Guarantee in more detail. Before turning to this, I should address one question which has been raised, which is whether the Guarantee, coupled with the reform of SERPS and the other proposals, could replace the basic National Insurance pension. The answer depends on the view that one takes of the National

Insurance system, since the abolition (or erosion) of the basic pension would represent a substantial diminution in the return to contributions paid. This diminution in turn could seriously undermine the ability of the government to raise revenue by this means, not least as a result of fiscal competition, the contribution principle providing a defence against competitive pressures to scale down the Welfare State (chapter 15). My personal view is that social insurance remains an important feature of our income maintenance system, particularly when viewed in a European context, and that this requires a significant element of pension provision from which people cannot contract out.

16.7 The Minimum Pension Guarantee

What would be involved in the Minimum Pension Guarantee (or MPG for short)? In its simplest form, the MPG would bring the total state pension, plus any occupational or personal pension, up to a minimum specified level. If we were to take £80 a week as this level, then a person with a basic pension of £56 plus an occupational pension of £14 would receive an additional £10 a week under the MPG.

The MPG would differ from means testing in two important respects: (i) it would be calculated on an individual basis, and (ii) the calculation would not involve other elements of income, or capital assets. There would be no need to know about the income from savings, dividend income, earnings, etc. The calculation could indeed be made at the date of retirement, with information being collected about the amounts of pension, annuity, etc., and about the provisions for indexation. This allows for the possibility that a person might not be eligible for the MPG at the outset, but become eligible at a later date: for example, a person choosing a level annuity at retirement might subsequently fall below the MPG level. The calculation would take account of any pension commuted in the form of a lump sum, so that this would not provide an avoidance device.

Two objections to the MPG are that, on the one hand, it would be paid to people with sizeable savings and hence not be 'targeted', and, on the other hand, it would discourage people from making their own pension provision. Both of these have some validity, but their significance should not be overstated. The first objection assumes that the sole purpose of pension provision is the abolition of poverty, whereas I have earlier stressed a wider view of pension objectives. I see the MPG as forming part of the pension provision, not as simply an alternative form of Income Support. The force of the second objection is mitigated by the requirement that membership of a defined benefit pension plan be compulsory for everyone in employment or self-employment. While it is possible that the existence of the MPG would affect the form in which benefits were taken, such as the choice between a level and an indexed annuity, avoidance provisions could be introduced such as those for commuted pensions. It would also be possible for the guarantee to be graduated, with the rate of withdrawal less than the 100 per cent which is implied by the MPG formula. At the same time, it should be noted that the 100 per cent rate does not apply to personal savings other than in the form of pensions, so that we would not have the savings trap shown in figure 16.6.

The costs and benefits of the simple MPG are illustrated in figure 16.7. The cost clearly depends on the level of the guarantee. A guarantee of £60 a week, which would provide particular benefit to those who do not qualify for a full National Insurance basic pension, would cost an estimated £2.3 billion according to the POLIMOD model. A guarantee of £70 a week would cost £3.8 billion and the target of £80 a week would cost £6.2 billion. This is a large amount, but less than I expected, reflecting the degree of targeting which is achieved. To raise the basic National Insurance pension, both Category A and Category B, to £80 a week, and to extend the coverage to all those aged 65 or over, would cost nearly £9½ billion.

The cost of the proposal is in part due to the adoption of an independent basis. If the guarantee were to be applied to the joint pension income of couples (where both aged 65 or over), at a rate of £128 a week, compared with £80 for a single person, then the cost would be more than halved to £2.8 billion. About half of couples would now gain, compared with three-quarters on an independent basis. It would be necessary in this case to collect regular information on the status of pensioners.

This addition to government spending would raise important issues of financing. In part, the proposals involve additional contributions as well as additional benefits. By partially reversing the exodus from SERPS, and by extending it to the self-employed, there would be an increase in contribution revenue of rather more than £1 billion. It would then be necessary, in order to finance the MPG on an independent basis at a rate of £80 a week, to raise the Class 1 National Insurance contribution by between 2 and 2½ percentage points. This would mean that a person on average male earnings would pay around an extra £6 a week. In years to come, the cost of the package as a whole would rise on account of the fact that the basic pension would be linked to earnings rather than prices, but the cost of the MPG would tend to fall as occupational, SERPS and other pensions increased.

The benefit is first that pensioners would have a guaranteed pension: for example £65 a week is some 40 per cent of average national income. Secondly, it would reduce the dependence of many pensioners on means-tested benefits. A minimum guarantee of £70 would mean that very

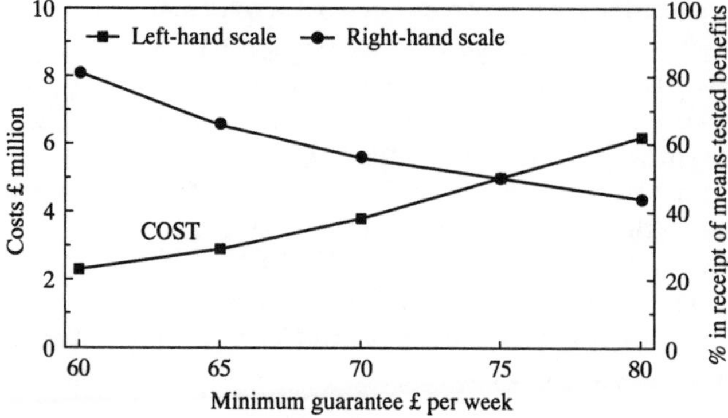

Figure 16.7 Cost and benefit of minimum guarantee

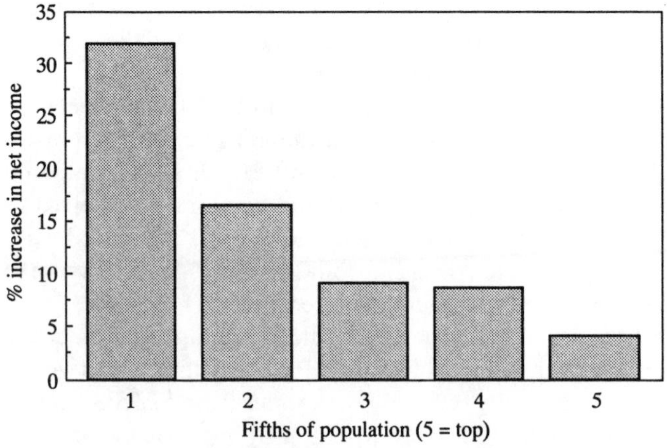

Figure 16.8 Gain from £80 a week minimum guarantee

few pensioners had to claim Income Support, which would radically transform their situation, particularly that of the sizeable minority who do not claim their entitlement. (The same would be true with a guarantee on an independent basis.) A number would remain dependent on housing benefit, but the proportion receiving any form of means-tested assistance would fall to a half or lower, as shown in figure 16.7.

Another way of expressing the targeting achieved by the MPG proposal is to look at the average gain in income by different income ranges as shown in figure 16.8 (it should be noted that these calculations are based on a different source from figure 16.4, and relate to all pensioners, rather than single and couples separately). Figure 16.8 shows that a MPG of £80 a week would increase the income of the bottom fifth by nearly a third. The gain is smaller for those further up the distribution and only 4 per cent for the top fifth. Introduction of the MPG would therefore go a long way to redressing the rise in inequality among the elderly in the past decade.

The MPG is not a new idea. It does indeed form part of the Chilean reform of pensions which has received much international attention. Nearer home, the proposals of Field and Owen (1993) include a Guaranteed Minimum Pension. Their proposal is however for its longer-term introduction, whereas I see it as essential that steps be taken now to provide for today's pensioners and those retiring in the next few years.

Conclusions

My conclusions are simple to summarise. Present policy towards pensions is a cause for concern not just on account of future cost and of the present budget deficit, but also because it cannot guarantee an adequate standard of living in old age. It needs to be reformed. Such reform is moreover quite possible, and I have described one route by which it could be achieved. This is not necessarily the only route. There are interesting proposals which I have not discussed, such as those of Falkingham and Johnson (1993) for a unified funded pension scheme, but the plan outlined here would I believe provide both for the pensioners of tomorrow and for the pensioners of today.

Notes

1 What is happening to the distribution of income in the UK?

A revised version of the Keynes Lecture presented at the British Academy, 15 October 1991. I am particularly grateful to Karen Gardiner and Holly Sutherland for allowing me to draw on our joint research. Most helpful comments on earlier versions have been made by Peter Hart, John Hills, Stephen Jenkins, Alan Milward, Henry Phelps Brown, Nick Stern and Holly Sutherland, but they are not to be held responsible in any way for the views expressed.

1 Some of the low incomes in the Blue Book estimates relate to tax units which exist for only part of the year:

> Part year units comprise women who are widowed or divorced for part of the tax year, new entrants to the work force, people who die during the year and immigrants and emigrants. The effect of including these part year incomes is to increase the measured inequality of the distribution. In 1978/79, their removal from the pre-tax distribution produced a reduction in the Gini coefficient of two percentage points (*Economic Trends*, November 1987, p. 98).

2 Around the trend, there was cyclical variation; for discussion of the relationship with the rates of unemployment and inflation – see Nolan (1987).

3 It would be helpful to attach a confidence interval to the estimated shares, in order to assess the statistical significance of this fall. The estimates are however the product of an elaborate process of adjustment to the initial survey results involving extensive use of extra-sample information – see Ramprakash (1975).

4 'The Commission has made a valuable contribution to improving our understanding of the trends in the distribution of income and wealth. As a direct consequence of its recommendations the government's own statistics are now providing better information in this area and should enable us to carry on the necessary up-dating of the Commission's reports' (Letter from James Prior, Secretary of State for Employment, 11 June 1979).

5 In the UK, the Royal Commission on the Distribution of Income and Wealth found that 'there is little doubt that if account were taken of employee benefits, working conditions and other aspects of employment, the dispersion of the earnings distribution would be increased. The effect within the top one per cent of employees must be particularly marked' (1979, p. 233).

6 For fuller accounts of the construction of the Blue Book estimates, see Stark (1972 and 1978) and Ramprakash (1975).

7 On the other hand, estimates based purely on the FES have certain advantages, including avoiding the problem of part-year units.

8 The composition of the non-household population was examined by the Royal Commission on the Distribution of Income and Wealth (1978, Appendix L) on the basis of information in the 1971 Census of Population. At that time, 'more than 70 per cent of the total of about 900,000 consisted of people in mental and other hospitals, old people's homes, hotels and boarding houses' (1978, p. 238), although this is likely to have changed since then. According to the Blue Book estimates of the distribution of income, in 1972/3 there were 1.2 million tax units living in institutions, out of a total of 28.4 million (Ramprakash, 1975, table D).

9 The results are derived from the FES Base Tapes. The data relate to family units, and relate to 9,253 family units in 1975 and 9,040 in 1985. Results given below for 1988 relate to 9,307 family units. The results have been adjusted for differential non-response by applying the grossing-up factors by family type for Great Britain used by the Department of Social Security with a proportionate adjustment for Northern Ireland.

10 An earlier study which takes net resources is that by Morris and Preston (1986) with results for 1968, 1977 and 1983. Our estimates differ in that we do not attempt here to construct a measure of *annual* income.

11 In particular, there is a problem with measures of disposable income *before* housing costs of securing consistent treatment of housing rebates (for rent and, at that time, rates). If income is defined to include such rebates, then we have the practical difficulty that in the FES data such rebates are not always recorded (the net rent being reported or the rebate being paid as a lump sum). It is also the case that between 1975 and 1985 the rents charged to local authority tenants increased substantially while at the same time rebates were increased. An income measure including rebates would give a misleading impression.

If income is defined to exclude housing rebates, then account has to be taken of the fact that, prior to April 1983, assistance towards housing costs was provided through Supplementary Benefit. It is necessary to deduct part of the latter payment, which involves additional assumptions (Johnson and Webb, 1990).

The Blue Book series in table 1.1 includes rent rebates in the definition of disposable income, but not rate rebates (Ramprakash, 1975, p. 81). No deduction is made of housing costs.

12 Another significant difference is that disposable income in the CSO series is net of rates (poll tax), but not rent (although rent rebates are included in income).

13 The invitation to give this Lecture emphasised that it did not have to be about Keynes, and I have followed this instruction to the letter, to the extent that I shall not even mention the contribution to the study of distribution for which Keynes is most famous – the supposed constancy of factor shares in national income.

14 The importance of looking at the joint distribution of income and work has been

emphasised by Piachaud (1987).

15 The contribution of demographic change to changes in overall inequality is discussed by, among others, Dinwiddy and Reed (1977) and Mookherjee and Shorrocks (1982). According to Stark (1988) and Jenkins (forthcoming), the experience of the 1980s has in this respect been different, the within-group changes dominating those due to changes in the age composition or in the profile of mean income by age.

16 These calculations refer to the FES sample, and classification of families, described in the next paragraph.

17 No allowance has been made in these calculations for the value of leisure. One way of treating this is to apply a 'discount' to labour income to allow for the disutility of work; equivalently, we might have a 'target' replacement rate for income out of work. Taking the replacement rate as 3/4, or the discount as a quarter, the increase in inequality between the two years is smaller, but it remains substantial. On the other hand, it does not seem appropriate to value at the same rate leisure which is chosen and leisure which is enforced.

18 The definition of labour market status poses a number of problems. The distinction here is based on the variable A201 in the FES, which refers to the status 'at present', whereas the income variables refer to past periods. A person who has recently started work may therefore be recorded as in work but not as receiving earnings.

19 It should be noted that they apply the tax and benefit structure for 1979 *uprated to take account of price inflation*; the results could well be different if they were uprated in line with average incomes.

20 The same kind of finding has been reached in other countries. In the US for example, Grubb and Wilson (1989) concluded that 'inter-sectoral shifts appeared to be of some importance, but that the trends seem to be driven chiefly by developments within labour force groups, rather than movements among them' (1989, p. 3).

21 The effect of this should not be exaggerated. The proportion of shareholders has indeed risen, but this still leaves the majority of the population without holdings. The most important privatisation has been that of council houses, but the Inland Revenue estimate that the maximum effect is likely to have been a 1 percentage point reduction in the Gini coefficient by 1988 (*Economic Trends*, October 1990, pp. 145–6). In fact the distribution of wealth, according to the Inland Revenue estimates, showed little change over the 1980s. This represents a departure from the long-run pattern, which had seen a fairly steady fall in the degree of concentration since the 1920s (Atkinson and Harrison, 1978).

2 Income distribution in European countries

This chapter draws on a project being carried out as part of the Luxembourg Income Study, of which a fuller account is given in Atkinson, Rainwater and Smeeding (1994). It also makes use of research carried out in conjunction with the Microsimulation Unit at the Department of Applied Economics in Cambridge, supported by the ESRC, the Newton Trust, the Department of Social Security and the European Community Human Capital and Mobility Programme. I am grateful to Holly Sutherland for valuable comments.

1 For further discussion of the sensitivity of the results, see Buhmann *et al.* (1988) and Atkinson, Rainwater and Smeeding (1994).
2 Throughout this chapter, 'Germany' refers to the former West Germany. For evidence about the distribution of income in East Germany, see Hauser *et al.* (1991) and Hauser (1992).
3 Usually known as the 'Blue Book' estimate, which combines information from the tax records with household survey data and other information.
4 The Luxembourg Income Study (LIS) project began in 1983 under the joint sponsorship of the government of Luxembourg and the Centre for Population, Poverty, and Policy Studies (CEPS) in Walferdange. It is now funded on a continuing basis by CEPS/INSTEAD and by the science foundations of its member countries. The main objective of the LIS project has been to create a database containing social and economic data collected in household surveys from different countries. The database currently contains information for some 25 countries for one or more years. Extensive documentation concerning technical aspects of the survey data, and the social institutions of income provision in member countries, is being made available to users.
5 Although differences in methods cannot be fully eliminated. An important example is that of bottom-coding, where in some data sets negative or very low incomes are either adjusted to a predetermined level or excluded.
6 Sawyer discusses the per-capita distribution, but his table (1976, table 7) is a mixture of pre-tax and post-tax data.
7 It would clearly be possible to calculate the sampling errors associated with the Lorenz curve, and require that one curve be significantly different from another at a specified level of confidence. However, this focuses on sampling error to the exclusion of other, non-sampling, error, which may be quantitatively more important.
8 Recent reviews of the evidence about trends in income inequality in different countries include Bourguignon and Morrisson (1992), Gottschalk (1993), Green, Henley and Tsakalotos (1992) and Gardiner (1993).

3 Poverty, statistics and progress in Europe

This chapter is a revised version of a Keynote Address delivered to the Seminar on Poverty Statistics in the European Community, 24–6 October 1989, at Nordwijk, Netherlands.

1 The situation may be contrasted with that at the time of the Berlin Symposium (Spahn, 1985). A revised version of my own paper is reprinted in Atkinson (1989).
2 The official figure was not available at the time of these comparisons, having only been published in 1990 (Department of Social Security, 1990).
3 The figure quoted refers to incomes before housing costs.
4 The median is about a tenth less than the mean: in 1979 49.3 per cent of the population had less than 90 per cent of the mean (Department of Social Security,

1990, annex 1, table C1). Buhmann *et al.* (1988) show that taking 60 per cent of the median gives a low-income figure of 18.7 per cent. Interpolating between 8.1 per cent and 18.7 per cent seems likely to give a figure of around 11–13 per cent for the low-income population.

5 According to estimates by the Institute for Fiscal Studies, in 1980–2 (averaging data for three years) the proportion of the population living in households with incomes below 50 per cent of the average was 24 per cent in Northern Ireland (House of Commons Social Services Committee, 1990, p. xxiv). The overall UK figure was 8.3 per cent. If those in Northern Ireland are excluded (but the cut-off still based on 50 per cent of UK average income) the percentage would fall to 7.9 per cent. Poverty in Northern Ireland is examined in greater depth by Borooah and McGregor (1989).

6 A further possible difference concerns the period over which income is assessed. The HBAI figures are based on current income, whereas the others may have employed 'normal' income. Johnson and Webb (1989, table 5) find that the use of current rather than normal income in 1983 led the estimated proportion living in households with less than 50 per cent of average income to rise from 7.7 per cent to 8.1 per cent.

7 Of course, this method may lead to absurd conclusions if applied slavishly: for example, the enlargement of the Community with the accession of Spain and Portugal would have lowered the poverty line.

8 As an aside, one can understand the appeal to politicians of a scale that is fixed in real terms, adjusted over time only in line with consumer prices. Growth in real incomes at 4 per cent per annum would soon lead to the elimination of poverty defined in this way.

4 Comparing poverty rates internationally: recent studies in OECD countries

I am grateful to Richard Hauser, Brian Nolan, the editor of the *World Bank Economic Review*, and the referees for helpful comments on the background paper (prepared for *World Development, Report 1990*) out of which this article grew, and to Sandrine Cazes of Observatoire Français des Conjonctures Economiques for allowing me to draw on our joint work (Atkinson and Cazes, 1990). I would also like to acknowledge that table 4.1 had its origins in a table presented by Stephen Jenkins at the meeting of the International Association for Research in Income and Wealth in Lahnstein, Germany, in August 1989.

1 The two studies in question are of Great Britain (excluding Northern Ireland), not of the entire United Kingdom. 'Germany' refers to the Federal Republic of Germany before reunification with the former German Democratic Republic.

2 This is of course an argument against relying solely on a headcount measure of poverty. The relative merits of different poverty measures are not considered here – see Atkinson (1987).

3 Strictly, the income definition for Great Britain is a mixture, with earned income and transfers relating to the current pay period but investment and self-employment typically relating to a previous year; see, for example, Atkinson and Micklewright (1983) and Nolan (1987, p. 69).

5 Two nations in early retirement? The case of Britain

The authors thank Jane Falkingham for her assistance.

1 The data used are not weighted for differential non-response.
2 *Sources*: *Employment Gazette*, January 1981 and January 1988, table 2.1 in both cases.
3 A less kindly statement is that of the Royal Commission on Population: 'It is clearly desirable that the old should, if possible, do more than hitherto to maintain themselves, or rather, contribute more by their exertions to the general economic effort of the community' (1949, p. 114). This passage is quoted by Abel-Smith (1953), who goes on to provide a critique.
4 The 'unoccupied' category includes persons out of work for more than five years who are not retired, sick or injured.
5 The proportions for 1985 are similar to those found by Laczko *et al.* (1988, table 1), but they are concerned only with the older part of the age group (men aged 60–4) and with an earlier date (1980–2), differences which operate in opposite directions.
6 For discussion of the reliability of the income data in the FES, see Atkinson and Micklewright (1983).
7 Family income is defined net of income tax and National Insurance contributions where these are deducted at source, but before tax where this is not deducted at source. Since the categories of income for which tax was deducted at source changed between 1975 and 1985, there are slight differences in definition in this variable for the two years.
8 *Source*: *New Earnings Survey 1983*, part B, table 30, and *1986*, part B, table 30, series linked at 1983.
9 In terms of simple *receipt*, there is a considerable degree of overlap. Of the 295 early retired in 1985 (A201 = 5–7), 56 received an occupational pension and no state transfers, and 111 were in the reverse position, but there were 115 in receipt of both (and 13 receiving neither).
10 The 1975 FES contained less extensive information on disability benefits, so that we may have understated the number in that year.
11 One reason why this is important is that, between 1975 and 1985, the rents charged to local authority tenants were increased substantially while at the same time rebates for low-income tenants were increased. An income measure which included the rebates would give a misleading impression, but with net resources the two items are offset. (Rent and rate rebates have been excluded from the benefit and total income variables used in the previous section.)
12 Resources can exceed the SB scale in these cases on account of additions for exceptional circumstances.
13 We should note that the SB scale increased sharply in 1975 (when inflation was high). Comparing the scale in force at the start of the year, we see that the 1985 scale represented a money increase by a factor of 3.43, or rather more than average earnings; comparing the end year figures, the factor was only 2.74, or about the rate of inflation. The scale applied to each observation is that in force at the date of interview.

14 *Source*: *New Earnings Survey 1983*, part B, table 30 and *1986*, part B, table 30, series linked at 1983.
15 We have not discussed here the position of the unemployed.
16 The relation is not purely proportional since there is other income (e.g., from savings).
17 The 'piling-up' of frequencies at the SB level has similarity with that caused by the minimum wage and has been treated by Meyer and Wise (1983). A similar approach could be adopted here.
18 Personal pensions are on a defined-contribution basis and cannot guarantee any specified proportion of earnings on retirement.

6 Is the Welfare State necessarily a barrier to economic growth?

An earlier version of this chapter was presented at the European Economic Association Annual Congress at Maastricht, September 1994. I am grateful to Edmond Malinvaud and Jacques Drèze for their comments.

1 As noted earlier, I am not considering government spending on goods and services, which may directly enter the production function (as in Barro, 1990) and positively affect the level of output.
2 Another version has been proposed by Blanchard (1985), where there is a constant probability of death and wages decline exponentially over the lifetime. This has been used by Saint-Paul (1992) to argue that an unfunded social security system reduces the growth rate.
3 Although it should be stressed that this policy is explicitly rejected in the case of Sweden by Lindbeck *et al.* (1994, p. 107).

7 A national minimum? A history of ambiguity in the determination of benefit scales in Britain

The author would like to acknowledge the stimulus which he has received from reading the papers (1989, 1989a and 1989b) of John Veit-Wilson, and has drawn heavily on his work. He is grateful to Dorothy and Tom Wilson, for their comments on the first version of this chapter.

1 There were twenty shillings (s.) in a pre-decimal pound and twelve pennies (d.) in a shilling.
2 Department of Employment (1971, table 40), with a deduction of 4s. 11d. for NIC and 16s. 7d. income tax.

8 The development of state pensions in the United Kingdom

1 The first version of this paper quoted from the Draft Version of the Charter. The differences are instructive. The Draft read:

> Every European Community citizen in retirement or early retirement shall be able to receive an income affording him or her a decent standard of living (para. 28).
>
> Any European Community citizen having reached retirement age but who is not entitled to a pension, for example owing to a very long period of exclusion from the labour market, and who does not have other adequate means of subsistence, shall be entitled to a minimum income (para. 29).

Note the removal in the final version of the reference to early retirement and of the explicit reference to a minimum income.

2 In calculating the number of years, there are provisions for years to be disregarded in which there was home responsibility protection or credited contributions.

3 These calculations are of a very simple kind. A more extensive analysis requires a detailed simulation model, such as that constructed for Canada by Wolfson (1987).

4 This calculation assumes that no other income is received other than earnings in work and pension in retirement. The net earnings in work are calculated for a single person below the age of 65 not contracted out of SERPS.

5 *Source*: CERC (1983, p. 73). In each case, the figures are based on the case with final salary nearest to the male average. The figures are gross of social security contributions.

9 Income maintenance for the unemployed in Britain and the response to high unemployment

Section 9.1 draws heavily on joint work with John Micklewright, of Queen Mary College, London, in conjunction with the ESRC Programme on Taxation, Incentives, and the Distribution of Income, but he is not to be held responsible for the views expressed. In preparing the revised version, I have benefited considerably from the comments of Brian Barry, Tom Campbell, Bob Goodin, Julian Le Grand and John Micklewright.

1 The estimate for Supplementary Benefit (which was the predecessor of Income Support) quoted in HM Treasury (1987, p. 244).

2 See, e.g., Hayek: 'In the Western world some provision for those threatened by the extremes of indigence or starvation due to circumstances beyond their control has long been accepted as a duty of the community.... The necessity of some such arrangement in an industrial society is unquestioned – be it only in the interest of those who require protection against acts of desperation on the part of the needy' (1960, p. 285).

3 It is assumed here that the unemployment insurance scheme must be self-financing in all periods. Keynesian macro-economic considerations may suggest that the fund be allowed to run a deficit when unemployment rises above the normal level. As was noted by Beveridge, 'the maximum effect of a social insurance scheme in stabilising employment would be obtained ... by increasing the contribution rates in good times and lowering them in bad times' (Beveridge, 1942, p. 164).

4 This kind of interdependence theory of redistribution has been criticised by Barry, who describes it as 'like a conjurer putting a rabbit in a hat, taking it out again, and expecting a round of applause' (1977, p. 279). The comparative static exercise performed here may not be a major piece of prestidigitation, but it is not entirely obvious whether – if it starts to rain – the rabbit will get wet inside the hat.

5 Such a shift may also reflect the changing composition of the electorate. By the

1987 election few of those of working age would have been in the labour force in the 1930s.

6 The term 'slack' is derived from that of 'organizational slack' in the theory of the firm, which indicates that there is scope for managerial discretion. The electors are in our case the counterpart of the shareholders in the firm, who can sack the management, or sell out, if performance is sufficiently unsatisfactory, but who cannot enforce full implementation of their wishes.

7 Differentiating with respect to δ, it may be seen that the sign depends on the difference between $(1-p)(1-\delta\theta)$, which is the proportion in employment and not receiving benefit, and $\theta[p+\delta(1-p)]$, which is the proportion receiving benefit. By assumption, the former is larger.

8 A Department of Health and Social Security minister has referred to the 'two navy principle' applied to social security spending being twice the next two departments in size. It was not clear that this constituted an upper limit but illustrates the way in which the total enters budgetary discussions.

9 'Minorities' here include not only the unemployed but also those, like the author, whose concern about inequality has not diminished in the past decade.

10 Note that we are not considering here the application of different judgements at different dates, as with the example of Parfit (1973), of a Russian nobleman who, in his idealist youth, views with horror the prospect of changing into a more cynical and – to him – altogether different self.

11 The source for the data in the Appendix is Atkinson and Micklewright (1989).

10 Institutional features of unemployment insurance and the working of the labour market

In writing this chapter I have drawn heavily on joint research with John Micklewright of Queen Mary College, London, and the European University Institute, Florence. He has made helpful comments on the chapter but is not to be held responsible for the views expressed. I am also grateful to Nicholas Barr, Andrea Brandolini, Douglas Gale, and participants in seminars at the Observatoire Français des Conjunctures Economiques and the Centre d'Etude des Revenus et des Coûts in Paris for their comments on the first version.

11 Social insurance

This chapter was presented as the Fifteenth Annual Lecture of the Geneva Association, 11 June 1991. I am grateful to the members of the Welfare State Programme for the stimulus they have given to my thinking and to participants in the Welfare State Seminar for their comments on an earlier version. In revising the chapter for publication, I have been helped by the remarks of the discussants at the Lecture: Denis Kessler, Pierre Pestieau and Agnar Sandmo.

1 This is well illustrated by the account given by Sandmo (1991) of how economic and social thinking in Scandinavia influenced the development of the Welfare State in those countries.

2 The definition of equilibrium needs to be made precise. For a fuller discussion, see

Rothschild and Stiglitz (1976), Wilson (1977) and Hellwig (1987).

3 The precise interpretation of Knight is a matter for debate – see LeRoy and Singell (1987), who argue that he in fact had in mind market failure due to adverse selection and moral hazard. As they point out, the distinction attributed to Knight was made by Keynes (1921).

4 For fuller discussion of the use of the term, see Harris (1972, p. 4) and the references given there.

5 According to Harris: 'personal and mutual savings which might be sufficient for short periods of unemployment were likely to be far less adequate during successive years of depression, such as occurred in certain industries and localities between 1884 and 1888. During those years the funds of many trade unions were severely strained' (1972, p. 52).

6 There has been controversy among historians in Britain as to how far retirement is a recent phenomenon. Whereas Thomson argues that 'for many centuries retirement has been a recognised feature of English life' (1986, p. 36), the view of Hunt appears more representative: 'most working men simply kept working for as long as they were able. Ageing was accompanied not by retirement and a pension but by increased sickness and falling earnings' (1981, p. 8).

7 Again we have to ask about other forms of transfer, notably provision by children for their parents. As argued by Kessler (1989), among the factors limiting such transfers were labour migration and, this century, the loss of life in the First World War.

8 After first writing this chapter, I learned of the closely related work in the development economics literature on two-tier labour markets in agriculture – see Eswaran and Kotwal (1985), and the references given there.

9 It is noteworthy that Peacock in his book *The Economics of National Insurance* says that 'At the present stage of evolution of national insurance, it is probably true to say that the traditional economic problems of this form of social security, e.g., the relationship between wage rates and insurance, the particular incidence of social security taxation, insurance as a deterrent of labour mobility, etc., are of less interest and importance than the relationship between it and general economic policy as directed by the State' (1952, p. 51). It was stabilisation that he considered first and then micro-economics. The stabilisation aspects of unemployment insurance were discussed by Malinvaud (1985).

12 On targeting and family benefits

This chapter is a development of a paper originally prepared for the World Bank. I am grateful to Nicholas Barr, Andrea Brandolini, John Hills, John Micklewright, and Dominique van de Walle for their helpful comments on the earlier paper.

1 Among the issues not examined here are the time period over which income is measured, and the consequences of changing circumstances over time, together with the related choice between income and expenditure as indicators of resources.

2 The poverty deficit is found by integrating $F(y)$ between y_{min} and z (see Atkinson, 1987).

3 This problem has been studied by, among others, Kanbur (1987), Ravallion and Chao (1989) and Bourguignon and Fields (1990).

4 With a uniform distribution, and a lowest income equal to zero, the poverty gap is $Hz/2$.

5 The cost of the minimum income guarantee is $(H/z)(g^*)^2/2$, which is equal to $(g^*/z)^2$ times the poverty gap. With a budget equal to one third of the poverty gap, the guarantee which can be financed is $\sqrt{(1/3)}z$.

6 See for example Sen (1976), Foster (1984) and Ravallion (1992).

7 This expression differs from that proposed by Foster *et al.* (1984), and from that generally used, in that P is expressed to the power of α. This is to ensure that, as α tends to infinity, the measure converges to the Rawlsian form. It may be noted that, with a uniform continuous density h, integrating to unity over the whole range, the expression P is equal to

$$[hz/(1+\alpha)]^{1/\alpha}\,[1-y_{\text{min}}/z]^{1+1/\alpha}$$

so that it converges to $[1-y_{\text{min}}/z]$ as α tends to infinity.

8 This means that the equivalent income of a person in a family with total income Y and size N is calculated as

$$Y/N^{\gamma}$$

9 See Goodin (1985). Cornia and Stewart (1992) refer to ‘F-mistakes’ (failure to reach the target population) and ‘E-mistakes’ (excessive coverage).

10 The comparison differs from that of Besley (1990), who assumes that the government expenditure is determined by setting the minimum income guarantee equal to the poverty line. As a result, the introduction of claiming costs, reducing take-up, reduces the total budget and hence the size of the uniform benefit. Here we follow the alternative approach suggested in Besley’s footnote 5, of taking a fixed budget, assumed here to be less than that necessary to fill the poverty gap.

11 As a result of non-claiming, the gross guarantee becomes

$$\sqrt{(t+c^2)}$$

12 The headcount is given by the density times w^*, where w^* is the level of w such that (12.5) holds with equality. The poverty gap is

$$(1+\beta)/(2+\beta)\;Hz$$

13 The transfer is received by all those with w such that

$$w^{1+\beta}\leq(1+\beta)\;g$$

If the budget is equal to t times the initial poverty gap, then the transfer which can be financed is

$$g/z=[t/(2+\beta)]^{(1+\beta)/(2+\beta)}\;(1+\beta)^{\beta/(2+\beta)}$$

14 The function assumed here does not allow for any income effect on labour supply, whereas both the minimum income and the universal benefit may have income effects.

15 See, for example, Akerlof (1978), Stern (1982) and Kanbur and Keen (1989).

16 As explained earlier, benefit may be assessed on past income, which means that a rise in earnings may have no immediate impact on benefit receipt.

13 The Western experience with social safety nets

Presidential Address as the Tenth World Congress of the International Economic Association, Moscow, August 1992. I am grateful to Gary Burtless and Tim Smeeding for help with the United States statistics, although they should not be held responsible for the use I have made of them.

1 The programme may be subject to a test of income, in which case it is usually referred to as *income tested*, or to a test of both income and assets, in which case it is said to be *means tested*.
2 This series is known as the 'Blue Book' series, and was published for many years in the *United Kingdom National Accounts*. Recent references are given in chapter 1 and in Atkinson and Micklewright (1992, statistical appendix).
3 In these calculations the low-income definition is maintained at 75 roubles a month for a single person, but applied on an equivalent adult basis to the families of different sizes. The results are only approximate, being linearly interpolated from the bottom interval for each family type.
4 Medicaid from table 14, p. 1652; food stamps from the same source, table 4, p. 1616; AFDC from table 19, p. 654; SSI from table 1, p. 779; earned income tax credit from table 18, p. 1019; federal housing assistance from table 29, p. 1681; 'other' includes the Women, Infants and Children Supplemental Food Program (table 34, p. 1689), job training (table 36, p. 1692), summer youth employment (table 37, p. 1693), Jobs corps (table 38, p. 1694), Head start (table 39, p. 1696), low-income home energy assistance (table 41, p. 1701) and veterans' pensions (p. 1704). Figures for transfer programmes include administrative expenditures.
5 Although strictly we need to look at their effectiveness in helping those in poverty *after* non-means-tested transfers, in order to assess the incremental contribution of the means-tested programmes.
6 It is also possible that families qualify on income grounds but are excluded by the assets test.

14 Towards a European social safety net?

I am grateful to my colleagues on the Welfare State Programme for their help, and particularly to Karen Gardiner and Holly Sutherland for allowing me to draw on our joint research.

1 The scale is 1 for the first adult, 0.7 for additional persons aged 14 or over, and 0.5 for those aged under 14. The number aged 0–14 is used from Feinstein (1976, Table 56), and the number of household heads estimated using the proportion of 1/2.78 found in the 1937–38 budget survey.

15 Beveridge, the national minimum and its future in a European context

A public lecture given on 2 December 1992 at the London School of Economics as part of the Suntory-Toyota Lectures to mark the fiftieth anniversary of the

Beveridge Report and presented to a Plenary Session of the Poverty Summit at Edinburgh, 6–8 December 1992.

1 The 1948 legislation in fact went further than the 1941 Act in that it abolished the latter's provision to withhold assistance from a single applicant without dependants living in the household of a parent or child (Report of the National Assistance Board 1948, p. 14).

16 State pensions for today and tomorrow

A revised version of the David Hobman Annual Lecture presented at King's College London in January 1994. I am most grateful to the Age Concern Institute of Gerontology for the invitation to deliver the lecture in honour of David Hobman, who has contributed so much to this field. My thanks are due to Judith Atkinson, Patricia Hewitt, Emma MacLennan, Holly Sutherland and Richard Thomas for their comments on earlier versions. The actuarial calculations in section 16.3 were kindly made available to me by Harvie Brown of William M. Mercer Ltd; the simulations using the microsimulation model POLIMOD in section 16.7 were carried out by Holly Sutherland. None of the above should be held responsible for the opinions expressed, which are my personal views.

Bibliography

Aaron, H., 1980, 'Rejuvenating US Social Security', *Economic Impact*, 32.

Abel-Smith, B., 1953, *The Reform of Social Security*, Fabian Research Series No. 161, Fabian Society, London.

1959, 'Social security', in Ginsberg, M. (ed.), *Law and Opinion in England*, Stevens, London.

1984, 'The study and definition of poverty: values and social aims', in Sarpellon, G. (ed.), *Understanding Poverty*, Angeli, Milan.

Abel-Smith, B. and Townsend, P., 1965, *The Poor and the Poorest*, G. Bell, London.

Adams, M., 1988, 'The distribution of earnings 1973 to 1986', Department of Employment Research Paper 64, London.

Akerlof, G. A., 1970, 'The market for "lemons"', *Quarterly Journal of Economics*, 83: 488–500.

1978, 'The economics of tagging as applied to the optimal income tax, welfare programs, and manpower planning', *American Economic Review*, 68: 8–19.

Akerlof, G. A. and Katz, L. F., 1989, 'Workers' trust funds and the logic of wage profiles', *Quarterly Journal of Economics*, 103: 525–36.

Alderman, H., 1987, 'Allocation of goods through non-price mechanisms: evidence on distribution by willingness to wait', *Journal of Development Economics*, 25: 105–24.

Altmann, R., 1982, 'The incomes of the early retired', *Journal of Social Policy*, 11: 355–64.

Altmann, R. M. and Atkinson, A. B., 1982, 'State pensions, taxation and retirement income, 1981–2031', in Fogarty, M. (ed.), *Retirement Policy: The Next Fifty Years*, Heinemann, London.

Ameline, C. and Walker, R., 1984, 'France: poverty and the family', in Walker, R., Lawson, R. and Townsend, P. (eds.), *Responses to Poverty: Lessons from Europe*, Heinemann Educational Books, London.

Anand, S. and Kanbur, R., 1984, 'Inequality and development: a reconsideration', in Nissen, H. P. (ed.), *Towards Income Distribution Policies: From Income Distribution Research to Income Distribution Policy in LDCs*, EADI, Padenburg.

Arrow, K. J., 1962, 'The economic implications of learning by doing', *Review of*

Economic Studies, 29: 155–73.

Assémat, J. and Glaude, M., 1989, 'Source Fiscale et/ou Enquête par Interview', paper presented at Seminar on Poverty Statistics in the European Community, Nordwijk, Netherlands.

Atkinson, A. B., 1969, *Poverty in Britain and the Reform of Social Security*, Cambridge University Press, Cambridge.

1970, 'On the measurement of inequality', *Journal of Economic Theory*, 2: 244–63.

1983, *The Economics of Inequality*, second edition, Oxford University Press, Oxford.

1987, 'On the measurement of poverty', *Econometrica*, 55: 749–64.

1987a, 'Social security harmonisation in Europe: evidence from Britain and France', in House of Lords, Select Committee on the European Community, *Social Security in the European Community*, HMSO, London.

1987b, 'Income maintenance and social insurance', in Auerbach, A. J. and Feldstein, M. S. (eds.), *Handbook of Public Economics*, vol. II, North-Holland, Amsterdam.

1988, 'The economics of unemployment insurance', Presidential Address to the Econometric Society.

1989, *Poverty and Social Security*, Harvester, Hemel Hempstead.

1991, 'The social safety net', Welfare State Programme Discussion Paper 66, STICERD, London School of Economics, London.

1994, What has happened to the macro-economic theory of distribution?, Caffè Lectures, University of Rome La Sapienza.

Atkinson, A. B., Bourguignon, F. and Chiappori, P-A., 1988, 'The French tax system and a comparison with the British system', in Atkinson, A. B. and Sutherland, H. (eds.), *Tax-Benefit Models*, STICERD Occasional Paper 10, London School of Economics, London.

Atkinson, A. B. and Cazes, S., 1990, 'Mesure de la pauvreté et politiques sociales: une étude comparative entre le Royaume-Uni, la R.F.A. et la France', *Observations et Diagnostics Economiques, Revue de l'OFCE*, vol. 33: 105–30.

Atkinson, A. B. and Champion, B., 1989, 'Family Income Supplement and two-parent families, 1971–1980', in Atkinson, A. B., *Poverty and Social Security*, Harvester Press, Hemel Hempstead.

Atkinson, A. B. and Harrison, A. J., 1978, *Distribution of Personal Wealth in Britain*, Cambridge University Press, Cambridge.

Atkinson, A. B., King, M. A. and Stern, N. H., 1989, 'The poverty trap in Britain', in Atkinson, A. B., *Poverty and Social Security*, Harvester Press, Hemel Hempstead.

Atkinson, A. B. and Micklewright, J., 1983, 'On the reliability of income data in the Family Expenditure Survey 1970–1977', *Journal of the Royal Statistical Society*, 46: 33–61.

1989, 'Tightening the screw: benefits for the unemployed 1979–1988', in Dilnot, A. W. and Walker, I. (eds.), *The Economics of Social Security*, Oxford University Press, Oxford.

1991, 'Unemployment compensation and labour market transitions: a critical review', *Journal of Economic Literature*, 29: 1679–727.

1992, *Economic Transformation and the Distribution of Income in Eastern Europe*, Cambridge University Press, Cambridge.

Atkinson, A. B. and Mogensen, G. V., 1993, *Welfare and Work Incentives*, Clarendon Press, Oxford.

Atkinson, A. B., Rainwater, L. and Smeeding, T., 1994, *Income Distribution in OECD Countries: the Evidence from the Luxembourg Income Study (LIS)*, LIS.

Atkinson, A. B. and Sutherland, H., 1990, 'Scaling the "poverty mountain": methods to extend incentives to all workers', in Bowen, A. and Mayhew, K. (eds.), *Improving Incentives for the Low Paid*, Macmillan, London.

Atkinson, A. B. and Sutherland, H. (eds.), 1988, *Tax-benefit Models*, STICERD Occasional Paper 10, London School of Economics.

Azariadis, C., 1975, 'Implicit contracts and underemployment equilibria', *Journal of Political Economy*, 83: 1183–202.

Bannock, G., Baxter, R. E. and Rees, R., 1979, *The Penguin Dictionary of Economics*, second edition, Allen Lane, London.

Barr, N. A., 1987, 'Strategies for income support', Welfare State Programme Research Note 3, STICERD, LSE, London.

1987a, *The Economics of the Welfare State*, Weidenfeld and Nicolson, London.

1988, 'The mirage of private unemployment insurance', Welfare State Programme Discussion Paper 34, STICERD, London School of Economics.

1990, 'Economic theory and the welfare state: a survey and reinterpretation', Welfare State Programme Discussion Paper 54, STICERD, London School of Economics.

1992, 'Economic theory and the welfare state: a survey and reinterpretation', *Journal of Economic Literature*, 30: 741–803.

1993, *The Economics of the Welfare State*, second edition, Weidenfeld and Nicolson, London.

Barro, R., 1974, 'Are government bonds net wealth?', *Journal of Political Economy*, 82: 1095–117.

1990, 'Government spending in a simple model of endogenous growth', *Journal of Political Economy*, 98: S103–S125.

1991, 'Economic growth in a cross section of countries', *Quarterly Journal of Economics*, 106: 407–43.

Barry, B., 1977, 'Justice between generations', in Hacker, P. M. S. and Raz, J. (eds.), *Law, Morality and Society*, Clarendon Press, Oxford.

Beckerman, W., 1979, 'The impact of income maintenance payments on poverty in Britain, 1975', *Economic Journal*, 89: 261–79.

1979a, *Poverty and the Impact of Income Maintenance Programmes*, International Labour Office, Geneva.

Beenstock, M. and Brasse, V., 1986, *Insurance for Unemployment*, Allen and Unwin, London.

Bégué, J., 1976, 'Remarques sur une étude de l'OCDE concernant la répartition des revenus dans divers pays', *Economie et Statistique*, No. 84: 97–104.

Bentolila, S. and Saint-Paul, G., 1992, 'The macroeconomic impact of flexible labor contracts, with an application to the case of Spain', *European Economic Review*, 36: 1013–47.

Berger, S. and Piore, M. J., 1980, *Dualism and Discontinuity in Industrial Societies*, Cambridge University Press, Cambridge.

Bergson, A., 1984, 'Income inequality under Soviet socialism', *Journal of Economic Literature*, 22: 1052–99.

Bertola, G., 1993, 'Factor shares and savings in endogenous growth', *American Economic Review*, 83: 1184–98.

Besley, T., 1990, 'Means testing versus universal provision in poverty alleviation', *Economica*, 57: 119–29.

Besley, T. and Coate, S., 1992, 'Workfare vs. welfare: incentive arguments for work requirements in poverty alleviation programs', *American Economic Review*, 82: 249–61.

Beveridge, Sir W. (Lord), 1942, *Report on Social Insurance and Allied Services*, Cmnd 6404, HMSO, London.

Bewley, T. F., 1988, *Knightian Uncertainty*, Nancy L. Schwartz Memorial Lecture, Northwestern University.

1989, 'Market innovation and entrepreneurship: a Knightian view', Discussion-papier A-233, University of Bonn.

Blanchard, O., 1985, 'Debt, deficits, and finite horizons', *Journal of Political Economy*, 93: 223–47.

Bodie, Z., 1990, 'Pensions as retirement income insurance', *Journal of Economic Literature*, 28: 28–49.

Booth, C., 1889–1903, *The Life and Labour of the People in London*, Macmillan, London.

1892, *Pauperism and the Endowment of Old Age*, Macmillan, London.

Borch, K., 1981, 'The three markets for private insurance', *Geneva Papers on Risk and Insurance*, No. 20: 7–31.

Borooah, V. K. and McGregor, P., 1989, 'Inequality and poverty in Northern Ireland', paper, University of Ulster.

Bosanquet, N., 1987, *A Generation in Limbo*, Public Policy Centre, London.

Bosanquet, N., Laing, W. and Propper, C., 1990, *Elderly Consumers in Britain*, Laing and Buisson, London.

Bourguignon, F. and Fields, G. S., 1990, 'Poverty measures and anti-poverty policy', *Recherches Economiques de Louvain*, 56: 409–27.

Bourguignon, F. and Morrison, C., 1990, 'Income distribution, development and foreign trade: a cross-sectional analysis', *European Economic Review*, 34: 1113–32.

1992, 'The Kuznets curve and the recent evolution of income inequality in developed countries', paper presented at conference on 'Growth and income inequality', Paris.

Bowles, S., 1985, 'The production process in a competitive economy: Walrasian, Neo-Hobbesian and Marxian models', *American Economic Review*, 75: 16–36.

Bowley, A. L., 1937, *Wages and Income since 1860*, Cambridge University Press, Cambridge.

Bowley, A.L. and Hogg, M.H., 1925, *Has Poverty Diminished?*, P.S. King, London.

Boyer, G.R., 1990, *An Economic History of the English Poor Law*, Cambridge University Press, Cambridge.

Bradbury, B. and Saunders, P., 1990, 'How reliable are estimates of poverty in Australia?', Social Policy Research Centre Discussion Paper 18.

Brandolini, A. and Sestito, P., 1994, 'Mutamenti nella distribuzione del reddito in Italia, 1977–1991', in Rossi, N. (ed.), *Secondo Rapporto CNEL sulla Distribuzione e Redistribuzione del reddito in Italia*, GRETA, Venice.

Briggs, A., 1961, 'The welfare state in historical perspective', *Archives européennes de sociologie*, 2: 221–59.

Buhmann, B., Rainwater, L., Schmaus, G. and Smeeding, T.M., 1988, 'Equivalence scales, well-being, inequality, and poverty', *Review of Income and Wealth*, 34: 115–42.

Bulow, J.I. and Summers, L.H., 1986, 'A theory of dual labor markets with application to industrial policy, discrimination, and Keynesian unemployment', *Journal of Labor Economics*, 4: 376–414.

Burdett, K., 1979, 'Unemployment payments as a search subsidy: a theoretical analysis', *Economic Inquiry*, 17: 333–43.

Burdett, K. and Mortensen, D.T., 1980, 'Search, layoffs, and labor market equilibrium', *Journal of Political Economy*, 88: 652–72.

Burtless, G., 1986, 'Public spending on the poor: trends, prospects and economic limits', in Danziger, S.H. and Weinberg, D.H. (eds.), *Fighting Poverty*, Harvard University Press, Cambridge, Mass.

1987, 'The adequacy and counter-cyclical effectiveness of the unemployment system', Testimony for the Committee on Unemployment and Means, US House of Representatives, 15 December 1987.

1990, 'The economist's lament: public assistance in America', *Journal of Economic Perspectives*, 4: 57–78.

Callan, T. and Nolan, B., 1993, 'Income inequality and poverty in Ireland in the 1970s and 1980s', ESRI Working Paper 43, ESRI, Dublin.

Callan, T., Nolan, B., Whelan, B.J., Hannan, D.F. with Creighton, S., 1989, *Poverty, Income and Welfare in Ireland*, Economic and Social Research Institute, Dublin.

Calvo, G. and Wellisz, S., 1979, 'Hierarchy, ability and income distribution', *Journal of Political Economy*, 87: 991–1010.

Camdessus, M., 1992, 'Address to UN Economic and Social Council', *IMF Survey*, 3 August 1992, p.255.

Campbell, D., 1988, *Personal Pensions and Occupational Schemes: An Employer's Guide*, Tolley, London.

Canceill, G. and Villeneuve, A., 1990, 'Les inégalités de revenus: quasi statu quo entre 1979 et 1984 pour les salariés et les inactifs', *Economie et Statistique*, No. 230: 65–74.

Cantillon, B., Marx, I., Proost, D. and Van Dam, R., 1994, 'Indicateurs Sociaux: 1985–1992', Centrum voor Sociaal Beleid, University of Antwerp.

Casey, B. and Laczko, F., 1989, 'Early retired or long-term unemployed?', *Work, Employment and Society*, 3: 509–26.

CERC (Centre d'Etude des Revenus et des Coûts), 1983, *Comparaison des régimes de Sécurité Sociale*, Document 68, Paris.

Clarke, J. J., 1939, *Social Administration*, third edition, Pitman, London.

Clarke, J. S., 1948, 'The Assistance Board' in Robson, W. A., (ed.), *Social Security*, third edition, Allen and Unwin, London.

Collet, C. E., 1919, Book Review, *Economic Journal*, 29: 241.

Collins, J., 1993, 'Occupational pensions for the less well off: who benefits?', *Watsons Quarterly*, Issue 28: 4–7.

Cornia, G. A., 1990, 'Child poverty and deprivation in industrialized countries: recent trends and policy options', Innocenti Occasional Papers, Number 2, UNICEF, Florence.

Cornia, G. A. and Stewart, F., 1992, 'Two errors of targeting', World Bank Conference on Public Expenditures and the Poor: Incidence and Targeting, Washington, DC.

Cowell, F. A., 1990, *Cheating the Government*, MIT Press, Cambridge, Mass.

Cowell, F. A. and Kuga, K., 1977, 'Additivity and the entropy concept: an axiomatic approach to inequality measurement', Institute of Social and Economic Research, Osaka University, Discussion Paper 96.

Creedy, J., 1982, *State Pensions in Britain*, Cambridge University Press, Cambridge.

Crijns, L. H. J., 1991, *The EC and Social Security*, European Institute of Public Administration, Maastricht.

Danziger, S., Haveman, R. and Plotnick, R., 1981, 'How income transfer programs affect work, savings and the income distribution: a critical review', *Journal of Economic Literature*, 19: 975–1028.

Dasgupta, P. S. and Maskin, E., 1986, 'The existence of equilibrium in discontinuous economic games I and II', *Review of Economic Studies*, 53: 1–41.

Dawson, A. and Evans, G., 1987, 'Pensioners' incomes and expenditure 1970–85', *Employment Gazette*, May: 243–52.

Deacon, A., 1976, *In Search of the Scrounger*, G. Bell, London.

de Koning, J., 1990, 'Opening address', in L. Betten (ed.), *The Future of European Social Policy*, Kluwer, Deventer.

Deleeck, H., 1989, 'The adequacy of the social security system in Belgium, 1976–1985', *Journal of Social Policy*, 18: 91–117.

Deleeck, H. and van den Bosch, K., 1989, 'The measurement of poverty in comparative context: empirical evidence and methodological evaluation of four poverty lines in seven EC-countries', paper presented at the Seminar on Poverty Statistics in the European Community, Nordwijk, Netherlands.

Denison, E. F., 1962, *The Sources of Economic Growth in the United States and the Alternatives Before Us*, Committee for Economic Development, Supplementary paper No. 13, New York.

Department of Employment, 1971, *British Labour Statistics*, HMSO, London.

1988, *Training for Employment*, Cm 316, HMSO, London.

Department of Health and Social Security, 1975, *Two-Parent Families in Receipt of*

Family Income Supplement 1972, Statistical and Research Report Series, No. 9, London.

1977, *Low Incomes*, Supplementary Benefits Administration Paper 6, HMSO, London.

1981, *Growing Older*, HMSO, London.

1984, *Population, Pension Costs and Pensioners' Incomes*, HMSO, London.

1985, *Reform of Social Security*, Cmnd 9517, HMSO, London.

1985a, *Reform of Social Security: Programme for Action*, Cmnd 9691, HMSO, London.

1986, *Low Income Families – 1983*, HMSO, London.

1988, *Low Income Statistics: Report of a Technical Review*, HMSO, London.

1988a, *Low-Income Families, 1985*, HMSO, London.

Department of Social Security, 1989, 'Supplementary Benefit Take-up 1985', House of Commons deposited paper.

1990, *Households Below Average Income: A Statistical Analysis 1981–87*, Department of Social Security, London.

1992, *Households Below Average Income: A Statistical Analysis 1979–1988/9*, Department of Social Security, London.

1993, *Social Security: The Government's Expenditure Plans 1993–94 to 1995–96*, Cm 2213, HMSO, London.

1993a, *Income-Related Benefits: Estimates of Take-Up in 1989*, Department of Social Security, London.

1993b, *Households Below Average Income, 1979–1990/1*, Department of Social Security, London.

Diamond, P. A., 1965, 'National debt in a neoclassical growth model', *American Economic Review*, 55: 1126–50.

1977, 'A framework for social security analysis', *Journal of Public Economics*, 8: 275–98.

1981, 'Mobility costs, frictional unemployment, and efficiency', *Journal of Political Economy*, 89: 798–812.

1982, 'Wage determination and efficiency in search equilibrium', *Review of Economic Studies*, 49: 761–82.

Dilnot, A. and Johnson, P., 1992, 'What pension should the state provide?', *Fiscal Studies*, 13 (4): 1–20.

Dinwiddy, R. and Reed, D., 1977, *The Effects of Certain Social and Demographic Changes on Income Distribution*, Royal Commission on the Distribution of Income and Wealth, Background Paper No. 3, HMSO, London.

Disney, R., 1982, 'Theorising the welfare state: the case of unemployment insurance', *Journal of Social Policy*, 11: 35–58.

Dispersyn, M., Van der Vorst, P., de Falleur, M., Guillaume, Y. and Meulders, D., 1990, 'La construction d'un serpent social Européen', *Revue Belge de la Sécurité Sociale*, 889–979.

Doeringer, P. B. and Piore, M. J., 1971, *Internal Labor Markets and Manpower Analysis*, Lexington Books, Lexington, Mass.

Drèze, J. H., 1979, 'Human capital and risk-bearing', *Geneva Papers on Risk and*

Insurance, No. 12: 5–22.

Drèze, J. H. and Malinvaud, E., 1994, 'Growth and employment: the scope for a European initiative', *European Economy*, No. 1: 77–106.

Duncan, G. J., 1984, *Years of Poverty, Years of Plenty*, Survey Research Center, University of Michigan, Ann Arbor, Michigan.

Empson, W., 1953, *Seven Types of Ambiguity*, third edition, Chatto and Windus, London.

Epland, J., 1992, 'Inntektsfordelingen i 80-årene', *Økonomiske analser*, No. 2: 17–26.

Ermisch, J., 1991, 'European integration and external constraints on social policy: is a Social Charter necessary?', *National Institute Economic Review* (May): 93–108.

Eswaran, M. and Kotwal, A., 1985, 'A theory of contractual structure in agriculture', *American Economic Review*, 75: 352–67.

European Commission, 1989, *Interim Report on a Specific Community Action Programme to Combat Poverty*, Brussels.

1990, *Social Protection in the Member States of the Community*, MISSOC, Brussels.

1991, *Final Report on the Second European Poverty Programme 1985–1989*, European Commission, Brussels.

1993, *Towards a Europe of Solidarity*, European Commission, Brussels.

1993a *Report of the Implementation of the Community Programme for the Social and Economic Integration of the Least Privileged Groups (1989–1994)*

Eurostat, 1990, *Inequality and Poverty in Europe (1980–1985)*, Rapid Report No. 7.

Falkingham, J. and Johnson, P., 1993, 'A Unified Funded Pension Scheme (UFPS) for Britain', Welfare State Programme Discussion Paper 90, London School of Economics.

Falkingham, J. and Victor, C., 1991, 'The myth of the woopie?: incomes, the elderly, and targeting welfare', *Ageing and Society*, 11: 471–93.

Feinstein, C. H., 1976, *Statistical Tables of National Income, Expenditure and Output of the UK 1855–1965*, Cambridge University Press, Cambridge.

Feldstein, M. S., 1976, 'Temporary layoffs in the theory of unemployment', *Journal of Political Economy*, 84: 937–57.

1976a, 'Social security and saving: the extended life cycle theory', *American Economic Review*, 66: 76–86.

Fenn, P., 1980, 'Sources of disqualification for unemployment benefit, 1960–76', *British Journal of Industrial Relations*, 18: 240–53.

Field, F. and Owen, M., 1993, 'Private Pensions for All', Fabian Society Discussion Paper 16, London.

Fields, G. S. and Jakubson, G. H., 1990, 'The inequality-development relationship in developing countries', Discussion Paper, Cornell University.

Fields, G. S. and Mitchell, O. S., 1984, *Retirement Pensions, and Social Security*, MIT Press, Cambridge, Mass.

Fisher, J. D., Nadler, A. and Whitcher-Alanga, S., 1982, 'Recipient reactions to aid: a conceptual review', *Psychological Bulletin*, 91: 27–59.

Flemming, J. S., 1978, 'Aspects of optimal unemployment insurance: search, leisure, savings and capital market imperfections', *Journal of Public Economics*, 10: 403–25.

Foster, J. E., 1984, 'On economic poverty: a survey of aggregate measures', *Advances in Econometrics*, 3: 215–51.

Foster, J. E., Greer, J. and Thorbecke, E., 1984, 'A class of decomposable poverty measures', *Econometrica*, 52: 761–6.

Foster, J. and Wan, H., 1984, 'Involuntary unemployment as a principal-agent equilibrium', *American Economic Review*, 74: 476–84.

Fraser, D., 1984, *The Evolution of the British Welfare State*, second edition, Macmillan, London.

Fuchs, V., 1965, 'Toward a theory of poverty', in *Task Force on Economic Growth and Opportunity, the Concept of Poverty*, Chamber of Commerce of the United States, Washington, DC.

Fulbrook, J., 1978, *Administrative Justice and the Unemployed*, Mansell, London.

Gannon, T. M., SJ, 1987, *The Catholic Challenge to the American Economy*, Macmillan, New York.

Gardiner, K., 1993, 'A survey of income inequality over the last twenty years – how does the UK compare?', Welfare State Discussion Paper 100, STICERD, London School of Economics.

Garraty, J. A., 1978, *Unemployment in History*, Harper, New York.

Giarini, O. and Stahel, W. R., 1989, *The Limits to Certainty*, Kluwer, Dordrecht.

Glaude, M., 1991, 'L'originalité du système du quotient familial', *Economie et Statistique*, No. 248: 51–67.

Goode, R. (chairman), 1993, *Pension Law Reform*, Cm 2342, HMSO, London.

Goodin, R. E., 1985, 'Erring on the side of kindness in social welfare', *Policy Sciences*, 18: 141–56.

1988, *Reasons for Welfare*, Princeton University Press, Princeton.

Goodin, R. E. and Dryzek, J., 1987, 'Risk sharing and social justice: the motivational foundations of the post-war welfare state', in Goodin, R. E. and Le Grand, J. (eds.), *Not Only the Poor*, Allen and Unwin, London.

Goodman, A. and Webb, S., 1994, *For Richer, For Poorer*, Institute for Fiscal Studies, Commentry No. 42, London.

Gordon, M. S., 1988, *Social Security Policies in Industrial Countries*, Cambridge University Press, Cambridge.

Goskomstat, 1990, *Sostav sem'i, dokhody i zhilishchnve usloviia semei rabochikh sluzhashchikh i kolkhoznikov* (Composition of the family, incomes and living conditions of workers, employees and collective farm workers), Moscow.

Gottschalk, P., 1993, 'Changes in inequality of family income in seven industrialized countries', *American Economic Review*, Papers and Proceedings, 83: 136–42.

Gottschalk, P. and Joyce, M., 1991, 'Changes in earnings inequality – an international perspective', LIS Working Paper 66, Luxembourg.

Government Actuary, 1981, *Occupational Pension Schemes 1979*, HMSO, London.

1990, *National Insurance Fund Long Term Financial Estimates*, HMSO, London.

Green, F., Henley, A. and Tsakalotos, E., 1992, 'Income inequality in corporatist and liberal economies: a comparison of trends within OECD countries', University of Kent Discussion paper 92/13, forthcoming in *International Review of Applied Economics*.

Green, G., Coder, J. and Ryscavage, P., 1992, 'International comparisons of earnings inequality for men in the 1980s', *Review of Income and Wealth*, 38: 1–16.

Grossman, S.J. and Hart, O.D., 1981, 'Implicit contracts, moral hazard and unemployment', *American Economic Review*, 71: 301–7.

Grubb, W.N. and Wilson, R.H., 1989, 'Sources of increasing inequality in wages and salaries, 1960–80', *Monthly Labor Review* (April): 3–13.

Gustafsson, B. and Palmer, E.E., 1993, 'Changes in Swedish inequality: a study of equivalent income 1975–1991', University of Gothenburg.

Gustafsson, B. and Uusitalo, H., 1990. 'The Welfare State and poverty in Finland and Sweden from the mid-1960s to the mid-1980s', *Review of Income and Wealth*, 36: 249–66.

Haddad, L. and Kanbur, R., 1990, 'How serious is the neglect of intrahousehold inequality?', *Economic Journal*, 100: 866–81.

Hagenaars, A.J.M. and de Vos, K., 1988, 'The definition and measurement of poverty', *Journal of Human Resources*, 23: 211–22.

Hahn, F.H. and Matthews, R.C.O., 1964, 'The theory of economic growth: a survey', *Economic Journal*, 74: 779–902.

Hamermesh, D.S., 1979, 'Entitlement effects, unemployment insurance and employment decisions', *Economic Inquiry*, 17: 317–32.

Hancock, R., 1985, 'Explaining changes in families' relative net resources: an analysis of the Family Finances and Family Resources Surveys', Taxation, Incentives and the Distribution of Income Programme Discussion Paper 84, London School of Economics.

Hannah, L., 1986, *Inventing Retirement*, Cambridge University Press, Cambridge.

Hansen, F.K., 1993, 'Social exclusion in Denmark', Center for Alternativ Samfundsanalyse, Copenhagen.

Harper, S. and Thane, P., 1989, 'The consolidation of "old age" as a phase of life, 1945–1965', in Jeffreys, M. (ed.), *Growing Old in the Twentieth Century*, Routledge, London.

Harris, J., 1972, *Unemployment and Politics*, Clarendon Press, Oxford.

1977, *William Beveridge: A Biography*, Clarendon Press, Oxford.

Harris, J. and Todaro, M., 1970, 'Migration, unemployment and development', *American Economic Review*, 60: 126–42.

Harsanyi, J.C., 1955, 'Cardinal welfare, individualistic ethics, and interpersonal comparisons of utility', *Journal of Political Economy*, 63: 309–21.

Hartmann, H., 1981, *Sozialhilfebedürftigkeit und 'Dunkelziffer der Armut'*, Kohlhammer, Stuttgart.

Hauser, R., 1990, 'Sozioökonomische aspekte der Sozialhilfe', in Kitterer, W. (ed.), *Sozialhilfe und Finanzausgleich*, R v Decker's Verlag, Heidelberg.

1992, 'Die personelle Einkommensverteilung in den alten und neuen Bundesländern vor der Vereinigung', in Buttler, F. (ed.), *Sozialpolitik im vereinten Deutschland II*, Duncker & Humblot, Berlin.

Hauser, R. and Becker, I., 1993, 'The development of the income distribution in the Federal Republic of Germany during the seventies and eighties', University of Frankfurt.

Hauser, R., Muller, K., Wagner, G. and Frick, J., 1991, 'Incomes in East and West Germany on the Eve of Union', Discussion Paper 34, DIW Berlin.

Hauser, R. and Semrau, P., 1989, 'Trends in poverty and low income in the Federal Republic of Germany', University of Frankfurt SFB3 Working Paper 306.

1990, *Poverty in the Federal Republic of Germany*, report prepared for the European Commission.

Haveman, R. H., 1987, *Poverty Policy and Poverty Research*, University of Wisconsin Press, Madison.

Hayek, F. A., 1960, *The Constitution of Liberty*, Routledge and Kegan Paul, London.

Hellwig, M., 1983, 'Moral hazard and monopolistically competitive insurance markets', *Geneva Papers on Risk and Insurance*, 8(26): 44–71.

1987, 'Some recent developments in the theory of competition in markets with adverse selection', *European Economic Review*, 31: 319–25.

Henderson, R. F., Harcourt, A. and Harper, R. J. A., 1970, *People in Poverty: A Melbourne Survey*, Cheshire, Melbourne.

Hennock, E. P., 1987, *British Social Reform and German Precedents*, Oxford University Press, Oxford.

Hey, J. D. and Mavromaras, K., 1981, 'The effect of unemployment insurance on the riskiness of occupational choice', *Journal of Public Economics*, 16: 317–41.

Hicks, J. R., 1932, *The Theory of Wages*, Macmillan, London.

Hills, J., 1993, *The Future of Welfare*, Joseph Rowntree Foundation, York.

Himmelfarb, G., 1984, *The Idea of Poverty*, Faber and Faber, London.

Hirschman, A. O., 1970, *Exit, Voice and Loyalty*, Harvard University Press, Cambridge, Mass.

HM Treasury, 1985, *The Government's Expenditure Plans 1985–86 to 1987–88*, HMSO, London.

1987, *The Government's Expenditure Plans 1987–88 to 1989–90*, HMSO, London.

1988, *The Government's Expenditure Plans 1988–89 to 1990–91*, HMSO, London.

1992, *Public Expenditure Analyses to 1994–95*, HMSO, London.

Holmans, S. K., 1987, *Social Security Systems in Selected Countries and their Integration with Tax Systems*, HM Treasury, London.

House of Commons Social Services Committee, 1989, *Minimum Income*, House of Commons Paper 579, HMSO, London.

1990, *Households and Families Below Average Income: A Regional Analysis 1980–1985*, HMSO, London.

Hunt, E. H., 1981, *British Labour History, 1815–1914*, Weidenfeld and Nicolson, London.

IMF, 1992, 'From the Executive Board ...', *IMF Survey*, 17 August 1992, p. 267.

IMF, World Bank, OECD and EBRD, 1991, *A Study of the Soviet Economy*,

OECD, Paris.

International Labour Office, 1984, *Into the Twenty-First Century: the Development of Social Security*, ILO, Geneva.

Jallade, J-P., 1988, 'Redistribution in the Welfare State: an assessment of the French performance', in Jallade, J-P. (ed.), *The Crisis of Redistribution in European Welfare States*, Trentham Books, Stoke on Trent.

Jaynes, G. D., 1978, 'Equilibria in monopolistically competitive insurance markets', *Journal of Economic Theory*, 19: 394–422.

Jenkins, S. P., 1991, 'Income inequality and living standards: changes in the 1970s and 1980s', *Fiscal Studies*, 12: 1–28.

forthcoming, 'Recent trends in UK income inequality', in Slottje, D. (ed.), *Research on Economic Inequality*, vol. IV, JAI Press, Greenwich, Connecticut.

Johnson, G. and Layard, R., 1986, 'The natural rate of unemployment: explanation and policy', in Ashenfelter, O. and Layard, R. (eds.), *The Handbook of Labor Economics*, vol. II, North-Holland, Amsterdam.

Johnson, P., 1986, 'The historical dimensions of the welfare state "crisis"', *Journal of Social Policy*, 15: 443–65.

Johnson, P. and Webb, S., 1989, 'Counting people with low incomes: the impact of recent changes in official statistics', *Fiscal Studies*, 10: 66–82.

1990, *Poverty in Official Statistics: Two Reports*, IFS Commentary 24, London.

1992, 'Recent Trends in UK Income Inequality: Causes and Policy Responses', Royal Economic Society conference.

1993, 'Explaining the growth in UK income inequality', *Economic Journal*, 103: 429–43.

Kaldor, N., 1956, 'Alternative theories of distribution', *Review of Economic Studies*, 23: 83–100.

Kanbur, R., 1987, 'Measurement and alleviation of poverty', *IMF Staff Papers*, 34: 60–85.

Kanbur, R. and Keen, M., 1989, 'Poverty, incentives, and linear income taxation', in Dilnot, A. and Walker, I. (eds.), *The Economics of Social Security*, Oxford University Press, Oxford.

Kanbur, R., Keen, M. and Tuomala, M., 1990, 'Optimal non-linear income taxation for the alleviation of income poverty', IFS Discussion Paper 91/2.

Kanellopoulos, C. N., 1986, 'Incomes and poverty in Greece: determining factors', Centre of Planning and Economic Research, Scientific Studies 22, Athens.

Kemsley, W. F. F., Redpath, R. U. and Holmes, M., 1980, *Family Expenditure Survey Handbook*, HMSO, London.

Kessler, D., 1989, 'But why is there social security?', in Johnson, P., Conrad, C. and Thomson, D. (eds.), *Workers versus Pensioners*, Manchester University Press, Manchester.

1990, 'Solutions to the coming crisis in social security: save today or work tomorrow?', *Geneva Papers on Risk and Insurance*, no 55: 122–38.

Keynes, J. M., 1921, *A Treatise on Probability*, Macmillan, London.

Kilpatrick, R. W., 1973, 'The income elasticity of the poverty line', *Review of Economics and Statistics*, 55: 327–32.

Kitterer, W., 1986, 'Die Einkommens- und Verbrauchs-stickproben des Statistischen Bundesamtes', in Lindner, H. (ed.), *Aussagefähigkeit von Einkommensverteilungsrechnungen für die Bundesrepublik Deutschland*, Institut für Angewandte Wirtschaftsforschung, Tübingen.

Klevmarken, A., 1994, 'Economic astrology or empirical science?', Inaugural lecture, Uppsala University.

Knight, F. H., 1921, *Risk, Uncertainty and Profit*, Houghton Mifflin, Boston.

Kohl, J., 1992, 'Minimum standards in old age security and the problem of poverty in old age', in Atkinson, A. B. and Rein, M. (eds.), *Age, Work and Social Security*, Macmillan, London.

Krupp, H-J. and Schupp, J., 1988, *Lebenslagen im Wandel: Daten 1987*, Campus, Frankfurt.

Kuznets, S., 1955, 'Economic growth and income inequality', *American Economic Review*, 45: 1–28.

Laczko, F., Dale, A., Arber, S. and Gilbert, G. N., 1988, 'Early retirement in a period of high unemployment', *Journal of Social Policy*, 17: 313–33.

Laffont, J-J., 1981, 'Asymétrie d'information et les trois marchés de l'assurance', *Geneva Papers on Risk and Insurance*, No. 20: 36–40.

Lazear, E. P., 1979, 'Why is there mandatory retirement?', *Journal of Political Economy*, 87: 1261–84.

1981, 'Agency, earnings profiles, productivity, and hours restrictions', *American Economic Review*, 71: 606–20.

Le Grand, J., 1984, 'The future of the welfare state', *New Society*, 68: 385–6.

Le Grand, J. and Winter, D., 1987, 'The middle classes and the defence of the British welfare state', in Goodin, R. E. and Le Grand, J. (eds.), *Not Only the Poor*, Allen and Unwin, London.

LeRoy, S. F. and Singell, L. D., 1987, 'Knight on risk and uncertainty', *Journal of Political Economy*, 95: 394–406.

Lindbeck, A., Molander, P., Persson, T., Petersson, O., Sandmo, A., Swedenborg, B. and Thygesen, N., 1993, 'Options for economic and political reform in Sweden', *Economic Policy*, No. 17: 219–64.

1994, *Turning Sweden Around*, MIT Press, Cambridge.

Lippman, S. A. and McCall, J. J., 1980, 'Search unemployment', *Scandinavian Journal of Economics*, 82: 253–72.

Loizides, I. and Giachalis, V., 1989, 'Poverty profiles in Greece: A probabilistic approach', Athens School of Economics and Business Science.

Lucas, R., 1988, 'On the mechanics of economic development', *Journal of Monetary Economics*, 22: 3–42.

Lydall, H. F., 1979, 'Some problems in making international comparisons of inequality', in Moroney, J. R. (ed.), *Income Inequality: Trends and International Comparisons*, D. C. Heath, Lexington.

Lynes, T., 1977, 'The making of the Unemployment Assistance scale', Appendix 1 in Department of Health and Social Security, *Low Incomes*, Supplementary Benefits Administration Paper 6, HMSO, London.

Macleod, W. B. and Malcomson, J., 1993, 'Wage premiums and profit maximisation in efficiency wage models', *European Economic Review*, 37: 1223–49.

Malinvaud, E., 1985, 'Unemployment insurance', *Geneva Papers on Risk and Insurance*, 10(34): 6–22.

Mankiw, N. G., Romer, D. and Weil, D., 1992, 'A contribution to the empirics of economic growth', *Quarterly Journal of Economics*, 107: 407–37.

Marris, R., 1964, *The Economic Theory of 'Managerial' Capitalism*, Macmillan, London.

Matthews, M., 1986, *Poverty in the Soviet Union*, Cambridge University Press, Cambridge.

McAlister, C., Ingles, D. and Tune, D., 1981, 'General revenue financing of social security: the Australian minimum income support system', *Social Security Journal* (December): 24–38.

McDonald, I. M. and Solow, R. M., 1985, 'Wages and employment in a segmented labor market', *Quarterly Journal of Economics*, 100: 1115–41.

Meade, J. E., 1991, *The Building of the New Europe: National Diversity versus Continental Uniformity*, Hume Occasional Papers No. 28, Edinburgh.

Mercader, M., 1993, 'The low income population in Spain and a comparison with France and the UK', Welfare State Programme Discussion Paper 95, STICERD, London School of Economics.

Meyer, R. H. and Wise, D. A., 1983, 'Discontinuous distributions and missing persons: the minimum wage and unemployed youth', *Econometrica*, 51: 1677–98.

Micklewright, J., 1990, 'Why do less than a quarter of the unemployed in Britain receive unemployment insurance?', Taxation, Incentives and the Distribution of Income Programme Discussion Paper 147, LSE.

MIL Research, 1988, Report to Department of Social Security, London.

Milano, S., 1989, *Le Revenu Minimum Garanti dans la C.E.E.*, Presses Universitaires de France, Paris.

Mill, J. S., 1843, *A System of Logic*, J. W. Parker, London.

Millar, J. and Jenkins, S. P., 1989, 'Measurement of the within household distribution: what is feasible?', paper presented at ESRC Workshop on Changing Definitions of Poverty, Policy Studies Institute.

Milner, E. and Milner, D., 1918, *Scheme for a State Bonus. A Rational Method of Solving the Social Problem*, State Bonus League, London.

Ministère des Affaires Sociales, 1990, *Annuaire des Statistiques Sanitaires et Sociales*, SESI Documentation, Paris.

Minister of Reconstruction, 1944, *Social Insurance*, Part I, Cmd 6550, HMSO, London.

Ministry of Pensions and National Insurance, 1959, *Improvements in National Assistance*, Cmnd 782, HMSO, London.

Moffitt, R. L., 1992, 'Incentive effects of the US welfare system', *Journal of Economic Literature*, 30: 1–61.

Mookherjee, D. and Shorrocks, A., 1982, 'A decomposition analysis of the trend in UK income inequality', *Economic Journal*, 92: 886–902.

Morris, N. and Preston, I., 1986, 'Inequality, poverty and the redistribution of income', *Bulletin of Economic Research*, 38: 277–344.

Mortensen, D. T., 1977, 'Unemployment insurance and job search decisions', *Industrial and Labor Relations Review*, 30: 505–17.

1988, 'The persistence and indeterminacy of unemployment in search equilibrium', Centre for Mathematical Studies in Economics and Management Science Discussion Paper 810.

Musgrave, R. A., 1959, *The Theory of Public Finance*, McGraw-Hill, New York.

National Assistance Board, 1949, *Annual Report 1948*, Cmd 7767, HMSO, London.

Nichols, A. L. and Zeckhauser, R., 1982, 'Targeting transfers through restrictions on recipients', *American Economic Review*, Papers and Proceedings, 72: 373–7.

Nichols, D., Smolensky, E. and Tideman, T. N., 1971, 'Discrimination by waiting time in merit goods', *American Economic Review*, 16: 312–23.

Nolan, B., 1987, *Income Distribution and the Macroeconomy*, Cambridge University Press, Cambridge.

Nolan, B. and Callan, T., 1988, 'Measuring Trends in Poverty over Time: Some Robust Results for Ireland 1980–87', ESRI Working Paper Number 7, Dublin.

NOSOSO, 1993, 'Social Security in the Nordic Countries', Nordic Social-Statistical Committee, Oslo.

Odagiri, H., 1981, *The Theory of Growth in a Corporate Economy*, Cambridge University Press, Cambridge.

OECD (Organisation for Economic Co-operation and Development), 1992, *Historical Statistics 1960–1990*, OECD, Paris.

O'Higgins, M. and Jenkins, S. P., 1989, 'Poverty in Europe, estimates for 1975, 1980 and 1985', paper presented at the Seminar on Poverty Statistics in the European Community, Nordwijk, Netherlands.

Orshansky, M., 1965, 'Counting the poor: another look at the poverty profile', *Social Security Bulletin*, 28: 3–29.

Oswald, A. J., 1986, 'Unemployment insurance and labor contracts under asymmetric information', *American Economic Review*, 76: 365–77.

Padoa-Schioppa, T. *et al.*, 1987, *Efficiency, Stability and Equity*, Oxford University Press, Oxford.

Pahl, J., 1983, 'The allocation of money and the structuring of inequality within marriage', *Sociological Review*, 31: 237–62.

Palmer, J. L., Smeeding, T. and Torrey, B. L., 1988, *The Vulnerable*, Urban Institute, Washington, DC.

Parfit, D., 1973, 'Later selves and moral principles', in Montefiore, A. (ed.), *Philosophy and Personal Relations*, Routledge and Kegan Paul, London.

Parker, H., 1989, *Instead of the Dole*, Routledge, London.

Parker, H. (ed.), 1991, *Basic Income and the Labour Market*, BIRG Discussion Paper 1, London.

Parker, S., 1980, *Older Workers and Retirement*, HMSO, London.

Pauly, M., 1973, 'Income redistribution as a local public good', *Journal of Public Economics*, 2: 35–58.

Peacock, A. T., 1952, *The Economics of National Insurance*, Hodge, London.

Pen, J., 1971, *Income Distribution*, Allen Lane, London.

Penrose, E., 1959, *The Theory of the Growth of the Firm*, Basil Blackwell, Oxford.

Persson, T. and Tabellini, G., 1994, 'Is inequality harmful for growth?', *American Economic Review*, 84: 600–21.

Peterson, P. E. and Rom, M. C., 1990, *Welfare Magnets*, Brookings Institution, Washington, DC.

Phelps Brown, E. H., 1977, *The Inequality of Pay*, Oxford University Press, Oxford.

Piachaud, D., 1986, 'Disability, retirement and unemployment of older men', *Journal of Social Policy*, 15: 145–62.

1987, 'The distribution of income and work', *Oxford Review of Economic Policy*, 3: 41–61.

Piore, M. J., 1987, 'Historical perspective and the interpretation of unemployment', *Journal of Economic Literature*, 25: 1834–50.

Pissarides, C., 1979, 'Job matchings with state employment agencies and random search', *Economic Journal*, 89: 818–33.

1984, 'Search intensity, job advertising, and efficiency', *Journal of Labor Economics*, 2: 128–43.

1985, 'Short-run equilibrium dynamics of unemployment, vacancies, and real wages', *American Economic Review*, 75: 676–90.

Poduluk, J. R., 1967, *Incomes of Canadians*, Ottawa: Dominion Bureau of Statistics.

Preston, S., 1984, 'Children and the elderly: divergent paths for America's dependents', *Demography*, 21: 435–57.

Privy Council, 1981, *Government Statistical Services*, Cmnd 8236, HMSO, London.

Quintin, Q., 1989, 'The Commission's political conclusions', European Conference on Basic Income, Windsor.

Ramprakash, D., 1975, 'Distribution of income statistics for the United Kingdom, 1972/73: sources and methods', *Economic Trends*, No. 262, 78–96.

Ravallion, M., 1992, 'Poverty comparisons: a guide to concepts and methods', Living Standards Measurement Study Working Paper No. 88, World Bank, Washington, DC.

Ravallion, M. and Chao, K., 1989, 'Targeted policies for poverty alleviation under imperfect information: algorithms and applications', *Journal of Policy Modeling*, 11: 213–24.

Reardon, T., 1988, *Allied Dunbar Pensions Guide*, second edition, Longman, London.

Rhys Williams, J., 1943, *Something To Look Forward To*, Macdonald, London.

Ribich, T. I., 1968, *Education and Poverty*, Brookings Institution, Washington, DC.

Riley, J. G., 1979, 'Informational equilibria', *Econometrica*, 47: 331–59.

Rodrigues, C., 1993, 'The measurement and decomposition of inequality in Portugal, 1980/81–1989/90', Microsimulation Unit Discussion Paper MU9302, Department of Applied Economics, Cambridge.

Room, G., 1989, 'Poverty statistics and European policy demands', paper presented at the Seminar on Poverty Statistics in the European Community, Nordwijk, Netherlands.

Rose, M. E., 1972, *The Relief of Poverty 1834–1914*, Macmillan, London.

Rothschild, M. and Stiglitz, J. E., 1976, 'Equilibrium and competitive insurance markets: an essay on the economics of imperfect information', *Quarterly Journal of Economics*, 90: 629–49.

Rowntree, B. S., 1901, *Poverty: A Study of Town Life*, Longman, London.

1922, *Poverty: A Study of Town Life*, new edition, Longman, London.

1937, *The Human Needs of Labour*, Longman, London.

1941, *Poverty and Progress*, Longman, London.

Rowntree, B. S. and Lavers, G. R., 1951, *Poverty and the Welfare State*, Longman, London.

Royal Commission on Population, 1949, *Report*, HMSO, London.

Royal Commission on the Distribution of Income and Wealth, 1978, *Report No. 6 Lower Incomes*, Cmnd 7175, HMSO, London.

1979, *Report No. 7 Fourth Report on the Standing Reference*, Cmnd 7595, HMSO, London.

Rubinow, I. M., 1913, *Social Insurance*, Williams and Norgate, New York.

Saint-Paul, G., 1990, 'Efficiency wage, duality and the dynamics of labour demand', DELTA Discussion Paper 9029.

1992, 'Fiscal policy in an endogenous growth model', *Quarterly Journal of Economics*, 107: 1243–59.

Salais, R., Baverez, N. and Reynaud, B., 1986, *L'invention du chômage*, Presses Universitaires de France, Paris.

Sandmo, A., 1991, 'Economists and the welfare state', *European Economic Review*, 35: 213–39.

Sarkisyan, G. S. and Kuznetsova, N. P., 1967, *Potrebnosti i dokhod sem'i, uroven', struktura, perspektivy*, Moscow.

Saunders, P., 1991, 'Selectivity and targeting in income support: the Australian experience', *Journal of Social Policy*, 20: 299–326.

Saunders, P. and Bradbury, B., 1989, 'Some Australian evidence on the consensual approach to poverty measurement', Social Welfare Research Centre Discussion Paper.

Saunders, P., Smeeding, T., Coder, J., Jenkins, S., Fritzell, J., Hagenaars, A. J. M., Hauser, R. and Wolfson, M., 1993, 'Noncash income, living standards, and inequality: evidence from the Luxembourg Income Study', in Bös, D. (ed.), *Economics in a Changing World*, Macmillan, London.

Saunders, P. and Whiteford, P., 1989, 'Measuring poverty: a review of the issues', Economic Planning Advisory Council, Discussion Paper 89/11.

Sawhill, I. V., 1988, 'Poverty in the US: Why is it so persistent?', *Journal of Economic Literature*, 26: 1073–119.

Sawyer, M., 1976. 'Income distribution in OECD countries', *OECD Economic Outlook*, OECD, Paris.

Schmähl, W., 1983, 'Income analysis based on longitudinal data from social security earnings records', in Atkinson, A. B. and Cowell, F. A. (eds.), *Panel Data on Incomes*, STICERD Occasional Paper 2, London.

Scholz, J. K., 1994, 'The Earned Income Tax Credit: participation, compliance, and antipoverty effectiveness', *National Tax Journal*, 47: 63–87.

Schultz, T. W., 1961, 'Investment in human capital', *American Economic Review*, 51: 1–17.

Seidman, L. S., 1990, *Saving for America's Economic Future*, Sharpe, Armonk, New York.

Sen, A. K., 1976, 'Poverty: an ordinal approach to measurement', *Econometrica*, 44: 219–31.

1977, 'Starvation and exchange entitlements: a general approach and its application to the great Bengal famine', *Cambridge Journal of Economics*, 1: 33–59.

1977a, 'Rational fools', *Philosophy and Public Affairs*, 6: 317–44.

1981, *Poverty and Famines: An Essay on Entitlement and Deprivation*, Clarendon Press, Oxford.

1983, 'Poor, relatively speaking', *Oxford Economic Papers*, 35: 153–69.

1985, *Commodities and Capabilities*, North-Holland, Amsterdam.

1992, *Inequality Reexamined*, Harvard University Press, Cambridge.

1992a, 'The political economy of targeting', World Bank Conference on Public Expenditures and the Poor: Incidence and Targeting, Washington, DC.

Shapiro, C. and Stiglitz, J. E., 1984, 'Equilibrium unemployment as a worker discipline device', *American Economic Review*, 74: 433–44.

Shorrocks, A. F., 1980, 'The class of additively decomposable inequality measures', *Econometrica*, 48: 613–25.

Sinclair, R. K., 1988, *Democracy and Participation in Athens*, Cambridge University Press, Cambridge.

Sinn, H-W., 1990, 'Tax harmonisation or tax competition in Europe?', *European Economic Review*, 34: 489–504.

Smeeding, T. M., O'Higgins, M. and Rainwater, L. (eds.), 1990, *Poverty, Inequality and Income Distribution in Comparative Perspective: the Luxembourg Income Study*, Oxford University Press, Oxford.

Smeeding, T., Torrey, B. B. and Rein, M., 1988, 'Patterns of income and poverty: the economic status of children and the elderly in eight countries', in Palmer, J. L., Smeeding, T. and Torrey, B. B. (eds.), *The Vulnerable*, Urban Institute, Washington, DC.

Solow, R. M., 1992, 'Siena lectures on endogenous growth theory', Dipartimento di Economia Politica, Siena.

1994, 'Perspectives on growth theory', *Journal of Economic Perspectives*, 8: 45–54.

Spahn, P. B., 1985, 'Report on a symposium on poverty statistics in the European Community', J-W. Goethe University, Frankfurt.

Stark, T., 1972, *The Distribution of Personal Income in the United Kingdom 1949–1963*, Cambridge University Press, Cambridge.

1978, 'Personal incomes', in Maunder, W. F. (ed.), *Reviews of United Kingdom Statistical Sources*, vol. VI, Pergamon Press, Oxford.

1988, 'The changing distribution of income under Mrs Thatcher', in Green, F. (ed.), *The Restructuring of the UK Economy*, Harvester, London, pp. 177–96.

Stern, N. H., 1982, 'Optimum taxation with errors in administration', *Journal of Public Economics*, 17: 181–211.

Stiglitz, J. E., 1983, 'Risk, incentives and insurance: the pure theory of moral hazard', *Geneva Papers on Risk and Insurance*, 8(26): 4–33.

1986, 'Theories of wage rigidity', in Butkiewicz, J. L., Koford, K. J. and Miller, J. B. (eds.), *Keynes' Economic Legacy*, Praeger, New York.

1988, *Economics of the Public Sector*, second edition, Norton, New York.

1989, *The Economic Role of the State*, Basil Blackwell, Oxford.

Stiglitz, J. E. and Weiss, A., 1981, 'Credit rationing in markets with imperfect information', *American Economic Review*, 71: 393–410.

Supplementary Benefits Commission, 1979, *Annual Report 1978*, HMSO, London.

Sutherland, H., 1990, 'The income of husbands and wives', Welfare State Programme, London School of Economics.

Tawney, R. H., 1913, *Poverty as an Industrial Problem*, Morris, London.

Thane, P., 1982, *The Foundations of the Welfare State*, Longman, London.

Thomson, D., 1986, 'Welfare and the historians', in Bonfield, L., Smith, R. M. and Wrightson, K. (eds.), *The World We Have Gained: Histories of Population and Social Structure*, Blackwell, Oxford.

1989, 'The welfare state and generation conflict', in Johnson, P., Conrad, C. and Thomson, D. (eds.), *Worker and Pensioners*, Manchester University Press, Manchester.

Tinbergen, J., 1952, *On the Theory of Economic Policy*, North-Holland, Amsterdam.

Titmuss, R. M., 1955, 'Pension schemes and population change', *Political Quarterly*, 26: 152–66.

1962, *Income Distribution and Social Change*, Allen and Unwin, London.

Townsend, P. B., 1979, *Poverty in the United Kingdom*, Allen Lane, Penguin.

1991, *The Poor Are Poorer: A Statistical Report on Changes in the Living Standards of Rich and Poor in the United Kingdom 1979–1989*, Statistical Monitoring Unit, Department of Social Policy and Social Planning, University of Bristol.

Trinder, C. G., 1989, *Employment over 55*, NIESR, London.

Tsakloglou, P., 1988, 'Aspects of inequality and poverty in Greece: 1974, 1982', Ph D thesis, University of Warwick.

1990, 'Aspects of poverty in Greece', *Review of Income and Wealth*, 36: 381–402.

US Bureau of the Census, 1981, *Characteristics of the Population Below the Poverty Level: 1979*, US Government Printing Office, Washington, DC.

US Council of Economic Advisers, 1964, *Economic Report of the President*, US Government Printing Office, Washington, DC.

US Department of Commerce, 1993, *Money Income of Households, Families, and Persons in the United States: 1992*, Current Population Reports, Series P-60, No. 184, Washington, DC.

US House of Representatives, Committee on Ways and Means, 1992, *1992 Green Book*, US Government Printing Office, Washington, DC.

Uusitalo, H., 1989, *Income Distribution in Finland*, Central Statistical Office of Finland, Helsinki.

1994, 'Changes in income distribution during a deep recession', unpublished paper.

Uzawa, H., 1965, 'Optimum technical change in an aggregative model of economic growth', *International Economic Review*, 6: 18–31.

1969, 'Time preference and the Penrose effect in a two-class model of economic growth', *Journal of Political Economy*, 77: 628–52.

van de Klundert, Th., 1988, 'Wage differentials and employment in a two-sector model with a dual labor market', unpublished paper.

van Ginneken, W. and Park, J., 1984, *Generating internationally comparable income distribution estimates*, ILO, Geneva.

Vanlerenberghe, P., 1992, chairman, *RMI – Le Pari de l'Insertion*, La Documentation Française, Paris.

van Oorschot, W., 1991, 'Non-take-up of social security benefits in Europe', *Journal of European Social Policy*, 1: 15–30.

Van Trier, W., 1990, 'Who framed social dividend: a tale of the unexpected', Discussion Paper, University of Antwerp.

Veit-Wilson, J., 1989, 'The concept of minimum income and the basis of social security scales', seminar paper.

1989a, 'Memorandum' in House of Commons Social Services Committee, 1989, *Minimum Income*, House of Commons Paper 579, HMSO, London.

1989b, 'Genesis of confusion: the Beveridge Committee's poverty line for social security', seminar paper.

Vielrose, E., 1978, 'Patterns of the distribution of earnings in Poland', in Krelle, W. and Shorrocks, A. F. (eds.), *Personal Income Distribution*, North-Holland, Amsterdam.

Villeneuve, A., 1989, 'L'Enquête Multidimensionelle sur les conditions de vie des ménages de l'INSEE', paper presented at the Seminar on Poverty Statistics in the European Community, Nordwijk, Netherlands.

Walker, A., 1993, 'Whither the social contract? Intergenerational solidarity in income and employment', in Hobman, D. (ed.), *Uniting Generations*, ACE Books, London.

Walker, A., Alber, J. and Guillemard, A-M., 1993, *Older People in Europe: Social and Economic Policies*, Report of the European Observatory, European Commission, Brussels.

Warlick, J. L., 1981, 'Participation as a measure of program success', *Institute for Research on Poverty Focus*, 5: 12–16.

Weinberg, D. H., 1987, 'Filling the "poverty gap", 1979–84', *Journal of Human Resources*, 22: 563–73.

Weisbrod, B. A., 1970, 'Collective action and the distribution of income: a conceptual approach', in Haveman, R. H. and Margolis, J. (ed.), *Public Expenditure and Policy Analysis*, Markham, Chicago.

Whiteford, P. and Doyle, J., 1991, 'The take-up of FIS in 1986', SPRC Discussion Paper 29, University of New South Wales.

Williams, C. A., Turnbull, J. G. and Cheit, E. F., 1982, *Economic and Social Security*, 5th edition, John Wiley, New York.

Wilson, C., 1977, 'A model of insurance markets with incomplete information', *Journal of Economic Theory*, 16: 167–207.

Wolfe, B., de Jong, P., Haveman, R., Halberstadt, V. and Goudswaard, K. P., 1984, 'Income transfers and work effort: the Netherlands and the United States in the 1970s', *Kyklos*, 37: 609–37.

Wolfson, M. C., 1987, 'Lifetime coverage: the adequacy of Canada's retirement income system', in Wolff, E. N. (ed.), *International Comparisons of the Distribution of Household Wealth*, Clarendon Press, Oxford.

Wolfson, M. C. and Evans, J. M., 1989, 'Statistics Canada's low income cut-offs', Statistics Canada Research Paper Series.

Woolf, S., 1986, *The Poor in Western Europe*, Methuen, London.

World Bank, 1990, *World Development Report 1990*, Oxford University Press, Oxford.

1994, *Averting the Old Age Crisis*, Oxford University Press, Oxford.

Name index

Subject index